Murders and Madness

Medicine, Law, and Society in the *Fin de Siècle*

RUTH HARRIS

CLARENDON PRESS · OXFORD
1989

Oxford University Press, Walton Street, Oxford OX2 6DP
Oxford New York Toronto
Delhi Bombay Calcutta Madras Karachi
Petaling Jaya Singapore Hong Kong Tokyo
Nairobi Dar es Salaam Cape Town
Melbourne Auckland
and associated companies in
Berlin Ibadan

Oxford is a trade mark of Oxford University Press

Published in the United States
by Oxford University Press, New York

British Library Cataloguing in Publication Data
Harris, Ruth
Murders and madness: medicine. law and society in the Fin de Siècle.—(Oxford historical monographs).
1. France. Crimes. Responsibility of mentally disordered persons
I. Title
344.405'4
ISBN 0-19-822991-7

Library of Congress Cataloging in Publication Data
Harris, Ruth, 1958–
Murder and madness.
(Oxford historical monographs)
Bibliography: p. Includes index.
1. Criminal justice, Administration of—France—History—19th century. 2. Medical jursiprudence—France—History—19th century. 3. Murder—France—History—19th century—Case studies. 4. Psychology, Forensic—History—19th century. I. Title. II. Series.
HV9960.F7H37 1989 364'.944 88-29140
ISBN 0-19-822991-7

Set by Grove Graphics
Printed in Great Britain
Biddles Ltd.,
Guildford and King's Lynn

ACKNOWLEDGEMENTS

Over the years many people and institutions have encouraged me to complete this volume. I was fortunate enough to have been awarded a Thouron Scholarship which enabled me to begin my graduate work at Oxford, a grant which was succeeded by a Wellcome studentship for another two years. St John's College offered me a unique opportunity to finish the degree and the book while enjoying the pleasures of being a Junior Research Fellow. Charles Webster, Margaret Pelling, and Paul Weindling of the Wellcome Unit in Oxford were constant in their provision of advice and support, while Roy Porter and William Bynum at the Wellcome Institute in London were generous with comments and practical help. The head of the *Archives de la Seine*, M. Ribot, graciously cut through a jungle of bureaucratic red tape to gain access to the manuscripts on which the study is based, while his colleagues turned a blind eye to my ordering up several times the daily allowance of boxes, enabling me to read them in record time. Mme Tridon of Nancy was exceptionally kind in allowing me to see and quote from her unpublished manuscript autobiography of Étienne Beaunis.

Innumerable friends and colleagues have helped me over the years. When I first arrived at Oxford, Ludmilla Jordanova proved to be an enthusiastic supervisor who cheerfully read several drafts of the doctoral thesis over the years, helping me to make essential revisions. While in Paris, Scott Haine and Joëlle Guillais were helpful colleagues and excellent companions, always eager to share with me their discoveries in the archives. In England, there were many people who flattered me with their inexhaustible interest, helping me to see some merit in the work when the writing became tedious. Colin Lucas at Balliol College made my return to Oxford much less painful than it might otherwise have been; Robert Gildea shared his knowledge of French history with me; Anne Jefferson provided constant intellectual stimulation, supplying much of the laughter during my years at St John's; Ying Chiang rekindled interest in the moral and philosophical dimensions of the study.

I would like to thank those who read drafts and offered comments, in particular Neil McWilliam, who read the work several times, Margaret Hunt, who read the conclusion, as well as Liz Loudon, Edward Berenson, and Celia Applegate, who read portions of it. Others such as Anne Harrington and Godileve Van Heteren were always available for critical comments and support. Special thanks go to my Oxford examiners, Roger Smith and Tony Judt, who took considerable time and trouble going over difficult theoretical and substantive issues.

In recent years, there have been particular individuals who have helped me turn the thesis into a book. I owe an enormous debt to Lyndal Roper, who made me understand the value of feminist history and read the whole book through when chapters came off the word processor. One of the greatest pleasures of recent months has been spending hours in collaborative discussion with Robert Nye, who knows the field inside and out. Barbara Taylor was an expert and incisive critic, opening my eyes to many unexplored themes. Finally, I must once again thank Tony Judt, who read the revised book manuscript, and was always available to give criticism, references, and friendly advice.

Special personal acknowledgement goes to my family, who never complained about my long stay away, encouraging me to carry on and bring this work to conclusion. George and Betty Pears gave me a home away from home, making those lonely, early years in England much more welcoming. Finally, my greatest debt goes to Iain Pears, the dedicatee of the work, who from the earliest days of our acquaintance has been an invaluable friend, companion, and intellectual helpmate. Not only did he quietly abide with me through the long hours of revising and rewriting—ready always with an editor's pen—but was also able to lighten the process through an unending stream of humorous asides.

All these people have contributed to the work and have made it better than it might otherwise have been.

Smith College R.H.

CONTENTS

ILLUSTRATIONS

NOTE ON THE CITATION OF CASES

In the following text I have been obliged to use two different forms of citations for the murder cases. I often refer to the criminals without using their proper names (e.g., the carpenter Joseph-Pierre C . . .) because of the conditions of an authorization provided by the *Archives de la Seine* which sought to protect the names of these defendants and their families. I have attempted in the footnotes to give as complete a reference as possible, including carton number and date of judgement. After 1893, when the dossiers of the cases at the Assizes court were destroyed, I have used trial reports, generally contained in published records such as the *Gazette des tribunaux*. In these instances the full names are cited. Occasionally, because of the notoriety of the offender, it was impossible to hide the identity of the criminals. In these rare instances, I have used the full names.

I

INTRODUCTION

> But today, with the scramble of systems, with popularized theories everywhere prevalent,—atavistic fatalism, determinism, the corrupting influence of the social milieu—who, then, will declare 'this man is guilty' with serenity, without emotion or doubt. . . . All the ideas of the century have been introduced into all minds, even the most narrow, and there reflect off each other like a troubled mirror. Schools, barracks, books, newspapers have affected peoples' minds; simple and absolute ideas have been shaken and all kinds of philosophical doubts slumber there which the words of the defence attorney and that of the expert awaken.
>
> Jean Cruppi[1]

In 1902, a hairdresser's assistant, Adrien Virgile Legrand, was sentenced in the Parisian *Cour d'assises* to hard labour for life for slitting his six-year-old son's throat.[2] On the surface the case appeared simple enough, as Legrand freely admitted the deed and received the harsh punishment prescribed. However, during the trial, he asserted that he had acted under the influence of a 'delirious crisis', a defence which seriously complicated the proceedings. As in many other murder trials in this period, the issue became not whether he was the author of the crime but rather if he could be punished for it. To determine his responsibility, the court sought to evaluate Legrand's defence by probing into his motivations, character, and past history.

To help in this evaluation, the court called in an expert, a representative of the speciality of *la médecine légale*. By 1900, such a disinterested witness, who spoke for neither the prosecution nor the defence, was a routine figure, his forensic role set

[1] *La Cour d'assises* (Paris, 1898), 58, 60.

[2] *Gazette des tribunaux*, 13 Nov. 1902.

out by the provisions laid down for the conduct of criminal investigations and trials. For the most part these 'medico-legists' were called in to assess physical evidence of sudden death, spending their time performing autopsies in the Parisian morgue. When the mental state of the defendant was at issue, as it was in Legrand's trial, it was customary to call an expert in the sub-speciality of *la médecine légale des aliénés* (lunatics) who were usually, if not always, notable Parisian psychiatrists.

Despite the different approaches and attitudes of the various experts and witnesses in Legrand's case, they all seriously considered the possibility of his diminished responsibility. The judge, although clearly in favour of a harsh sentence, was none the less keen to demonstrate open-mindedness by assessing evidence of mental derangement. Perhaps more understandably, the medico-legist called in as an expert witness, stressed Legrand's 'degeneracy', alcoholism, and hysteria, developing a subtle portrait of abnormality which suggested that illness, as much as evil inclination, had caused the crime. Even his bereaved and embittered wife pointed to his drunken habits and recurring migraines as possible symptoms of mental disorder.

Although everyone agreed that Legrand was personally reprehensible and socially dangerous, the court still equivocated, fearful that a lunatic might be unjustly condemned. In this book, I want to explain this reticence and to analyse the theories, assumptions, and techniques that came into play when determining the responsibility of defendants and deciding what to do with them. Underlying the enquiries into the 'badness or madness' of individual defendants was the deeper issue of whether these opposing conceptions within the French legal system still possessed validity in an age pervaded by subversive medical and social-scientific theories.

I will argue that the debate surrounding crime and madness reached a new and important turning-point in the *fin de siècle*. In this era, psychiatric notions of mental activity, revised analyses of the 'criminal mind', and changing strategies of crime prevention and control undermined the traditional bases of the French judicial system. The period saw a thorough-going reassessment of the principles of punishment and a marked shift towards deterministic explanations of anti-social behaviour, most forcefully and coherently articulated by psychiatrists who routinely intervened in court as expert witnesses. Their psycho-social analyses, based largely on deterministic theories of hereditarian degeneration and neurophysiological automatism, had a profound impact on interpretations of both individual and social pathology. Such ideas insistently militated against a criminal code that was founded on moral responsibility, free will, and legal theories of fault-based contractual obligation.

I will examine the impact of medical approaches on legal developments, to show how jurists sought to take account of scientific findings in the development of the new field of criminology. The revised account of crime and punishment that medical and legal collaborators produced increasingly moved away from the evaluation of moral responsibility towards one which emphasized professedly neutral social-scientific factors. This shift altered the orientation of judicial theory and practice and had a lasting effect on the aims and administration of the penal system. The result was the elaboration of a radical *politique criminelle* which proposed wide-ranging measures of intervention and potentially challenged many of the libertarian guarantees inscribed in criminal law.

This book is not, however, primarily an exercise in intellectual or professional history. I intend to break down the boundaries which conventionally tend to isolate these areas from broader social, political, and cultural trends. The emergence of criminology can only be understood as part of a process of constant interaction between different social groups and their diverging approaches to the problem of responsibility. Hence, the work examines the judicial culture of magistrates and judges, the clinical and scientific world of medical men as well as the milieu of the defendants themselves, whose cases provided the raw material on which discussions of social pathology were based. I will concentrate on specific problems analysed in court that reveal the key anxieties of the era, issues relating to sexual antagonism, class tension, and concerns over moral and political authority in 'mass' society. In these cases, discussion tended to expand from an analysis of the individual on trial to encompass more generalized concerns about female hysteria, hypnotism, and women's sexuality; male alcoholism and its relationship to industrial indiscipline, revolutionary politics, and national degeneration; and, finally, crimes of passion, anarchist terrorism, child murder, and crowd violence. In sum, the work not only examines the intellectual and professional evolution of a new type of knowledge, but also attempts to uncover the social and political factors that influenced and helped direct its formation.

The debate over crime and madness originated in the 1820s when a small group of physicians spoke on behalf of a series of defendants accused of brutal crimes such as murder, cannibalism, rape, and mutilation. Although the defendants showed none of the traditional signs of madness, the physicians nevertheless categorized them as 'instinctive monomaniacs', thereby claiming an unprecedented expertise in the identification of insanity. These audacious assertions were opposed by jurists who sought to prevent interference with what they considered to be the proper workings of justice.

They rejected the doctors' claims because they adhered to the principles underpinning the 1810 penal code. This legal system reflected the contributions of utilitarian penal philosophy and Kantian moral theory. The utilitarian strand was elaborated in Cesare Beccaria's *Dei delitti e delle pene* in 1764 (translated into French in 1766), and expanded in the highly influential penal philosophy of Jeremy Bentham.[3] Believing human beings capable of calculating their own interests, they and their followers maintained that the role of criminal justice was to threaten criminals with inevitable punishment, dispensed in quantities which exactly matched the seriousness of the deeds. They argued that, through a process of psychological association, the coupling of crime and punishment would ultimately produce a self-interested tendency to obey the law.

Neither sympathy for the penniless driven to theft, nor outrage against a brutal killer, would alter the exact and mathematical dispensation of penalties. Rather than a system based on public retaliation and brutal vengeance, utilitarians proposed an uncompromising moral arithmetic. Judges were

[3] See Elie Halévy, *The Growth of Philosophic Radicalism*, trans. Mary Morris (Clifton, NJ, 1972), 3–36, 54–74.

to hand out similar sentences to all individuals who committed equivalent offences, thereby divesting the process of emotionalism, arbitrariness, and injustice.

The penal codes ideally provided both a 'just measure of pain' and a 'promise of punishment'. This system of justice was to accompany a programme of rehabilitation. Designed to remove the dangerous criminal from circulation, it would demonstrate to both the individual and his peers that 'crime did not pay', and, it was hoped, reform criminals, returning them to society after the prescribed period of imprisonment. The penitentiary of the early nineteenth century was founded on a belief in discipline that would require convicted felons to judge their interests more accurately through a programme of surveillance, work, and silence conducive to moral reflection.[4]

In line with utilitarian recommendations, the French penal code emphasized deterrence, matched specific crimes to irrevocable penalties, left judges no discretionary power in sentencing, and refused to countenance the existence of either extenuating or aggravating circumstances until 1832. However, at the same time that the Code's authors gave it a strong utilitarian flavour, they were also influenced by very different, Kantian, notions of retribution.[5] In this view, punishment was necessary to do justice, conceived of on absolute moral grounds rather than in terms of the greatest happiness for the greatest number. All people were enjoined to act morally by certain categorical imperatives which were susceptible to their understanding. Confusion resulted because many simultaneously espoused utilitarian and retributivist arguments, that punishment was necessary both to deter others from crime and

[4] For a provocative analysis of the history and ideas behind this movement see Michel Foucault, *Discipline and Punish: The Birth of the Prison*, trans. Robert Hurley (New York, 1980) and Michael Ignatieff, *A Just Measure of Pain: The Penitentiary in the Industrial Revolution, 1750–1850* (New York, 1978). For more detailed historical accounts of the prison system in France see Patricia O'Brien, *The Promise of Punishment: Prisons in Nineteenth-Century France* (Princeton, 1981); Michelle Perrot (ed.), *L'Impossible Prison: Recherches sur le système pénitentiaire au XIXe siècle* (Paris, 1980); and Gordon Wright, *Between the Guillotine and Liberty: Two Centuries of the Crime Problem in France* (New York, 1983), which surveys differing management strategies and theoretical positions concerning criminality.

[5] See Bruce Aune, *Kant's Theory of Morals* (Princeton, 1979), 169–70.

to retaliate for the threat to another's dignity, property, or life.[6]

While both penal theories opposed each other in principle, each none the less rested firmly on a belief in rationality as a constant and universal feature of human nature.[7] Accordingly, individuals were to be punished not just for breaking the law, but because they possessed awareness of wrongdoing and had intentionally committed crimes. Consequently, the code made special provision for individuals who could not be held responsible by virtue of their irrationality. The insane, who were deprived of reason, were hence considered to be dispossessed of moral agency and of responsibility. Article 64 stated that 'there is neither a crime nor a misdemeanour when the defendant was in a state of insanity at the moment of the act, or when he was constrained by a force against which he could not resist'.

It appears that, initially, this article was not a cause of struggle or dispute. The identification of the insane was based on a consensual appraisal of disordered or diminished intelligence, that is, an inability to make reasoned judgements about the world. Tentative attempts to claim a special place for medical expertise were hardly pressed, since the defendant's neighbours and associates of long standing were deemed to be as qualified as physicians, if not more so.[8]

However, such an easy agreement on human rationality, moral responsibility, and the attributes of insanity were not to continue, and it is out of the breakdown of consensus that the controversies and reorientations described in this book derived. As Goldstein has shown,[9] a shift in the cultural perception of insanity occurred between the 1780s and the mid-1820s, the latter date marking the beginnings of the monomania

[6] For an early nineteenth-century discussion of the perceived problems associated with the inclusion of both utilitarian and Kantian perspectives see Adolphe Chauveau and Faustin Hélie, *Théorie du code pénal*, vol. ii (Paris, 1836), 4–26.

[7] For more on the Enlightenment project for the justification of morality see Alasdair Macintyre, *After Virtue: A Study in Moral Theory* (London, 1981), in particular, 43–8; on utilitarianism see Amartya Sen and Bernard Williams (eds.), *Utilitarianism and Beyond* (Cambridge, 1982), in particular, the article by Charles Taylor, 'The Diversity of Goods', 130–2.

[8] See Jan Ellen Goldstein, *Console and Classify: The French Psychiatric Profession in the Nineteenth Century* (New York, 1987), 162–3.

[9] For an illuminating and scholarly account of this transformation see ibid., in particular, 41–196.

controversies. The physicians who engaged in this struggle were inspired by the founding father of French psychiatry, Philippe Pinel (1745–1826), and were fired by a vision of themselves as the torch-bearers of a humanitarian tradition summed up by the legend of Pinel's (probably mythical) shattering of the chains shackling the inmates of the Bicêtre and Salpêtrière hospitals. This image identified alienism with a libertarian mission aimed at alleviating the lot of one of the most pitiable elements of society who, in their view, were unjustly and brutally maltreated.[10]

Their programme of improvement was linked to novel philosophical and therapeutic considerations which Pinel had hammered out in his various writings. He was credited with several key achievements, the most important of which were the application of sensationalist philosophical precepts to the study of insanity and the synthetic enunciation of a special form of therapy for the insane. In the path-breaking *Traité médico-philosophique* (1801), he brought together an impressive array of clinical studies to demonstrate the effectiveness of his so-called 'moral treatment'. In contrast to the bleedings, purgings, punishments, and baths which had hitherto formed the rigorous regimen of the insane patient, he advocated techniques of *douceur*, psychological methods which hoped to persuade the lunatic back to sanity. Above all, Pinel emphasized the moral authority of the doctor, whom he portrayed as a firm, but just, pedagogue who would redirect the patient's straying reason. Still very much a man of the Enlightenment endowed with a Rousseauian sensibility, Pinel advocated that these techniques be applied in a controlled environment, away from the corrupting and artificial passions engendered by civilization, in which the *esprits aliénés* would be returned to their 'natural' state. Physicians who came to specialize in the treatment of medical illness were called 'alienists', a term which will be used interchangeably throughout this work with 'psychiatrists'.[11]

[10] For analysis of the condition of lunatics in France before the law of 1838 see G. Lamarche-Vadel and Georges Préli, 'Généalogie des équipements psychiatriques au XIXe siècle', in Foucault (ed.), *Généalogie des équipements de normalisation, les équipements sanitaires* (Paris, 1976), 85–107.

[11] See Goldstein, *Console and Classify*, 90–107, for the medico-philosophical underpinnings; for the elaboration of moral treatment see 64–119. For more on the subject, see also Gladys Swain, *Le Sujet de la folie: Naissance de la psychiatrie* (Toulouse, 1977);

The shifts were essential to the young physicians surrounding Pinel's disciple, J.-E.-D. Esquirol (1772–1840), when they came to defend the murderers described above.[12] However, there was little in Pinel's legacy which would have suggested an inevitable conflict with legal and commonsense notions of insanity. On the whole, Pinel elaborated upon a Lockean and Condillacian tradition and continued to associate insanity with a generalized condition of disordered or diminished intelligence. However, there was one diagnosis which seemed to contain more ambiguous implications. Pinel had observed an instance of a condition which he called *manie sans délire*, a term which described a circumscribed intellectual misapprehension. Such patients appeared to reason well except on certain limited subjects and, when questioned in these areas, demonstrated incoherence or extreme exaltation. This disease description suggested the possibility of a localized intellectual insanity.[13] Esquirol, from 1819 onwards, extended Pinel's work with the notion of monomania, confining its application once again to isolated intellectual deliriums in which the patient often demonstrated extreme, and sometimes outrageous, behaviour and preoccupations.[14]

Such subtleties of medical diagnosis might well have stayed within the confines of the profession but for their use in modified form by Esquirol's disciple, Étienne Georget (1795–1828). It was he who, in a series of pamphlets,[15] identified the condition

Marcel Gauchet and Swain, *La Pratique de l'esprit humain: L'Institution asilaire et la révolution démocratique* (Paris, 1980); Klaus Doerner, *Madmen and the Bourgeoisie* (Oxford, 1982), 98–163; Henri Baruk *La Psychiatrie francaise de Pinel à nos jours* (Paris, 1967), 3–24.

12 For biographical accounts of Esquirol and his major contribution in forming the first generation see René Sémélaigne, *Les Grands aliénistes francais*, vol. i (Paris, 1930), 124–40; see also Goldstein, *Console and Classify*, 128–47.

13 For the complete analysis of the debates concerning madness and law in this period, particularly in relation to the monomania concept, see Goldstein, *Console and Classify*, 152–96; for Pinel's discussion of *manie sans délire* see his *Traité médico-philosophique sur l'aliénation mentale*, 1st edn. (Paris, 1801), 13–14.

14 See J.-E.-D. Esquirol, 'Monomanie', in C.-C.-F. Panckoucke (ed.), *Dictionnaire des sciences médicales* (Paris, 1819), xxxiv. 114–25.

15 See Étienne Georget, 'Examen médical des procès criminels des nommés Léger, Feldtman, Lecouffe, Jean-Pierre et Papavoine, dans lesquels l'aliénation mentale a été alléguée comme moyen de défense', *Archives générales de la médecine*, 8 (1825), 148–214; 'Quelques considérations médico-légales sur la liberté morale', ibid., 317–85; and 'Discussion sur la folie en aliénation mentale', ibid., 11 (1826), 497–558.

of *monomanie instinctive*, a radical diagnosis which contradicted both the received wisdom concerning insanity and the findings of his clinical *maîtres*. In effect, he went beyond Esquirol's analysis and proclaimed that the murderers were insane even though they showed no signs of intellectual disturbance. Georget acknowledged that they reasoned perfectly well, and were even morally repelled by their deeds. He still maintained that the murderers had been propelled by an irresistible urge, committing crimes with full knowledge of their horror.

Georget argued that, rather than demonstrating an isolated intellectual misapprehension, 'homicidal maniacs' were afflicted by a 'lesion of the will' which left the rational faculties intact and moral discernment unimpaired. His diagnosis suggested that insanity and moral awareness were no longer mutually exclusive. Suddenly, the distinction between 'madness and badness' became exceedingly problematic, requiring specialist knowledge to make an accurate distinction.[16] Despite the initial ridicule to which their claims were subjected, alienists none the less immediately put into doubt the moral authority of the judiciary. They implied that to reach verdicts in such cases without the assistance and advice of medical experts was tantamount to wilful injustice.

The debate over the management of these few offenders—important for their symbolism more than for their numbers—derived from two seemingly incompatible interpretations of human nature. While the majority of Restoration jurists regarded such wrongdoers as the apotheosis of criminality, the alienists saw them as hapless victims of disease. One proposed a moralistic and voluntaristic account, while the latter insisted on a medicalized and deterministic interpretation.[17] From this fundamental split arose a plethora of disturbing questions, often articulated at the moment of the monomania controversies and raised with increasing frequency thereafter. If madness could exist unseen except by trained medical men, then was the

[16] After initial hesitations, Esquirol soon endorsed his disciple's views and even developed them in his mature and synthetic work; see his *Des maladies mentales considérées sous les rapports médical, hygiénique et médico-légal*, 2 vols. (Paris, 1838), ii. 94–129.

[17] For a seeming incompatibility of psychiatric and legal perspectives see Michael S. Moore, *Law and Psychiatry: Rethinking the Relationship* (Cambridge, 1984), 1–5 and 113–54. For more on these theoretical problems see Roger Smith, 'Expertise and Causal Attribution in Deciding between Crime and Mental Disorder', *Social Studies of Science*, 15 (1985), 67–98.

judiciary competent to reach correct verdicts on any defendant? Could those who committed the most abominable deeds go unpunished because an expert witness identified insanity invisible to others? Or should rationality as the essential factor determining eligibility for punishment be abandoned in favour of some other criterion? In effect, such questions set the terms for sustained medical and legal conflict, with the same arguments and rhetorical flourishes repeatedly marking out respective positions throughout most of the century.

Although the monomania controversies in the 1820s and 1830s earned practitioners a judicial role, alienists continued to enounter obstacles right through the Second Empire. They were still harassed by both Church and State for their materialist explanations of the mind/body problem. Nor did their position significantly improve under the regime of 'moral order', as all attempts were made to stifle the opposition and to keep Republican medical men out of positions of power and influence.[18]

After the elections of 1877, however, the medical profession benefited markedly from the resulting anticlericalist atmosphere, which proved congenial to many of their most cherished aspirations. Doctors promoted and supported a Republic based on universal male suffrage, educational reform, meritocratic values, and a release from religious 'superstition'. Medical men felt the impact of political changes keenly, particularly later through the heightened visibility attained by many colleagues—Georges Clemenceau and Émile Combes being the most famous—in the mainstream of Republican politics. Doctors entered the *Chambre des députés*, occupied important ministerial posts, and overfilled the ranks of the Republican, Opportunist, Radical, and Socialist parties. Their loyalty was rewarded by the 30 November 1892 law on medical practice that provided a more favourable educational, institutional, and corporate base from which to extend their virtual monopoly over the healing arts.[19]

Now free to disseminate and develop their scientific analysis

[18] See Goldstein, 'The Hysteria Diagnosis and the Politics of Anti-Clericalism in Late Nineteenth-Century France', *Journal of Modern History*, 54 (1982), 209–39.

[19] See Jacques Léonard for the physicians' important political power in *La Médecine entre les pouvoirs et les savoirs: Histoire intellectuelle et politique de la médecine française au XIXe siècle* (Paris, 1981), 279–84; for the specific provisions of the law see 293–8.

of 'mind', psychiatrists were aided by such potent allies as Paul Bert, Professor of Physiology at the Sorbonne, and later Léon Gambetta's Minister of Public Instruction. Jean-Martin Charcot and his associate D.-M. Bourneville together made a frontal assault on institutionalized clericalism, with the latter leading the successful campaign in the early 1880s for the laicization of public hospitals.[20] Finally, psychiatrists' intellectual labours were recognized by the state in 1879 when a chair in mental maladies was established in the Paris Medical Faculty,[21] an appointment matched by a second in diseases of the nervous system created especially for Charcot in 1882 under the premier's patronage.

The increased public presence of both psychiatrists and physicians was symptomatic of the way medical knowledge provided some special defining role in *fin de siècle* society. Medical ideas had long focused on the importance of moderation, on the inescapability of punishment for the sins of drunkenness, gluttony, and sexual excess, notions which had provided an important physiological correlate to religious and moral doctrines. This approach was maintained in the 1870s and 1880s, but the anticlericalist climate and emphasis on civic morality increasingly detached their positivist evangelicism from any religious underpinning, science itself becoming the independent determinant of the reformist movement and of its political ideology.

Medical men were thus not seen simply as doctors healing the sick, but were rather discussed—favourably and unfavourably—as the embodiment of certain moral and social philosophies, ideals, and aspirations.[22] Physicians were prophets of progress, positivists who espoused a theory of knowledge which rejected metaphysical explanation. Instead they embraced an experimental method which sought an orderly and predictable

[20] Goldstein, 'The Hysteria Diagnosis'.

[21] For the story of its closure in 1821 and the problems caused by its lack in ensuing decades see Charles Martin, *La Dégénérescence dans l'œuvre de B. A. Morel et dans sa postérité*, Ph.D. thesis (L'École pratique des hautes études, 1983–4), 39.

[22] For more on this defining role see Macintyre's discussion of social *characters* in *After Virtue*, 27–30. For Macintyre, '*characters* are the masks worn by moral philosophies . . . a whole cluster of attitudes and activities', a description which could be readily applied to physicians and their outlook in the last decades of the nineteenth century in France.

pattern for natural processes.[23] Science provided an optimisitic perspective, a rationale for interventionist procedures to improve the health of the 'social organism'. Moreover, the doctors were early and persuasive advocates of evolutionary theory. If the record of biological transformation demonstrated a tendency towards a greater and more perfect division of labour and specialization, then similar progressive tendencies were shaping contemporary evolution and human history, affecting the development of individuals and that of races and nations.

But if evidence of improvement abounded, there were an equal number of indications that processes of reversion were in operation. As the century drew to a close, doctors acted increasingly as secular Cassandras stressing the imminence of decline and degeneration. As Robert Nye has shown,[24] they provided a compelling language and conceptual system for describing the moral and social implications of racial debilitations, nervous exhaustion, and cultural despair. Their analyses centred on the problems of urbanization and working-class life, concentrating on endemic overcrowding in insalubrious '*taudis*' as well as on the growing scourges of alcoholism, prostitution, and crime. Such urban outcasts as vagrants and beggars were afflicted by neurasthenic conditions which determined their idleness, while striking workers were disturbed by hysterical inclinations that made them susceptible to the destabilizing impact of revolutionary demagogues. Moreover, their defects appeared even more worrying in the light of economic and imperial competition from the 1890s onwards, as army officers surveyed the sorry state of their recruits, and politicians—of diverse sectarian affiliations—fretted over the problem of France's relative depopulation.

But the disease went deeper and also touched the bourgeoisie, as the refinement of civilization required great adaptive energy, forcefulness, and willpower, qualities that the middle classes were not always seen to possess. Men of the

[23] For a critical philosophical account see Leszek Kolakowski, *Positivist Philosophy*, 2nd edn. (Harmondsworth, 1972), chaps. 2–5; see also Maurice Mandelbaum, *History, Man and Reason: A Study in Nineteenth-Century Thought* (Baltimore, 1971), 1–20.

[24] *Crime, Madness and Politics in Modern France: The Medical Concept of National Decline* (Princeton, 1984).

middle classes were subject to ever greater exertions as they sought to prove themselves worthy of their place in the new meritocratic social order. For those striving towards social advancement the strains of competitive examinations produced an unhealthy '*surménage*', as intellectual achievement was often bought at the price of mental and physiological health. The privileged sons of the well-to-do were prone to the sins of idleness and dissipation, temptations which the Belle Epoque world of the café-concert, the theatre, and the automobile provided in dangerous abundance. Finally, middle-class women, often reduced to a debilitating idleness, were prone to nervous illness, their disorders a symptom both of the 'advance of civilization' and of the heavy toll imposed by evolutionary development which had refined their psychic constitutions to an exquisite frailty.

In sum, physicians' vision of social progress often competed unsuccessfully with the more depressing view of the need to restore the equilibrium of a dangerously sick patient. Everywhere medical men saw danger, in the collapse of moral values within the bourgoisie, as well as in a resistance to authority among the lower orders, and recommended sometimes radical intervention to avoid further destabilization. In the past they had often championed the extension of rights and responsibilities to all sectors of society; in the *fin de siècle*, as will be seen, they increasingly insisted on curative procedures which tended to threaten the liberal vision with which they had long been associated, justifying their campaigns in the name of national survival.

This pessimistic current in their theorizing and social philosophy was, to a large extent, the fruit of scientific investigation. The examination of heredity, environment, and 'unconscious' processes opened up a Pandora's box, out of which jumped undeniable proof of the power of the 'irrational' in psychic and social life. Their faith in the revelation of natural processes paradoxically led them to deterministic accounts of human nature and ultimately to increasing philosophical pessimism.[25] Moreover, this gloomy outlook was

[25] For a general evocation of this cultural climate see H. Stuart Hughes, *Consciousness and Society: The Reorientation of European Social Thought, 1890–1930*, 2nd ed. (New York, 1977), in particular, 3–66. For a more contemporary account see Lucien Lévy-Bruhl, *History of Modern Philosophy in France*, trans. anon. (Chicago, 1924), chap. 15. Chap. 6 and 8 will discuss these themes in more detail.

repeatedly reinforced by the unstable tenor of French political life.

The concentration on decadence and degeneration, already an age-old theme, took on added attractions after 1848 with the failure of liberal aspirations and the repressive intellectual climate of the early Second Empire.[26] Each successive political crisis embellished and intensified the perception of disorder. The defeat by Germany in 1870 and the ensuing Commune and civil war had a particularly decisive influence on a whole generation of intellectuals and literati.[27] Alive to the implications of social Darwinist reasoning, an entire generation asked whether or not France was indeed sufficiently fit to survive. The optimism associated with the foundation of a liberal regime after 1877 and the promise of reform soon dissipated. Recurring disturbances—from the Boulanger episode to anarchist bombings and strikes—indicated the difficulty of establishing the Republic on an enduring footing.[28] The Dreyfus affair was equally important in emphasizing the already existing divisions and tensions in French intellectual life, as associates and erstwhile colleagues found themselves in opposing political camps. The experience undermined the ideals of the Republic and generated new kinds of political ideologies on both the left and right as new, and sometimes radical, reassessments of Enlightenment ideas of rational improvement and material progress were advocated.[29]

A common feature of the intellectual and philosophical climate was a 'revolt against rationalism', a revolt which, despite its aims, drew strength and inspiration from positivist investigation. Even the most extreme theories—the revolutionary apostasy of Georges Sorel and the radical nationalism

[26] See Koenraad Swart, *The Sense of Decadence in Nineteenth Century France* (The Hague, 1964), chap. 4.

[27] For the impact of the defeat on French intellectual life see, for example, Claude Digeon, *La Crise allemande de la pensée francaise* (Paris, 1959), chap. 5.

[28] For more on this, particularly in relationship to the development of crowd theory, see Susannah Barrows, *Distorting Mirrors: Visions of the Crowd in Late Nineteenth-Century France* (New Haven, 1981); and Nye, *The Origins of Crowd Psychology: Gustave LeBon and the Crisis of Mass Democracy in the Third Republic* (London and Beverly Hills, 1975).

[29] For the most comprehensive introduction to the many opposing ideologies and shifts in political orientations see Stephen Wilson, *Ideology and Experience: Anti-Semitism in France at the Time of the Dreyfus Affair* (London, 1982).

of Maurice Barrès, for example—were redolent with scientific language and ideas. For the former, the 'myth' of the general strike would harness the 'unconscious' yearnings and utopian vision of a revolutionary class; for the latter, the potential of French genius was to be found in racial blood, attachment to the native soil, ideas embedded in broader currents of social evolutionism. Those attracted to the aesthetic tenets of the decadent movement in the 1880s and 1890s—although self-consciously opposed to the disenchanting effects of science—none the less used techniques of 'positive' psychology in rendering their portraits of inner thought processes. In effect, they dissected in careful detail the obsession with sensuality and presented psychophysiological arguments to justify their attack on conventional morality.

Within the academic mainstream of moral, social, and political theory, the 'revolt against rationalism' was little more than the self-conscious inclusion of the 'irrational' into pre-existing positivist systems of thought and explanation. Rather than relegated to the sidelines of inquiry, the impact of the 'unconscious',[30] of heredity, and of the environment became the focus of scientific investigation. In the broader sphere of philosophical speculation, for example, greater emphasis was placed on intuitivist explanations of human understanding, as pragmatism in England and America and Bergsonianism in France gained increased ascendency. Durkheim sought to found his sociology, not on an understanding of individual moral agency or contractual obligation, but rather on a belief in social solidarity, emphasizing the law-like processes of the division of labour and the underlying values which constituted the *conscience collective*. Finally, in political theory, much attention focused on the role of charismatic leadership, on the importance of unconscious manipulation of groups and crowds in mass democratic societies. As will be seen, this aspect of theory owed much to medical and particularly psychiatric ideas and concepts, with clinical models of unconscious suggestibility often readily transposed to larger social phenomena.

The critique provided by the criminal specialists who

30 For an introduction to the primacy of this discussion and its relationship to broader philosophical trends see Henri F. Ellenberger, *The Discovery of the Unconscious: The History and Evolution of Dynamic Psychiatry* (New York, 1970).

emerged in the 1880s also reflected concern with the moral agent, liberal values and interventionist strategies, although specific debates over crime and madness sharpened their particular approach. The system of classical jurisprudence—the penal code and its reliance on the doctrine of free will and moral responsibility—became the object of fundamental criticism and revision for this loose collection of physicians, jurists, and penal reformers. This new breed of social-scientific specialists distrusted the rigid categories set out by the penal code, and suggested that technical, rather than moral, considerations be deployed in order to foster a more efficacious programme of social management.

Often criticizing retributivism, as well as Bentham's moral arithmetic, they would claim that there was neither a self-evident retaliatory principle nor a natural taxonomy of crimes and penalties. Like the utilitarians, they argued that justice for the sake of retribution was both socially useless and unnecessarily brutal. They differed, however, by insisting that the ostensibly scientific classes of crimes and penalties were nothing more than the imposition of rigid and abstract categories in a managerial field which in fact required infinite flexibility. Even more, they would object to the view of human rationality embodied in both penal philosophies, demonstrating in this area a selective affinity for psychiatric concepts.

For example, the Benthamite world view presumed that people could judge their interests through a process of rational calculation, that the constant association of crime and punishment would convince citizens of the harm breaking the law would cause them. However, half a century of penitentiary experience along these lines had produced nothing more, it seemed, than incorrigibles, degenerates, and, above all, 'moral imbeciles'. Hence, professionals involved in criminological debate criticized the psychology of deterrence, remarking on the apparent intractability of criminal behaviour, the growth and persistence of antisocial networks, and the expanding number of repeat offenders. Like the monomaniacs of the 1820s, this large category of individuals was deemed able to understand the difference between right and wrong, but incapable of experiencing that difference or acting upon it. Overwhelmed by the 'objective' study of the 'irrational' in human behaviour, the criminologists suggested a system which would diagnose the extent of each criminal's malady and the possibility of containing his or her antisocial impulses.

The more radical criminologists argued for a system of criminal management divorced from the concept of moral responsibility. They contended that the 'natural' taxonomy which linked crimes and penalties did not guarantee justice, but rather imposed an outmoded, and indeed metaphysical, system that only scientific knowledge could properly reform. Indeed, the more radical argued that justice itself was an antiquated notion, and instead advocated a programme of social defence to neutralize those elements which were deleterious to society. The healthy and adaptive functioning of the 'social organism', rather than the rights and responsibilities of the individual, would become the cornerstone of the criminological position. This way of conceptualizing the problem of crime and its prevention owed much to medical, and particularly psychiatric, concepts and practices. Their primary concern was to investigate the 'psycho-social state', of the criminals, and to measure their dangerousness by probing the recesses of their minds, bodies, and social habits. As I will demonstrate, this psycho-social state was a fragmented entity, a composite of unconscious urges, automatic responses, conflicting identities, and dangerous social influences. The area in which moral agency could operate effectively was increasingly circumscribed although, as will be seen, not entirely extinguished, through the pressure of criminological criticism.

I focus primarily on the capital for several reasons. Although other cities, such as Lyons, were important centres for criminological research, Paris was the hub of scientific activity to which all leading provincial intellectuals ultimately referred. I concentrated on this one city, too, because I intended to elucidate the complex network of connections between theory and practice in the development of the criminological approach. The key experts who intervened in court were also central figures in the movement for reform, as were many of the Parisian magistrates and judges.

My early interest in the topic was generated, above all, by

a problem in the historical sociology of knowledge.[31] I wanted to analyse competing systems of values as incorporated in divergent medical and legal perspectives on human nature. I was also concerned to discuss the impact of this struggle on perceptions of social authority in nineteenth-century France, where psychiatry was broadly recognized as integral to the administration of the deranged and dangerous. This concentration emerged out of a preoccupation with the 'medicalization of morality' which the evaluation of criminal offenders most strikingly brought to the fore. I was struck by the implications for the construction of paternalistic social theory that the medical description of human behaviour contained. By describing processes of illness, rather than imputing fault and responsibility, psychiatric ideas consistently undermined a view of individuals as self-conscious moral agents and insisted on the need for expert intervention and curative procedures.

Equally noticeable was the constant reiteration that such an enterprise was consistently associated with humanitarian considerations for the socially marginal, the sick, or the deranged. I became determined to distinguish between the self-professed motivations and claims made for and by physicians, and the half-hidden implications of their knowledge, which, in many respects, opened up unprecedented areas for manipulative social relations. This is not to suggest that the humanitarian rhetoric rang hollow or had no real effect, but rather that the impact of medical knowledge was multifaceted, and was to some extent obscured even to contemporary participants.

For this reason, I pay particular attention in chapter 2 to the content of medical ideas and their impact on the judicial domain. Too often dismissed today as the naïve and dangerous champions of a narrow scientism, psychiatrists elaborated highly sophisticated theories, the persuasive power of which can be judged by the use of their medical vocabulary and concepts on all levels of society. I aim neither to debunk their positivist pretensions nor to reiterate their claims to

[31] In the early years of this project I was inspired by the work of Roger Smith, who had investigated these issues in his study *Trial by Medicine: Insanity and Responsibility in Victorian Trials* (Edinburgh, 1981), as well as by Foucault's, *I, Pierre Rivière, Having Slaughtered*, which elucidates the process whereby an example of personal tragedy was reduced to a problem of social management.

scientific truth; rather, I hope to demonstrate the impact of their formulations on specific individuals and to explain their effect by analysing psychiatric knowledge within the common cultural preoccupations of the era.

As will be seen in the next chapter, psychiatric concepts were constructed around certain key dichotomies—normal and pathological, mind and body, higher and lower, right and left, equilibrium and destabilization, economy and excess, control and disinhibition. These polarities provided the boundaries of scientific debate, containing within them deeper cultural tensions. According to where the boundaries were drawn along the implied continuum, such designations generated intense controversy both within the medical community and from those outside it who were concerned with the implications of scientific knowledge for moral, social, and political authority.[32] As chapter 3 will show, the doctors' chief antagonists and collaborators in this period were jurists who, through their own confrontation with developments in the social sciences, found some common ground with medical men in revising interpretations of moral responsibility.

However, while exposing the broader cultural and political dimensions of medical and legal argument, this volume is not intended to be a historicized account of the clash and subsequent exchange between legal and medical interpretations of human agency and social interaction. Further study of the documents of pre-trial investigation and courtroom reporting —to be discussed in greater detail in chapter 4—made me realize that the emergence of criminology was tied very much to the way in which professional men interpreted their interaction with defendants. The defendant's *manière de vivre*, a technical term used in criminological discussion, was one which was readily accessible to lay observers in constructing a portrait of social dangerousness or, alternatively, confirming the absence of a 'criminal personality'.

32. For more on the importance of boundaries to social structure and systems of belief see Mary Douglas, *Purity and Danger: An Analysis of Concepts of Pollution and Taboo* (London, 1966); *Natural Symbols: Explorations in Cosmology* (London, 1970); and *Implicit Meanings: Essays in Anthropology* (London, 1975). For an illuminating discussion of the significance of dichotomies in scientific debate see Ludmilla J. Jordanova (ed.), *Languages of Nature: Critical Essays on Science and Literature* (London, 1986), particularly her introd., 34–6.

Through face-to-face confrontation during the process of judicial interrogation and clinical observation, the subjects of analysis played a central role in narrating personal accounts of motivation, life-style, work habits, and character. They also shared in the common cultural context which shaped the debate over crime and madness, altering their recitations for varying audiences, and switching back and forth between languages of determinism and voluntarism, illness and morality, in representing their mental states at the moment of the crime. The decision to convict or exonerate was rarely based on whether the defendant was the author of the crime, as almost always the accused had confessed to the deed. The evaluation undertaken went beyond this simple test of fact. The question of moral responsibility acted as a lens through which important issues regarding the civil and political status of individuals in a democratic society were refracted. Each court decision fixed a temporary moment in social and political history, with defendants playing a key role in their own assessment.

The inclusion of the defendants' narratives in the process of evaluation is intended to offer another dimension to the understanding of the debate, as hitherto the historiography of the medical and legal conflict and of the penal sciences in France has largely relegated the criminals to a secondary position.[33] They are either used as exemplars of changing penal strategies, or dispensed with altogether in favour of elucidating intellectual and philosophical debate. Their neglect seems to me all the more problematic precisely because of the experts' emphasis on 'knowing' the individual on trial, and using this knowledge to determine effective management strategies.

These decisions were profoundly influenced by questions of gender and class. Whenever possible, I will show how this emphasis was interwoven into the analysis of medical and legal thinking and practice, with the four final chapters dealing explicitly with the diverging treatment of women and men of different social classes and political affiliations. Conceptions of

[33] For these works see above n. 5. The work of Patricia O'Brien, *The Promise of Punishment*, makes a more concerted attempt to uncover the lives of the criminals, as do selections in Perrot's *L'Impossible Prison*. References to lesser works concerned specifically with the lives of criminals will be cited throughout.

social dangerousness and of the 'criminal personality' were largely defined by perceptions of femininity and masculinity, of individual responses to family, work, and political activity. The servant maid and the bourgeois lady received very different responses in court, as did the male working-class labourer and the refined Parisian aesthete. The work will illuminate the often shifting boundaries of respectability, the concessions made to working-class men and women in some circumstances, and the often harsh imposition of bourgeois values in other instances, particularly in the sphere of sexual morality.

Hence, in any discussion of the defendant, be it legal, medical, or journalistic, emphasis was placed on the success or failure of the woman or man to live up to certain prescribed social roles. For example, the legal system envisaged different rights and responsibilities for both sexes. Civil capacity was determined by gender, with men holding rights to property, freedom of movement, and political power, which were all denied to women. Although important first measures were undertaken in this period to alter slightly their position in the Napoleonic Code, women largely remained subservient to men and were denied control over their property and affairs. While the system of criminal justice did not make such distinctions—both men and women were subject to the code's directives and were seen as appropriate objects for punishment when they broke the law—in practice women were only rarely perceived of as responsible for their crimes. When they were tried in court, a very different standard of judgement came into play, and one key object of this book is to analyse the responses of judges and jurors and to determine their impact on the women involved.

Finally, the attention given here to medical knowledge necessitates a further investigation of gender relations. From the Enlightenment onwards[34] medical knowledge played an increasingly important role in devising prescriptive systems for

[34] See Maurice Bloch and Jean H. Bloch, 'Women and the Dialectics of Nature in Eighteenth-century Thought', and Jordanova, 'Natural Facts: An Historical Perspective on Science and Sexuality', in Carol M. MacCormack and Marilyn Strathern (eds.), *Nature, Culture and Gender* (Cambridge, 1980), 25–41 and 42–69 respectively; see also Thomas Lacquer, 'Orgasm, Generation and the Politics of Reproductive Biology', in Catherine Gallagher and Thomas Lacquer (eds.), *The Making of the Modern Body: Sexuality and Society in the Nineteenth Century* (Berkeley, 1987) 1–41.

women and men based on their differing 'natural' capacities. Throughout the nineteenth century, the attractiveness of medical formulations increased, as religious justifications for feminine inferiority were matched, and indeed often superseded, by scientific accounts of womanly incapacity in nearly all fields except the domestic. The end of the nineteenth century provided an unprecedented amount of 'natural' knowledge purporting to give a scientific account of women's innate incapacity, a programme of research strengthened and given focus in France by the particular circumstances of the anticlerical struggle. Nowhere was the impact of medical formulations more accessible than in the courtroom, where psychiatrists presented an account of womanly nature endorsed time and time again by both legal and lay participants. It is because of this key emphasis that chapters 5 and 6 concentrate exclusively on the medico-legal conflict surrounding women, focusing first on hysteria and hypnotism and then on feminine crimes of passion, two areas of investigations which aroused considerable professional and lay commentary.

There were also key areas in which medical knowledge had an important impact in undermining the perception of masculine moral agency. Chapter 7 will discuss the contemporary debate surrounding alcoholism, a disease concept which, in contrast to hysteria, was almost always associated with the working-class male. The conclusion will attempt to speculate further on why and how such distinctions in medical knowledge and broader cultural conceptions of disease and gender were represented. An important characterization of a morally depraved and biologically degenerate working man impinged significantly on the outcome of individual cases. It also contributed, as chapter 7 will show, to the development of criminology as a specialized *politique criminelle*, which was more concerned to eradicate undesirables than to reform the seemingly irretrievable according to the dictates of social defence philosophy. Further observations on masculine responsibility will be provided in the last chapter, as male crimes of passion, notions of masculine honour, and the critique of middle-class decadence are examined. In all these discussions I will attempt to unravel the relationship between prescriptive statements made by medical men and jurists on appropriate sexual and class behaviour on the one hand and the infinite complexity of the perception of social reality on the other, particularly as it relates to the problem of moral responsibility and the penalties meted out to defendants in court.

2

THE MEDICAL APPROACH

In writing their reports to the investigating magistrates in the thirty years before 1910, physicians incorporated a wealth of clinical and experimental evidence, basing their conclusions on the findings of pathological anatomy, physiological principles, and neurological investigation. In their search to understand 'mind', they conducted experiments on animals, collected brains and crania for examination, and wrote masses of clinical reports on afflicted individuals. Their scientific work was closely allied to their social and political interests, as they examined criminals in the prison and police establishment and actively sought public recognition by talking to journalists and lobbying for new institutional positions.

There is no way of doing full justice here to the variety of medical theories and debates which impinged on the medico-legal sphere. My intention is merely to give prominence to those aspects of the medical viewpoint which most consistently featured in reports to the magistrature. Physicians brought a unique array of conceptual tools and clinical orientations, specialist knowledge, and a professional stance to their task. At the same time, however, their knowledge was embedded in a common cultural context and in a language which, despite its esoteric qualities, was often readily understood by judicial and lay audiences. It is this double-edged nature of medical discourse, both elusive and accessible, which I hope to explore here. Moreover, the chapter will also attempt to show the connection between theoretical and clinical knowledge on the one hand, and the way that knowledge was deployed in the courtroom on the other.

The diagnoses doctors gave to the court were largely shaped by their attempt to provide an account of insanity as a 'bodily' illness. This long-standing feature emerged as early as the 1820s and from the outset partially contradicted both Pinel's medical-philosophical synthesis and his system of disease classification. An inheritor of a nominalist tradition, Pinel had proposed the study of the various forms and mutations of mental pathology with a view towards establishing a truly scientific taxonomy of its classes, genres, and species.[1] However, while he, and later Esquirol, continued to concentrate on the collection, observation, and classification of mental disorder (describing forms of mania, melancholia, deliria, dementia, idiocy, and later monomania), other contemporaneous trends in scientific medicine militated against such an exclusive preoccupation.

Instead, work in the Paris hospitals increasingly focused on pathological anatomy, developing a body of disease descriptions based on wholly different criteria.[2] More precisely, the anatomical approach led to a search for a 'physicalist' understanding of the bases of mental illness, a tradition which tended to equate mind with brain and suggested that all mental operations would ultimately be revealed as combinations of physical processes. In the 1820s, this new medical 'gaze' was known as the 'anatomo-clinical' method and concentrated on the links between localized organic lesions and the clinical 'tableau' seen as mere external manifestations of an underlying, somatically based pathology. This partial rebellion had generational overtones, with Esquirol's disciples—Georget, Calmeil, Rostan, Bayle, and Falret—eager to apply the new methods to their own speciality.[3] Much of their optimism was based on the belief that the investigation of 'this multitude of open crania, dissected meninges, and brains exposed and examined with a feverish attention'[4] would link alienism to the most prestigious contemporaneous trends in scientific medicine. One element of this work was the research of A.-L.-J. Bayle, who, as early as 1822, correlated stages of degenerative brain

[1] For this and other aspects of Pinel's work see Paul Bercherie, *Les Fondements de la clinique: Histoire et structure du savoir psychiatrique* (Paris, 1980), 25–39.

[2] See Erwin Akerknecht, *Medicine at the Paris Hospitals, 1794–1848* (Baltimore, 1967) and Michel Foucault, *The Birth of the Clinic: An Archeology of Medical Perception*, trans. A. M. Sheridan Smith (New York, 1975).

[3] For Georget's 'organicist' position see *De la folie* (Paris, 1820); for the evangelical ardour characterizing psychiatric research into pathological anatomy see J.-P. Falret *père*, *Des maladies mentales* (Paris, 1864), pp. i–iv.

[4] Antoine Ritti quoted in Anon., *Inauguration des bustes de Baillarger et de Falret à L'Hospice de la Salpêtrière* (Paris, 1894), 20.

tissue and linked these with a picture of progressive insanity. Several seemingly distinct clinical entities thus became part of one malady, the stages and evolution of which were united by the single underlying physical lesion. Starting with a period of exalted monomania in which the patient at least partially conserved his judgement and reason, there followed a period of '*agitation maniaque extravagante*', which ultimately degenerated into an '*affaiblissement démentiel*' and ended in death.[5]

This anatomo-clinical entity, called general paralysis of the insane (GPI), was to be repeatedly applauded as a major milestone. As late as the French Congress of Mental Medicine held in Paris in 1889, for example, the alienist J.-P. Falret *fils* declared that GPI 'constitutes the most important discovery of the century'.[6] A whole range of new work conducted from the 1820s through to the turn of the century extended this aspect of neuro-psychiatric investigations, with clinicians waiting, with often indiscreet enthusiasm, for the death of promising patients in order to continue the search for inflammations, haemorrhages, and lesions. Using the methods of histology promoted by men like Charles Robin and J. Luys, the fine anatomical structure of the central nervous system was subjected to the ever more intense focus of the microscope. Not only was the clinical tableau of GPI fleshed out, but other work also sought to distinguish it from, for example, senile dementia, always with the aim of restructuring the classificatory map of mental illness along ostensibly more rigorous and scientific lines.

This component of psychiatric research was largely successful in attaching the medico-psychological specialism more securely to neurological investigation. The connections between the two fields were perhaps strongest at the Salpêtrière, where, between the 1860s and 1880s, Charcot and his neurological associate G.-B.-A. Duchenne de Boulogne (1806–75), studied locomotive ataxia, miliaanry aneurysms, the degeneration of the spinal cord, and brain softening in an attempt to correlate lesions with clinical portraits of motor, sensory,

[5] See A.-L.-J. Bayle, *Nouvelle doctrine des maladies mentales* (Paris, 1825); id., *Traité des maladies du cerveau et de ses membranes* (Paris, 1826); for an analysis of Bayle's work see Bercherie, *Les Fondements de la clinique*, 71–9.

[6] Antoine Ritti, editor of Comptes rendus, 'Discours d'ouverture', *Congrès international de médecine mentale* (Paris, 5–10 Aug., 1889), 25.

and mental pathology.[7] Many readily interchanged their psychiatric and neurological caps and, in so doing, helped to further an increasingly monist interpretation of the mind/body relation, a perspective strengthened by other neurophysiological research exemplifying a similar philosophical tendency.

Even this seemingly esoteric aspect of medical research had its medico-legal implications. For example, the behavioural symptoms of GPI led the more adventurous to suggest that those in the early, or so-called 'prodromic', period of the disorder could be medically identified, thus sparing an afflicted defendant unjust punishment and protecting society from his dangerous proclivities. Here was an example of the profession's dreams of accurate prediction made possible by the identification of the ineluctable stages of pathology. The chief physician of the Paris public asylums, E. Marandon de Montyel, recalled a case in 1886 of an unnamed man of distinguished background who, after a lewd scene of self-exhibition, shot at his best friend. Manifesting the characteristic features of the disease—difficulty in speaking, trembling, and spasms—he was placed in a lunatic asylum where his outrageous behaviour and symptoms worsened until he was as docile as a gentle child. Immediately after his death, an autopsy satisfactorily revealed that the corpse, as Marandon remarked, 'showed all the classical lesions of general paralysis in the meninges and brain'.[8]

There were other areas where this strand of medical research enlivened criminological and even political debate. For example, post-mortems of guillotined murderers were eagerly awaited. These investigations were generally conducted by the Professor of Legal Medicine and Dean of the Faculty, Paul Brouardel, one of his associates at the Morgue, or other physician-anthropologists at the *École anthropologique*—men like Paul Topinard and Léonce Manouvrier, who oversaw the school's impressive collection of brains and crania.[9] Any signs

[7] For Duchenne de Boulogne's eccentric career and important work see P.-J.-L. Guilly, *Duchenne de Boulogne* (Paris, 1936).

[8] E. Marandon de Montyel, 'Homicide et assassinat à la période prodromique de la paralysie générale', *Annales d'hygiène publique et de médecine légale*, 3rd ser., 20 (1888), 151.

[9] Robert Nye, *Crime, Madness and Politics*, 287n.

of physical illness boosted the arguments of advocates for the abolition of the death penalty and were interpreted as proof of the unenlightened nature of a judicial system which could countenance meting out irrevocable penalties to possibly sick, abnormal, and irresponsible individuals.

Moreover, this was a position which defence attornies were keen to exploit. For example, Louis Menesclou was tried in 1880 for the murder, rape, and dismemberment of a four-year-old girl and was guillotined in 1881. The guilty verdict was due, at least in part, to the fact that the examining psychiatrists refused to recommend indulgence on medical grounds despite finding numerous abnormalities.[10] His attorney, Henri Robert, the most famous advocate of the day, had unsuccessfully called for a second medico-legal report and years later remembered bitterly the result of the post-mortem when, during a meeting of the *Société des prisons* in 1905, he criticized judicial haste: 'This is how surgical justice operates—first cut his head off and look inside. In fact, the autopsy did show a particular adhesion of the meninges which indicated that Menesclou was a sick man!'[11]

However, for all the emphasis placed on pathological anatomy, the findings which it yielded were often disappointing. Despite the most fastidious investigations, lesions persistently eluded the physicians, and a prominent doctor such as J. Falret *père*—a disciple of Esquirol and a key psychiatric clinician and theorist in mid-century—even went so far as to repudiate his own earlier adherence to the technique in a critical account published in the 1860s.[12] Similarly, while important as a rhetorical gambit in advancing a 'physicalist' interpretation of mental disorder, reference to the proof provided by an organic '*siège*' was rarely of use in the courts. In the case cited above, Marandon de Montyel was fortunate both in his diagnosis and in the timely demise of the patient. However, when called to give expert testimony, medico-legists

[10] See D^2U^8 98, 30 July 1880, for the medico-legal report which was also reprinted in Charles Lasègue, Paul Brouardel, and Auguste Motet, 'Affaire Menesclou: Examen de l'état mental de l'inculpé', *Annales d'hygiène publique et de médecine légale*, 2nd ser., 4 (1880), 439–53.

[11] Henri Robert, in the discussion of the 'Traitement à appliquer aux délinquents à responsabilité limitée', *Revue pénitentiaire*, 29 (1905), 326–7.

[12] Falret *père*, *Des maladies mentales*, pp. i–iv.

could not produce such conclusive evidence, able only to examine the symptoms of living subjects rather than their remains.

The search for lesions in the central nervous system was far from being the only way in which alienists demonstrated their commitment to a 'physicalist' interpretation of mental disorder. Rather, they resorted often and with great persuasive power to a wide array of functional abnormalities. Accounts of the etiology of mental illness had long indicated a series of physiological disturbances which predisposed individuals towards mental illness. Pinel, for example, cited the importance of such traumatic episodes as a knock on the head as a cause of mental instability, as well as a range of 'sympathetic' factors which affected the brain through other organs of the body, be they cutaneous infections, haemorrhages altering the blood supply, fevers, and so on. He also noted the influence of heredity as a factor in the evolution of mental disorder, as well as numerous 'moral' causes, ranging from political disturbances and vicious education to bad habits and an irregular lifestyle. This last set, considered crucial in Pinel's system, were seen to disturb the person's physiological 'economy' and through the action of the passions—anger, fear, and sadness—to alter the function of the viscera as well as the processes of circulation and respiration.[13]

Throughout the century there is a remarkable continuity in the nature of the causes adduced by psychiatrists to account for the rise of mental disorder. What changed and shifted crucially was first the growing and pervasive emphasis on heredity as key factor. A second change affected the nature of the medical theory employed to explain the processes of physiological destabilization through the production of diffuse, unlocalized 'functional disturbances', or the existence of so-called 'dynamic lesions'. For the moment the discussion of heredity will be set aside and emphasis placed on the broader currents of psychiatric theory and practice which concentrated on physiological theory and experimentation.

The 'emergence' of physiology in the early decades of the nineteenth century has preoccupied historians, as they seek to trace the way in which the practitioners both were indebted to,

[13] Bercherie, *Les Fondements de la clinique*, 32–3.

and sought to distinguish themselves from, the clinical and patho-anatomical methods ascendant in the Paris hospitals in these years. Marie-Xavier-Bichat (1771–1802) described physiological processes as 'assemblages of different organs which, each performing its own function, contribute in their own ways to the conservation of the whole. There are so many specialized machines in the general machine which constitutes the individual.'[14] This perception was intimately linked to an appraisal of anatomical differentiation, based on an analysis of a variety of tissues. Identifying twenty-one organized elements, Bichat explained how they were distinguished by their structure and varying vital properties which combined to form the complexity and unified activity of organic life.

Through the work of such physiologists as François Magendie, however, these aspects of Bichat's system were subjected to increasing attack in the 1810s and 1820s.[15] Magendie based his own notion of physiological explanation on a *unitary* vital force and saw the enumeration of various vital properties (always identified with some morphological unit) as militating against such a conception.[16] Claude Bernard continued in this direction, describing physiological functioning as 'a series of acts or phenomena in harmony, grouped together to attain a predetermined result'.[17] He sought to demonstrate these precepts by using new techniques of animal vivisection. In studies on nutrition, particularly his famous experiments on

[14] Quoted in Joseph Schiller, *Claude Bernard et les problèmes scientifiques de son temps* (Paris, 1967), 47.

[15] See John E. Lesch, *Science and Medicine in France: The Emergence of Experimental Physiology, 1790–1855* (Cambridge, Mass., 1984), 50–79; Lesch has carefully sought to reinterpret Bichat's 'two physiologies'. The first emphasized the vital-properties doctrine and was inspired by vitalist physiological currents in the eighteenth century and later developments in tissue anatomy. The second focused on surgical intervention, employing an experimental technique going as far back as Harvey. He argues that the essential duality in these distinctive, but complementary, modes of analysis left an enduring legacy of ambiguity in the interpretation of Bichat's system both for historians and for succeeding generations of physiologists who would find the first strand of analysis both puzzling and annoying; see, in particular, 76–9. For another interesting discussion of the political implications of Bichat's and Majendie's physiology see John Pickstone, 'Bureaucracy, Liberalism and the Body in Post-Revolutionary France: Bichat's Physiology and the Paris School of Medicine', *History of Science*, 19 (1981), 115–42.

[16] See Lesch, *Science and Medicine*, 93–4.

[17] Quoted in Schiller, *Claude Bernard et les problèmes scientifiques de son temps*, 47.

the glycogenetic function of the liver,[18] he sought to demonstrate the interplay of opposing physiological forces, the process of analysis and decomposition followed by one of synthesis and absorption.

However, it was not only in the experimental arena that Bernard made an impact. As a powerful theoretician who opposed both vitalism and physiochemical determinism, he constructed in the seven years after 1850 a model denoted by the term *milieu intérieur*, an ideal arrangement of physiological relationships within the organism which enabled it to react successfully to changing external conditions. The organism mobilized its internal resources through a dynamic process of physiological integration, at each moment actively adjusting its internal environment to the stimulus provided by the external milieu. This set of relationships was

> . . . the pre-condition for a free and independent life. The mechanism which facilitates this . . . maintains all the conditions necessary for organic life in the *milieu intérieur*. . . . The stability of this milieu presupposes an ongoing improvement of the organism in which external changes are constantly compensated for and counterbalanced. Consequently, far from being indifferent to the external world, the animal is, on the contrary, in a skilful relationship with it, in such a way that its equilibrium stems from continual and delicate readjustments, establishing the most sensitive of balances.[19]

This orderly account of the development of physiological theory, concentrating on the contributions of a few 'great' men, gives an inadequate representation of the desultory and indeed often incomplete nature of the changes taking place. The identification of vital energy with certain organs and tissue groups did not disappear until well past the middle of the century. Equally, Bernardian notions did not immediately pervade the entire medical profession, and older humoral ideas lived on happily until 1900 and beyond in popular medical literature.[20] None the less, the effects of the Bernardian approach for many

[18] For the detailed examinations of Bernard's experimental work see Frederic Lawrence Holmes, *Claude Bernard and Animal Chemistry* (Cambridge, Mass., 1974); Mirko Drazen Grmek, *Raisonnement expérimental et recherches toxicologiques chez Claude Bernard* (Geneva and Paris, 1972) and Georges Canguilhem, *Études d'histoire et de philosophie des sciences*, 5th edn. (Paris, 1983), 127–62.

[19] Quoted in Schiller, *Claude Bernard et les problèmes scientifiques*, 173.

[20] I would like to thank Robert Nye for clarification on this point.

of the élite mid-century alienists were unmistakable. Bernard was a close friend and associate of the important medico-legist Charles Lasègue (1816–83) and shared rooms with Auguste Morel, who used his concepts in his elaboration of the theory of degeneration.

However, to explain the impact of such ideas solely through a network of personal association would unduly minimize their significance. Key mental pathogists used Bernard's experimental techniques with a self-conscious desire to emulate both his methodological prescriptions and the vivisectional work done on animals. In his famous and much-cited *L'Introduction à la médecine expérimentale*, Bernard made an important distinction between observation and experiment. Passive observation of nature was deemed insufficient; rather, the scientist was required to test an idea of 'hypothesis' during controlled experiments which provoked the necessary conditions for proper observation. In this way, Bernard lent primacy to theory and envisaged the experimental method as a necessary precondition for the production of scientific knowledge. Although very much a self-serving account of his own career and outlook, *L'Introduction* none the less became an almost inspirational text for young medical men as well as a philosophical treatise extolling the benefits of positivism.

Valentin Magnan, for example, was widely known for the little laboratory he had attached to the Asile Ste Anne, 'one of the sanctuaries of modern science', where he took 'a pre-eminent place among physicians who, in accordance with the doctrine promoted at the time by C. Bernard, were engaged in furthering the close and therefore productive alliance between physiology and the clinic.'[21] There Magnan injected dogs with alcohol, cocaine, and morphine and, through the extreme spasms and convulsions leading to their untimely death, obtained vivid illustrations of the toxic physiological effect of these drugs. Similarly, it will be suggested that some of the impetus behind hypnotic research at the Salpêtrière—to be described in chapter 5—was the possibility of experimenting on living subjects. Hypnosis was often described as a kind of

[21] M le professeur Gley, 'Discours', *Jubilé du Docteur V. Magnan, 15 Mars 1908* (n.p., n.d.), 18.

psychophysiological vivisection during which the effect of magnets, bright lights, noises, metallic substances, and electric prods could all be examined.

Perhaps more importantly, however, Bernardian conceptions increased the weight doctors gave to the unified nature of physiological process—'life is not concentrated in one particular place; it is everywhere distributed'[22]—and enabled them to explain why discrete lesions of the central nervous system were not always readily identifiable during post-mortem examinations. At the same time, however, they were able to defend with confidence a view of mental disorder based on a physiological and hence 'physical' interpretation of its nature. Physiology in general, and the concept of the *milieu intérieur* in particular, provided a treasure trove of metaphorical expressions for talking about animal, human, and social organisms. Checks and balances, the division of labour, equilibrium and disequilibrium, reduction and recombination —these were the polarities which structured physiological explanation. They also provided a descriptive language in medico-legal discourse, which resonated with moral associations by describing the individual's 'disequilibrated' and 'disinhibited' propensities in a readily accessible fashion. The recourse to such polarities also suggests the extent to which medical ideas both contributed to, and were infused by, other contemporary debates in political theory, political economy, and sociology.[23]

Physiological principles were most commonly used to produce a sophisticated etiological system which shaped not only psychiatrists' techniques of clinical observation, but also their medical-legal interventions. For example, in the compendious *Traité de pathologie mentale* published in 1903 by the medico-legist and psychiatrist Gilbert Ballet, the article dealing with 'general etiology of mental disorders' concentrated on a wide range of physiological pre-conditions—'the psychopathic substratum [*terrain*]'—to explain the onset of mental disorder. Not only did he include heredity in all its various possibilities—'direct or individual, consanguineous or atavistic . . .'—but also a wide array of other causes

22 Quoted in Schiller, *Claude Bernard et les problèmes scientifiques*, 54.

23 For an analysis of this interpenetrability see Paul Quentin Hirst, *Durkheim, Bernard and Epistemology* (London, 1975).

that ranged from infantile maladies to cerebral traumas, from rheumatism and gout to nutritional deficiencies and thyroid conditions.[24] Although some of these ailments were considered more likely than others to predispose an individual to mental illness, in each case the emphasis rested on the destabilizing physiological effect produced. All were regarded as potentially deleterious factors operating on the general animal economy, disturbing the functioning of the central nervous system, and hence possibly modifying mental functioning.

In their medico-legal analysis of predisposing causes, psychiatrists again cited a virtually limitless array of prior organic illness which were seen as crucial indicators in the pathological portrait they were painting. When the prominent medico-legist Henri Legrand du Saulle examined Hippolyte F . . . for trying to kill his wife, he found his subject irresponsible because of a cerebral trauma suffered three years previously when the man was hit on the head with an iron bar in a café. Once known for his gentle, diligent nature, F . . . had become irritable and increasingly wayward after the fight. Unable to tolerate army discipline, argumentative with his wife and at work, he committed his crime after getting totally drunk on only one drink. Legrand du Saulle's assessment was indulgent, and his opinion was matched by that of the man's wife and of the jury which acquitted him in 1884.[25]

The extent of this physiological view of destabilization can perhaps be best illustrated by the case of the Italian immigrant worker, François-Louis M . . ., who murdered a total stranger and injured three others while on a drunken rampage through the streets of Paris in 1885. Confronted with an apparently genuine inability to remember the incident, the medico-legists Paul Brouardel and Auguste Motet maintained that, although he appeared in adequate health, he had none the less been subjected to damaging physiological influences by spending the fifty days before the attack in a compressed air chamber laying pylons for the Pont D'Austerlitz. The constant changes in air pressure had been so extreme that the physicians believed that 'M . . .'s cerebral activity [*la vie cérébrale de M . . .*] is not normal and it is possible to suggest that his brain's constantly changing circulation makes it more likely

[24] See Gilbert Ballet *et al.*, *Traité de pathologie mentale* (Paris, 1903), 22–64.
[25] See Hippolyte F . . . D^2U^8 164, 4 Sept. 1884, medico-legal report.

to suffer from the toxic effect of alcohol than a healthy one.'[26] Although they did not recommend a conclusion of irresponsibility, they none the less suggested that these factors, combined with a heredity that indicated a tendency to convulsive attacks, be taken into account. M . . . was sentenced to five years' forced labour.

Equally striking was the effect of physiological reasoning on the analysis of women. Beset by a biological life cycle that was deemed to be fraught with periods of instability—menstruation, pregnancy, childbirth, and lactation—women were considered to go through periods of insanity which sometimes led to horrifying crimes against themselves, their children, or their mates. In 1858, the psychiatrist L.-V. Marcé devoted an entire volume to the physiological disturbances associated with women during the pregnant and post-partum periods.[27] Discussing the problem of 'puerperal insanity', Marcé cited differences in medical opinion, some limiting the period of madness associated with the post-partum state to between two weeks and a month, and others insisting on evidence of physiological disturbance from the moment of conception, through pregnancy, labour, and wet-nursing. Whatever the preferred duration, however, the doctors agreed that the biological life cycle associated with reproduction caused 'a profound modification of the blood', and hence left women open to periods of intense mental instability, an attitude which continued to mark medical appreciations well into the *fin de siècle* and beyond.

This perception of womanly derangement associated with childbearing regularly cropped up in court cases. When, for example, the wet-nurse Marie C . . ., newly arrived from the country, attempted to poison the baby of her bourgeois Parisian employers, the the leading Parisian psychiatrist, Auguste Motet, sought to determine whether the deed was due to a 'morbid impulsion', to an unstable character, or to the physiological changes produced during lactation. Although Motet ultimately decided that antagonism, not insanity, was the cause of the crime, his line of inquiry exemplified the common medical approach to women who committed crimes while 'disturbed' by the physiological processes associated with childbirth.[28]

[26] François-Louis M . . . D^2U^8 176, 25 Apr. 1885, medico-legal report.

[27] See L.-V. Marcé, *Traité de la folie des femmes enceintes des nouvelles accouchées et des nourrices et considérations médico-légales qui se rattachent à ce sujet* (Paris, 1858).

[28] Marie C . . . D^2U^8 178, 9 June 1885; she received a penalty of 8 months' imprisonment, and a 10 francs fine.

Perhaps the clearest example of the medical and lay appreciation of temporary female insanity can be seen in the 1897 case of Femme Charmillon, who, after an evening at the local *débit de vins*, murdered her beloved child with a hatchet, tried to do the same to her husband, and then attempted to injure herself with a triangular file, finishing her deed by trying to jump out of the window. The intervening psychiatrist suggested that the defendant deserved judicial indulgence, 'as her pregnancy may have produced that particular state of excitability and impressionability that one observes in women at such times'.[29] She herself hastened to present a similar explanation for her deeds, an account of womanly derangement which was unhesitatingly seconded by judge and jury. Mme Charmillon was acquitted.

It was not only in relation to states associated with pregnancy, labour and lactation that women were seen to go through bouts of dangerous temporary insanity. As will be seen, the 'scientific' study of hysteria had ostensibly moved the focus of medical investigation from the womb to the nervous system, although there were many important relics of the uterine interpretation, with virtually all commentators inevitably returning to the relationship between hysterical behaviour and menstruation. Regularly, physicians sought to determine when women had begun menstruating and used this evidence in shaping their medico-legal arguments. When three physicians examined Gabrielle Bompard before her trial for murder in 1890, they effectively dismissed her defence that she had acted under hypnotic suggestion and referred instead to what they considered her 'moral imbecility' and hysterical disposition. For Auguste Motet, she was nothing more than a prostitute, a girl of rudimentary moral development whose precocious menstruation from the age of eight had encouraged vicious tastes and habits.[30]

Although medical men concentrated in this instance on an ostensibly depraved woman,[31] all members of her sex were

29 Femme Charmillon, *Gazette des tribunaux*, 26 June 1897.

30 'Rapport de MM. Brouardel, Motet et Ballet, Affaire Gouffé', *Archives d'anthropologie criminelle*, 6 (1891), 72.

31 There was considerable medical and criminological discussion of the relationship between prostitution and menstruation. In their *La Femme criminelle et la prostituée*, trans. L. Meille (Paris, 1896) the Italian criminal anthropologists, Cesare Lombroso and

considered prone to madness and violence during the menstrual period. S. Icard, a pupil of Benjamin Ball, compared menstruating women to animals on heat. Through a long-examination of the intimate details of domestic life, often garnered, through his own admission, by questioning husbands, Icard gave examples of any number of extravagant masturbatory practices during menstruation as well as a shocking list of murder, cannibalism, and defilement indulged in during this state. The implication of such an inventory was that all women were potentially and periodically insane, reduced to animality because of their bodily functions.[32]

EVOLUTIONARY NEUROPHYSIOLOGY, HUMAN AUTOMATISM, AND THE 'UNCONSCIOUS'

Physiological analysis was particularly important for theories of nervous functioning, an area of investigation most obviously connected to the study of insanity. Medical research on the disorders of the cerebro-spinal axis in this period posited a continuous, but hierarchical, view of nervous functioning that ranged from the lower reflexive levels to the highest mental operations of the cerebral hemispheres. Moreover, it incorporated a view of the heterogeneity of cerebral function based on the localization of various mental faculties and sensory and motor centres. When this finely tuned system was destabilized by degeneration, the various levels of vertical co-ordination and centres of horizontal communication no longer operated in tandem, neither along the cerebro-spinal axis nor across the cerebral hemispheres. Time and again, reference was made to the 'disarray' of the system, its disequilibration and the subsequent appearance of symptoms of uncontrollability,

Guglielmo Ferrero, saw menstruation as a condition which unleashed the latent and universal fund of erotic perversity underlying women's characteristic frigidity. Prostitutes, above all, demonstrated the dangerousness of this combination. They bled precociously and in excessive amounts, 'natural facts' which showed links between external signs and internal, degenerative qualities. For a discussion of their analysis see Hilde Olrik, 'Le sang impur: Notes sur le concept de prostituée-née chez Lombroso', *Romantisme*, 31 (1981), 168–78.

32 Séverin Icard, *La Femme pendant la période menstruelle: Étude de psychologie morbide et de médecine légale* (Paris, 1890).

'disinhibition', and automatism which were characteristic of the mentally ill.

Doctors had long supplied a vision of irresistible behaviour which experimental neurophysiology ultimately began to confirm. In the 1820s, Charles Bell and François Magendie revealed the differentiation of the spinal cord into posterior sensory and anterior motor nerves. In the 1830s Marshall Hall and Johannes Müller supplied a general formulation of the sensory-motor reflex arc, identifying it as fundamental to nervous functioning, with organisms reacting purposively, although automatically, to their internal and external words. Müller was also responsible for laying the groundwork for the so-called 'law of specific nervous energies', while in 1850 his student, Hermann Helmholtz, measured the speed of nervous impulses and suggested that vital processes, like other physical systems, could be measured by the laws of theoretical mechanics.[33]

Earlier investigators had tended to apply such concepts only to the lower, 'mindless' levels of the nervous system and suggested that the cerebrum, the seat of the highest mental faculties, was of an entirely different structure. However, it was not long before it was hypothesized that the encephalic ganglia had their own form of reflex action and that brain reflexes were responsible for a large proportion of highly complex conscious and unconscious mental functions. In England, William Carpenter proposed the term 'unconscious automatism' in the 1850s and applied it to such things as dreaming, reverie, and hallucinations. Clinical descriptions increasingly tended to make use of the perspectives of sensory-motor psychophysiology and a wide range of behaviours associated with the 'higher' cerebral centres were incorporated within the same explanatory framework. Indeed, by 1870 the doctrine of nervous continuity had become the hallmark of modern neurophysiology.[34]

[33] Good general outlines of the state of neurophysiological knowledge during the first half of the nineteenth century may be found in Edwin Clarke and Charles Donald O'Malley, *The Human Brain and Spinal Cord: A Historical Study Illustrated by Writings from Antiquity to the Twentieth Century* (Berkeley, 1968). See also Canguilhem's seminal article, 'Le Concept de réflexe au XIXe siècle', in K. E. Roshschuh (ed.), *Die Entwicklung der kontinentalen Physiologie im 18. und 19. Jahrhundert mit besonderer Berücksichtigung der Neurophysiologie* (Stuttgart, 1964) and Edwin Boring, *A History of Experimental Physiology* (New York, 1950).

[34] See Roger Smith, 'The Background of Physiological Psychology in Natural Philosophy', *History of Science*, 11 (1973), 75–123. For a French interpretation of the

By mid-century, speculation on the central nervous system became increasingly tied up with an evolutionary conception of the development of 'mind' particularly associated with Herbert Spencer's *Principles of Psychology*.[35] Such ideas exerted a strong influence in France especially through the work of the philosopher–psychologist, Théodule Ribot (1839–1916),[36] who combined a knowledge not only of Spencer's psychological writings but also of the most recent developments in experimental neurophysiology, clinical neurology, and psychiatry.[37] By establishing the *Revue philosophique* in 1877, moreover, he provided the single most important interdisciplinary forum for the examination of 'mind' during the French *fin de siècle*.

Ribot saw himself as a rebel, determined to bury the legacy of official 'eclectic' psychology in France[38] and establish the field on a new, postivist foundation by paying proper attention to the findings of clinical research, the studies of German experimentalists, and the psychology of British 'associationists' such as Bain and Mill. He sought to establish the evolutionary origins of traditional categories of psychological analysis, namely memory, will, and emotion. In three classic monographs published in the 1880s,[39] he concentrated on the development of such 'higher' faculties and tried to establish the

history of neurophysiology see Jules Soury, *Le Système nerveux central, structure et fonctions: Histoire critique des théories et des doctrines* (Paris, 1899).

[35] For a general analysis of Spencer's psychological and evolutionary ideas see John David Yeadon Peel, *Herbert Spencer: The Evolution of a Sociologist* (New York, 1971), 112–65. For the specific impact of Spencer's ideas on British medico-psychological ideas see Michael J. Clark, ' "A Plastic Power Ministering to Organisation": Interpretations of the Mind-Body Relation in Late Nineteenth-century British Psychiatry', *Psychological Medicine*, 13 (1983), 492.

[36] Ribot translated Spencer's *Principes de psychologie* with A. Espinas in 1876.

[37] For discussions of Ribot's philosophy and impact see M. Reuchlin, 'The Historical Background for National Trends in Psychology: France', *Journal of the History of the Behavioural Sciences*, 1 (1965), 115–23; Pierre Janet, 'L'Œuvre psychologique de Ribot', *Journal de Psychologie*, 11 (1915), 268–82; Raymond Lenoir, 'The Psychology of Ribot and Contemporary Thought', *The Monist*, 30 (1920); J. Alexandre Gunn, 'Ribot and his Contribution to Psychology', *The Monist*, 34 (1924), 1–14; Georges Dwelshauvers, *La Psychologie française contemporaine* (Paris, 1920), 110–26.

[38] See Ribot's somewhat polemical 'Philosophy in France', *Mind*, 2 (1877), 366–86.

[39] id., *Les Maladies de la mémoire* (Paris, 1881); *Les Maladies de la volonté*, 2nd edn. (Paris, 1884); and *Les Maladies de la personnalité* (Paris, 1885).

basic building blocks out of which human consciousness emerged.[40]

In analysing the development of the cerebro-spinal axis, Ribot relied on the elemental unit of neurophysiological analysis, reflex action: 'The very basis of an intelligent act is effectively found in reflex action . . . [it] thus embodies everything that constitutes a psychological act apart from consciousness itself.'[41] According to this view, consciousness was merely the product of an organic process set in motion by evolution, with the higher functions being nothing more than complex and specialized conglomerations of cerebral reflexes. From the spinal cord to the cerebral hemispheres, reflex activity became increasingly complex and specialized, with consciousness itself nothing more than an incidental or epiphenomenalist phase resulting from underlying psychophysical processes. Reason, memory, feeling, or will were mere abstractions, the subjective aspect of co-ordinated neurophysiological reaction.[42]

How Ribot perceived the evolutionary development of consciousness may be seen through his examination of 'will', the crucial element which enabled normal individuals to inhibit their automatic urges and adapt positively to the environment. An infant was a 'spinal being' whose activity was 'purely reflexive', and the primary object of education was to suppress and restrain its automatic urges. Infants, he argued, 'only really express the activity of the species, that which is acquired, organized, and fixed by heredity.'[43] Children and 'savages' demonstrated most obviously the next stage, that of desire, which was tempered in normal civilized adults by 'education, habit, reflection' which 'mutilate or brake it'.[44]

For the successful acquisition of 'will', the reasonable,

[40] Ribot took inspiration from the psychological studies of Hippolyte Taine (1828–93), whose *L'Intelligence* (Paris, 1870) proposed an 'atomistic psychology' which sought to reduce psychic life to its basic constituents.

[41] Ribot, *De l'hérédité* (Paris, 1872), 309; for his analysis of the development of the nervous system see 305–56.

[42] For an illuminating discussion of similar theories in England see Clark, 'The Data of Alienism: Evolutionary Neurology, Physiological Psychology, and the Reconstruction of British Psychiatric Theory, *c.*1850–1900', D.Phil. thesis (Univ. of Oxford, 1982), 67–79.

[43] Ribot, *Les Maladies de la volonté*, 5.

[44] Ibid., 6.

healthy adult needed perfect hierarchical co-ordination of the lower reflexive and instinctual urges with higher intellectual and moral development. What was necessary was '*une coordination avec subordination*' which enabled the nervous system to operate like a well-ordered society, all its parts working in consort and the higher capacities quelling the dangerous lower elements.[45] While this idea offered the possibility of heightened neurophysiological advance, reaching such a level of development was neither inevitable nor easily accomplished. On the contrary, the laws of nature seemed stacked against its realization, as the nervous system was liable to a cumulative functional disequilibrium due to the tendency of the more fixed and stable lower levels to overrun the higher, but more fragile and recently acquired, intellectual and moral capacities.[46] In cases of lunacy, particularly when degeneration was present, the higher capacities were 'swamped' by the more bestial qualities lurking beneath the surface of civilized behaviour, an age-old description of insanity articulated, refined, and modified by the evolutionary and neurophysiological perspectives in which it was conveyed.

The language describing the nervous system was pervaded with metaphorical expressions juxtaposing control and disinhibition, struggle and harmony, as well as higher and lower tendencies. Ostensibly a neutral explication of neurophysiological processes, such analyses were pervaded with moral, philosophical, and political warnings on the dire consequences of the breakdown of necessary regulatory mechanisms in either individuals or society. It may be suggested that in describing thus the fragility of the neurophysiological system, men like Ribot created a rich language of organic metaphors to describe the perilous predicament of a society burdened by an increasingly complex and at times seemingly uncontrollable civilization.

Hence, by systematizing a framework for understanding the

[45] Ibid., 136–69 for Ribot's analysis of this hierarchical view.

[46] As Ribot described it: 'deux . . . tendances antagonistes luttent pour se supplanter réciproquement. En fait, tout le monde le sait, cette lutte a lieu entre les tendances inférieures, dont l'adaptation est bornée, et les tendances supérieures, dont l'adaptation est complexe. Les premières sont toujours les plus fortes par nature; les secondes le sont par artifice. Les unes représentent une puissance enregistrée dans l'organisme, les autres une acquisition défraîchissante.' (Ibid., 66.)

ontogenetic and phylogenetic development of human consciousness, Ribot conveyed both an esoteric scientific conception and a readily accessible moral and social vision. Although using comparable linguistic expressions and engaging in similar philosophical musings, psychiatrists focused primarily on clinical evidence, on the 'dissolution' of neurophysiological co-ordination observed among individual sufferers.[47] The most striking example was that of epilepsy, in which subjects were portrayed as dangerous machines gone haywire. In a wide-ranging debate on the neurological description of the condition,[48] clinicians from mid-century expended a great deal of time and energy describing syndromes ranging from dizziness, through amnesia, to full-blown convulsive seizures in which descriptions of gnashing teeth and flailing limbs provided a clinical portrait of total disinhibition.

Epilepsy figured prominently in the medico-legal domain during the *fin de siècle*, with doctors constantly enquiring whether or not its presence could explain periods of amnesia or lack of control. Despite the sympathy expressed towards those afflicted, psychiatrists were wary of becoming the dupes of simulators, and reticent about excusing the wide range of less extreme 'epileptoid' syndromes which seemed often associated with querulousness, mental debilitation, and general antisocial habits. When discussing the case of a certain R . . ., for example, the psychiatrist Charles Vallon described his tainted maternal heredity, his frequent stays (since the age of 11) in the Salpêtrière for a range of unspecified *crises de nerfs*, as well as a previous condemnation for vagabondage. Caught burgling an apartment, R . . . was examined by the physicians at the Préfecture de Police, declared a lunatic, and sent first to the Asylum at Ste-Anne and then to Villejuif. There he was put under Vallon's care but, despite diagnosing R . . . as an epileptic suffering from 'petit mal', he opposed his continual confinement in a mental hospital. According to his report, R . . . was

[47] The most famous expression of this problem was articulated by the renowned British neurologist John Hughlings Jackson (1835–1911) in his 'Evolution and Dissolution of the Nervous System', *Selected Writings of John Hughlings Jackson*, vol. ii (London, 1932), 76–91.

[48] For the difficulty of arriving at an agreed nosological description of various epileptoid phenomena in the period before 1860 see Oswei Temkin, *The Falling Sickness*, 2nd edn. (Baltimore, 1971), 285–91; see also his analysis of John Hughlings Jackson's contribution to the study of epilepsy, 328–9.

'cunning, a liar, argumentative; he is perpetually trying to plot with the other patients against the warden and makes repeated escape attempts; he is a dangerous person'.[49] Obliged as a result to stand trial, R . . . received a penalty of five years' imprisonment.

Such models of neurophysiological disinhibition were applied with equal readiness to those who abused drugs and alcohol, the narrative stressing the unaccountable behaviour produced while simultaneously condemning the subject for acquiring and persisting in bad habits. As chapter 7 will show, alcohol was seen as a key factor for producing violence and allowed enormous scope for medico-legal intervention, with the description of *delirium tremens* providing as extreme a portrait of disinhibition as any associated with epilepsy. The morphinomaniac also sporadically appeared in medico-legal literature and in trials, and was described as an individual who was 'antisocial . . . [C]ompletely dominated by a fierce egotism, he is essentially lazy and unproductive'.[50] Morphine addicts would stoop to the lowest expedients—thieving, prostitution, and the corruption of friends—to support their habit. This complete destruction of moral sense was accompanied by a state of cerebral disequilibration in which the higher faculties were no longer in command and were instead directed by the excitation of the lower, emotional instincts housed in the lower, posterior reaches of the brain.

The state of nervous debilitation in which morphine addicts found themselves needed to be taken into account when they were judged in court. Sometimes medico-legists showed indulgence, as in instances of bourgeois women who were reduced to stealing to support their habits.[51] In other instances, however, there was little sympathy for such individuals who seemed to a large extent responsible for their own state of dangerous automatism. When G.-L.-J. Aubert was tried in

[49] Charles Vallon, 'De la responsabilité des épileptiques, *Annales d'hygiène publique et de médecine légale*, 3rd ser. 29 (1893), 471.

[50] Henri Guimbal, 'Crimes et délits commis par les morphinomanes', *Annales d'hygiène publique et de médecine légale*, 3rd ser., 25 (1891), 481.

[51] For more on the kleptomaniacs see Patricia O'Brien, 'The Kleptomania Diagnosis: Bourgeois Women and Theft in late Nineteenth-century France', *Journal of Social History*, 17 (1983), 65–77. See also Michael B. Miller, *The Bon Marché: Bourgeois Culture and the Department Store, 1869–1920* (London, 1981), 197–206.

October 1896 for murder and the theft of a valuable stamp collection—thereby demonstrating the most despised combination of violence and avarice—he was unable to sit through his trial because of his craving for a shot of morphine. His excessive twitching during the proceedings, the nervous tic 'which makes his two small, quite lively, eyes blink', was seen as evidence of his debilitated mental condition, with the judge asking the defendant: 'The question is to know whether this tic is an excuse for your crime'. Not only would the judge not give Aubert the drug during his pre-trial incarceration, he also unusually denied him a medico-legal investigation. Despite his attorney's defence that he was an irresponsible degenerate, Aubert received a penalty of forced labour for life.[52]

In all these accounts of neurophysiological processes, emphasis has been placed on the vertical axis of integration and hierarchy. Equally important, however, was the study of localized centres in different regions of the cerebral hemispheres. In 1860, the physical anthropologist and neuroanatomist Paul Broca (1829–80) 'discovered' the seat of 'articulate language' (a term which referred specifically to the locomotive capacity for speech) in the third convolution of the left frontal lobe after a post-mortem investigation on an aphasic patient named 'Tan'.[53] Although basing his findings on a single, ambiguous autopsy, Broca extravagantly proclaimed that his work confirmed previous speculation on the organic '*siège*' of the faculty, no doubt basing his own assertion on several decades of corroborative work which associated speech capacity with this region of the brain. The ideological implications of the 'discovery' were automatically grasped. Once language—a distinctively human capacity—was given a material substratum, a wholly evolutionary conception of the development of 'mind' became an imminent possibility, an ideological position which brought controversy in its wake.

Following the discovery, a programme of clinical research was devoted to motor and sensory deficiencies associated with

[52] *Gazette des tribunaux*, 26–7 Oct. 1896.

[53] See Francis Schiller, *Paul Broca: Founder of French Anthropology, Explorer of the Brain* (Berkeley, 1979), 165–211 and Robert Young, *Mind, Brain, and Adaptation in the Nineteenth Century* (Oxford, 1970), 134–49.

language, cases which revealed a loss of speech, but not understanding; the retention of spoken language but the inability to formulate coherent phrases; the ability to read, but an incapacity to write. All these observations suggested to observers the existence of centres in the hemispheres responsible for each sensory, motor, or cognitive process.[54] Increasingly, work was directed towards understanding the different capacities of the right and left hemispheres and their directing influence on opposing parts of the human organism. For example, a range of experiments conducted on hysterical subjects at the Salpêtrière attempted to hypnotize different 'brain halves', evoking hallucinations of sensation and emotion on differing sides of the face and body.[55]

The research into the differing capacities of the 'brain halves' was also important for stimulating the medical view of the left hemisphere as the material home of the higher, 'civilized' qualities. Such research was important to psychiatry in different ways, with the 'demonstration' of left-brain dominance providing a potent explanatory system for interpreting the symptoms of mental pathology. As Anne Harrington has shown, the right side was increasingly associated with femininity, passivity, and emotion while the left generally corresponded to masculinity, activity, and rationality. Hysteria, for example, was seen as left-brain deficiency. Since the occipital lobe (or posterior region) had been traditionally associated with right-brain functioning, anthropological analysis identified the 'lower', black races with these posterior areas and the 'higher', white races with the anterior portions of the brain. It was possible therefore to divide and oppose halves of the human central nervous system along a number of axes: higher/lower, front/back, left/right. As Harrington has explained,

> the nineteenth century's model of lateralised cerebral functioning—with its two antagonistic brain halves poised within a single skull—. . . stand(s) with [the] hierarchical brain model as one important

[54] For an example of this work by Gilbert Ballet, one of the most prominent medico-legists of the era, see *Le Langage intérieur et les diverses formes de l'aphasie* (Paris, 1886).

[55] See Anne Harrington, *Medicine, Mind and the Double Brain: A Study in Nineteenth-Century Thought* (Princeton, 1987), chap. 6, in particular, 166–205.

way in which neurologists . . . reflected their society's awareness (and fear) of the thorough and primitive duality of mind.[56]

The division of the central nervous system into horizontal and vertical axes provided mental pathologists with ready tools for understanding the various kinds of 'disequilibration' affecting the insane and degenerate. Valentin Magnan, for example, believed sexual disturbances could be ascribed to differing lapses and instabilities in various nervous centres. Sexual functioning demanded the simultaneous co-ordination of 'psychic, sensory, and spinal centres'. If one was disturbed, a psycho-physiological disorder was bound to occur. Inhibition of the spinal centre caused impotence, its disinhibition satyriasis. Inhibition of the 'sensory centres' caused frigidity in women, while their excessive excitation caused nymphomania. Psychic disturbances in the cerebral hemispheres might result in a wide array of perversions and inversions, fetishism and bestiality, where a disordered conception of love might lead the sufferer to realize 'abnormal' desires.[57]

Indeed, the broad contours of the clinical approach to insanity can be gleaned from the attempt to provide a cerebro-spinal topography of mental pathology. Idiots, for example, represented degeneration *par excellence*, since nervous life was reduced to the action of the spinal cord. Theirs was a reflexive existence in which they responded like 'an automatic machine' to internal and external excitation. Others, such as the 'feeble-minded, the mentally defective, or backward' (*les faibles d'esprit, les débiles, les arriérés*), were slightly better equipped than idiots, although they still lacked the ability to synthesize the information they acquired. 'Superior degenerates' demonstrated advanced abilities in discrete areas, but none the less showed a multitude of strange and bewildering behavioural and emotional propensities, once again indicating some imbalance between the left and right sides and between higher and lower functioning. In describing such a person Magnan asserted that

[56] Id., 'Hemisphere Differences and "Duality of Mind" in Nineteenth-Century Medical Science, *c.*1860–1900', D.Phil. thesis (Univ. of Oxford, 1985), 119.

[57] V. Magnan and P.-M. Legrain, *Les Dégénérés* (*État mental et syndromes épisodiques*) (Paris, 1895), 95–100.

'in everything he says, he displays a lack of logic . . . The most faultless reasoning leads to the most incomprehensible actions and grandiose ideas are effaced by petty resolutions'.[58] He equally included the category of 'fous moraux'—so important in the medico-legal domain—who reasoned well but were unable to *experience* the difference between right and wrong. There was also the large category of 'impulsives' and 'obsessives' who were unable to restrain themselves, and who hence often found themselves in trouble for a range of anti-social, even murderous acts.

In analysing this apparent 'automatism', mental pathologists were preoccupied with the workings of the 'unconscious' which, despite the pioneering work of men like Pierre Janet on psychological analysis from the 1880s onward,[59] were not generally cast in psychodynamic terms. In Charcot's researches, for example, dreams and fantasies were not considered crucial material for 'decoding' the unconscious, but rather as evidence of 'disinhibition', always potentially pathological if left unchecked. As will be seen, despite the intense fascination with the content and range of hysterical hallucinations, these manifestations of the 'unconscious' were regarded as mere symptoms of the larger psychophysiological malady. The psychological traits of the hysterical patients were scrutinized, but in themselves were not yet seen as the key for either understanding or curing their illness (see chapter 5).

The history of this perspective can be traced to medico-psychological research on hallucinations and dreaming. An extended medico-psychological discussion in mid-century regarded these states as either approaching madness or as virtually indistinguishable from it.[60] In the 1840s, for example, J.-G.-F.

[58] Ibid., 107.

[59] For an introduction to Janet's intellectual development see Henri F. Ellenberger, *The Discovery of the Unconscious: The History and Evolution of Dynamic Psychiatry* (New York, 1970), 331–418.

[60] For a short history of this writing and its relationship to a contemporary literary and artistic discussion see Anthony R. W. James, 'L'hallucination simple?' *Revue d'histoire littéraire de la France*, 6 (1986), 1024–37; for the medico-psychological debate see Henry Ey, 'La Discussion de 1855 à la Société Médico-psychologique sur l'hallucination et l'état actuel du problème de l'activité hallucinatoire', *Annales médico-psychologiques* 15th ser. 1 (1935), 584–613; see also Theodore R. Sarbin and Joseph B. Juhasz, 'The Historical Background of the Concept of Hallucination', *Journal of the History of the Behavioural Sciences*, 3 (1967), 339–58.

Baillarger sought to make a distinction between the powers of imagination and memory directed by a controlling 'moi', and those mental reveries which were automatic and unrestrained. Quoting the spiritualist philosopher Théodore Jouffroy—whose school, as will be seen, impinged significantly on the orientation of a few key nineteenth-century psychiatrists—he described the process as one in which '. . . the individual withdraws but our *nature continues to exist on its own*; everything which happens within us *is inevitable* and we fall under the influence of the *law of necessity* which *trifles with us* . . .'.[61]

Several leading doctors were interested in the effects of the unconscious disorganization of the mental faculties during hallucinatory states. J.-J. Moreau de Tours experimented on himself in the 1840s with hashish, a drug which enabled him to observe the uncontrollable flow of his unconscious imagination without entirely depriving him of conscious awareness.[62] He was particularly interested in the relationship he perceived between drug-induced hallucinations and those experienced by the insane. In 1855, he went even further and maintained that there was 'from the psychological point of view, an absolute identity between the state of dreaming and insanity.'[63] Moreau hence regarded the sleeping state as one in which the inhibitory centres were dangerously relaxed.

The devout Catholic physician, A.-J.-F. Brierre de Boismont, dissented from this majority view in a widely discussed volume on apparitions, visions, ecstasies, and dreams first published in 1845 and reprinted in 1852 and 1862. He asserted that hallucinations were not always pathological, seeking to make distinctions between the truly divine visitations recorded in Scripture and other, later manifestations of religious experience, some of which were pathological and others not.[64] Significantly, however, he conceded that hallucinations might unconsciously induce crime, and cited a range of deeds to prove

[61] Quoted by J.-G.-F. Baillarger, 'Théorie de l'automatisme', in his *Recherches sur les maladies mentales* (Paris, 1890), i. 495.

[62] See his *Du hachish et de l'aliénation mentale* (Paris, 1845).

[63] Id., 'De l'identité de l'état de rêve et de la folie', *Annales médico-psychologiques*, 3rd ser., 1 (1855), 302.

[64] A.-J.-F. Brierre de Boismont, *Des hallucinations ou histoire raisonnée des apparitions, des visions, des songes, de l'extase, des rêves, du magnétisme et du somnambulisme* (Paris, 1845), 7–10.

his point. He recorded instances of women who killed their babies when called upon to do so by beckoning angels and of men who felt pursued by imaginary enemies, evidently defending themselves before they were attacked.[65]

In later decades, psychiatrists and neurologists were even more fascinated by the pathological dimensions of the 'unconscious', their attention as much generated by a clinical preoccupation with hallucinations, deliriums, and apparent 'double personalities' (*dédoublement de la personnalité*) as by widespread popular interest in spiritualist interpretations of altered states of consciousness. As Ellenberger has shown, from the 1830s and 1840s accounts of divided consciousness—observed through hypnotism, faith healing, automatic writing, and mediumistic seances—provided a means of probing and analysing a whole range of mental phenomena.[66] Mental pathologists were keen to produce a self-consciously scientific analysis of these seemingly inexplicable experiences and to contrast their approach to the popular enthusiasm for occult experience. The hostility of some key practitioners to '*spiritisme*'—seances, popular performances of magnetism, and so on—will be seen in chapter 5 to have animated their extended campaign against a whole range of 'amateur' practitioners.

Despite this rivalry, however, the worlds of medical clinic and spiritualism were not entirely separate, there being an important network of personal contact and communication between the two spheres.[67] Equally, both shared styles of self-presentation which revelled in their virtually 'magical' powers. While amateur magnetizers gave widely attended public performances to paying audiences of remarkable acts, medical and legal mandarins displayed similarly extravagant feats. Janet, for example, conducted famous experiments in which he hypnotized the peasant woman Léonie B . . . at a distance of several hundred metres;[68] the Nancy jurist and experimenter,

65 Ibid., 542–600.

66 Ellenberger, *The Discovery of the Unconscious*, 53–181.

67 For an analysis of a similar kind of interpenetration in Britain see J. Perry Williams, 'Psychical Research in late Victorian Britain: Trance as Ecstasy or Trance as Insanity', in William F. Bynum, Roy Porter, and Michael Shepherd (eds.), *The Anatomy of Madness: Essays in the History of Psychiatry* (London, 1985), i. 233–54.

68 Bert S. Kopell, 'Pierre Janet's Description of Hypnotic Sleep Provoked from a

Jules Liégeois, triumphantly did the same over the telephone;[69] and Charcot used a range of metallic substances and magnets to transfer hysterical symptoms from one side of the body to the other.[70] Although each of these investigations was predicated on a belief in the experimental method, they were as deeply pervaded by a love of the fantastic as any number of spiritualist seances featuring talking hats and levitating chairs.

In the medico-legal domain, psychiatrists regularly pointed to the existence of *dédoublement de la personnalité*, hypnotism, and 'second states' to explain a wide range of criminal deeds. Otherwise upright men were known to walk into shops in self-induced somnambulistic trances and wreck the premises.[71] A range of degenerates would commit fetishistic acts, over-powered by an irresistible impulse often likened to a second, pathological personality.[72] The dramatic effect of such episodes was perhaps best demonstrated in January 1881 in the *Chambre des appels de police correctionnelle*, which revoked a judgement against a man called Didier for an offence against public decency after an experiment carried out by Auguste Motet. The doctor claimed that this 'poor devil' had been in a spontaneous *condition seconde* similar to a hypnotic trance when the police arrested him for masturbating in a public urinal. Motet had the man relive the crime by inducing a somnambulistic state, releasing him from his commands only when the defendant was about to commit the offence again in

Distance', followed by trans. of 'M. Pierre Janet, Report on Some Phenomena of Somnambulism', in *Journal of the History of the Behavioural Sciences*, 4 (1968), 119–31.

[69] For references to these experiments see the Nancy newspaper *L'Est républicain*, 21 Dec. 1890 and Liégeois's *Hypnotisme téléphonique*—lecture delivered to the Académie de Stanislas during the meeting of 4 Dec. 1885.

[70] Harrington, 'Hemisphere Differences and "Duality of Mind" ', 205–45.

[71] See Paul Garnier, 'L'Automatisme somnambulique devant les tribunaux, prévention de vol—Rapport médico-légal—Non-lieu', *Annales d'hygiène publique et de médecine légale*, 3rd ser., 17 (1887), 334–54.

[72] The range of obsessive sexual behaviour was enormous and figured prominently in the medico-legal domain. See, for example, Garnier, *Les Fétichistes, pervertis, et invertis sexuels, observations médico-légales* (Paris, 1896); Valentin Magnan, *Des exhibitionnistes . . . travail communiqué du 12 mai 1890* (Paris, 1890); and Charles Féré's more synthetic *L'Instinct sexuel, évolution et dissolution* (Paris, 1899); for an interpretive account, see Georges Lanteri-Laura, *Lecture des perversions: Histoire de leur appropriation médicale* (Paris, 1980).

front of the appalled, but none the less convinced, judges on the bench.[73]

Degeneration

There was nothing novel about a medico-psychological discussion of heredity. On the contrary, psychiatrists from Pinel onwards had cited it as a predisposing cause in the production of mental disorder. It was not until mid-century, however, that the subject acquired a heightened urgency, with men like Prosper Lucas, one of Magnan's clinical *maîtres*, producing his noted *Traité de l'hérédité* (1850), which amassed a long and impressive list of clinical case studies to demonstrate its crucial role. Heredity increasingly gained priority in the long list of biological and moral causes cited by physicians, a shift in attitude summed up by the psychiatrist Ulysse Trélat, who declared in 1856 that 'in speaking of the hereditary component of insanity, we are far from claiming to say something new, but we wish to attribute all the importance and value which is due to this great and important question.'[74]

In 1857, Auguste Morel published his *Traité des dégénérescences* in which he sought to present a novel synthesis that linked heredity, the environment, and racial decline.[75] These were in turn related to an analysis of the rise of mental disorder, with the discussion then broadening to present an account of regressive tendencies in both individuals and modern societies. Morel's work was on the one hand the product of a wide range

[73] Motet, 'Accès de somnambulisme spontané et provoqué', *Annales d'hygiène publique et de médecine légale*, 3rd ser., 5 (1881), 214–25.

[74] Ulysse Trélat, 'Des causes de la folie', *Annales médico-psychologiques*, 3rd ser., 2 (1856), 21.

[75] See Georges Genil-Perrin, *Histoire des origines et de l'évolution de l'idée de dégénérescence en médecine mentale* (Paris, 1913); and Francoise Bing, 'La Théorie de la dégénérescence', in J. Postel and C. Quétel (eds.), *Nouvelle histoire de la psychiatrie* (Toulouse, 1983), 351–6. For hereditarian ideas in nineteenth-century French science and society see Jean Borie, *Mythologies de l'hérédité au XIXe siècle* (Paris, 1981); see articles discussing the implications of 'degeneration' in various intellectual and artistic fields in Edward J. Chamberlain and Sander L. Gilman (eds.), *Degeneration: The Dark Side of Progress* (New York, 1985); see also Daniel Pick's comparative appraisal, 'The Conception and Descent of Degeneration, 1848–1914', Ph.D. thesis (Univ. of Cambridge, 1987).

of anthropological, physiological, and natural historical ideas and, on the other, a creation pervasively marked by his religious convictions, metaphysical preoccupations, and philanthropic inclinations. Perhaps more than any other notion, the degeneration theory he helped shape pervaded the clinical, social, and moral vision of the medico-psychological speciality in the second half of the century, its impact intensifying with each passing decade.

Morel was born in Vienna, was raised by a priest, entered a Catholic seminary when 12, and was expelled seven years later when he participated in a student disturbance ostensibly linked to liberal ideas.[76] A poverty-stricken student, he studied medicine in Paris between 1831 and 1839 and formed a close friendship with Phillipe Buchez, a physician and deputy during the 1848 Revolution, whose Christian socialism and metaphysical ideas played a large role in the development of Morel's later medical theories and personal political outlook.[77] During the same period he shared rooms with Claude Bernard, whose intellectual influence also left an important imprint.

Appointed *Médecin en chef* at the *Asile St-Yon* outside Rouen in 1856, Morel was struck by the impact of industrialization on 'the city of attics', notorious for its poverty, filthy living quarters, the difficulty of the working conditions imposed on the dye-workers, as well as the high rates of infant mortality.[78] In looking at the problem of insanity in terms of an interactive relationship between the individual and society, Morel was working in a tradition of hygienic investigation which dated back to the eighteenth century.[79] In this earlier period, a conception of medical police—having a less exclusive association with law

[76] For Morel's biography see Ruth Friedlander, 'B.-A. Morel and the Theory of Degeneration: The Introduction of Anthropology into Psychiatry', Ph.D. thesis (Univ. of California, 1973); and Motet, 'Eloge de Morel', *Annales médico-psychologiques*, 5th ser. 12 (1874), 4–111.

[77] For Buchez see François-André Isambert, *Politique, religion et science de l'homme chez Philippe Buchez, 1796–1865* (Paris, 1967).

[78] C. Martin, *La Dégénérescence dans l'œuvre de B. A. Morel et dans sa postérité*, Ph.D. thesis (L'École pratique des hautes études, 1983–4), 104–5.

[79] For the story of the *Société royale de médecine*, founded in 1775 and designed to further the collaboration between medical men and the enlightened absolutist state in promoting the health of the rural population, see Harvey Mitchell, 'Rationality and Control in French Eighteenth-century Medical Views of the Peasantry', *Comparative Studies in Society and History*, 21 (1979), 82–112.

enforcement—envisaged a widespread system of restraint and intervention to improve the circulation of goods, control dangerous individuals such as vagrants and criminals, as well as provide a more hygienic supply of water and food.[80] Such perspectives were strengthened by the Napoleonic wars, where physicians were obliged to confront unprecedented problems of social hygiene in the army. Their experience influenced profoundly the hygiene movement in the 1820s and 1830s which was interested in epidemics, the impact of industrial capitalism on the work-force, and the role of urban environments in producing crime, mental illness, and prostitution. Its members catalogued a seemingly endless list of causal factors ranging from climate to moral character in the attempt to understand the onset of disease. Playing a crucial role in shaping the movement for prison and asylum reform, they also advanced the cause of legal medicine and, through their contacts in politics, learned societies, and philanthropic bodies, helped form the bases of social investigation and the nature of nineteenth-century public assistance institutions.[81]

The earlier hygienists counted important alienists among their numbers, with Esquirol and his followers explaining insanity's causes by reference to the same factors seen to produce ill health in every other sphere. They pointed to the damaging effects of excess passions, immoderate living, climate, political upheavals, bad working conditions, religious exaltation, and poverty on the equilibrium of the individual and social organism. Through his observations of the inhabitants of Rouen, Morel extended and refined this interpretation, noting how the conditions peculiar to 'modern' civilization produced

80 For the tradition of eighteenth-century 'environmentalism', which underpinned the programme of medical policing, see Jordanova, 'Earth Science and Environmental Medicine: The Synthesis of the Late Enlightenment', in Jordanova and Porter (eds.), *Images of the Earth* (Chalfont St Giles, 1979), 119–46); and her 'Policing Public Health in France, 1780–1815', in T. Ogawa (ed.), *Public Health: Proceedings of the Fifth International Symposium on the Comparative History of Medicine, East and West* (Tokyo, 1981), 15–17, 23–5. See also Foucault, 'The Politics of Health in the Eighteenth Century', in *Power/Knowledge, Selected Interviews and Other Writings, 1972–1977*, ed. Colin Gordon (London, 1980), 166–82, and Charles Rosen, *From Medical Police to Social Medicine: Essays in the History of Health Care* (New York, 1974).

81 For the first full-length study of the 'hygiene movement' see William Coleman, *Death is a Social Disease, Public Health and Political Economy in early Industrial France* (Madison, 1982); for an interesting, but different approach, to similar subjects, see Alain Corbin, *Le Miasme et la jonquille: L'Odorat et l'imaginaire social, XVIIIe–XIXe siècles* (Paris, 1982).

a wide array of physical, moral, and social infirmities. Those working in urban conglomerations were obliged to subsist in a cesspit of physical and moral squalor, producing an interlocking set of deleterious circumstances which gave rise to the degenerative process:

> . . . [w]orking in dangerous or insalubrious occupations and living in unhealthy, over-populated cities, the human organism is subjected to unprecedented agents of debilitation [*dépérissement*] and consequently degeneration. I know well what man's spirit is capable of when struggling against harmful influences. However, his strength is limited. Despite all the progress science has made, it is impossible that he should not be transformed by bad working conditions in the factories and the mines where he extracts toxic substances and is forced to spend most of his days in the bowels of the earth. Now, add to these generally bad conditions the profoundly demoralizing influence of poverty, lack of education, want of thrift, abuse of alcohol, sexual excess, and inadequate nourishment, and you will have some idea of the complex circumstances which tend to modify unfavourably the temperaments of the poor classes.[82]

For Morel, degeneration was the production of 'morbid varieties of the human species',[83] deviations from the primordial human type created by God and exemplified by Adam. His narrative of biological degeneration was a scientific examination of 'the new conditions which ought to have recreated the great event of Man's original fall'.[84] The account of degeneration thus sought to underpin rather than destroy the scriptural account of creation. Although psychiatrists of the early Third Republic almost entirely jettisoned this aspect of his work, the close affiliation between scientific and religious preoccupations in Morel's formulation perhaps helps explain the theory's ready accessibility. By being expressed in a manner which evoked a range of Christian, moralistic precepts, it may be said to have provided a scientific assessment of how 'the sins of the father were visited on the sons'.

The analysis of degeneration emphasized the process of regressive development, or 'progressive . . . debilitation'.

[82] Morel, *Traité des dégénérescences physiques, intellectuelles et morales de l'espèce humaine et des causes qui produisent ces variétés maladives* (Paris, 1857), p. vii.

[83] Ibid., 46.

[84] Ibid., 4.

When 'the major functions of the [animal] economy are successively compromised',[85] he argued, infirmities in the psychophysical constitution of individuals resulted. Morel's account of the destabilization of the animal economy owed much to the idea of adaptation implicit in physiological conceptions. Although animals made what were in his view constant, and moreover valiant, attempts to adjust to and counteract lethal influences, they were not always successful. Labourers obliged to work surrounded by noxious substances were under constant physiological pressure. The effects of such disruptions were generally temporary but sometimes more long-lasting. When researchers found 'a lot of copper or lead in the organs of copper or lead workers'[86] they concluded that the effect of such toxic substances could become 'fixed'.

Similarly, alcoholic intoxication, reaching full strength in *delirium tremens*, would radically destabilize the animal economy. Repeated abuse would alter the individual's psychophysiological make-up and the debilitated tendencies could then be transmitted to offspring. The process of hereditarian transmission itself was not specified, with emphasis placed instead on the pathological characteristics observable in succeeding generations. Morel believed that the regressive effects of the degenerative process would strike the fourth generation sterile, a view which demonstrated his belief in the capacity of the natural economy ultimately to extirpate deleterious elements. Nature's healing powers, however, were no cause for complacency, as the process of degeneration was an extremely dangerous one, evidenced by its dynamic acceleration in the face of environmental pressures.

Morel was as much concerned with providing an overarching perspective on regression in modern societies as with shifting the terms of reference within psychiatry. Rather than enumerating an array of distinct clinical types each existing independently as disease entities on the nosological map, he devised a classificatory system in which all mental disorders were the mere manifestation of the underlying pathological substratum of degeneration. This somatically based foundation of debilitation was made observable to the physician through the afflictions

[85] Ibid., 320. [86] Ibid., 313 n.

affecting the subject's forebears through the revelation of various 'stigmata' ranging from club-foot through strabismus to scrofula. In effect, Morel asserted that general pathological tendencies rather than specific traits were transmitted. The theory thus provided a subtle means of interpreting mental pathology by implying a continuum in which infinitely variable strengths and combinations of environmental, psychological, and physiological conditions could produce behavioural patterns ranging from quaint eccentricity to homicidal mania. Through the theory of degeneration, physicians sought a probabilistic model for understanding the course of disease, which they both hoped and claimed would aid a programme of preventive intervention against dangerous individuals and deleterious conditions in the environment. However, the gap between aspiration and reality was wide indeed, as the theory often only provided an account of diverse and seemingly disparate symptoms after they had already appeared.

While the theory of degeneration held out great professional prospects for the future, it also provided a convincing explanation for alienists' difficult institutional position during mid-century. Their quandaries can be traced back to the law of 1838 when psychiatrists became administrators of a nationwide asylum system. This victory effectively represented an official endorsement of a medical solution to the problem of insanity by requiring a public institution in every department, or arrangements with other kinds of hospitals nearby.[87] The momentous reform not only gave them an institutional domain, it also empowered them to impose an obligatory confinement on the insane in the name of 'therapeutic isolation'. Through the so-called *placement d'office*, the prefect of police—later aided by a

[87] The law of 1838 was the culmination of several decades of reformist efforts led by Esquirol, with his embryonic conception for the management of lunatics already contained within his *Des établissements des aliénés en France et les moyens de l'améliorer le sort de ces infortunés* (Paris, 1819). For illuminating accounts of the passage of the law see Robert Castel, *L'Ordre psychiatrique, l'âge d'or de l'aliénisme* (Paris, 1976), 191–230; he has also included a text of the law on 316–24; and Goldstein, *Console and Classify: The French Psychiatric Profession in the Nineteenth Century* (New York, 1987), chap. 6, 276–321. For a succinct account of the legal position of lunatics during their internment see Ballet *et al.*, *Traité de pathologie mentale*, 1364–413. For a general survey of the legal and institutional condition of the insane in France from the eighteenth century to the twentieth see Foucault (ed.), *Généalogie des équipements de normalisation, les équipements sanitaires* (Paris, 1976).

physician—confined lunatics in an asylum when they posed a threat to public order. Rather than being arrested and tried, they were held at departmental expense with their release depending on the doctors' assessment.[88]

The passage of this law had been associated with professional *élan* and therapeutic optimism. Those who had followed Pinel—particularly Esquirol and his disciples—had argued from a deeply felt polemical position which they had successfully advanced during their struggle for legislative innovation. By the 1850s, however, this buoyancy was weighted down by institutional realities, with psychiatrists spending considerable time and energy defending themselves from detractors instead of enjoying the fruits of their success. The law itself equally remained in many respects statutory, and its first article—requiring an asylum in every department—was never properly put into effect.[89] Moreover, there were worrying signs that their position was being eroded. An imperial decree of 1851, for example, moved powers of appointment from the Minister of the Interior in Paris to the less sympathetic provincial *préfets*, who seemed more inclined to keep a tighter reign on the administrative purse-strings.[90]

Such governmental neglect was, however, a minor irritation compared with the demoralization doctors faced in their clinics, where a range of difficulties rapidly dampened their most cherished aspirations. The supply of patients provided by the *placement d'office* confronted them with a barely treatable clientele of generally poor, uneducated, violent, and physically repulsive inmates with whom they could hardly sympathize.[91] As the decades advanced, the ineffectiveness of many of their procedures became a source of both disquiet and embittered

[88] In addition to the *placement d'office* there was the *placement volontaire* which put therapeutic services at the disposal of those who were insane but not dangerous, and obliged relations to pay towards the patient's upkeep. The catch in this procedure, however, was that if patients became disorderly and dangerous during their stay, then the physician in charge was able to change the voluntary confinement into an obligatory one.

[89] Castel, *L'Ordre psychiatrique*, 232–41.

[90] See Iain Dowbiggan, 'Degeneration and Hereditarianism in French Mental Medicine, 1840–1890', in Bynum, Porter, and Shepherd (eds.), *The Anatomy of Madness*, i. 225 n. 85.

[91] Castel explains that by 1853 the number of *placements d'office* had reached 6,473 while the rate for *placements volontaires* stood at a meagre 2,609.

frustration. The much-vaunted programme of moral treatment—the revolutionary clarion call of the profession—was also subject to revision. Reflecting on the intractability of their charges, mid-century alienists like F. Leuret commended measures which smacked more of coercion than persuasion, advocating authoritarian, if not intimidating, tactics to persuade the madman to recover his sanity:

> My aim is not to cure him [the lunatic] by one fixed method but by any means possible. If, in order to move him, I must appear harsh and even unjust . . . why should I shrink from using such methods? Should I be afraid of causing him pain? A strange kind of pity indeed! It would be the same as tying a surgeon's hands when he is about to perform an operation essential to the life of his patient because it cannot be performed without pain.[92]

While the majority were disinclined to adopt Leuret's 'genuine regime of terror', the sheer numbers involved meant doctors were unable to give the kind of personalized attention that the Pinelian programme had envisaged. Having once expected a rapid turnover of mental patients ready to take up their normal lives after a salutary period of 'isolation', alienists were instead confronted with chronic disorders requiring even longer periods of internment. The result in the 1850s and 1860s was a permanent problem of 'overcrowding' [*surencombrement*] which led to their activities becoming more akin to a dreary round of custodial routine than to a gratifying professional calling.[93]

In analysing their situation, some alienists recognized that the law of 1838, by providing a managerial 'solution' to the problem of insanity, had put in place a new bureaucratic and

[92] See Castel, 'Le Traitement morale: thérapeutique mentale et contrôle social au XIXe siècle', *Topique*, 2 (1970), 125, citing François Leuret, *Du traitement moral de la folie* (Paris, 1840), 120–1.

[93] For the history of the increasing 'fossilization' of moral treatment and the drudgery of daily routine see Mark Alexander, 'The Administration of Madness and Attitudes Towards the Insane in Nineteenth-Century Paris', Ph.D. thesis (Johns Hopkins Univ., 1976), 83–129; Gérard Bleandonu and Guy Gauffey, 'Naissance des asiles d'aliénés (Auxerre-Paris)', *Annales: Économies, Sociétés, Croyances*, 20 (1975), 93–121; G. Lamarche-Vadel and G. Préli, 'Généalogie des équipements psychiatriques', chaps 4, 5, 6 in Foucault (ed.), *Généalogie des équipements*; for the impact of the asylum system on the alienists' therapeutic pessimism see G. Lanteri-Laura, 'La Chronicité dans la psychiatrie française moderne', *Annales: Économies, Sociétés, Croyances*, 27 (1972), 548–68.

policing structure which, by tracking down and treating lunatics, tended to emphasize the problem of insanity. They insisted, however, that the accelerating statistical trend of admissions was not a mere medical construction, but rather reflected a real increase in the incidence of insanity for which they could not be held responsible. When Morel spoke about the effects or the 'ills of civilization' on the production of mental disorder, he was merely reiterating a consensus view. It is purely a matter of speculation as to whether the nature of industrial work in early factories and mines, the deteriorating living conditions of overcrowded and under-serviced urban centres, and the dislocation of communal networks of mutual support did indeed produce an increased level of temporary and permanent mental illness. What is certain, however, is that the *Annales médico-psychologiques* of the 1850s and 1860s were peppered with commentaries on the 'fact' of the increase of mental disorder, as a wide range of practitioners expressed a growing sense of helplessness. As one alienist, Dumésnil, remarked: 'Experience has shown us that the number of lunatics is rising very rapidly in all countries and that everywhere provisions which seemed largely worked out have been found insufficient.'[94] With such an appraisal of the individual and epidemiological dimensions of insanity, it is perhaps easier to understand the growing acceptance of Morel's account of degeneration.

At the same time that alienists faced difficulties in their asylums, they also had to contend with a range of problems in the courtroom when they were called upon to assess the responsibility of defendants. Morel's category of *folies héréditaires* directly aided the solution of some of these difficulties by ridding physicians of the unwieldy monomania diagnosis. Although key in carving out a judicial role for alienists, monomania had also left them with an extremely ambiguous legacy. Between the 1820s and 1850s, it had continued to operate as an important classificatory category, describing conditions marked by the apparent paradox of irresistibility and rational awareness. Included under its umbrella was a range of intellectual, affective, and instinctual monomanias, each manifesting itself through an isolated aberration of reason, emotion, or urges. Equally,

94 Quoted in Martin, *La Dégénérescence*, 52.

later elaborations denoted other seemingly localized disorders such as *lypémanie* (depressive mania), *érotomanie* (romantic obsession detached from sexual love), and 'religious monomania'. Further varieties figuring prominently in the medico-legal domain were dipsomania, pyromania, kleptomania, and, especially, homicidal mania, all invoked in court to explain a wide range of reasoned, but none the less, impulsive and irresistible behaviours.

When assessing individuals in court, alienists often came to a conclusion of 'partial' responsibility and had their evaluation rigidly rejected by jurists. For the latter, responsibility was an indivisible entity, and hence in requesting medical advice they desired a straightforward yes or no answer. This was precisely, however, what alienists felt unable to provide, not possessing, as they constantly reiterated, a strictly calibrated *phrénomètre* which could measure such delicate matters.[95] Their reports detailed psychic anomalies, physical defects, as well as moral and social attributes, but, while citing numerous proofs of impairment, often concluded that these did not necessarily preclude moral awareness. Alienists' refusal to translate into terminology understandable to the court in turn provoked complaints that they were hindering judicial proceedings by giving no clear answer and compromising their public image by appearing indecisive.[96] Placed in the awkward position of having to explain how an individual could be irresponsible and responsible at the same time, alienists came to regard legal requirements as a series of *questions mal posées* necessitating inconclusive answers simply because the terms were unenlightened by scientific findings.

None the less, psychiatrists themselves expressed increasing disillusionment with monomania, its virtual abandonment around mid-century being enmeshed in a series of philosophical debates on the mind/body relation which were intertwined with political polemic. The concept had become increasingly associated with

[95] Falret *père*, 'De la responsabilité morale et la responsabilité légale des aliénés', *Annales médico-psychologiques*, 4th ser., 2 (1863), 243.

[96] For discussions of the problem see A.-J.-F. Brierre de Boismont, 'De la responsabilité générale des aliénés et de leur responsabilité partielle', ibid., 174–96 and Eugène Dally, 'Considérations sur les criminels et sur les aliénés criminels au point de vue de la responsabilité', ibid., 260–95, and the 'Discussion sur la responsabilité partielle', during the meeting of 29 July 1863, ibid., 462–4.

the phrenological movement embraced by many of Esquirol's followers in the 1820s and 1830s.[97] The apparent affinity was based on the way monomania seemed to split the human *moi* into a series of differentiated faculties which could operate in isolation from each other. Phrenology, by seeking to present a topography of distinct faculties of the 'mind', appeared to present a parallel, if not similar, interpretation. In their neuroanatomical work, for example, the phrenologists Gall and Spurzheim sought to determine the nature and relative strength of such faculties through examining the external contours of the cranium. The approach attempted to distinguish between twenty-eight innate faculties of the brain and provide an ostensibly empirical methodological programme for understanding propensities which varied among individuals. By thus speaking in terms which often seemed to equate 'mind' with 'brain', the phrenologists seemed to be proposing a materialist, and hence politically radical, explanation of human consciousness.

During the July Monarchy, the entire edifice of late eighteenth- and early nineteenth-century medical theorizing —often called 'physiology'—was consistently attacked by the philosophical establishment headed by Victor Cousin and the 'spiritualist' or 'psychological' school. Through a self-consciously eclectic combination of eighteenth-century Scottish moral philosophy and Kantianism, he and his followers emphasized the independence of the human *moi*, philosophical doctrines which sought to militate against the perceived determinism of medical theorizing from Condillacian sensationalism right through to phrenology. If 'physiological' doctrines seemed inclined to imply an intimate connection between 'mind' and the organization of brain and nervous tissue, then the 'psychologists' proposed an entirely dualistic conception of the mind/body relation in which the former—the '*moi*'—was a distinct, unfettered reality, discoverable through the 'psychological' method of introspection.[98] Their account of the human personality was as much shaped by political interests as that which they opposed, and from the 1840s was

97 See Lanteri-Laura, *Histoire de la phrénologie* (Paris, 1970).

98 For a most illuminating discussion of the early nineteenth-century discussions relating to 'physiology' and 'psychology' see Goldstein, *Console and Classify*, chap. 7, 240–75.

perceived as the 'official' philosophy of the July Monarchy underpinning moral agency and the values of the *juste milieu*.

By mid-century, several key alienists repudiated their 'physiological' heritage—particularly their earlier adherence to phrenology—and sought to apply the 'psychological' approach to the study of mental alienation. The concept of monomania particularly came under attack, as it was accused of causing difficulties in the medico-legal domain and of being based on faulty philosophical principles.[99] They increasingly stressed instead the 'solidarity' of the mental faculties and sought to provide a unified conception of disease processes. The 'spiritualist' psychiatrists J.-P. Falret *père* and J.-G.-F. Baillarger demonstrated this trend when in 1854 they engaged in a vicious priority dispute over the 'discovery' of the 'manic-depressive' syndrome which joined together into a single disease entity the previously isolated conditions of mania and melancholia. In line with this perspective, Falret—an advocate of phrenology in his youth—self-consciously sought to repudiate his past and encourage a unified 'psychological' approach to understanding mental disorder.[100]

Morel also shared in this trend towards a unified view of disease processes, although he differed from Falret in key areas, particularly by continuing to emphasize the role of organic disturbance in the central nervous system.[101] As a religious man believing in an indivisible *moi*, however, he made a distinction between disordered organic processes and human consciousness itself, rejecting the materialist implications of the 'physiological' systems which monomania was deemed to represent. He argued that the varying symptoms of

[99] See J.-A. Bariod, 'Études critiques sur les monomanies instinctives—non-existence de cette forme de maladie mentale', DM thesis (Paris, 1852); Louis Delasiauve, 'De la monomanie au point de vue psychologique et légale', *Annales médico-psychologiques*, 2nd ser., 5 (1853), 353–71; Brierre de Boismont, 'De l'état des facultés dans les délires partiels ou monomanies', ibid., 567–89; Auguste Ott, 'De la folie générale et de la folie partielle et des questions médico-légales que soulève l'aliénation', ibid., 317–38; and the 'Discussion sur la monomanie' meetings of 30 May and 27 June (ibid., 2nd ser., 6 (1854), 99–118 and 273–98 respectively).

[100] Motet quotes Falret and discusses his method in *Inauguration des bustes*, 36–7.

[101] For example, Morel did not include Falret's designation of *folie à double forme* in his own classification. By focusing above all on the affiliated mental and behavioural symptoms of the disorder, Falret had not taken into consideration the underlying degenerative substratum.

mental disorder—even the periods of apparent lucidity—were only part of a series of evolving stages that made up a unified whole. 'Partial delirium' thus became merely one element or stage in a 'systematized delirium' in which periods of incubation, manifestation, and remittance were ineluctably followed by the generalization of the delirium, the material substratum of which was the degeneration itself. The seemingly localized symptoms therefore merely pointed to a diffuse 'constitutional insanity' predicated on a view of degeneration which deprived individuals of their 'moral liberty'.

Through such an analysis, Morel wished to dispense with the notions of both 'partial insanity' and 'partial responsibility' and present a medical case to the judiciary based on a single, developing notion of mental disorder. These theoretical perspectives concentrated on human wholeness, a view which maintained a tense coexistence throughout the century with an equally strong fascination with the divisibility and fragmentation of human consciousness. Although phrenology and Esquirol's classifications were attacked, later studies such as the investigations of Broca and others into cerebral localization, the 'double brain' and the 'dual personality', demonstrated the continuing attraction of the second strand of theorizing.

The medico-legal impact of the theory of degeneration can be best seen by the way in which the monomanias of earlier decades associated with specific antisocial acts—suicide, homicide, arson, drinking, and a growing range of sexual perversions—were classed as 'instinctive maniacs' or 'precocious perverts' under the category of *folies héréditaires*.[102] Such individuals were antisocial and exemplified a 'double hereditary degeneration, which is both moral and physical, and makes up a large proportion of the population in prisons and juvenile penitentiary institutions'.[103] This perspective therefore strengthened the long-standing links between criminality and madness, making it ever more difficult to determine the difference between the two.

It may seem at first glance that the theory of degeneration should have increased the disenchantment between the medical

102 See Morel's classification system as laid out in his *Traité des maladies mentales*, in particular, 513–70.

103 Quoted in Martin, *La Dégénérescence*, 86.

and legal professions. By implying that this large class of abnormal and dangerous individuals be handed over to medical supervision and treatment, it seemed to launch an almost imperialistic assault on traditional legal authority. In this instance, however, such an argument holds few attractions, as the alienists' embrace of the theory was as much an attempt to consolidate their medico-legal role as to encroach on the prerogatives of others. Moreover, the broad social interpretation of insanity contained within the theory will be shown to have opened up avenues of approach and areas of possible *rapprochement* which encouraged a dialogue between the medical and legal professionals in later, altered political circumstances. Their exchange never reconciled opposing voluntaristic and deterministic accounts of human behaviour. Rather it provided a possibility for the discussion of altered management strategies particularly designed to cope with the wide range of degenerate 'impulsives' and 'moral imbeciles' which the psychiatrists so regularly identified.

Degeneration and Evolutionism, 1880–1910

The lure of hereditarianism in the medico-legal domain can be seen by the way in which the alienist Auguste Motet clearly relished the reconstruction of a defendant's family history in a case of attempted parricide in 1890. In analysing the moral and intellectual deficiencies evident in this degenerate *débile*, Motet pronounced enthusiastically on finding a confirmation of current theories: 'One rarely finds a man more oppressed by his heredity than C . . .'. In demonstrating C . . .'s diminished 'resistance to instinctive urges', he supplied the magistrature with a geneological table of 'marriages between blood relations . . . and finally the end of his family line with the appearance of an idiot'.[104] Although not all nineteenth-century physicians emphasized the debilitating consequences of consanguinity, Motet's stress in this instance underscores the importance ascribed to heredity.

In his analysis, Motet was using an already substantially

[104] Charles François C . . . D^2U^8 261, 30 Dec. 1890, medico-legal report.

revised version of Morel's theory. The refinement was a communal process, exemplified best by the work of the clinician Valentin Magnan, whose influence was particularly strong among his many disciples and associates. The dominance that the theory of degeneration achieved in the final part of the century can only be understood in the context of the French neo-Lamarckian perspective on inheritance and species transformation, an approach which opposed the Darwinian emphasis on natural selection. At the outset, however, it is important to recognize that no single, absolute conception of either 'Darwinism' or 'neo-Lamarckianism' may be offered. For example, Darwin, as well as many self-professed Darwinists, often readily conceded an important role for the inheritance of acquired characteristics, a doctrine generally associated with neo-Lamarckianism. Moreover, Darwinism represented more than the English naturalist's corpus of writings on evolution. For example, Huxley's popularization of Darwin's theories, and the use of such highly polemical terms as 'survival of the fittest', (a term first coined by Spencer) meant that Darwinism immediately conjured up a range of moral, social, and political associations which French scientists would often reject.

So, while evolutionism was the order of the day in France as elsewhere in the scientific communities of Europe and America after 1870, the discussion did not focus on controversies surrounding the *Origin of Species* (1859). Instead, it centred on specifically French scientific concerns,[105] particularly the polemic between Pasteur and Pouchet on spontaneous generation[106] (a scientific theory which suggested that organisms could arise independently from any parent), and on the debates among anthropologists over polygenist or monogenist interpretations of human descent.[107] The majority of the anthropologists in the *Société d'anthropologie* (almost all of

105 For a summary of the French response see Pietro Corsi and Paul J. Weindling, 'Darwinism in Germany, France and Italy', in David Kohn (ed.), *The Darwinian Heritage* (Princeton, 1985), 683–711.

106 John Farley and Gerald L. Geison, 'Science, Politics and Spontaneous Generation in Nineteenth Century France: The Pasteur-Pouchet Debate', *Bulletin for the History of Medecine*, 48 (1974), 161–98.

107 For the most extensive account of this debate see Claude Blanckaert, *Monogénisme et polygénisme en France de Buffon à P. Broca, 1749–1880*, 3 vols., Ph.D. thesis (Univ. of Paris I, 1981).

whom were medically trained and active in the same neurological debates which preoccupied psychiatrists) accepted *transformisme*, the French word for evolution. However, they rejected the primacy of natural selection, either relegating it to an extremely limited role, or denying entirely its influence in evolutionary change.[108] In sum, the work of the English naturalist either went unnoticed or was interpreted as a mere, and indeed faulty, elaboration of the ideas of the eighteenth-century Frenchman, Jean-Baptiste Lamarck.

The initial hostility to the *Origin* may be partially ascribed to its translation in 1862 by the radical feminist Clémence Royer, who provided a polemical fifty-page introduction on the social and political implications to be drawn from Darwin's work. Despite the appearance of a second, more sober, version, the response to Darwin's theories produced nothing more than a reiteration of transformist credos. As the monumental work by Yvette Conry has explained, this indifferent response cannot be explained away as mere chauvinism. To understand the reception of Darwin's work, Conry has investigated the fundamental postulates underpinning the French biological sciences which were infused by an ontological conception of natural economy. Rather than random conflict, they stressed the 'laws of proportions, rules of exchange and principles of justice'.[109]

Instead of natural selection and the struggle for existence, they emphasized Milne-Edwards' notion of the physiological division of labour, the *solidarité* of the organism's constituent elements and its ability to adapt to the milieu which 'solicits the primordial activity'. In the period between 1868 and 1873, the development of cellular physiology underpinned this view of smaller elements working in 'association', a formulation which was readily expanded to understand the ideal way in which a liberal society should function. Similar notions of harmonious differentiation and developmental integration were most persistently applied in embryology. The development of the embryo, its growth from a single cell through the many stages of

[108] See Robert E. Stebbins, 'France', in Thomas F. Glick, *The Comparative Reception of Darwinism* (Austin, 1972), in particular, 152–6.

[109] Yvette Conry, *L'Introduction du darwinisme en France au XIXe siècle* (Paris, 1974), 400.

'intermediate' life forms to the final human product, was one of the most oft-repeated analogies for the evolutionary process.

In none of these analyses could random variation or natural selection play any major role. Instead, biological investigation concentrated almost exclusively on the organism's purposive, and therefore directed, attempts to adapt to the ceaselessly changing milieu. Underpinned by Bernard's notion of the *milieu intérieur*, physiological theory concentrated on the organism's attempt to marshal its internal labour force to best advantage and implied that it might be able to determine its own 'conditions of existence' through an elective process.[110] At every turn, in other words, Darwinism encountered a 'non-monolithic neo-Lamarckianism' which attributed 'creativity and directivity, not to natural selection but to the environment', thereby 'merely transpos[ing] the old convictions about a natural order into a transformist framework'.[111]

The French discussion of mental pathology was also keenly affected by the contemporary debate over heredity and evolution. First, and perhaps not surprisingly given the strength of the neo-Lamarckian tradition, was the relatively small impact made by the publication in 1883 of Weissman's theory of the continuity of the germ plasm. This theory maintained that the germ plasm of the cell contained the substance of heredity and was transmitted intact to succeeding generations without interfering with the sotoplasmic cells. Such assertions reduced the role of the environment and hence greatly undermined the doctrine of the inheritance of acquired characteristics, a cardinal feature of neo-Lamarckianism. During the last decades of the century, this was one of the most hotly contested areas of biological investigation, with Weissman, for example, chopping off the tails of white mice for five generations to see if such acquired characteristics were passed on.

The legacy of neo-Lamarckianism was so strong that there was a concerted effort to reshape Weissman's theory and adapt it within a more suitably French tradition.[112] The mental

110 Ibid., 336.

111 J. R. Moore, 'Could Darwinism be Introduced in France?' (Essay Review of Yvette Conry, *L'Introduction du darwinisme en France* . . . , in *British Journal for the History of Science*, 10 (1977), 249.

112 See Denis Buican, *Histoire de la génétique et de l'évolutionnisme en France* (Paris, 1984), 39–45.

pathologist, Charles Féré, exemplified the French response by suggesting that the germ plasm was also affected by the environmental pressures which buffeted the somotoplasm:

> At the same time that they act on the individual organism, environmental conditions [*les conditions de la vie*] affect the germ plasm . . . To put it another way—and to speak Weissman's language—external conditions are, to a certain extent, capable of modifying the *Déterminants* both of the organism and of the germ plasm which is permanently contained within the organism's cells. The persistence of this influence on many successive generations will make the modifications of these *Déterminants* permanent, that is to say, will create a new and hereditary character.[113]

With such arguments, French scientists could retain their neo-Lamarckian approach and advance their own perception of the 'laws' governing both normal and morbid heredity. In an article published in 1894, Féré explained how normal heredity operated (1) in a 'direct' or 'immediate' fashion whereby parents tended to pass on specific physical and moral attributes to their offspring; (2) in 'predominant' form whereby the legacy of one rather than both parents prevailed; (3) in an atavistic form, in which the descendant was marked by heredity going back several generations; and (4) the *loi de l'hérédité homochrone*, whereby the manifestation of hereditary traits appeared through the developmental process, with similar characteristics appearing at the same life intervals among both parents and offspring.[114]

Morbid heredity, however, did not always operate in the same manner. Like capital, it needed to be accumulated and then discharged through the manifestation of pathological symptoms, neither necessarily observable in the next generation nor consistent in appearance. For example, a degenerate moral imbecile who found himself in court accused of murder and theft might have had forebears who were only imperceptibly tainted. A suicidal father, a fanatically religious uncle, or a reclusive mother might be sufficiently debilitated to transmit their mild form of a deleterious condition, and this might then resurface as a more severe and dangerous illness:

113 Charles Féré, *La Famille névropathique* (Paris, 1884), 7–8.

114 id., 'L'Hérédité morbide', *Revue des deux mondes*, 126 (1894), 436–52.

Often enough, the family taint manifests itself only gradually, with one or several generations, showing small disturbances, preparatory ones, so to speak. [Morbid] heredity needs to be accumulated, capitalized in some way, before becoming an identifiable defect . . . Among the forebears of lunatics one often finds individuals afflicted with a habitual state of over-excitation, enthusiasts, eccentrics, unsuccessful inventors, spendthrifts, unusual people affected by intellectual and moral tics.[115]

In addition to this notion of capital accumulation was the related concept of 'collateral' transmission. For example, a diabetic father could produce an ataxic son, a hysterical daughter, or an epileptic offspring: there was no simple reproduction of the parents' affliction but a higher probability that some kind of disorder would be present in the children. Not only was this important in understanding the innumerable, interconnected affiliations within *la famille morbide*, it was also a significant analytical tool in understanding particular social 'types'. For example, criminals were widely believed to come from families marked by 'madness, imbecility, idiocy, etc.'. Such individuals were part of a seemingly permanent class of antisocial individuals whose pathological symptoms were given full rein during those periods of revolutionary outburst which marked the history of nineteenth-century France:

By providing an opportunity for criminal instincts and stimulating predispositions to insanity, great social upheavals can bring to light hereditary, psychic abberations [*monstruosités*] and demonstrate the link between these two defects in an almost experimental fashion. One can cite among those who took a particularly evil role in the insurrections of the century a good number of individuals who were treated for insanity or had lunatics in their family.[116]

Similar disturbing links could be found among the *tempérament artistique*, 'genius', and madness. Following an older vein of psychiatric speculation it was noted that genius was often nothing more than a 'neurosis', an indication of an inherited tendency towards cerebral disequilibration. There were those who were only 'partial geniuses', possessing remarkable aptitudes in one particular field, but otherwise demonstrating a

115 Ibid., 438. 116 Ibid., 440.

range of mental, moral, and emotional deficiencies. Civilization encouraged unusual variations, hence providing an explanation both for the excess of madmen and criminals as well as the superabundance of intellectuals and artists. The fact that women, less advanced than men, demonstrated fewer varieties was evidence of the paradoxical implications of heightened evolutionary development which threw up exceptional individuals at the same time that it created a class of antisocial ones.

Morbid heredity operated in other ways as well. For example, it was admitted that 'tainted families' were sometimes lucky enough to produce perfectly healthy children. This could be explained by the law of *hérédité en retour*, or atavism, in which such descendants resembled individuals in their ancestral past. Other families showed no evidence of morbid heredity but none the less sometimes produced offspring afflicted by illnesses. In such cases the disorders were ascribed to a 'deficiency [*vice*] of development', an acquired propensity brought on by, for example, an accident in the womb. When a foetus was conceived during a drunken or drugged state, when the mother's physiological economy was disturbed by an 'alcoholic poisoning' or an 'emotional drunkenness', by 'bad nutrition' or 'defective hygiene', then the child might well be born with some congenital abnormality or develop pathological tendencies later. As Féré concluded: 'Popular opinion is rarely mistaken in its judgement when it says, for example, "He was a *breech baby*" to explain both his abnormality and the absence of morbid heredity.'[117] There was therefore no direct link between degeneration and heredity, a perspective which once again underpinned the emphasis on the milieu in understanding pathological processes.

These notions concerning the workings of morbid heredity give some preliminary indication not only of the way the process of degeneration was envisaged, but also of the potentially large class of individuals affected by it. Magnan's evocation of degeneration was not only more far-reaching, but also more pessimistic than any preceding version. He denied the existence of a Morellian 'primitive type', the starting-point of a

[117] Féré, op cit. 443.

creationist assessment of the origin of Man, and instead underscored the ongoing march towards perfection directed by the process of evolution. When, however, obstacles were put in the way of advance, a reverse process instituted 'progression from *a more perfect to a less perfect state*'. Such individuals were 'regressive' or 'inversive' (*reversif*) but none the less still attempted to marshal 'all the power of resistance necessary for [their] future perfection' (*perfectionnement*),[118] a position which suggested the need for reform, intervention, and therapeutic treatment.

In contrast, degenerates no longer possessed the ability to regenerate themselves and were, in essence, members of a lost generation. They fatally carried their pathological capital with them from cradle to grave, making it impossible for the clinician to hold out hope for a cure. Indeed, so apocalyptic was the vision, it appeared that even if the symptoms of degeneration could be momentarily vanquished, the fund of latent pathology would soon manifest itself in some other form. For example, the kleptomaniac (almost always a woman) might be kept from stealing but was none the less likely to show subsequently some other impulsive tendency, becoming, perhaps, a morphinomaniac or dipsomaniac. As Magnan explained:

> Degeneration is the pathological state of an individual who is constitutionally diminished in his psychophysical resistance in comparison with his immediate predecessors and who only partially achieves the biological conditions necessary for the struggle for life. This weakening is manifested by permanent stigmata and is essentially progressive unless halted in the interim by regeneration. When this does not occur [the negative progression] results sooner or later in the extinction of the species.[119]

However, deciding who was or was not a degenerate was far from easy. French clinicians saw no direct correlation between physical and moral stigmata, a position held in opposition to rival Italian specialists that had important implications for criminological debate (see next chapter). An individual could seem entirely normal and in perfect health but still be afflicted with latent intellectual and moral disorders which the alienist needed to ferret out through long clinical investigation. There

118 Magnan and Legrain, *Les Dégénérés (État mental et syndromes épisodiques)*, 7.
119 Ibid., 79.

were, however, some striking physical symptoms which automatically indicated degeneration. When a baby was an *anencéphale*—that is lacking the frontal lobes of the cerebrum—he or she quickly perished and had no chance of passing on the morbid heredity. But there were many other characteristics—club-foot and polydactyl, for example—which were not fatal and allowed degenerates to transmit their inheritance. Degeneration was indicated primarily by some kind of physical asymmetry, such as cranial malformation and other traits such as hare lips or a 'wolf face' (*gueule de loup*), which made the subjects either unpleasant or repulsive to look at. They were also typified by a wide range of sensory and motor incapacities such as stuttering, problems with language, or a lack of motor co-ordination (*zézaiement*). Finally, they demonstrated disordered sexual properties such as hermaphrodism or men with overdeveloped breasts.[120]

Although clearly an important rationalization for the alienists' therapeutic inadequacy, degeneration was equally a source of perverse optimism, its grounding in 'scientific truth' a positivist balm for the wounds of a beleagured profession. The existence of morbid heredity was supported not only by science but, perhaps more importantly for their public image, by 'common-sense' observation. The theory also reinforced the alienists' links to other more prestigious biomedical fields. By linking their own accounts to the lively debate over hereditarian transmission, as well as by actively participating in the most up-to-date debates in neuro-anatomy and neurophysiology, the psychiatrists could quite legitimately claim an important role in advancing the cause of scientific knowledge.

However, while the theory of degeneration linked alienism more firmly to these advances, at the same time it was also what distinguished psychiatrists' outlook from all other specialities. On the one hand, the hereditarian explanation of mental disorder tied them securely to the anchor of 'physicalism' which underlay their special competence to treat the insane; while on the other, it allowed enormous scope for the consideration of moral, social, and psychological phe-

120 Magnan and Legrain, op cit. 88–91.

nomena in producing the taint or sparking off latent degenerative tendencies.

In sum, despite the many efforts made to produce classificatory tables based on the functioning of the cerebro-spinal axis, their discussion of psychological symptoms—abnormalities of thought, behaviour, and emotion—still largely preoccupied them when analysing the characteristics of the mentally ill. The theory of degeneration thus enabled them to repudiate dualist interpretations of the mind-body relationship and to regard even the highest mental operations as the product of underlying evolutionary and neurophysiological processes. At the same time, however, it justified their unique preoccupation with the study of the disorders of 'mind'—volitional incapacities, delusions, moral and emotional perversions—which ostensibly militated against their increasingly rigid somatic interpretation of mental disorder.

This remarkable versatility should not, however, be seen as intellectual flimsiness. Rather, it demonstrates the psychiatrists' peculiar ability to straddle these tensions, no matter how uncomfortably, a capacity crucial for enhancing the conceptual power of psychiatric discourse. In the medico-legal domain, their analyses simultaneously contained discussions of both mind and body as well as of morality and science. While they were still obliged to do battle with sceptical jurists, such language also made their descriptions accessible to laymen who readily grasped the elements of moral condemnation attached to the 'stigma' of physical disease.

While degeneration theory was thus extremely congenial for views on mental pathology, there were also more specifically institutional reasons for its widespread appeal. If the 1850s had represented a crisis in the psychiatrists' clinical practice, the period after 1880 showed their attempt to fight back.[121] The institutional history of psychiatry in this era reveals a harshly pragmatic attitude which was intimately tied up with its medico-legal role. While in court, psychiatrists tirelessly cited the stigmata of degeneration, but were none the less disinclined to see such offenders under their own supervision. Such individuals disrupted asylum routine, often attacked the

121 For the increasingly disturbing implications of the management of madness in this period see Quétel, 'L'Asile d'aliénés en 1900', *L'Histoire*, 7 (1978), 25–34.

doctors, and made it impossible for them to devote themselves to the more rewarding task of treating patients with better prognoses.[122] Instead, alienists wanted such individuals to be either transported or gaoled, even though they were vividly aware that the pathological taints that partially deprived them of their 'moral liberty' made such a course strictly speaking unjust. As the next chapter will show, this managerial dilemma was a key preoccupation of medical, legal, and penal specialists who grappled with the problem of how best to deal with 'degenerates'.

Psychiatry was also the object of successive legislative projects during the period, partly due to a series of highly publicized cases under the late Second Empire during which alienists were accused of wrongfully confining sane individuals who had virtually no means of legal redress. The campaign was continued by Gambetta and Joseph Magnin under the Third Republic as a civil libertarian crusade against the confinement procedures contained in the law of 1838.[123] Almost every decade, from 1872 onwards, the movement boiled up into a series of bills presented to parliament which invariably failed to be enacted. More important for this discussion, however, is the gradual change in emphasis which can be detected. Although the wish to impose safeguards on procedures of internment continued, the campaign became dominated by the search for more effective strategies to cope with the dangerous and/or incurable by placing them in special security and custodial institutions. Although the healing aspects of the asylum system were championed by such Republican reformers as Joseph Reinach, increasing attention was paid to the need to separate the 'criminally insane', the 'degenerate' and the chronically ill (particularly the senile) from less offensive and more easily treated patients.[124]

[122] This category included not only those afflicted by hysteria, but also by neurasthenia, a disorder affecting both working- and middle-class sufferers. For the classic French elaboration of this neurosis see Ballet and Proust, *The Treatment of Neurasthenia* (London, 1897). In the late nineteenth century increasing demands were made by 'progressive' psychiatrists for a policy of 'open-door' to break the cycle of chronicity.

[123] Lamarche-Vadel and Préli, 'Généalogie des équipements psychiatriques', in Foucault (ed.), *Généalogie des équipements*, 137–84; see also Albert Mairet, *Le Régime des aliénés: Révision de la loi de 1838* (Paris, 1914).

[124] Nye, *Crime, Madness and Politics*, 227–47.

Already inherent in Morel's theory, but progressively extended in later elaborations, was an emphasis on medicine's role in preventing the onset of degeneration, which was stimulated by the 'ills of modern civilization', industrial conditions, bad housing, deficient nourishment, and defective education. Such an outlook provided enormous scope for hygienic intervention, refining and deepening the programme of medical policing established in the eighteenth century. The prominence of physicians in the mainstream of Republican and Radical politics of the 1880s and 1890s, as well as their intimate association with many of the social-welfare programmes associated with *solidarisme* during those decades and after, meant that degeneration theory provided an overarching biological rationale for the alleviation of a wide variety of 'social pathologies'. Indeed, most of the medico-legal specialists, as their biographies show (see chapter 4), placed an immense emphasis on the hygienic aspect of their work.

In addition, the theory of degeneration impinged radically upon social and political analysis in which the organism/society analogy was applied to the interpretation of colonial expansion, class division, and class struggle.[125] As Nye has demonstrated,[126] the appeal of degeneraton theory was all the greater after 1890 when France was increasingly obliged to compete in the world economic and imperial struggle. With a population declining in relation to its Teutonic neighbour, as well as with alarming increases in suicide, crime, alcoholism, syphilis, and a whole range of other social ills, the process of national degeneration seemed to be accelerating at a dangerous rate. Medical techniques and concepts appeared particularly well adapted to aid the struggle against such debilitating influences through a hygienic model of non-sectarian treatment designed to restabilize the balance of modern society.

By admitting and indeed stressing the importance of the milieu, the theory of degeneration proposed the necessity of ameliorative social measures to halt the spread of contagion.

125 See for a summary, Linda L. Clark, *Social Darwinism in France* (Birmingham, Ala., 1984).

126 Nye, 'Degeneration and the Medical Model of Cultural Crisis in the French Belle Epoque', in Seymour Drescher, David Sabean, and Allan Sharlin (eds.), *Political Symbolism in Modern Europe* (New Brunswick, NJ, 1982), 19–41.

The extended nature of the process of 'regeneration', however, implied a lengthy time-scale, the delicate and fragile nature of the social organism's balance precluding any rapid social or political transformation. Indeed, this idea pervaded the social theory of the *fin de siècle* and was an important aspect of the development of Durkheim's early work.[127] Consequently, the most appropriate, scientifically valid approach was prevention, a massive intervention to moralize and sanitize, to isolate dangerous individuals and study those populations at risk, a strategy which presupposed a strong, medically influenced outlook on patient care and treatment. As will be seen, this set of attitudes was also central to the development of criminology in France.

In practical terms, degenerationist ideology was integrally tied up with a reform movement between approximately 1890 and 1910 that was heavily influenced by an ideal of hygiene and prevention. The French Anti-Alcoholic Union, the National Alliance for the Growth of the French Population, the French Society for Sanitary and Moral Prophylaxis, as well as a score of others dealing with issues as diverse as tuberculosis and physical fitness, all sought to unite different classes against common moral/biological enemies which threatened the health of the nation.[128] These single-issue groups generally struck an apolitical stance—although including activists of numerous political affiliations—even though the ideology of hygiene in fact contained enormous potential for authoritarian intervention justified in the name of more effective technical management.

[127] For the importance of these notions in the formulation of Durkheim's view of sociology see Nye, 'Heredity, Pathology and Psychoneuroses in Durkheim's Early Work', *Knowledge and Society*, 4 (1982), 103–42.

[128] For information on the nature of these reformist campaigns see Jacqueline Lalouette, 'Le Discours bourgeois sur les débits de boisson aux alentours de 1900', *Recherches: L'Haleine des faubourgs*, 29 (1977), 315–46; Paul-Maurice Legrain, *Hygiène et prophylaxie: Dégénérescence sociale et alcoolisme* (Paris, 1895). For the major work on depopulation see Jacques Bertillon, *La Dépopulation de la France, ses conséquences, ses causes, et des mesures à prendre pour la combattre* (Paris, 1910); see also A. Corbin, 'Le Péril vénérien au début du siècle: Prophylaxie sanitaire et prophylaxie morale', *Recherches: L'Haleine des faubourgs*, 29 (1977), 245–83; Paul Brouardel, *La Lutte contre la tuberculose* (Paris, 1901); and Pierre Guillaume, *Du désespoir au salut: Les Tuberculeux aux 19e et 20e siècles* (Paris, 1986). For the general problem of chronic illness in late nineteenth-century France see Jacquemet, 'Médecine et "maladies populaires" ', *Recherches: L'Haleine des faubourgs*, 29 (1977), 349–65.

The theory of degeneration, therefore, was intimately tied to a series of professional campaigns which both reflected and contributed to the pre-World War I movement for social reform. However, to explain the appeal of degeneration solely in terms of professional interest sharpened by the demands of imperial policy would be to neglect the broad, internal political backdrop which influenced its development. Increasingly, degeneration theory was expressed in strident terms, revealing an array of anxieties about social disorder and the potential for recurring revolution.

Indeed, it is perhaps not surprising that the theory of degeneration was articulated in sophisticated form in the aftermath of the 1848 Revolution. As a devout Catholic convinced of the radical social mission of the Church, Morel was perhaps disillusioned with the outcome of the revolution. It seems likely that he shared the disenchantment of his medical and political associate Buchez, who, at first gladdened by the Republican experiment, subsequently wrote fearfully about the barbarity of the crowd during the June Days.[129] It may be suggested that in his *Traité* Morel provided not only a refined biological and social portrait of the mythical 'dangerous classes, working classes',[130] but also expressed his own pessimistic appreciation of the Revolution and its consequences, sharing in a broader trend of cultural despair which marked an important strand of French intellectual life in the 1850s.[131]

If disillusionment followed the era after 1848, then genuine despair characterized the bourgeois appreciation of the events of 1870–1. Indeed, it may be suggested that the refinement of crowd theory in this period emerged partly as a response to the terrors of the Commune and the perceived irrational reactions of the Parisian crowds, portrayed as drunken, frenzied rioters, hypnotized by unscrupulous leaders and bent on destruction. These phantasmagoric images found vivid expression in the historical studies of Hippolyte Taine on the origins of

129 See Pick, 'The Conception and Descent of Degeneration', chap. 4.

130 The phantom of the 'dangerous classes' was mythologized by literary men and hygienists in the first part of the nineteenth century. For the classic, although correctly much disputed, evocation of Paris's poor, see Louis Chevalier, *Laboring Classes and Dangerous Classes in Paris During the First Half of the Nineteenth Century*, trans. Frank Jellinek (Princeton, 1973).

131 See Swart, *The Sense of Decadence in Nineteenth Century France*, chap. 4.

contemporary France (in which the recent Commune was made to mirror the horrors of the Terror during the French Revolution) and in the work of Émile Zola, particularly in his view of striking miners in *Germinal*.

As important to crowd theorists as the increasingly distant memory of the Commune was the Boulanger affair of 1886–9, which swept across France, catching in its populist net such unlikely political allies as *revanchiste* Catholics and the miners of Décazeville (Aveyron). Analysis by criminologists and psychiatrists focused on the general's success in manipulating an irrational, suggestible, and degenerate mob who were impressed by this regal (if not very intelligent) military man astride a horse. Such a figure resonated with images of Napoleonic Caesarism, the man of action so dear to the French national *âme* as Gustave LeBon, the most renowned and influential popularizer of crowd psychology, would call the repository of national visions.[132] Similarly, during the anarchist bombings of the early 1890s, psychiatrists and criminologists stressed the 'degenerate' nature of those who resorted to what was perceived of as the politics of terrorism. Indeed, repressive measures were called to stop the anarchist contagion, legitimated by the belief that other 'degenerates' would imitate their acts.

In sum, the theory of degeneration enjoyed its immense popularity precisely because it provided a secular, scientific language for talking about the problem of recurring revolution and intractable criminal and antisocial tendencies. Political instability, class struggle, and social injustice were reassuringly translated into medicalized terminology and explained as part of a wider psycho-sociological pathology amenable to scientific investigation. However, to show how degeneration was deployed as a polemical weapon to political struggle still does not explain the specific discursive terms in which the theory was cast. As has been seen, degeneration was elaborated in esoteric medical language shaped by neo-Lamarckian evolutionary concepts

[132] See Susannah Barrows, *Distorting Mirrors: Visions of the Crowd in Late Nineteenth-Century France* (New Haven, 1981); in this work Barrows discusses the entire range of work from Taine to Zola, and the analyses of the Boulanger affair by crowd theorists. See also Nye, *The Origins of Crowd Psychology: Gustave LeBon and the Crisis of Mass Democracy in the Third Republic* (London and Beverly Hills, 1975), for his detailed account of LeBon's life and work.

and physiological theories of destabilization and debilitation. Through the complexities of technical language, however, it is clear that it focused above all on the inescapable 'fact' of the accumulation of morbid capital and its unpredictable, although inexorable, eruption across generations. In a provocative and compelling argument, Daniel Pick[133] has suggested that, as a discourse about the reproduction of deforming traits and pathological tendencies, degeneration theory unconsciously expressed fears about the course of nineteenth-century French history. Each revolutionary crisis was deemed to leave a hereditary imprint on the national consciousness which only worsened as it accumulated over generations. In other words, history was seen to be repeating itself, albeit in transmuted form, in a way homologous to the biological reproduction of degenerate individuals. Read in this light, the fearful, sometimes strident, but always sorrowful terms in which degeneration was discussed becomes, perhaps, more readily understandable.

133 D. Pick, 'The Conception and Descent of Degeneration', 72–188.

3

MEDICINE, LAW, AND CRIMINOLOGY

Despite the inevitable wrangles over the issue of criminal insanity which periodically marred the relationship between jurists and psychiatrists in court, the *fin de siècle* was none the less distinguished for the collaboration between the two professions in forging new directions in the field of criminal management. Their sometimes esoteric formulations had a vital impact on the progress of criminal trials. For example, when discussing a 'degenerate' alcoholic accused of murdering his family, intervening medico-legists, investigating magistrates, and even judges on the bench demonstrated certain areas of consensus. Rather than attempting to determine defendants' moral responsibility, they were often content to analyse their 'social dangerousness' by determining if they had 'criminal personalities' and posed a 'risk' to society.

THE ITALIAN AND FRENCH SCHOOLS

Such practical manifestations of criminological precepts both contributed to and were an integral aspect of international debates centring on the reassessment of classical penal codes in the last quarter of the nineteenth century, a movement intimately connected with an attempt to recast procedures of sentencing and rehabilitation. The central focus of this discussion—which engaged progressive jurists, penal specialists, legislators, and mental pathologists interested in the 'criminal mind'—was the establishment of a more efficacious and, above all, scientific conception of criminal control. The debate centred on the problem of the 'moral responsibility' of offenders and the attack launched on this 'metaphysical' notion by the Italian School of Criminal Anthropology.

The leading figure was Cesare Lombroso, who in 1876 painted a refined portrait of the 'born criminal', a reversion of a primitive subhuman creature described as an atavistic remnant of an ancestral type. He claimed to have identified significant anatomical and physiological characteristics which distinguished the criminal from his normal counterpart, and cited a range of indicators—facial asymmetry, irregular teeth, large jaws, dark facial hair, and twisted noses—denoting an unbalanced psychophysiological economy that could indicate insensitivity to pain, a tendency to epilepsy, and an instinctive urge towards antisocial behaviour.[1] With his delineation of the 'criminal type', Lombroso self-consciously sought to construct a scientific system in which such diagnostic signs would provide the basis for a preventive model of criminal control. Once the characteristics of innate criminality were identified, it was possible to know in advance those predestined towards antisocial behaviour and eliminate or treat them before they became a danger to society.

Lombroso entered the debate concerned with issues particular to the political and intellectual context of post-Risorgimento Italy. An avowed anticlericalist, he opposed the Catholic interpretation of crime as sin and claimed to eschew all 'metaphysical' accounts of antisocial behaviour. As Pick has shown,[2] his major political preoccupation was with the progress and unification of the nation state, a concern which linked his perception of criminality to the future of Italy. If criminal anthropology was the search for atavism—or inherited backwardness—then the investigation was linked to a similar attempt to identify the areas of 'regression' plaguing his country.

Faced, like many Italian intellectuals, with the disjunction between new-found political unity on the one hand and the persistence of social, cultural, and linguistic fragmentation on the other, Lombroso concentrated on the 'inherited backwardness' of the Italian peninsula. He focused on southern Italy,

1 See Stephen Jay Gould, *The Mismeasure of Man* (New York, 1981), 122–45; see also Marvin E. Wolfgang, 'Cesare Lombroso', in Hermann Mannheim (ed.), *Pioneers in Criminology* (London, 1960), 168–227.

2 See Daniel Pick, 'The Faces of Anarchy: Lombroso and the Politics of Criminal Science in Post-Unification Italy', *History Workshop*, 21 (1986), 60–86.

debilitated by poverty, an antiquated social system based on noble and church privilege, malaria, illiteracy, and its dangerously close contact with Africa. In constructing his evolutionary conception of social processes, Lombroso was concerned to classify the various pathologies afflicting the nation, unifying an assortment of evils—ranging from superstition and hysteria to prostitution and crowds—which seemed to oppose the march towards unification and political stability. Lombroso sought to identify those who were not worthy of citizenship, using a scientific account of atavism to underpin their exclusion from civil and political power. In his discussion, key political anxieties were embodied in representations of biological abnormality. Their emphasis on the inherent 'savagery' of brigands, for example, underscored the problem of recurring peasant and regional dissent, while other discussions of working-class crowds—particularly by one of his school, Scipio Sighele—pointed to another set of destabilizing influences in mass, urban society.

Although Italy's problems of cultural and political disunity were undoubtedly more extreme than those of France, governments of the early Third Republic faced a similar set of concerns. They too were attempting to 'civilize' and even 'colonize' the nation's outlying regions, to consolidate the regime through education, the army, and economic integration.[3] Indeed, Morel's earlier formulation of degeneration reflected such preoccupations during the 2nd Empire. Not only did he identify the distinguishing features of the 'dangerous classes, working classes', he also demonstrated the degenerate tendencies of the French peasantry, plagued by such seemingly endemic conditions as goitre and cretinism.[4] The criminology that emerged in France in the 1880s may also be seen as part of this broader attempt to identify and then eliminate elements of 'savagery' and political instability inimical to national

[3] Perhaps Eugen Weber gives the most evocative representation of the perception of 'savagery' and the need to civilize the hinterlands in his *Peasants into Frenchmen: The Modernization of Rural France, 1870–1914* (Stanford, 1976).

[4] See B.-A. Morel, *Considérations sur les causes du goître et du crétinisme épidémiques à Rosières-aux-Salines (Meurthe)* (Nancy, 1851); and *Du goître et du crétinisme, étiologie, prophylaxie, traitement, programme médico-administratif* (Paris, 1864). For more on the development of this research, see Pick, 'The Conception and Descent of Degeneration, 1848–1914, Ph.D. thesis (Univ. of Cambridge, 1987), chap. 3.

solidarity. In more specific terms, however, French criminology, unlike that of Italy, was almost exclusively preoccupied with urban problems. Despite the occasional interest in Corsican vendettas, rural crime was not seen as having the potential for disruption that the urban variant possessed. However, as with Lombroso's criminal anthropology, French discussions also sought to provide secular and 'positivist' criteria to legitimate measures that aimed at the political, economic, and indeed physical exclusion of a wide range of dangerous individuals.

Given the similarity of the concerns—if not particular conditions—of French and Italian theorists, it may be surprising that they engaged in strident confrontations during the International congresses of 1885 and 1889. Lombroso's characterization of the criminal 'type' became the focus of a struggle between his school and French opponents—such as Magnan, Brouardel, the Lyonnese Professor of Legal Medicine Alexandre Lacassagne, and the jurist, criminal statistician, sociologist, and philosopher Gabriel Tarde.[5] As Nye has shown,[6] the debate at first concentrated on the concept of the *criminel-né*, with the French anthropological response combatting Lombroso's 'ideal harlequin'.[7] By describing the 'born criminal' in this fashion, the French were implying that the Italian's formulation was a pastiche, bearing all the marks of scientific rigour but none the less merely reifying the 'vulgar' representation of inveterate criminals. To counter this assault the Italians called for a comparative examination of normal and criminal skulls and were so angered by the French refusal to participate in the investigation that they voted to boycott the next international conference in Brussels in 1882. In sum, the French implied that the Italians' anatomical reductionism would prove nothing, no matter what the results.

[5] See Henry Geisert, *Le Système criminaliste de Tarde* (Paris, 1935) and Terry N. Clark, *Gabriel Tarde: On Communications and Social Influence* (Chicago, 1969).

[6] Robert Nye, 'Heredity or Milieu: The Foundations of Modern European Criminological Theory', *Isis*, 67 (1976), 335–55.

[7] For the congress proceedings, see Émile Magitot, 'Deuxième Congrès international d'anthropologie criminelle', *Archives d'anthropologie criminelle*, 4 (1889), 517–651. For Manouvrier's paper see 'Existe-t-il des caractères anatomiques propres aux criminels?', ibid., 590–98. For his response after the Rome congress of 1885 see 'Les Crânes des suppliciés', ibid., 1 (1886), 119–41.

This position was advanced despite the strength of the tradition of French physical anthropology, shaped by one of the most distinguished and applauded scientists of his day, Paul Broca. Through a rigorous programme of craniometric measurement, Broca had aimed in the 1860s and 1870s to distinguish the varying physical characteristics of French regional groups and of all human races to establish an anthropological *échelle* demonstrating the various levels of human perfectability.[8] However, this tradition of French craniometry had passed its zenith by the time of Lombroso's appearance.[9] Broca's successors were unwilling to assert a direct link between the characteristics of gross anatomical abnormality and a psychological portrait of inveterate criminality, asserting that even an honest man might be unfortunate enough to possess unbecoming features and a distorted head.

Instead, all were profoundly influenced by the theory of degeneration which, with its elaborate account of morbid heredity, implied an only limited role to the mechanism of 'atavism', or the reappearance of an ancestral type. They regarded the degenerative process as operating through a complex combination of possible environmental and hereditarian influences in which diseased hereditary capital, accumulated over generations, appeared in polymorphous manifestations. They sought to identify the dangerous individual by identifying a range of competing and sometimes hidden moral, social, and physical symptoms.[10] In 1893, the French *criminaliste*, Charles DeBierre, summed up what had become the overriding consensus on the Italians' anatomical emphasis.

Even if the criminal has a crooked nose, jug ears, a prominent jaw, broad cheek bones, drooping eyebrows, a narrow and receding forehead, and large eye sockets set very far apart; even if his head and face are assymetrical, if his eyes are wild, shifty, and sinister-looking, if

[8] Francis Schiller, *Paul Broca: Founder of French Anthropology, Explorer of the Brain* (Berkeley, 1979), 136–64.

[9] Donald Bender, 'The Development of French Anthropology', *Journal of the History of the Behavioural Sciences*, 1 (1965), 139–51, and Fred W. Vogt, 'Progress, Science, History and Evolution in Anthropology', ibid., 3 (1967), 132–55.

[10] In later publications even Lombroso increasingly moved towards the theory of degeneration. It is not clear whether or not he responded to foreign criticism or if he adopted the theory because it coincided with his increasing pessimism, in which the criminal type could no longer be so easily identified. See Pick, 'The Conception and Descent of Degeneration', 234–58.

his lips are thin and his beard wispy; even if his appearance is suspicious, his characteristics unusual, with defects doubtless due to some problem of cranial development, his features pathological or teratological, it is no less true that at present it is still impossible to establish any causal relationship between a cranial or cerebral abnormality and criminal behaviour. Anatomical study of the individual is still powerless in determining whether he has been or will become a villain.[11]

It was not only through their concentration on the 'born criminal' that the Italians irritated their French opponents. The former also regularly resorted to metaphors of biological struggle, employing a lexicon replete with atavism, elimination, and regression. In Italy, the social uses of Darwinism and evolutionism were broadly interpreted from the 1860s onwards and produced some savage debates over Man's place in nature.[12] Lombroso himself had read Darwin and supplemented his evolutionary training with perusals of Morel, Haeckel, and Spencer. None the less, his relationship to Darwinism was as ambiguous as that of the English naturalist himself, as Lombroso also shared neo-Lamarckian perspectives about the inheritance of acquired characteristics.

The French, however, implied that the Italian position rested on a set of pernicious Darwinian associations. For Gabriel Tarde, this emphasis on struggle and 'atavism' was a dangerous error[13] and throughout his career he waged a battle against 'biologism', although he too was profoundly influenced by psycho-biological thinking.[14] For him, as well as for many other French thinkers pervaded by neo-Lamarckian ideas, 'Darwinian theories would be belied by the established fact of social solidarity that prohibits the founding of biology on

[11] Charles DeBierre, 'La Tête des criminels', *Archives d'anthropologie criminelle*, 8 (1893), 136.

[12] See Pietro Corsi, 'Recent Studies on Italian Reaction to Darwin', in D. Kohn (ed.), *The Darwinian Heritage* (Princeton, 1985), 711–29. See also Giuliano Pancaldi, *Darwin in Italia: Impresa Scientifica e Frontiere Culturali* (Bologna, 1983) and Giovanni Landucci, *Darwinismo a Firenze: Tra Scienze e ideologia, 1860–1900* (Florence, 1977).

[13] See 'L'Atavisme moral', *Archives d'anthropologie criminelle*, 4 (1889), 236–65.

[14] For his polemical position against the perceived 'biologism' of sociology see Steven Lukes, *Émile Durkheim: His Life and Work: A Historical and Critical Study* (Harmondsworth, 1973), 302–12. For his psycho-biological perspective see *Les Lois d'imitation* (Paris, 1890).

universal war.'[15] Indeed, Tarde's scepticism *vis-à-vis* the Italian approach was indicative of a wider French perspective, which was shared in varying degrees by many medico-legists and psychiatrists:

> The positivist school has developed a biological perspective but has not yet developed a sociology of its own. By this, I mean a sociology likely to regenerate penal law . . . This school is mentally intoxicated with the wine of the natural sciences but it must still eat the dry, substantial bread of the historical and social sciences . . . if it is to avoid the excesses of what one might call philosophical alcoholism.[16]

By invoking Darwin as an intellectual influence, the Italians were also seen as indicating certain political affiliations. Evolutionary arguments were taken up by partisans of many political persuasions, but were espoused particularly by those in the radical and socialist camps. One of Lombroso's most influential associates, the law professor Enrico Ferri, was a committed socialist[17] who regarded the evolutionary process as one of fierce competition which would guarantee an auspicious outcome to the class struggle. In his analysis, Darwinism and Marxism became inextricably entwined as two mutually reinforcing scientific theories.[18] Such heady doctrines, in which biological reductionism, naïve hereditarianism, Darwinism, and Marxism all seemed to blend, were ideal for alienating French criminologists, many of whom focused in contrast on environmentalism, neo-Lamarckianism, and concepts of social solidarity.

With the battle lines drawn, it is perhaps not surprising that Lombroso's claims set off a brushfire of intellectual debate, as an attempt was made to construct a 'criminal sociology' more attuned to French intellectual styles and specific professional traditions. The field was in large part formed through a succession of international congresses which met every four years

[15] Yvette Conry, *L'Introduction du darwinisme en France au XIXe siècle* (Paris, 1974), 400.

[16] Gabriel Tarde, 'Les Actes du congrès de Rome', *Archives d'anthropologie criminelle*, 3 (1888), 75.

[17] See Thorsten Selin, 'Enrico Ferri', in Hermann Mannheim (ed.), *Pioneers in Criminology* (London, 1960), 277–300.

[18] See Ferri's *Socialism and Positive Science: Darwin, Spencer, Marx*, trans. E. C. Harvey (London, 1902).

from 1885 onwards. A 'positivist' approach dominated all aspects of intellectual debate on the subject, with articles appearing in élite lay journals such as the *Revue des deux mondes* as well as in a variety of specialized periodicals which reflected the interdisciplinary emphasis of the field. In France, the most notable journal was the *Archives d'anthropologie criminelle*, which was self-consciously dedicated towards bringing together 'doctors, jurists, professors of criminal law, and magistrates'[19] and mobilizing their combined expertise to recast legal formulas and programmes of criminal management. Equally, a wider, European forum was provided for jurists in the Franco-German *Bulletin de l'Union internationale de droit pénal*. Older periodicals, such as the *Bulletin de la société des prisons*, rechristened the *Revue pénitentiaire* in 1892, also published criminological debates and discussed at length each new reform proposal on, for example, cellular confinement in prisons, repeat offenders, or the management of the 'criminally insane'.

The institutional location of criminology was equally diffuse, with interested professionals scattered throughout France's medical facilities, law schools, and specialized institutes. To take a few examples, the psychiatrist and medico-legist Paul Garnier was the head of the *Infirmerie spéciale du Dépôt de la Préfecture de Police* where Paris's deranged and dangerous were processed before being sent to other facilities in the capital. In 1900 he started the Préfecture's *vendredis du Dépôt*, weekly presentations of the 'malades' which aimed to educate physicians and jurists in the exacting art of medico-legal observation (see chapter 4). In addition, a *cours libre*[20] was started at the Paris Law Faculty in 1899, out of which ultimately grew the Paris *Institut de science pénale* founded in 1906. Around 1888 the jurist Georges Vidal began teaching a course on criminology at the Toulouse Faculty of Law which eventually formed the basis of the *Institut de criminologie et des sciences pénales*.[21]

In shaping their science the French persistently used the Italians as convenient foil to distinguish their own progressive

19 See the 'Avant-propos', *Archives d'anthropologie criminelle*, 1 (1886), 1.

20 The man who started this course was Henri Joly, who had a particular interest in juvenile delinquency. His most influential works were *Le Crime: Étude sociale* (Paris, 1888) and *La France criminelle* (Paris, 1889).

21 Nye, *Crime, Madness and Politics*, 118.

moderation from the extravagance and bombast of the rival position. Historical accounts have tended to reinforce this view of the conflict, with the Italians represented at worst as dangerous extremists and at best as objects of quaint antiquarian interest due to their naïve positivist zeal. In characterizing the debate in this manner, however, the broad similarities between the two schools have been largely overlooked, above all the mutual acceptance of deterministic explanations of criminal behaviour.

In effect, the French 'sociological' perspective proved to be a more flexible, and ultimately more efficacious, opponent of classical jurisprudence than the Italians' biological hereditarianism. In analysing the processes underlying criminogenesis, French theorists envisaged a constant interaction between pathological agents and susceptible environmental conditions. Their perspective was expressed in the language of Pasteurian microbiology, envisaging the criminal as a microbe and the environment as a breeding-ground or *bouillon* which sustained the contagion. As Alexandre Lacassagne remarked: 'The social milieu . . . is the culture [*bouillon de culture*] of criminality; the microbe is the criminal, an element of no importance until the day it finds the broth which makes it grow [*fermenter*].'[22] As will be shown, the 'environmentalism' which this epigrammatic statement encapsulates provided a sophisticated theoretical underpinning for a series of interventionist measures which were as far-reaching, if not more so, as any inspired by the Italians.

In addition, while they rejected the Italians' conception of the 'born criminal', the French were similarly concerned to construct typologies of various mental and physical states seen to predispose an individual to crime. Again, like the Italians, they increasingly regarded crime as a social pathology rather than as an individual moral failing, focusing on the offender's *état psycho-social* to determine the best means of eliminating or rehabilitating him. As René Garraud, a jurist and editor of the *Archives d'anthropologie criminelle*, remarked: 'In criminal sociology the objective changes: the crime is considered as a social phenomenon, where the thing that matters is to

[22] Quoted in Tarde, 'Les Actes du congrès de Rome', 72.

investigate the causes and determine the remedies; [in this perspective] the crime is seen as a social function.'[23]

The 'criminal sociology' they intended to construct was based on a wide variety of methodological orientations. Studies to be undertaken included statistical analysis to trace broad criminal trends. Researchers were encouraged to examine a wide set of causal factors that ranged from environmental conditions such as climate and geography, through social factors such as poverty, occupation, and education.

They were even interested in the 'professional psychology' of white-collar criminals. For example, the Lyonnese criminologist, Henri Coutagne, using a neo-Lamarckian perspective, suggested that occupational groups performed a series of mental operations which generated particular mentalities, potentially enabling the criminologist to examine 'the mechanism of the laws which govern cerebral adaptations strong enough to be transmitted and even reinforced through heredity'.[24] Rather than stressing a purely 'anthropological' account of criminality, Coutagne emphasized a social and economic interpretation, taking into consideration the new criminal opportunities opened up by 'modern' society in which rapid communication systems helped to promote new and more ingenious forms of theft and fraud. Work on the social underpinnings of juvenile crime, investigations of antisocial behaviour in the colonies, and comparative studies of crime, all typified the sociological approach which Lacassagne had done so much to promote.[25]

Although ostensibly centring on the widest social dimensions, interest in sensational, extravagant crimes remained a staple feature of criminological investigation, one marked heavily by the tradition of psychiatric intervention. The stigmata of degeneration, the biological, social, and moral characteristics of petty as well as notorious criminals, investigations into the increasingly troubling problem of juvenile

[23] René Garraud, 'Rapports du droit pénal et du la sociologie criminelle', *Archives d'anthropologie criminelle*, 1 (1886), 15.

[24] Henri Coutagne, 'De l'influence des professions sur la criminalité', ibid., 4 (1889), 617.

[25] Émile Raux, *Nos jeunes détenus: Essai sur l'enfance coupable* (Paris, 1890); Armand Corre, *L'Ethnographie criminelle* (Paris, 1894); Tarde, *La Criminalité comparée* (Paris, 1886).

delinquency,[26] all featured regularly in the *Archives* in an attempt to pin down those elements which made up the 'criminal personality'. Such investigations were self-consciously undertaken to categorize classes of criminal malefactors—to make demarcations between the retrievable and the incorrigible—as well as to examine the effect of prison life on inmates and to see what, if any, rehabilitative practices were effective. At the same time that such 'scientific' aims were pursued, another set of less well analysed fantasies were explored. Occasionally criminological discourse was infused with a baroque, self-consciously literary fascination with the 'other'. Thus one observer, who had gained access to six prisons with Lacassagne's help and masqueraded as an inmate, later explained the morbid preoccupation with criminality before proceeding with his '*Notes d'un témoin*'.

> There is [in the study of the prison world] a sort of complex and mysterious attraction, arising at once from the overwhelming taste that we all have to a greater or lesser extent for the horrible, the abnormal, and the monstrous, from the morbid pustule which leads us to scratch and rub away at badly healed wounds and to find in this strange habit I don't know what sort of treacherous pleasure, and finally from the confused belief in the enormous social importance of a problem that it would perhaps be immediately dangerous to leave unresolved.[27]

Entry into the prison world enabled men like Henri Joly, the Catholic writer on crime and social issues, to understand what methods of moralization were open to the criminologists. He recognized that imprisonment did not quell what he saw as the false love of the heroic and daring, with inmates preferring adventure stories to the vast multitude of bibles and works of morality which in prison libraries 'seem to be arranged like mummies in a necropolis.'[28] Inmates' drawings and writings, seemingly replete with pornographic representations, were analysed in order to understand 'the erroneous conceptions which haunt them'[29] and as diagnostic tools which pointed

[26] See Joly, 'Jeunes criminels parisiens', *Archives d'anthropologie criminelle* 5 (1890), 393–406.

[27] See Émile Gautier, 'Le Monde des prisons (Notes d'un témoin)', ibid., 3 (1888), 417.

[28] Joly, 'Les Lectures dans les prisons de la Seine', ibid., 307.

[29] Max Simon, 'Les Écrits et les dessins des aliénés', ibid., 318.

towards certain pathological tendencies such as mania, depression, and hysteria.

Criminal 'subcultures' in both their masculine and feminine forms were also the subject of considerable commentary, with the findings contributing crucially to the critique of contemporary penal strategies. Among men, unintelligible *argot*, ribald songs, and homosexual encounters all indicated to investigators the strengthening of an alternative system of antisocial values and beliefs. Tattoos fascinated particularly and, rather than indicating artistic leanings and self-expression, were represented instead as evidence of a self-mutilating tendency, an insensitivity to pain and a regressive strand of cultural imitation which prison life tended to reinforce rather than extirpate.[30]

Similarly, women's prison life was studied with keen interest and the inmates' inscriptions, love poems, and diaries taken to indicate the particularly 'sentimental' qualities of female psychology. From the inception of the penitentiary system, the penal regime for female moralization was based on a particular view of womanly 'nature', in which 'the fallen woman' was to be re-educated into proper conceptions of domestic morality. Indeed, the system of cellular confinement, the emphasis on silent and, above all, private forms of occupation, were seen as being particularly conducive to the feminine disposition.[31]

Despite the often crude and vulgar expressions scribbled on the walls, the fits of hysteria, jealousy, and rage which sometimes troubled prison decorum, women were perceived as better targets for reform than men. Not only did they still possess rather fierce maternal feelings (babies were sometimes born in prisons only to be given up after the period of wet-nursing), they also retained some sentiment for religion, particularly towards the Virgin Mary, whose favourable intercession was regularly sought during the gruelling months of pre-trial investigation.[32] Although such inclinations were

[30] For tattooing and criminal counter-cultures see Patricia O'Brien, *The Promise of Punishment: Prisons in Nineteenth-Century France* (Princeton, 1981), 90–8.

[31] See Claudie Lesselier, 'Les Femmes et la prison, 1820–1939', in Jacques Petit (ed.), *La Prison, le bagne et l'histoire* (Paris, 1984), 115–28.

[32] See Claude Langlois, 'L'Introduction des congrégations féminines dans le système pénitentiaire français, 1839–1880', ibid., 129–40; after 1880 a rapid de-christianization of the prison system was undertaken, probably for many of the same anticlericalist reasons which inspired a similar movement in the Paris hospitals.

sometimes condemned as female 'superstition' (depending on the political perspective of the author) Catholic belief was none the less often regarded as an ally in the moralizing enterprise. As the investigating magistrate, Adolphe Guillot, explained:

> In men's prisons the defendant hardly dares to show his religious feelings and the altar is gloomy and deserted, but the constant sound of entreaty rises from women's prisons. In a touching show of solidarity, every time a defendant is called for interrogation [by the examining magistrate] or when she is sentenced, her companions pray and burn candles for her.[33]

Such matters were not the only concerns which animated criminologists. For example, the *Archives* encouraged the science of criminal detection by including articles on sudden death, strangulation, and poisoning—work traditionally associated with the *Annales d'hygiène publique et de médecine légale*. It also reported regularly on the anthropometric techniques introduced by Alphonse Bertillon in 1883, whose bureau in the *Préfecture de police* fastidiously recorded the measurements and cranial indices as well as the arm and leg measurements of thousands of individuals. The results of these efforts were contained in an enormous 'catalogue of anthropometric particulars' as a means of tracking down repeat offenders who sought to hide their true identity,[34] a technique later transformed by the adoption of fingerprinting.[35]

Fingerprinting, as much a part of '*positive*' criminology as more obscure debates over moral responsibility, represented a sensational advance in detection. Moreover, it was identified, and hence praised, as part of a trend which spurned the gross anatomical characteristics redolent of Lombroso's criminal anthropology by concentrating instead on the smaller, even imperceptible, indices of identification.[36] For example, in

[33] Adolphe Guillot, *Les Prisons de Paris et les prisonniers* (Paris, 1890), 274–5.

[34] See, for his description of the technique, 'Sur le fonctionnement au service des signalements anthropométriques', *Archives d'anthropologie criminelle*, 3 (1888), 138–57.

[35] See also Henry T. F. Rhodes, *Alphonse Bertillon: Father of Scientific Detection* (London, 1956).

[36] For a most illuminating discussion of the epistemological basis of fingerprinting and its relationship to other forms of detection, for example, the analysis of dreams and art forgeries, see Carlo Ginsburg, 'Signes, traces, pistes. Racines d'un paradigme de l'indice', *Le Débat*, 6 (Nov. 1980), 3–44.

1905 Louis Gale was convicted of murder and theft and sentenced to ten years' hard labour on the evidence of Bertillon, 'who, methodically and scientifically, with an imperturbable calm, demonstrated to the jurors how he was able to discover that Gale had placed his hand on a litre jar seized at the Widow Mick's house'. Jurors reached their decision solely on the basis of his evidence, with the presiding judge remarking that such scientific verification was superior to the fickle testimony of witnesses: 'This is not mere personal testimony. It is scientific finding that does not lie.'[37]

Finally, criminal experts also examined the social-psychological mechanisms that would aid in understanding criminal fashions, collective criminality, mass demonstrations, and crowd behaviour. While virtually all specialists referred to the dangerous effects of criminal suggestion, the man who developed and refined the concept was Gabriel Tarde, whose work on 'interpsychology', the processes of unconscious imitation, pervaded criminological theorizing in this period. Legally trained and conservative in political outlook, Tarde was instrumental in providing a view of human action which emphasized the 'double personality' and took into account psychiatric writings on 'unconscious' and hence unpredictable behaviour when formulating ideas on moral responsibility. This stress can be seen in his discussion of such disparate antisocial phenomena as suicide, anarchism, and criminal activity under hypnotic suggestion.[38]

While it is clear that the 1880s marked a watershed in the interpretation of crime and punishment, the reasons behind the appearance of such intellectual and institutional initiatives at this particular historical juncture are harder to determine. However, it is clear that the 1880s saw the rise of an

[37] *Gazette des tribunaux*, 29 Oct. 1905.

[38] See Tarde, *La Philosophie pénale* (Paris, 1890). In this work he wrote extensively on the theory of responsibility, trying to find some revised interpretation of human action which took account of new philosophical and medical writing. He sought to bypass what was for him a sterile debate between determinism and spiritualism, maintaining that the evaluation of responsibility should be based on the degree to which an offender's *'identité personnelle'* had been integrated with his *'identité sociale'*. How such a process of evaluation was to be inserted into judicial practice is not entirely clear, but the attempt indicates the influence of psychological and sociological writing on his perception of criminal activity. See 85–114 and his discussion of *dédoublement de la personnalité*, 155–86.

acknowledged social problem and with it a dark chapter in French history, the 1885 law on recidivism, which stayed on the books until 1970 but effectively ceased to operate in 1942. When using the term recidivism to designate repeat offenders, criminologists harked back to a sixteenth-century legal concept, *récidive*. The word '*recidiviste*' only entered the mainstream of penological discussion in the 1840s. It was finally accepted by the *Académie française* in 1878. Middle of the road Republicans, headed by the young and ambitious René Waldeck-Rousseau, used this new term in supporting the bill to rid France of *gens sans aveu* flooding into large cities and the capital in search of employment during the agricultural depression. The conjunction of the Opportunist concern for moral order, the fear of repeated revolutionary upheaval, and the increasing conviction that recidivists were biological misfits, made possible the passage of a draconian measure which condemned vagrants and beggars to perpetual exile in New Caledonia and Guyana, the most insalubrious colonies of the empire.[39]

If the specific problem of petty offenders in the early 1880s gave buoyancy to criminological discussion, more general anxieties thereafter persistently supported its development. As suggested, the increasingly lurid portrayals of crowds, political offenders, and criminal bands demonstrated the unabated attraction for bourgeois commentators of the mythology of the 'dangerous classes'.[40] Each passing decade produced new stereotypes of possible threat, successive incarnations tending to appear as the French passed through the upheavals of the Third Republic. For example, as late as the first decade of the twentieth century, popular alarm concentrated on the so-called *apaches*, named after the American Indians they were deemed to resemble. These bands of juvenile delinquents—with their 'tribal' customs, sobriquets, and warring factions who roamed the *barrières* of the capital—were represented as dangerous savages ready to strike at the heart of bourgeois society.[41] The

[39] Nye, *Crime, Madness and Politics*, 49–96.

[40] Louis Chevalier, *Laboring Classes and Dangerous Classes in Paris During the First Half of the Nineteenth Century*, trans. Frank Jellinek (Princeton, 1973).

[41] Nye, *Crime, Madness and Politics*, 171–226; see also Michelle Perrot, 'Dans la France de la Belle Époque, les "apaches", premières bandes de jeunes', in *Les Marginaux et les exclus dans l'histoire, Cahiers Jussieu*, 5 (Paris, 1979), 387–407.

grande peur between 1906 and 1908, associated with strikes at home and sabre-rattling abroad, was matched by a similar alarm about *apache* violence at home. The effect of such associations between external threat and internal violence was a noticeable hardening of criminological rhetoric, which increasingly stressed social defence.

While the discussion of individual and social pathology was stimulated by these general anxieties, there were also more particular reasons of professional interest animating the major participants. Perhaps the most eager contributors were the medico-legists and psychiatrists who, from the earlier days of the monomania controversies, implicitly and sometimes explicitly demanded a reorientation of judicial principles. While in earlier decades their intervention had been more strongly guided by the humanitarian rationale of sparing the sick from the guillotine, later preoccupations emphasized 'social defence', an attitude which they unselfconsciously cultivated in court. When, for example, they examined Louis Menesclou, mentioned earlier for the probable rape and dismemberment of his four-year-old victim, Brouardel, Lasègue, and Motet flatly refused to recommend a conclusion of either partial or full irresponsibility, despite extensive evidence of physical debilitation and mental disequilibration.[42]

Such an assessment not only indicated the repulsion they felt for the man, but also exemplified an attitude which they expressed repeatedly and with increasing severity during criminological debates. While Menesclou might well have represented the epitome of the monomaniac to Esquirol and to his disciples, for these men he was nothing more than a degenerate. They were unwilling to see him consigned to an asylum and seemed little troubled by the probability of his execution. The reasoning behind his approach becomes clearer when it is put alongside the movement for the reform of the asylum system discussed in the last chapter, in which an increasing attempt was made to separate incurable from curable, dangerous from inoffensive. There was no facility like Broadmoor in England to receive those 'not guilty by virtue of

[42] Charles Lasègue, Paul Brouardel, and Auguste Motet, 'Affaire Menesclou: Examen de l'état mental de l'inculpé', *Annales d'hygiène publique et de médecine légale*, 2nd ser., 4 (1880), 439–53.

insanity', and 'deranged' offenders in France were generally consigned to asylums through the law of 1838 where their disruptive activities were a source of constant frustration. There was also the distinct possibility that violent lunatics would be freed once they were seemingly cured, with any recurrence of violence after their release tending to be blamed on the doctors (see chapter 7).

From the 1870s, medico-legal psychiatrists such as Garnier, Motet, and Ballet were key figures lobbying for the creation of special *asiles de sûreté*, where a regime of tranquillization and surveillance through the rigorous application of 'showers, pills, and quinquina' would effectively reduce these 'degenerates' to a suitable level of docility. Gone were considerations of humanitarian treatment and even possible cure; what remained was solely a distasteful custodial task. In a remark during one of the meetings of the *société des prisons*, Ballet summed up the psychiatric viewpoint, narrating a tale of biological, psychological, and social debilitation, the tone of which exemplified the ineluctable progress of degeneration. Such people were the epitome of those considered to be incurable:

> . . . individuals whom doctors, rightly or wrongly, call *degenerates* are people who have malformed [*mal ourlées*] ears, a squint, bad teeth and, in short, can be recognized as abnormal by certain outward defects. Examine their past: often they had infantile convulsions, experienced developmental difficulties during childhood, were aggressive, unsociable, hit their school-fellows; they show not only physical but also psychic defects. After being bad pupils, they become bad parents, bad sons and brothers, and fall easily and rapidly into crime. They make their debut either in a prison or a lunatic asylum, depending on whether or not they have the good or bad fortune to start with a straightforward crime or with a delirium (often alcoholic in nature). If they were lucky enough to begin with the asylum, they return there after every crime. They are, however, not always so fortunate, as often they are not delirious, but start-by going to prison after the first offence, after the second, third, and the tenth, and we end up by seeing these unfortunate outcasts over and over again.[43]

Like these psychiatrists, penal administrators and a wide range of philanthropists and legislators similarly concerned

[43] Gilbert Ballet, 'Traitement à appliquer aux délinquents à responsabilité limitée', *Revue pénitentiaire*, 29 (1905), 202–3.

themselves with criminological arguments. Their interests were indissolubly linked to the perceived failure of the penitentiary system, a view which was strengthened in the 1880s.[44] As with its sister institution, the asylum, the penitentiary was born out of an overriding belief in its reformist potential. As suggested, the model of cellular confinement which emerged in the early nineteenth century was to transform criminals into law-abiding citizens and oblige them to examine their evil inclinations in solitude. The rhythm of discipline, work, and silence was designed to impress upon the subject the need for rehabilitation. This vision, however, rarely found expression in practice until the 5 June law of 1875, virtually the last gasp of a movement dedicated to this ideal. Under the aegis of this measure, building projects began to convert *maisons centrales* into cellular institutions. The law was underpinned by free-will philosophy and supported by liberal Catholic reformers such as Othénin D'Haussonville who, still believing in the potential and value of moral expiation, sought to encourage penitence as the surest path towards rehabilitation. However, although this viewpoint derived support from both the Right and the Left, it increasingly lost ground to the Opportunists who, with the 1885 law on recidivism, called for an unsentimental politics of elimination.[45]

Although conflicting appraisals over the best means of rehabilitation continued to arouse debate, there was none the less an increasing emphasis on the seeming irretrievability of many subjects. More precisely, penologists recognized that the prison system seemed merely to reinforce criminals' antisocial tendencies, to refine deviant habits of mind, and create stronger criminal networks once they were released. There was a growing consensus that the prison system was nothing more than a factory for recidivism, with the statistics for petty crime being particularly revealing of this trend.[46] Increasingly, the

44 See Michelle Perrot, 'Délinquence et système pénitentiaire en France au XIXe siècle', *Annales: Économies, sociétés, croyances*, 30 (1975), 67–91 and O'Brien, *The Promise of Punishment*, 258–96. For the history of the reform movement as well as various penal experiments see M. Perrot (ed.), *L'Impossible Prison: Recherches sur le système pénitentiaire au XIXe siècle* (Paris, 1980).

45 Nye, *Crime, Madness and Politics*, in particular, 60–94.

46 Ibid., 57. Nye shows how vagabondage and mendicity averaged 10,893 cases a year between 1856 and 1860, climbed to 20,456 in 1880, and peaked at 35,301 in 1890. The average for the decade between 1891 and 1900 was 29,088 but fell to 22,500 for the decade to 1910.

penological movement concentrated on moving punitive practices from inside the prison walls into civil society, through programmes of parole and measures taken for the supervision for juvenile offenders, all strategies which, as will be seen, were imbued with criminological perspectives based on ideals of depenalization and indeterminant sentencing.

Although a substantial minority of jurists resisted criminology, the 'progressive' among them endorsed it with varying degrees of enthusiasm. As will be seen, the era was marked by broad alterations in legal approach which not only affected their view of penal process but also their appreciation of civil and administrative law. They were keen to participate in what was called a more 'positive' approach to legal studies, to assimilate the findings of the social sciences—particularly history, sociology, and political economy—into legal education, and to provide more flexible and pragmatic legal formulas to cope with new industrial combinations, labour unions, state power, and finally, the containment of social pathology. They regularly enjoined the psychiatrists and medico-legal community to make their knowledge more comprehensible to them,[47] and even admitted that the problem of degeneration made the classical administration of justice increasingly difficult. However, rather than transferring power and the management of the criminal offender to medical and administrative personnel, jurists were keen to carve out a large niche for themselves: displeased with their role as the executors rather than interpreters of the law, they worked for increased discretionary power on the bench, a movement which was to have a key effect on their role during sentencing.

Criminology, Hygiene, and the 'Microbe'

Criminology was partially conceived of as a kind of public hygiene, with its rhetoric marked by the contemporary enthusiasm for bacteriology, demonstrated above all by the frequent and handy use made by criminologists of the microbe-

[47] See, for an example of this, A. Abadane, 'Le Barreau français et la criminologie positive', *Archives d'anthropologie criminelle*, 3 (1888), 113–37.

bouillon metaphor. The adoption of such ideas was neither total nor concerted but rather helped to clarify ideas about the relationship between individual and social pathology and to justify new programmes of criminal identification and containment.

The word 'microbe' was invented in 1878 to denote a new object of scientific enquiry. Although now enshrined as another 'scientific revolution', bacteriology was in fact accepted only very gradually by the majority of French medical practitioners and indeed seems to have had little impact until the anti-diphtheria serum was effectively introduced in 1894. Still, there were early and important evangelists centring on Paris called *pastoriens*, a word coined in 1887 to designate those who were ready to impose microbiological ideas on medical education, the clinic, the operating theatre, and public hygiene. What is important is that there was a significant overlapping in personnel and theoretical orientation between this group and those interested in criminology.

Perhaps the most famous was Paul Brouardel, who not only acted as the leader of legal medicine in France, but was elected as the head of the Paris medical faculty by a vote of thirty-seven to two precisely because of his ready support of bacteriology. He perceived connections between a wide cluster of social and biological ills, and found little difficulty in moving from writing about typhoid epidemics in Clermont-Ferrand in 1886 to discussing hypnotism in an 1890 murder trial, as in both cases the aims pursued, if not the techniques, were the same. He thus campaigned against alcoholism, smallpox, and tuberculosis as well as convincingly demonstrating that typhoid bacteria were water-borne, a finding he used to contain the disease by imposing hygienic measures on the army. Finally, he also played a critical role in securing the passage of the law of 15 February 1902, which defined state powers on matters of public health and provided for obligatory vaccination, the notification of contagious diseases, and the sanitation of cities.[48]

While Brouardel was the most prominent in this arena, there were others who also recognized the potential of microbiological

[48] For more on Brouardel see Léon-Henri Thoinot, 'La Vie et l'œuvre de Paul Brouardel, 1837–1906', *Annales d'hygiène publique et de médecine légale*, 4th ser., 6 (1906), 193–235.

ideas. Charcot, for example, wanted to set up a microbiological laboratory at the Salpêtrière; the psychiatrist Jules Bergeron was also a keen *pastorien*, as he and many of his colleagues recognized the impact of environmental conditions in producing all forms of illness.[49]

However, it is not only through identifying key medical figures and their mutual interests that the pervasiveness of such ideas may be grasped. Criminal specialists were intrigued by the seemingly more rigorous methods of conquering disease. Bacteriologists, at least in theory, advocated an elegant three-stage process, a search for (1) the general etiology of disorder; (2) the identification of a specific disease agent (the microbe); and finally (3) interventionist measures to produce an acquired immunity in the diseased host.[50]

For example, the much-applauded identification of the tubercular bacillus by Koch seemed to fulfil at least two of these prescriptions. His analysis suggested a strongly environmentalist orientation which stressed the invasion of a germ into a susceptible *terrain*. This view was easily and congenially reconciled with the hereditarian emphasis of late nineteenth-century medicine,[51] a process which was most revealingly described in Brouardel's account of tubercular infection:

> . . . the combination of two indispensable factors is needed for a man to become a consumptive. First, Koch's bacillus or the *seed*; and second, the *breeding-ground* [*terrain*], which is the organism's ability to nurture [*développer*] it. This *individual receptivity* is either *innate* or *acquired*.[52]

Once incorporated into the discussion on crime, such an analysis explained why certain individuals were susceptible to antisocial influence, to the noxious germs of a debilitated society. From real microbes contaminating the waters of society, it was but a leap in scale to seeing criminals and other undesirable elements as having a similar nature and effect on the metaphorical waters which they inhabited. The perspective

[49] Jacques Léonard, 'Comment peut-on être pastorien?', in Claire Salomon-Bayet (ed.), *Pasteur et la révolution pastorienne* (Paris, 1986), 152–3.

[50] See Salomon-Bayet (ed.), 'Penser à la révolution pastorienne', ibid., 26.

[51] Ibid., 147.

[52] Brouardel, *La Lutte contre la tuberculose* (Paris, 1901), 22.

therefore implied two requirements: first to root out the criminal microbe—hence the concentration on his anatomical and psycho-social characteristics—and second to determine those elements in the milieu which exacerbated or contributed to his nocivity. In such an analysis, the offender was regarded as the host rather than the microbe, with the aim of the specialist being to isolate those disease agents in his biological and psycho-social constitution which were the 'germs' of disorder, a procedure deemed necessary to determine strategies of treatment.

Both of these criminological aims were, therefore, suffused with a desire to identify, manage, and, ultimately, to eradicate the criminal 'microbe' from the social body. The language which described Pasteur's own 'heroic', 'conquering' scientific quest used a series of battle metaphors which were readily transposed to discussions of social pathology. The campaigners sought adherents for a crusade against the invisible, but ultimately identifiable, microbes which pervaded all living systems. Pasteur's methods were also compared to a police or judicial enquiry which emphasized detective work and careful tracking. One of his disciples described him as a man who had undertaken 'ten great investigations (which can be compared to judicial enquiries) which ten times out of ten discovered the harmful agent and, even more remarkably, indicated [*sic*] the remedy'.[53] One eminent *pastorien* similarly used language which was virtually indistinguishable from that employed by criminologists when they discussed a prognostic system to identify certain dangerous 'psycho-social' types:

> If one could know the microbe behind each illness, . . . its favourite places, habits, its method of advance, it would be possible, with a *bonne police médicale*, to catch it just at the right moment, stop its progress and prevent its homicidal attack [*intervention*].[54]

The conceptual homologies between the bacteriological, hygienic, and criminological spheres can be further demonstrated. The tradition of medical policing described in chapter 2 envisaged public hygiene in the widest possible sense: water, air, soil, buildings, food, as well as social and political

53 Salomon-Bayet, 'Penser à la révolution', 34.

54 Bruno Latour, 'Le Théâtre de la preuve', in Salomon-Bayet (ed.), *Pasteur et la révolution pastorienne*, 352, quoting Trélat.

organization were all seen as elements which interacted in infinite combination. The medical policeman's role was thus to ensure a smooth regulation of biological and social relations in all these areas. The hygienic movement which assimilated bacteriological concepts continued to envisage this wider whole, while at the same time narrowing and sharpening the focus of enquiry to the various stages of the microbe's trajectory. Hence, in following and describing the microbe's path through its numerous hosts, the hygienist made the specific disease agent the supreme object of attention, the bodies, cultures, and societies through which it passed taking second place to the *technical* appreciation of the microbe's contagious journey. For example, an infected sailor ill with cholera died in Toulon. His clothes made the journey back to Yport where his sister washed them; after throwing the water into the street, seven people died. The hygienist could follow the pathogenic agent from ship, to train, to city neighbourhood, and in so doing place the new microbiological actor in the floodlights.[55]

Despite the environmentalism which bacteriological concepts seemed to underscore, the emphasis still remained on the disease agent rather than on the squalid or dangerous properties of the milieu. In the sphere of housing, for example, readily recognized as a breeding ground for contagion in the great urban centres, repeated efforts to oblige property owners to promote improvements and to encourage the state or municipal authorities to initiate building projects met with continual obstruction.[56] Instead, *ad hoc* and extremely invasive measures were occasionally employed to fumigate working-class living quarters, leaving undisturbed the interests of those with property and money.[57] The representation of the mythic microbe, therefore, was curiously detached from a search for a pervasive political and social solution to the problem of disease. This technical approach was also readily applied in criminological analysis, as experts pointed to the conditions which produced the 'degenerate' criminal. While highlighting

[55] Ibid., 351–2.

[56] For this story see Anne-Louis Shapiro, *Housing the Poor of Paris, 1850–1902* (Madison, 1985).

[57] Jacques Léonard, 'Comment peut-on être pastorien?', in Salomon-Bayet (ed.), *Pasteur et la révolution pastorienne*, 173.

the impact of unemployment, poverty, inadequate education, and so on, *criminalistes* none the less persistently targeted their interventionist strategies against the offender rather than on the 'diseased' milieu which had produced him. In sum, the environmentalism apparent in bacteriology and French degeneration theory did not lead reformers to advocate the structural reordering of society, a stance indicative of a broader political atmosphere which will be discussed more fully in the conclusion.

Instead, the solution they offered was a limited programme of technical assessment which followed the microbes' path and reacted with strategies of intervention to sanitize and eradicate the germs. Necessarily, this implied a wider role for the hygienist whose expertise could devise the necessary counter measures. Indeed, the appearance of the microbe not only justified past campaigns—such as quarantine and sanitization—taken against the nebulous *miasmes* which produced epidemics, but suggested the possibility of wider intervention, veritable *cordons sanitaires* stretching across Europe in an attempt to control and isolate disease. In 1901, Brouardel described the sense of achievement and clarity which bacteriology had brought:

> Although international sanitary conferences had been meeting for half a century, they never led to anything because doctors from different countries had no common doctrine. I studied medicine at a time when . . . the means of propagation of typhoid fever, cholera, and plague were unknown.
>
> Success was not possible until, thanks to the discoveries of Pasteur, we were able to replace the uncertainties and debates on spontaneous generation [*spontanéité*] with the specificity of disease agents and the sureness of experiments which everyone could repeat and the accuracy of which was acknowledged, after further checks, by researchers throughout the world.[58]

For the *pastoriens*, bacteriology and the potential for large-scale remedial action it implied meant that physicians were to be drawn into an increasing number of projects which would also further enhance their role as expert managers of society. Brouardel maintained that the physician should not merely treat but should also

58 Brouardel, *La Profession médicale au commencement du XIXe siècle* (Paris, 1903), 216–17.

point out to government, town councils, various communities, and the individual himself the way to be protected against those illnesses recognized as avoidable. The role of the doctor in society is no longer only curative; it is above all preventive [*prophylactique*].[59]

By demonstrating that microbes were everywhere, hygienists suggested that they and their interventionist practices should also be ubiquitously present.

The use of the metaphor of the microbe and the bouillon helped the doctors redefine the conception of individual liberties in matters of public health, underscoring the political concerns which imbued this revised hygienic perspective.[60] The recognition of the microbe's importance implied that individuals afflicted by contagious maladies might need to give up their rights in order to stop the disease spreading, a practice adopted by the 15 February 1902 law on public health requiring the public registration of a wide range of illnesses which, when updated the next year, included typhoid, typhus, smallpox, scarlet fever, measles, diphtheria, cholera, yellow fever, dysentery, and cerebral meningitis.[61]

While physicians sometimes sought to ignore these provisions, fearing the wrath of patients who might be obliged to enter hospital or close down businesses, the law was none the less an important erosion of the sanctity of the *secret professionnel*, or the contractual obligation of secrecy governing the doctor's relationship to his patient. Although limited local public health powers had previously been exercised during epidemics, the 1902 law legally enshrined the state's *obligation* to promote public health. The balance between individual liberty and social defence was increasingly tilted towards the latter so that a wider view of social responsibility compelled the sufferer to be 'isolated, disinfected, in short, to be placed in a situation where he can do no harm, like convicts'.[62]

[59] Brouardel, op. cit. 7; for the preventive movement, the dissemination of the 'goutte de lait', and the importance of chronic illness in public hygiene during this period, see Gérard Jacquemet, 'Médecine et ''maladies populaires'' dans le Paris de la fin du XIXe siècle'. *Recherches L'Haleine des faubourgs*, 29 (1977) 349–65.

[60] Bruno Latour, 'Le Théâtre de la preuve', in Salomon-Bayet (ed.), *Pasteur et la révolution pastorienne*, 375.

[61] Raymond Villey, *Histoire du secret médical* (Paris, 1986), 85–6.

[62] Latour, 'Le Théâtre de la preuve', 375.

Once again, the similarity in language between the emerging system of hygienic disease control and criminal management is very striking. Perhaps the most succinct demonstration of the matching of language, interpretation, and method between hygienic aspirations and criminological methods was provided by Adolphe Prins, a Belgian prison reformer who took an active role in both practical and theoretical debates: 'Take a housewife who throws her rubbish into the street. A policeman passes, makes out a report on the infringement and we fine her without asking if she is deranged . . .'[63] Extending his example into crime proper, he contended that when dealing with the criminal spreading his antisocial refuse about, society should also concern itself with 'propriety, hygiene, salubriousness, security' to prevent the spread of contagion,[64] rather than with any extraneous or metaphysical notions such as moral responsibility or individual liberty.

SOLIDARISM, LEGAL THEORY, AND THE CONCEPT OF RISK

The refined hygienic perspective infusing criminology must be placed alongside sometimes competing, but more often overlapping, developments within legal and political theory, both of which are equally important for understanding the new science of criminal management. In legal studies, perhaps the most important shift centred on the revision of notions of contractual obligation based on fault, new ideas which were profoundly shaped by the impact of debates in sociology, political economy, and history.[65] None of the discussions, equally, can

[63] Adolphe Prins, 'Traitement à appliquer aux délinquents à responsabilité limitée', in *Revue pénitentiaire*, 29 (1905), 474.

[64] Ibid.

[65] For an introduction to the changing concerns of legal education see George Weisz, *The Emergence of Modern Universities in France, 1863–1914* (Princeton, 1983), 188–90. For some of the polemical discussions surrounding the relationship of law to sociology and history see Fernand Faure, *La Sociologie dans les facultés de droit de France* (Paris, 1893); M. Hauriou, *Les Facultés de droit et la sociologie* (Paris, 1893); Raymond Saleilles, *Quelques mots sur le rôle de la méthode historique dans l'enseignement du droit* (Paris, 1890). For an important discussion on the need to introduce political economy in the law faculties see Alfred Jourdan, *Des rapports entre le droit et l'économie politique ou philosophie comparée du droit et de l'économie politique* (Paris, 1885).

be adequately understood without reference to political philosophy, particularly the growing influence of theories of social obligation and solidarism. At first glance, such considerations seem far indeed from criminology and the attempts to recast penal procedures. On the contrary, however, legal debates in civil, administrative, and penal law interpenetrated to a hitherto unimaginable extent and it was out of this exchange that a revised concept of moral responsibility emerged.

The legal debate was part of a discussion concerned to establish new terms of reference for state intervention and was animated by several interlocking preoccupations.[66] Perhaps the most overriding was an attempt to reassess the concept of popular sovereignty, the legitimating ideal underpinning the Republican regime which, perhaps paradoxically, was at the time the rallying cry of revolutionary movements. Because the state's sovereignty emanated from the consent of every (male) individual, it could be challenged by any one of them.[67] The history of nineteenth-century France, with its succession of revolutionary campaigns each claiming a legitimate right to overthrow the reigning government, pointed to the fearful and destabilizing political consequences of the concept.

During the Third Republic a whole range of theorists attempted to discover a surer, more stable basis for the Republican regime and found a solution in the notion of *solidarité*, a term which began to pervade political and legal discourse from the beginning of the 1880s. Third Republican philosophers such as Alfred Fouillé[68] regarded social solidarity

66 For a survey of the changing role of the state see Michael Halbecq, *L'État, son autorité, son pouvoir, 1880–1962* (Paris, 1965); for key debates over public and constitutional law and their relationship to social theory in this period see Jaques Donzelot, *L'Invention du social: Essai sur le déclin des passions politiques* (Paris, 1984), which surveys the important impact of two key legal theorists, Léon Duguit and Maurice Hauriou, 86–102. For an introduction to Hauriou see Albert Broderick (ed.), *The French Institutionalists, Maurice Hauriou, Georges Renard and Joseph T. Delos*, trans. Mary Welling (Cambridge, Mass., 1970). For more on Duguit see William Logue, *From Philosophy to Sociology: The Evolution of French Liberalism, 1870–1914* (Dekalb, Ill., 1983), 180–24; see also Steven Lukes and Andrew Scull, *Durkheim and the Law* (Oxford, 1984), in particular, 1–33.

67 Donzelot, *L'Invention du social*, 74.

68 For Fouillé's perspective on social science and law see respectively his *La Science sociale contemporaine*, 6th edn. (Paris, 1922) and *L'Idée moderne de droit*, 2nd edn. (Paris, 1923).

as the mobilization and harmonization of the various and increasingly specialized functions of society so that all could work in a 'common effort for a final end which is the maintenance of the whole'.[69] Émile Durkheim in his *La Division du travail social* (1893) sought to demonstrate the greater specialization of function in complex societies, interlocking systems of association, and interchange which increasingly transcended the idea of a *contrat libre* and were seen, in contrast, as constitutive of a *solidarité organique*.

Fully developed as the 'official' philosophy of Radical and Radical-socialist rule by Léon Bourgeois in 1897, this reformist doctrine stressed the need for state intervention to further programmes of social welfare. It aimed to reconcile morality and science—particularly Rousseauian theories of the contractual nature of society with those based on a deterministic conception of social organicism—in order to find *le juste milieu* between capitalism and socialism. Hence, 'solidarism' aimed to replace class struggle with conflict-free interdependence, a goal to be achieved through the suppression of the most flagrant abuses of capitalism.[70] Hitherto, society in general and the state in particular had been seen as the trustee of individual and corporate rights. 'Solidarism' in contrast presupposed a series of *devoirs* as well as rights, social debts which all individuals owed towards the better maintenance and amelioration of the social organism. The movement was revealingly described as the 'designated patron of the laws of social hygiene and public assistance'.[71] It was therefore endowed with many of the same managerial ideals discussed above, although it was only very partially realized through legislation such as the 1892 law regulating the employment of women and children in factories, the 1893 law on safety

69 Fouillé quoted in John A. Scott, *Republican Ideas and the Liberal Tradition in France, 1870–1914* (New York, 1966), 164.

70 J. E. S. Hayward, 'The Social History of an Idea in Nineteenth-Century France', *International Review of Social History*, 4 (1959), 261–84; 'The Official Philosophy of the French Third Republic: Léon Bourgeois and Solidarism', ibid., 6 (1961), 20–32; and 'Educational Pressure Groups and the Indoctrination of the Radical Ideology of Solidarism, 1895–1914', ibid., 8 (1963), 1–17. See also for the relationship of Durkheim's work to the movement Lukes' *Émile Durkheim: His Life and Work*, 350–4.

71 Célestin Bouglé quoted in Scott, *Republican Ideas and the Liberal Tradition*, 179.

conditions at work and for communal medical assistance, the 1898 bill on industrial accidents, and a scheme for old-age pensions in 1905.

The debate over the role of the state in improving social relations was integral to legal evolution. Several key legal theorists who engaged in the transformation of civil, administrative, and penal law in this era were *not* Radicals or Radical-socialists. Prominent men such as Maurice Hauriou[72] and Raymond Saleilles were avowed Catholics who remained closer to the tradition of Le Play's sociology[73] and the more conservative economic orientation of the *Société d'économie sociale*, but none the less shared a similar appreciation of the need to restrain capitalist abuses and promote social harmony.[74]

The forum for the elaboration of new legal principles and modifications in penal law was the *Union internationale de droit pénal*, a body self-consciously dedicated to gathering jurists from across Europe with the aim of reforming existing penal codes. The Frenchmen involved included such notable jurists as René Garraud, Paul Cuche, and Émile Garcon,[75] all *au courant* with criminology and acquainted with the slightly more radical ideas of other participants such as Adolph Prins, the Dutchman Gerard Anton Van Hamel, and the German Franz Eduard von Liszt. The most important legal concept to emerge

[72] The conservatives included men like Maurice Hauriou (see above, n. 66). In opposing Duguit—who was inspired by Durkheimian sociology—Hauriou shows tendencies closer to those of Gabriel Tarde, an interest in the individual and the psychological aspects of social relations. While concerned to establish public institutions designed to further common social ends, he became increasingly disturbed by what he perceived as the authoritarian implications of Duguit's formulations on the state. Hariou was received positively among more traditionally minded jurists, Catholic reformist circles, and industrialists. Another jurist, Raymond Saleilles, to be discussed in detail below, was associated with Catholic liberalism, having direct personal connection with one of the most important contemporary exponents of this political position, the deputy Abbé Lemire; see Jean-Marie Mayer, *Un Prêtre démocrate: L'Abbé Lemire, 1853–1928* (Paris, 1968).

[73] See Sanford Elwitt, *The Third Republic Defended: Bourgeois Reform in France, 1880–1914* (Baton Rouge, 1986), in particular, 19–51.

[74] For a summary of the union of diverse political affiliations in an effort to promote social harmony see Elwitt's 'Social Reform and Social Order in Late-Nineteenth Century France: The Musée Social and its Friends', *French Historical Studies*, 11 (1980), 431–51.

[75] See Paul Cuche, *De la possibilité pour l'école classique d'organiser la répression pénale en dehors du libre arbitre* (Grenoble, 1897) and his *Traité de science et de législation pénitentiaire* (Paris, 1905); René Garraud, *Le Problème moderne de la pénalité* (Paris, 1889) and Maurice Garcon, *Histoire de la justice sous la IIIe République*, 3 vols. (Paris, 1957).

from the Union's deliberations was the notion of the *état dangereux*, or criminal risk, an idea adapted from the newly developed system of employer liability which compensated workers for industrial accidents that was incorporated into the 1898 law on *risques professionnels*. The innovators in this field came from Bismarckian Germany[76] where the discussion surrounding social insurance legislation was already greatly advanced, but Raymond Saleilles in France was instrumental in extending the ideas and developing them so that they could enter French civil and criminal law virtually simultaneously.

Saleilles was an academic jurist of international reputation, concerned both with the most esoteric aspects of legal theory and with a range of practical initiatives focusing on penal reform, the rights of women within the family, as well as labour and industrial law. He was a well-respected figure in criminological circles, appeared at meetings at the *Société générale des prisons* and was a personal friend of Gabriel Tarde who wrote the preface to his path-breaking *L'Individualisation de la peine* (1898). One of the leading juridical figures in the so-called '*Nouvelle École*', Saleilles was the inspiration, 'the breath of life',[77] of the *Revue trimestrielle de droit civil*, a journal dedicated to bringing legal theory into line with 'positivist' developments in the social sciences. Maintaining that the study of economics, politics, and sociology should be an essential element of legal education, along with a wide array of progressive jurists, he encouraged historical and comparative studies of law to aid the process of adjusting and bending classical principles to the working of 'modern' societies.[78] He provoked what was called 'a real dramatic coup'[79] in 1890 when he published his

[76] For the history of social insurance in Germany and its relationship to occupational medicine see Dietrich Miller, 'From Workers' Diseases to Occupational Diseases: The Impact of Experts' Concepts on Workers' Attitudes', in Paul Weindling (ed.), *The Social History of Occupational Health* (London, 1985), 55–78; see also Yves Saint-Jours, 'France', in Peter A. Kohler and Hans F. Zacher (eds.), *The Evolution of Social Insurance, 1881–1981: Studies of Great Britain, France, Switzerland, Austria and Germany* (London, 1982), 93–149.

[77] Edmond-Eugène Thaller (ed.), *L'Œuvre juridique de Raymond Saleilles* (Paris, 1914), 4.

[78] See, for example, Raymond Saleilles, *Quelques mots sur le rôle de la méthode historique dans l'enseignement du droit* (Paris, 1890); Paul Fournier, 'Raymond Saleilles, historien de droit', in Thaller (ed.), *L'Œuvre juridique de Raymond Saleilles*, 155–83.

[79] Thaller (ed.), *L'Œuvre juridique de Raymond Saleilles*, 13.

seminal work, *Essai d'une théorie générale des obligations d'après le projet du code civil allemand*, in which he examined the legal formulations developing in Imperial Germany.

He concentrated on the best means of altering the underlying principles and legal provisions of the Napoleonic codes, criticizing the concept of sovereignty, the belief in natural law, as well as the simple contractual formulae which, in his view, incorporated an erroneous appreciation of atomistic, unconnected individuals entering into personal arrangements heedless of wider social consequences. His appreciation of the problems affecting 'antiquated' administrative and civil law is an important ingredient in understanding his evaluation of similar difficulties in the criminal justice system. In both, he counselled jurists to examine the particular problems of the 'modern' age and adjust classical formulae to take account of novel social conditions. In civil law he recognized the need for new 'juridical postulates' which would better supervise the problems generated by the 'industrial movement':

> . . . electricity can be generated through the power of waterfalls, but the use of this new force provokes a legal conflict between the legitimate claims of national industry and local landowners' opposing interests. Once electricity has been produced in this way, it has to be carried over long distances, a process which requires the support of people's homes to secure the cable along which it travels, and which provokes alarm amongst home-owners. In addition, under the vast pressure of movement caused by strikes and institutionalized through union activity, labour contracts have been transformed. Is it enough to know the theories of property or contract to resolve such problems? It is necessary to have the science of the engineer, the economic facts of an industrialist and all the knowledge indispensable for regulating the conflicts that arise between capital and labour . . .[80]

In surveying this extensive field of opposing rights and obligations, Saleilles chose to concentrate on the problems particular to 'great industries'. In examining the project for the German civil code, he maintained that large-scale manufacturing concerns and massive transportation networks, particularly the railroads, represented a different level of social evolution and organization which contained 'eventual risks', likelihoods

80 Saleilles, 'Les Méthodes d'enseignement de droit et de l'éducation intellectuelle de la jeunesse', *Revue internationale de l'enseignement*, 44 (1902), 318.

of damage and harm that were the inevitable result of 'the fact of exploitation',[81] of the technology and productive system. When accidents occurred it was rarely clear who should be held responsible for them, so complicated and diverse were the variables at work. Traditional notions of contract were hence irrelevant to new social conditions which produced 'obligations resulting from the very organization of large-scale industry that have nothing in common with the ordinary principles of private law, which only regulates individual agreements . . .'.[82] The clearest example of this was posed by recurrent and seemingly inescapable railway accidents: if a train full of people fell off the tracks it was uncertain whether fault lay with the driver, some other employee charged with making sure the train operated smoothly, or with the rail company which theoretically should have made the system proof against disaster.[83]

Similar legal difficulties surrounded the more general area of industrial production where accidents caused hostile stand-offs between workers complaining of unnecessary dangers and employers accusing their employees of causing accidents through inattention, drunkenness, and so on. Saleilles argued that fault in such instances lay with neither party; rather it was an integral inescapable aspect of the insecurity, unpredictability, and uncontrollability of the machine age. The industrial order itself was characterized as a dangerous, ever more fast-paced automaton, ready to erupt against workers who succumbed to the numbing effects of mechanical repetition. Employing the master and servant imagery which traditionally represented the relationship between man and machine, Saleilles suggested that the 'modern' age had reversed the relationship, with the machine now dominant and man the slave.[84]

There was no cure, however, for this state of affairs. The only remedy was to limit and repair the damage as much as

[81] Id., *Essai d'une théorie générale des obligations d'après le code civil allemand* (Paris, 1880), 339.

[82] Ibid., 398.

[83] Ibid., 377–80, 397–8; here Saleilles discusses the 7 June 1871 law introduced in Germany on the liability of rail companies for the 'faults' of their employees.

[84] Saleilles, 'Le Risque professionnel dans le code civil', *Réforme sociale*, 4th ser., 5 (1898), 636.

possible through a scheme of compensation which recognized responsibility without imputing fault. Notions of intention were hence deemed irrelevant. As one jurist explained:

> It was [Saleilles] who showed us for the first time that the effects of a judicial act do not all stem from the internal will [*volonté interne*] of its author, not only because economic and social necessities affect and diminish individual autonomy, but also because every act—however inadequate a reflection of the intention behind it—creates a risk, that is to say responsibility, which is a possible source of obligation.[85]

Consequently, instead of finding persons and requiring them to pay compensation, the obligation to repair damage lay with society as a whole, a duty to be discharged through a programme of insurance to which both sides would contribute, although the employer would be required to pay the larger share.

The use of the notion of *risque professionnel* in civil law to encompass all potential variables which conspired to cause harm found its approximate criminological equivalent in the *état dangereux* transferred to criminal law through Saleilles's *L'Individualisation de la peine* (1898). He examined the plethora of psychiatric and sociological writing on criminality and concluded that its evidence suggested the need to revise and modify the traditional assessment of moral responsibility. In line with his broader view of social relations—in which an infinite combination of social pressures acted on the autonomy of the individual—he increasingly relegated the question of fault and the imputation of moral responsibility to a secondary position.

The increasing number of 'degenerates' and 'moral imbeciles' suggested to him that the code's traditional reliance on a psychology of rational calculation was sorely outmoded. Indeed, he implied that the calculus between penalties and crimes was the product of a 'metaphysical' system based on antiquated eighteenth-century ideals which, through being applied automatically and without consideration of the offender's nature, personality, or potential for reform, would only hamper attempts at efficacious criminal management. Instead,

[85] Eugène Gaudemet, 'Raymond Saleilles et le code civil allemand', in Thaller (ed.), *L'Œuvre juridique de Raymond Saleilles*, 127.

Saleilles urged society to recognize the risk of crime and devise a system of 'social defence' to contain its dangerous effects. As harmful by-products of the advance of civilization and its complex division of labour, criminals were little different from the inevitable accidents which afflicted large-scale capitalist concerns. So identical was his appreciation of the two phenomena that when speaking of the 'facts' of degeneration and psychic disequilibrium evident among offenders he remarked that:

There are permanent states which in and of themselves restrict and reduce, without suppressing entirely, the will's capacity . . . to resist evil — neurasthenic states of all sorts, partial degeneration, cerebral excitation similar to monomania in the medical sense of the term. All the states of this kind in some respect diminish the capacity to be free, that is, the capacity to be responsible.[86]

The impact of these formulations can be seen from centrality accorded to the notion of the *état dangereux* in the *Bulletin de l'Union internationale de droit pénal*, as well as in the numerous managerial strategies proposed by 'progressive' jurists in its name. Developed during the meetings of the *Union de droit international* between 1897 and, approximately, 1910, the *état dangereux*, like its civil equivalent, sought to encompass all potential variables which conspired to cause harm. Theorists insisted that the line dividing civil and criminal law be softened, that 'a myriad of facts fall into the shifting boundaries between civil and criminal law, and the development of contemporary life—in its intensity, breathlessness, rapidity, and agitation—increase the analogies and points of contact'.[87] In 1909, after thirty years of discussion, Adolph Prins summed up the conceptual modifications that had taken place by pointing out the links between the rise of civil and criminal risk and the relative decline of concepts of fault and contractual agreement:

. . . classical penal law, by force of circumstance, has come to abandon the notion of individual responsibility to lean towards the idea of social defence . . .

And it is important to point out that this new bias shows up in all fields.

86 Saleilles, *L'Individualisation de la peine* (Paris, 1898), 76.

87 Adolphe Prins, 'La Liberté morale dans le droit pénal nouveau', *Bulletin de l'Union internationale de droit pénal*, 16 (1909), 489.

> In the face of the ever-increasing difficulty experienced in identifying where fault and responsibility lie, and [determining] the degree of responsibility, such discussions are avoided as much as possible.
>
> The vanishing [tendency] to demand proof of fault in either the employer or the worker and the birth of the notion of professional risk in Bismarckian labour legislation arises out of this . . .
>
> The same causes have given rise in penal law to the doctrine of social defence that gives the modern state the mission to protect society against all harm, whether civil or criminal . . .[88]

The programme of social defence envisaged focused on the sources of risk contained within the offender's *état psycho-social*. Legal guidelines hence required an individual assessment in order to treat each offender according to the risk he posed, a programme which contrasted with the classical system of a predetermined penalty linked to a crime instead of an individual. In thus emphasizing the 'individualization of penalties', the French had accepted a fundamental precept of Italian Criminal Anthropology, succinctly summed up by Rafaelle Garafalo as early as the Second International Congress of Criminal Anthropology in 1889: 'Penal law acknowledges only two terms, the *crime* and the *penalty*, while the new criminology acknowledges three, the *crime*, the *criminal*, and the *penalty*.'[89]

While articulated as a novel and an eminently scientific aspect of the new criminology, Garafalo's epigram in fact was confirming a trend towards the individualization of penalties which had its roots in the responses of juries throughout the nineteenth century. The penal code's rigid equation between penalties and crimes had meant that jurors not infrequently let offenders go free rather than risk a grave punishment that a verdict of guilty would necessarily entail, letting in the very 'sentimentality' which Enlightenment thinkers had done so much to exorcize. In the early nineteenth century this undirected trend was matched by increasing agitation among prominent liberals and literati for the abolition of the death penalty, or at least the reduction of the number of offences covered by it. The result was the introduction of the law of 1832

[88] Adolphe Prins, 'La Liberté morale dans le droit pénal nouveau,' *Bulletin de l'union internationale de droit pénal*, 16 (1909), 489.

[89] 'Deuxième congrès international d'anthropologie criminelle', *Archives d'anthropologie criminelle*, 4 (1889), 636.

permitting the consideration of extenuating and aggravating circumstances, thereby enabling penalties to be more closely tailored to the court's assessment of the individual. Further movement in this direction was achieved when the death penalty was abolished in 1848 for political offences, with mandatory punishment for infanticide also abandoned in 1901.[90]

These innovations were seen as responding to the perceived softening and civilizing of the *conscience collective* which recoiled before excessive punishment. This reasoning demonstrates the extent to which criminology was far from being an attempt to impose a system of criminal management from above, but was rather perceived of as an attempt to take account of and refine broader cultural attitudes, to harmonize the workings of the judicial system with social evolution. However, the individualization which such legislative innovations contained was of a very different order from the programme of criminal management which the specialists envisaged. While the strategies of criminal containment they advanced sometimes took a similarly lenient approach, at others their social-scientific perspective implied a number of far-reaching preventive measures which the classical criminal code never encompassed.

Some indication of their approach can be seen from a discussion held during a jurists' congress in Hamburg where the French contingent appeared. Prins asked: 'Should the delinquent be punished for what he did, for what he wanted to do or for what he is?', a rhetorical question which he then proceeded to answer himself:

The modern school is concerned not only with the crime, but also with the 'psychic and social state' of the offender. Enlarging the notion of punishment, it includes among its measures ones aimed at defence

[90] For a survey of jury behaviour in the nineteenth century see James M. Donovan, 'Justice Unblind: The Juries and the Criminal Classes in France, 1825–1914', *Journal of Social History*, 15 (1981–2), 89–105. For the changes in the penal code see A. Lacassagne, 'La Peine de mort et la criminalité', *Archives d'anthropologie criminelle*, 22 (1907)' 61–74. See also Paul Savey-Casard, *La Peine de mort* (Geneva, 1968), chap. 4 in particular for the early nineteenth-century discussion; Patricia Moulin in Michel Foucault (ed.), *I, Pierre Rivière, Having Slaughtered my Mother, my Sister, and my Brother . . .* (London, 1978), 212–18.

[*mesures de préservation*] . . . and their adaptation against an individual not only for what he has done but for what he is.[91]

Such an assertion opened up the possibility of action not only against those demonstrating an *état dangereux* by virtue of repeated offences, but also those who were deemed to possess a dangerous *état psycho-social*. Such reasoning encouraged jurists to ask themselves 'if one ought not to consider first-time offenders or even those who have not committed a crime as dangerous'.[92] They argued that once such individuals were spotted it was unwise—and moreover unnecessary—to wait for them to prove the diagnosis correct by committing a crime.

Out of such an extravagantly confident claim came a series of reform proposals which together represented a fundamental assault on all the libertarian safeguards against tyranny and arbitrariness. A range of practical programmes—some implemented and others not—was suggested in the discussions of the *Union*, the *Société générale des prisons*, as well as in the legislature and all were underpinned by the twin principles of indeterminate sentencing and de-penalization. The first was justified in the name of therapeutic efficacy. As doctors could not predict in advance how long it would take to heal their patients, so criminologists increasingly shied away from fixed penalties on the grounds that they too had to cure people, this time of antisocial tendencies, and similarly could not be expected to say how long a treatment would be required: 'If he is capable of being improved, then he must be cured [entirely]; but is it possible to imagine a sick man being sent to the hospital for a predetermined period?'[93] Such therapeutic considerations were always finely balanced with defensive preoccupations. For example, when considering new penal strategies, specialists often invoked the law of 1838 as a key precedent which, by imposing a hospital stay and not accusing

[91] Prins, Congrès de Hambourg, 'Extension pour certaines catégories de récidivistes de la notion de l'état dangereux', *Bulletin de l'Union internationale de droit pénal*, 13 (1905–6), 78.

[92] Émile Garçon, 'Dans quels cas déterminés par la loi, la notion de l'état dangereux du délinquent peut-elle substituée à celle de l'acte délictueux', *Bulletin de l'Union internationale de droit pénal*, 17 (1910), 186.

[93] Gabriel Tarde is explaining the ideas of Raffaele Garafalo in 'Positivisme et pénalité', *Archives d'anthropologie criminelle*, 2 (1887), 38.

the madman of any fault, provided a model for other rehabilitative strategies in the penal sphere.[94]

The principle of de-penalization was based on the view that offenders who acted unintentionally, negligently, in self-defence or in accord with more permissive social mœurs were unsuitable candidates for prison. Rather than being subjected to the contaminating effects of incarceration, a system of fines was advanced as an appropriate 'defensive' response to their crimes, a move which once again indicated the increasing unity of approach between penal and civil law. Garafalo, a forceful advocate of the death penalty,[95] for example, went so far as to suggest that a system of monetary restitution should be introduced for murder committed in brawls (when the killer had been the object of an assault), duels, death through negligence, insults, libel, seduction, adultery, abduction of minors, trespassing, breaking of professional secrets, and public outrages against decency without violence.[96] This attitude was to figure largely in the response given to both male and female *criminels passionnels* in the *Cour d'assises*, as defendant after defendant was acquitted because no 'criminal personality' was in evidence and imprisonment deemed an inappropriate response to an episode of 'temporary insanity' (see chapters 6 and 8).

An important measure designed to take such cases into account was the 1891 law of *sursis* which permitted suspended sentences, a measure specifically designed to prevent recidivism by prescribing *aggravated* penalties for those who none the less committed a second offence.[97] The 1885 law on recidivism also introduced a programme of conditional libera-

94 There was even recognition that the indiscriminate use of the law of 1838 was a way of providing long-term incarceration for individuals who had not committed serious offences. For an example of concern about such practices see the strong remarks of the head of the penitentiary administration, P. Grimanelli in 'Traitement à appliquer aux délinquents à responsabilité limitée', *Revue pénitentiaire*, 29 (1905), 332.

95 See A. Allen Francis, 'Rafaelle Garafalo', in Mannheim (ed.), *Pioneers in Criminology* (London, 1960), 254–76.

96 Baron de Garafalo, 'Quelles mesures peut-on recommander au législateur pour restreindre le rôle de la prison en ce qui concerne les condamnations prononcées pour les infractions légères?', *Bulletin de l'Union internationale de droit pénal*, 1–2 (1889–91), 60.

97 For the details of the *loi de sursis* see E. Glaucker, 'Loi du 26 mars 1891 sur l'atténuation et l'aggravation des peines', ibid., 3–4 (1892–94), 75–80.

tion, rewarding well-behaved prisoners with early release and a more agreeable regime of supervision by a *société de patronage*. Designed to remove the reformable as quickly as possible from the prison's contaminating influence, the measure aimed at separating the 'true' criminal from the redeemable offender.[98]

In these instances, the move towards de-penalization and indeterminancy demonstrated the indulgent strand of criminological thinking. However, at the same time another set of harsh and far-reaching measures was suggested against *potential* offenders, or those with records of repeated petty offences. As suggested, the most dramatic indication of this trend was the 1885 law on recidivists, which proposed to punish individuals not for what they had done but rather *for what they were*. The passage of this law was not universally applauded. Many a criminal specialist criticized it for being insufficiently infused by criminology, by prescribing combinations of offences which *required* judges to impose a penalty of lifelong transportation. Instead, they preferred a less mandatory system which would allow the court to decide when an individual was incorrigible. Equally, when the atmosphere of political hysteria in which it was passed had dissipated somewhat, judges tended to exercise their discretionary power to ignore its strict provisions and allow repeated beggars and vagrants to go free rather than impose lifelong exile on such degraded and dispossessed individuals.[99]

None the less, the attitude towards vagrancy and begging remained intensely condemnatory and fearful. In 1891, for example, a Belgian law converted the erstwhile misdemeanours

[98] For the terms of the 14 August 1885 law on conditional liberation see Victor Édouard Dalloz, *Les Codes annotés, supplément du code pénal, annoté et expliqué d'après la jurisprudence et la doctrine* (Paris, 1889). Later measures fleshed out the practical details of the law. A consulting committee working under the auspices of the Minister of the Interior—composed of representatives from the penitentiary administration, the police, and the section dealing with pardons at the Ministry of Justice—determined whether or not the prisoner was worthy of conditional liberation. Prisoners were then to be turned over to special *sociétés de patronage* responsible for investigating and watching over their activities until the termination of their sentences. These societies were to be subsidised by the government.

[99] See Nye, *Crime, Madness and Politics*, 95–6. In 1886, 1,737 were sent, although this figure was much lower than the predicted one of 5,000. In 1889, only 1,109 were transported, and under a thousand in the next two years; by 1911 only 477 were sent. Indeed, after 1907, women prisoners escaped this fate, as the dangerous climate of Guyana was deemed unsuitable for the frailties of the female constitution.

of vagrancy and begging into instances of the *état dangereux* and encouraged the incarceration of the potential criminals in special *maisons de travail* for between two and seven years, the length of stay depending on the display of disciplined tendencies.[100] Similar proposals were widely advocated in France, as medical men condemned the neurasthenic propensities of such miscreants and jurists described with disgust 'these malleable and apathetic natures, these idlers whose indolence and misconduct sent them down the wrong path'.[101] In sum, while a movement was afoot to 'de-moralize' and hence 'de-penalize' the crimes of begging and vagrancy, the indeterminate measures proposed were more far-reaching in scope than any the classical system had ever proposed. Similar measures were proposed against alcoholics who, rather than being convicted for public drunkenness or other offences while under the influence, were to be obliged to enter a special facility where they would be cured: 'Here, above all, indeterminancy is imposed, because one is treating an illness in the true sense of the word and the judge does not have the necessary specialized knowledge to assess the gravity of the patient's condition'[102] (see chapter 7).

Undoubtedly, the most important impact of the notion of the *état dangereux* was felt in the sphere of juvenile justice. Children were key subjects of criminological discussion. Not only did they lack discernment[103] because of their age, but also special measures seemed necessary to nip any 'criminal personality' in the bud. In 1912, after several decades of discussion and debate,[104] the juvenile courts were introduced distinguished

[100] Prins, 'Extension pour certaines catégories de récidivistes de la notion de l'état dangereux', 79.

[101] Alfred Gautier, 'À quelles catégories de détenus le système des sentences indéterminées pourrait-il être appliqué?', *Bulletin de l'Union internationale de droit pénal*, 5 (1895–6), 75.

[102] Ibid.

[103] See Maurice Levade, *La Délinquance des jeunes en France, 1825–1968* (Paris, 1972); for a survey of the discussion of children, particularly those who turn to crime because of 'irregular' family relations, see Philippe Meyer, *The Child and the State: The Intervention of the State in French Family Life*, trans., Judith Ennew and Janet Lloyd (Cambridge, 1983), 40–80.

[104] For the contemporary legal preoccupation with juvenile delinquence and the philanthropic concern to find new judicial and corrective measures for them see Adolphe Guillot, *Observations pratiques au sujet des enfants traduits en justice* (Paris, 1890); Georges Bonjean. *Enfants révoltés et parents coupables: Études sur la désorganisation de la famille et ses conséquences sociales* (Paris, 1895).

by the obvious use of the principles of de-penalization and indeterminacy, as well as the concentration of specialist personnel hoping to act upon the child before the age of responsibility. Donzelot[105] has shown how the system operated, with a series of graded layers designed to reform youths of varying intractability. Starting with the cajoling influence of the judge who paternalistically sought to steer youths away from antisocial behaviour, there then followed a sequence of monitoring, special educational establishments, and reformatories that culminated in prison as the last resort.

The essence of the treatment was not so much the punishment but rather the persistence of threatened chastisement that was meant to tempt the wayward back to good behaviour. At any moment, offenders had two roads available to them—they could respond to the attention and concern with which the experts surrounded them, or they could resist and be moved to progressively more unpleasant types of treatment. The arduous but none the less clear-cut collision with authority gave way to treatment based on ostensibly more humane and flexible criteria. However, the authorities extracted from this system a degree of power to move, restrain, or liberate that was inconceivable in a classical system of jurisprudence based on fixed sentences and unchangeable principles.

THE AMBIGUITIES OF NEO-CLASSICISM

Despite these numerous proposals and the real impact of new sentencing and rehabilitative procedures, one of the most striking features of the period was the remarkable resilience of the system of classical jurisprudence which weathered the attacks launched against it and emerged still firmly in control of many of its courtroom tasks, using criminological precepts but never becoming completely subservient to them. Throughout the debates, conservative jurists battled against their more 'progressive' counterparts, arguing that the major danger to social security came not from any fundamental inadequacy in the law

[105] Jacques Donzelot, *The Policing of Families*, trans. Robert Hurley (London, 1979), 99–117.

but rather from science's excessive claims to expertise and authority. The technical management of criminality, they maintained, could be either too lenient in its misguided desire to treat criminals or too random and ruthless in incarcerating the innocent who fell into their psycho-social categories. As the conservative jurist Louis Proal exclaimed in 1890:

> . . . if punishment is replaced by treatment and the prison by the asylum, then society's security is compromised and honest people are turned over to wrongdoers. If, on the other hand, the determinists wish to protect life, honour, the property of respectable people, the modesty of women and children, by preserving punishment—even at the risk of inconsistency—then it is no longer just, effective, or proportionate. Instead, punishment becomes a blind instrument of terror, arbitrariness, and cruelty . . . Impunity or barbarism, these are the two contradictory consequences of determinist theories.[106]

Indeed, throughout the debates, many of the 'progressives' distinguished themselves from the excesses of Italian positivism by calling themselves 'neo-classicists'. They steered a path between the advantages and potential of social defence theory on the one hand and guarantees of justice embodied in the classical system on the other. If such men as Saleilles, Tarde, Cuche, and Garçon were overwhelmed by the scientific evidence of the feebleness of man's moral agency, they none the less refused to advocate a full revolutionary programme of social defence by preventive incarceration. Indeed, they quite explicitly stated that such a programme would pose an even greater risk than did the vast number of degenerate potential criminals on the loose in society, as such extended state powers would completely compromise the freedom even of those whom such measures were designed to protect.

Unwilling to jettison the notion of free will and moral responsibility entirely, therefore, they were none the less eager to participate in the general movement for a '*politique criminelle*'. In wondering whether the 'Universe is ultimately mechanism and chance, or intelligence and liberty',[107] the

106 Louis Proal, 'Le Déterminisme et la pénalité', *Archives d'anthropologie criminelle*, 5 (1890), 391; see also A.-F.-A. Hamon, 'De la définition du crime', ibid., 8 (1893), 242–67.

107 Prins, 'La Liberté morale dans le droit pénal nouveau', *Bulletin de l'Union internationale de droit pénal*, 16 (1909–10), 488.

neo-classical jurists decided that such mysteries were beyond them, and instead directed themselves to a *pragmatic* implementation of social defence policies. As will be discussed more fully in the conclusion, both jurists and medico-legists held extremely ambivalent positions on the relationship between free will and determinism and, while eager to advance their professional position through institutional and procedural innovation, at the same time were also wary of dispensing entirely with the criminal justice system.

As a result, there developed between the traditional legal system and the new ideas which ostensibly opposed it a mutually complementary *modus vivendi* which extended official supervision over a much wider area. From the outset the jurists, concerned that a potential ally could easily change into a substantial threat, were at some pains to ensure that criminology did not step too far outside the strictly administrative sphere. Medico-legists continued in their role as expert witnesses without substantial change, although capital offenders were increasingly subjected to psychiatric assessment.[108] The court was, then, happy to countenance the aid of criminological perspective while its theories offered a substantial increase in judicial power. Despite evident caution there emerged a realm of shared perspectives and objectives between judges, psychiatrists, and those empowered to apply new penal strategies. This *rapprochement* was based on an acknowledgement that medicalized evaluations and rehabilitative methods contained elements of punishment and were aimed first at society's protection and only then at the improvement of the individual criminal.

In all of these activities the notion of the *état dangereux* was the subject of careful analysis in which the criterion for treatment was what the individuals were rather than on what they had done. In such a system, the high-risk offender—such as the poor, the foreigner, the recidivist—was less likely to receive leniency than other kinds of offenders, who, it was argued, were less likely to repeat their crimes. But to explain criminology in this manner

[108] With the introduction of the *Code de procédure pénale* in 1958 an inquiry into 'la personnalité des inculpés ainsi que sur leur situation matérielle, familiale ou sociale', was made obligatory, an innovation which signified the growing strength and institutional recognition of the medico-psychology tradition. See Jean Imbert and Georges Levasseur, *Le Pouvoir, les juges et les bourreaux* (Paris, 1971), 191.

is to reproduce the language of professed objectivity which the experts themselves employed. As will be seen, courtroom debate did focus on the *état dangereux* both explicitly and implicitly; however, the construal of social dangerousness was hardly an objective process, but was rather based on class, politics, and gender, on the offender's life-style (*manière de vivre*) and his or her self-representation in court.

It is clear, however, that criminological measures designed to individualize at the same time tended to have the effect of categorizing, introducing new, psycho-social categories which could be as implacable as those which they were meant to modify. It was perhaps ironic that the fervent desire to individualize also had the tendency to dehumanize, a point not lost on contemporaries who often viewed the trend with some trepidation. As Gabriel Tarde astutely remarked:

> Strangely enough, when modern criminologists . . . investigate the causes of crime, they discover only impersonal *factors*, climate, . . . race, cranial, or other abnormalities, suggestions arising from the social environment. In other words, they naturalize and socialize the crime; they de-personalize it. Then, when it comes to the question of a penal application for their theories, it is astonishing to see how they exaggerate the case for individualization which, like the individual, was nothing before and now is everything.[109]

Even more distressing was the way in which the slow but peristent destruction of moral responsibility began to call into doubt society's right to punish offenders at all, because the psycho-social portrait emphasized that extraneous social factors were as much the cause of crime as any evil and harmful desires on the part of the criminal. As the physician M. Legrain explained:

> The comparative study of *crime*—a *sociological* issue—and of the *criminal*—an *anthropological* one—is important in revealing the antagonism between the individual and society which produces crime. This finding has many implications. On which side does the crime lie? It can be blamed on the individual as much as on society, but it can also be produced by the harmful activity of the mass on the individual as well as vice versa. In most instances it can be blamed on both at once.[110]

109 Gabriel Tarde in the preface to Saleilles, *L'Individualisation de la peine*, p. v.

110 Paul-Maurice Legrain, 'La Médecine légale du dégénéré', *Archives d'anthropologie criminelle*, 9 (1894), 16–17.

Through a mountain of documents and interrogations, the infinite variables deemed to elucidate the reasons behind the criminal and the deed became the focus of scrutiny. Family relationships, work habits, political associations, and so on were all seen as much responsible for the antisocial make-up as the offender. With such a view the defendant perhaps had reason to resent any punishment/treatment, since much of the investigation seemed designed to demonstrate that society was largely responsible for his deed.

In sum, perhaps the greatest effect of criminology was to alter substantially the notion of what real justice was. No longer a discussion of events surrounding the crime, with the question of motive brought in only to help decide who had committed it, justice increasingly came to depend on an equally profound analysis of psycho-social disposition. Those accused of crimes were consequently given a vital role to play. To ensure that the legal system did its job properly, they and the experts who examined them were required to pour forth a steady stream of information which, if denied, meant that the court had to reach a verdict on inadequate evidence. By accepting criminological precepts, representatives of the law, psychiatry, and penal administration created an area in which the criminal and not the crime was the supreme object of judicial workings.

4

LEGAL PROCEDURE AND MEDICAL INTERVENTION

French psychiatrists were obliged to present the intricacies of medical argument within a very specific judicial context which they frequently considered to be less than ideal. On the one hand, their aid was increasingly requested by legal personnel investigating criminal trials, particularly when capital crimes were involved. On the other, they remained mere adjuncts in a process governed by complex conventions of interrogation, investigation, and courtroom procedure over which they had little control. These processes affected the reception of their ideas and impinged significantly on the way the problem of moral responsibility was assessed.

Judicial procedure was laid out in the 1808 *code d'instruction criminelle*, which, unlike the penal code itself, was only slightly modified through the course of the century.[1] The key figure in the process was the *juge d'instruction*, or investigating magistrate, who conducted his long interrogation in the privacy of his office (*cabinet du juge d'instruction*). He was often portrayed as a redoubtable figure, the resurrected version of the royal magistrate under the *ancien régime*, mandated to prepare a case against the defendant which his superiors would use in the prosecution. Although generally a youthful jurist on the way up the ladder of promotion (with the young stars trying to secure positions in the capital), he was none the less in a uniquely powerful position. He was

> invested with the most wide-ranging and unlimited powers in his professional sphere . . . the investigating magistrate must take every

[1] See A. Adhémar Esmein, *A History of Continental Criminal Procedure, with Special Reference to France*, trans. John Simpson (Boston, 1913), 528–69. Except for particularly important measures introduced in 1880 and 1897, to be discussed below, changes focused on the rules governing jury selection, the extent of the majority needed for conviction, and procedures surrounding bail.

possible step that might lead to the discovery of the truth. He must initiate research, verify the slightest piece of evidence, ascertain the facts, carry out searches and seizures, order expert testimony, call and hear witnesses, and juggle with the whole arsenal of summonses.[2]

The interrogation procedure was conducted very much at his direction, as defendants were not entitled to be told of the charges against them, to see the *pièces*—or documents—relating to the case, or to confront witnesses, although such meetings were frequently arranged. Most importantly, perhaps, the defendants were not allowed to be represented by counsel.

Their only right was to submit letters and memoirs. In fact, the judicial dossiers frequently contain autobiographical accounts of the defendants' lives and deeds. Such narratives varied among individuals and between the sexes—ranging from the barely literate through the ponderous to the eloquent—but all shared the aim of touching the magistrate's sensibilities. They were, therefore, documents important to the evaluative process, building up a portrait of the state of mind and motivation of the accused. Some conducted a veritable campaign of accusation and self-righteous invective from their cells. Often such behaviour resulted in their being submitted to medical examination to see if they were suffering from persecutory delirium.[3] Others spoke in more plaintive tones,[4] seeking to justify violence by referring to the behaviour of a wayward mate, a tactic that often produced an acquittal in cases of a crime of passion.

The psychological state of the defendant before and during the crime was of intense interest to investigating magistrates. For example, they regularly examined the love letters, poems, and diaries of women who killed their lovers, hoping to find in these documents evidence of the 'sentimental' nature of female violence. In sum, while they did not discourse on disorders of the mind, as did physicians, they were none the less 'psychologists' in their own right, seeking to elicit information in order to assess motive, intention, and desire. When, for

[2] Anon., *Le Palais de Justice: Son monde et ses mœurs*, pref. by Alexandre Dumas *fils* (Paris, 1892), 340.

[3] Eugène Jean P . . . D^2U^8 159, 13/14 June 1884. *pièce* 214.

[4] Jean Alphonse L . . . D^2U^8 148, 22 Oct. 1883, *pièce* 40.

example, a particularly heinous crime was committed, as in the case of Menesclou,[5] they would ask the defendant to write a memoir of self-explanation. In this instance they were disappointed by the dull quality of the text. The request, however, was indicative of the magisterial mentality which sought to 'know' the subject in all his dimensions.

The evidence provided by the pre-trial dossiers testifies to the magistrates' often tireless activity and zeal for information, summoning the aid of distant jurisdictions to examine the behaviour and past life of defendants in the *pays natal*, and sometimes assiduously scrutinizing their career in school, associates, and past habits. For example, when examining Gabrielle Bompard in 1890 on the charge of committing murder under the hypnotic influence of her older lover, the investigating magistrate received an account provided by the nuns at the convent where she had been a pupil, the sisters testifying to her lewd tongue and obstreperous behaviour.[6] Nor were the daily habits of the accused off-limits: when the young left-wing activist Pierre Eugène D . . . was accused of trying to murder his boss after a quarrel in the office, the police questioned the *marchand de vins* where the defendant usually ate, and reported on the way in which D . . . impressed his fellow-diners with the brilliance of his political rhetoric,[7] a characteristic that was held against him.

In such a system, the rules of evidence were non-existent. All kinds of information, including hearsay, were admissible, and anonymous denunciations were habitually incorporated. Indeed, during the examination of the case of Mme Clovis-Hughes, the wife of the Radical deputy, who killed a private investigator who had falsely charged her with fornication, several dozen anonymous letters were sent to the investigating magistrate. Among these where obscene statements about the accused, as well as discourses on marriage, the family, and the politics of the early Third Republic.[8] What is remarkable

[5] Louis Menesclou D^2U^8 98, 30 July 1880, *pièce* 139.

[6] Gabrielle Bompard, D^2U^8 263, 20 Dec. 1890, *pièces* 7lle, 713.

[7] Pierre Eugène D . . . D^2U^8 254, 5 June 1890, *pièce* 106.

[8] Jean Royannez Clovis-Hughes D^2U^8 169, 8 Jan. 1885. There was a weighty parcel of letters and postcards contained in the dossier; see, for example, *pièces* 171, 172.

perhaps is that such missives were included in the official dossier rather than discarded and, like the rest of the interrogations and experts' reports, were used in the preparation of the indictment ultimately read out in court.

The magistrature was dominated by men of Republican political persuasion. In 1883 a statute was passed which enabled the *Cour de cassation*—the highest court in the land able to order a retrial but not a change in judgement—to dismiss any magistrate who demonstrated 'hostility to the principles of Republican government', a measure which meant the prompt expulsion of 614 members unwilling to execute the anticlerical laws. The extent of the purge can be seen by the fact that 82 per cent of the prosecutors (1,763 out of 2,149) were dismissed between 1879 and 1882 as the conservative elements that had predominated during the July Monarchy and Imperial government were removed.[9] Although they, like many medical men, would become increasingly conservative in later years, their mutual affinity for Republican values and anticlericalism in the early 1880s *may* have provided a sympathetic basis for some collaboration.

In more specific terms, however, the importance of Republican patronage meant that magistrates occasionally suppressed evidence or even dismissed affairs entirely when they were politically damaging. However, these were rare and often notorious examples of corruption[10] and, in general, the intricacies of Republican politics affected few cases. If investigators went to extreme lengths to discover evidence of guilt—some dossiers included over 2,000 *pièces*—they were equally ready to drop charges when testimony suggested the defendant's innocence. This, however, is not to suggest that they were 'objective'. Their constant association with professed criminals meant that they were prone to assume illegal activity. Moreover, they were more than likely to be examining a member of Paris' poorer classes and were hence susceptible to a variety of moral and social judgements. As the rest of the work will demonstrate, when confronted with the facts of

[9] Benjamin F. Martin, 'The Courts, The Magistrature, and Promotions in Third Republic France, 1871–1914', *American Historical Review*, 87 (1982), 984–5.

[10] See ibid., 988–1009 for other examples of corruption. For more on famous trials see Martin, *The Hypocrisy of Justice in the Belle Époque* (Baton Rouge, 1984).

working-class cohabitation, illiteracy, café frequentation, periods of unemployment—often marked down through prior convictions for vagrancy, begging, or insults to the police—the magistrates demanded justifications for such 'shortcomings'.

It was only in 1897 that the role of the *juge d'instruction* was modified, and then only slightly. Repeated criticism of the system ushered in a series of minor reforms which gave defendants the right to be examined within forty-eight hours, informed of the charges against them, and allowed to see the judicial dossier on request.[11] In addition, defence attorneys were now permitted to attend the interrogations, although they were only allowed to interrupt if the magistrate gave permission. The magistrate's prerogatives, therefore, were left largely intact, the excessive intervention of a lawyer seen as hampering the inquisitorial process and turning the investigation into a form of adversarial wrangling.

The written documents of judicial interrogations are very specialized texts which require careful interpretation. The privacy of the interview was hampered only by the presence of the secretary who recorded the interrogation, by the appearance of other witnesses, or even more dramatically by the entry of the surviving victim. The record of the interaction was signed by the attending parties—including the defendant—to establish its accuracy. These are extremely stylized documents, which sometimes reflect spoken language—with its hesitations, indelicacies, ungrammatical phraseology, and even argot—but which also often contain extremely eloquent and formally phrased questions from the *juge d'instruction*. Although it is impossible to determine precisely, it may be that these documents were only distillations rather than word-for-word reproductions, and that this literary construction had a profound impact on the public prosecutor's perception of the case.

Finally, they appear in the form of questions and answers in which the proficiency of the judge was demonstrated by his building up of a portrait of guilt or mitigating circumstances. Necessarily, therefore, the defendant was almost always, quite

[11] James W. Garner, 'Criminal Procedure in France', *Yale Law Journal*, 25 (1916), 258.

literally, on the defensive, unable to direct or change the line of questioning. Early interrogations are marked by emotional excitation or exasperation, avowals of murderous intention, despair, but, perhaps surprisingly, rarely remorse. However, later in the interrogation this often gives way to a mature, developed, and often coherent self-representation in which defendants sought to explain their deeds to themselves, the magistrate, and to the world. For example, in 1886, the self-professed anarchist Charles Auguste G . . . exploded a bottle of poison gas in a bank occupying the main hall of the Bourse, following this by wildly brandishing his revolver. At this first interrogation he merely proclaimed his intention, refusing even to give his name: 'I will not give you my name. I am an anarchist and I wanted to teach the exploiters of the people a lesson. I did not succeed in doing what I wanted, but I set an example to those who will come after me.'[12] But in a later interview, after careful examination over several months by the investigating magistrate, Alphonse Guillot, he provided a refined self-portrait of moral rectitude, freedom from petty hatreds and a burning sense of social responsibility:

> I have been very unhappy in my life and was a victim of injustice. I was blocked because I was illegitimate and saw that careers which I deserved to enter through personal effort and education . . . were closed to me.
>
> I could justifiably take my revenge on the many people in the world who have wronged me, but a hateful thought has never entered my heart; I don't bear a grudge against individuals but rather against society as a whole.[13]

Although G . . .'s crime was unusual—anarchist offences, although notorious, were few in comparison to domestic violence or café brawls—the manner of self-characterization, the attempt to find a reasoned and carefully-elaborated justification, was common to virtually all. Such narratives were important for forming the psychiatrists' perception of the defendant's mental state and the magistrate's determination of a vicious or 'comprehensible' motive. Moreover, the interactive process which marked the lengthy pre-trial judicial

[12] Charles Auguste G . . . D^2U^8 199, 15 July 1886, *pièce* 2.

[13] Ibid., *pièce* 147; G . . . received a penalty of twenty years' hard labour.

investigation became crucial for preparing the defendant to face examination in court, and indeed the President's questions closely resembled those of the magistrate.

The actual trials always began with the reading of the indictment, which was a voluminous exposé rather than a terse rendition of the charges. 'The law wanted a summary but a novel was provided instead.'[14] This recitation was inevitably an extremely partisan essay which sometimes luridly portrayed the defendant as evil incarnate. However, in a very few cases, generally involving so-called crimes of passion, the indictment openly sympathized with the defendant, turning the trial itself into a mere exercise that ended in the acquittal of the defendant to the apparent satisfaction of everyone present.

In the Assize Court, the President was appointed by the Minister of Justice and seconded by two other judges. He wielded enormous power, questioning the defendant and witnesses as well as pronouncing the penalty. The interrogations that were conducted at the outset of the trial tended to be elaborate, a judicial convention perhaps reinforced by an 1881 statute which prevented the judge from providing a summary of the case to the jury at the end.[15]

However, even before the interrogations began, defendants were to some extent judged, as their demeanour and physical appearance were crucial to the trial's outcome. Women's faces—their '*traits fins*' or '*traits vulgaires*'—'*toilettes*', expressions of despair or defiance were regularly recorded in the newspapers. The description of the widow Groitzinger, accused of murdering her husband, gives some flavour of the vivid, if sometimes less than flattering, portrayal of female defendants: '. . . brunette, with exaggerated features and extremely stout. She was dressed in deep mourning'.[16] The features of men, their brutish or dandified qualities, were all presented as somehow having a bearing on the case. Indeed, the more famous criminal personages were often caricatured in the illustrated press, the ferocity or gentleness of their physiognomies conveying important impressions of personality and character.

[14] Jean Cruppi, *La Cour d'assises* (Paris, 1898), 72.
[15] Garner, 'Criminal Procedure in France', 264.
[16] *Gazette des tribunaux*, 26 July 1901.

Such portraits perhaps explain the accessibility of esoteric anthropological descriptions, as anyone with an asymmetrical head, close-set eyes, and a malignant expression was potentially identifiable as a 'criminal type'. For example, a young offender named Charles Kurter, already condemned on several past occasions and accused of murder in 1894, was described in the following manner: 'He is small and stocky; his features seem to embody the born criminal described by certain physiologists'.[17] Sometimes the descriptions were embellished even further. This is the way the journalist of the *Gazette des tribunaux* described the pimp, Louis Genty, accused of murdering someone in a brawl:

> Short and deformed, he conceals his forehead behind a thick fringe [*bandeau*] of carefully slicked hair that almost falls on to his eyebrows. If you have the misfortune to lift up this fringe you can read the following inscription tattooed on the wretch's forehead, 'Death to the tarts' [*Mort aux vaches*] and beneath it another inscription so base that decency does not allow me to repeat it.[18]

It was during these presidential interrogations that the pre-trial 'preparation' of the defendant emerged, as the accused provided autobiographical details, defended honourable intentions, explained past peccadilloes, and responded to the searching exploration of previous life, romantic adventures, and work habits. Sometimes they failed the 'test', as in the case of Jean-Baptiste Mettaz who claimed throughout the course of the pre-trial investigation to be in love with the mistress he had killed. However, at the 'trial [Mettaz] had a rather tiresome attitude. Instead of repenting his crime, he seemed only preoccupied with reproaching his victim for the money he had spent on her.'[19] He was sentenced to five years in prison, a surprisingly high sentence for a crime of passion which might ordinarily have resulted in an acquittal.

While certain presidents were careful to keep to a sober, unemotional tone when questioning the defendant, others were manifestly probing and could become hostile in style, being particularly severe with those whom they believed were trying

[17] *Gazette de tribunaux*, 25 Oct. 1894.
[18] Ibid., 12 July 1906.
[19] Ibid., 18 Mar. 1905.

to pass off an avaricious or vengeful murder as a crime of passion. In other instances, however, they would clearly side with the defendant. There were even suggestions that, during the trial in 1914 of Mme Caillaux, the second wife of the prime minister, who murdered the editor of *Le Figaro* for printing their love-letters, Jean-Marie-Louis Albanel demonstrated his political partisanship by calling for a recess at the very moment when her defence was about to collapse.[20]

The significance of the president was also demonstrated by his intervention when witnesses took the stand. They were called and asked to speak spontaneously, with the presiding judge asking them questions (*éclaircissements*) which he believed would illuminate their sometimes hesitant or incomplete presentations. Because there was no system of cross-examination in France—attorneys were obliged to put questions through the president—the repeated adversarial objections typical of the Anglo-American context were absent. The defence attorney often took a more active role than the prosecutor but, in general, the major contribution of both came during final speeches when they let loose their rhetorical powers in a burst of argument and emotion in a last attempt to sway the jury.

There were some famous defence counsel who dominated Parisian court proceedings during the era. Charles Lachaud at the beginning of the Third Republic was known for his theatrical style, one which was slightly modified by the simpler, yet still eloquent, pleas of one of the most famous criminal advocates of the day, Henri Robert.[21] Fernand Labori was also a prominent presence at the *Cour d'assises* and was distinguished for the way in which he sought to counteract the hostile questioning of the president during the trial of Émile Zola, accused of *délit de presse* in 1898 after the publication of his letter *J'accuse* defending Dreyfus.[22] Finally, the young Waldeck-Rousseau made an early reputation for himself by an

20 Martin, 'The Courts, The Magistrature, and Promotions in Third Republic France, 1871–1914', 991.

21 See Léopold de Leymarie, *Les Avocats d'aujourd'hui* (Paris, 1893). Other important defence attorneys included F.-A.-B. Décori, L.-C.-A. Danet, and C.-G.-E. Demagne, who defended Dreyfus. These men virtually monopolized high criminal proceedings during this period.

22 For Zola's trial, letters to Labori, and his summation to the jury, see his *La Vérité en marche*, introd. and annot. by Colette Becker (Paris, 1969).

'affectation of Anglo-Saxon dryness', a style which was not copied by other criminal lawyers who remained determined to play on the sympathies of the jury.[23]

Despite these specific instances, however, such a career was not the best means of acquiring status or distinction within the profession. While criminological ideas infused new energy into criminal law, it continued to occupy the second rank. For defence attornies,

> generally, the client appears in a scarcely sympathetic manner—as a beggar or a professional vagrant, a wrongdoer who admits the crime or denies it against all the evidence. Such examples of the dregs of society can still inspire pity, but how can one inject any passion into their defence?[24]

Jurists were acknowledged to be more interested in the legal problems posed by civil law. While the judge was often visibly distracted in the *tribunal correctionnel* (which tried lesser criminal cases), the same jurist became an altered man once transferred to the civil court: 'His interest turns into passion and he and the attorney have a feverish competition of research and subtleties.'[25] Repeated criticism was voiced against the lack of professional concern with criminal cases (popular fascination remained high), an apathy seen to be inimical to the maintenance of liberty in any civilized, democratic society.

Despite the power of the presiding judge, perhaps the key actors in the *Cour d'assises* were the twelve male jurors. To them the President's partiality might appear as excessively lenient and hence evoke a condemnatory verdict; on the other hand, a judge's severity towards the defendant, disadvantaged through the alliance of judge and prosecutor (who both appeared as red-robed and imposing servants of the state) might provoke them to a fit of indulgence. The jury brought an element of unpredictability into every court and was therefore a constant source of possible frustration for the professional judiciary.

The jury evoked extremely ambivalent feelings. It was not

[23] See Maurice Garçon, *La Justice contemporaine, 1870–1932* (Paris, 1933), 571–3.

[24] Émile Garçon, in the preface to Paul Saillard, *Le Rôle de l'avocat en matière criminelle* (Paris, 1905), p. xii. This preface was published separately as a pamphlet and the pages cited correspond to this edition.

[25] Ibid., p. viii.

an age-old institution upheld, despite recurring quibbles, as a cherished feature of national heritage and traditional rights. On the contrary, the jury was often seen as the child of the Revolution introduced in 1791, a relatively recent legal novelty and foreign import giving extensive—and for critics, excessive—power to the citizenry.[26] In line with his more authoritarian tendencies, Napoleon suppressed grand juries and restricted criminal juries to the Assize jurisdiction. His distrust of the jury was echoed by conservative jurists throughout the century who saw their indulgence as an affront to public order and morality. Indeed, Tarde was openly sceptical of jury trial and believed that it militated against a more efficacious technical administration of justice dispensed by a scientifically trained magistrature.[27] In contrast, precisely because of its association with the Revolution, defence of the jury was often linked to other liberal causes such as freedom of the press and association as well as universal suffrage.[28]

Whatever the political connotations surrounding the jury, there were particular procedures which increasingly limited its power. More cases were sent to the Correctional Tribunal, where they were decided by a panel of three judges who meted out lesser, but more consistent, penalties for minor charges, a procedure recognized as producing 'high-speed justice' (*à tout vapeur*). The statistics are particularly revealing of this trend, as the growing bulk of offences made it virtually impossible to send them all to the *Cour d'assises*. Between 1826 and 1850, 5,000 cases went to jury trial; in 1891, 2,932 were tried before the *Cour d'assises*, while 200,000 sentences were handed down by the correctional tribunals.[29] Hence, cases tried at the *Cour d'assises* represented only the very tip of the iceberg, with the professional magistrature executing daily justice with virtually no aid from laymen. The significance of these serious crimes was, therefore, largely symbolic, and the debates which revolved around them generated a mass of discourse entirely out of proportion to their number.

[26] See Cruppi, *Napoléon et le jury* (Paris, 1896).

[27] See Gabriel Tarde, *La Philosophie pénale* (Paris, 1890), 435–49.

[28] Adolphe Guillot, *Le Jury et les mœurs* (extrait de la *Gazette des tribunaux*) (Paris, 1885), 22.

[29] Cruppi, *La Cour d'assises* (Paris, 1898), 2–6.

In this period the jury was subjected to a range of criticism both from supporters who sought reform as well as from detractors who wanted it abolished. In 1872, a statute transferred the power of jury selection from the prefects to the judiciary, a move generally approved in theory but condemned in practice. It was claimed that the local *juge de paix*, in league with municipal counsellors, doled out favours, proposing friends or political associates. Jury lists were full of 'merchants or manufacturers, clerks or shop–assistants'. Added to this number were 'property owners or persons of independent means' (*propriétaires ou rentiers*), many of whom, it seemed, lived on modest rather than grand incomes. There was also a sprinkling of men from the 'liberal professions', including engineers, teachers, lawyers, and 'civil servants', as well as even fewer veterinarians, physicians, or pharmacists.[30]

Criticism focused on the low intellectual ability and social narrowness of these citizen-judges, willing to be swayed by the sentimental arguments of defence attornies and the tearful justifications of the accused. The jury contained virtually no 'elevated personages . . . that is to say the elements which constitute the richness of society, the blood and brains of the city'[31] to provide guidance and lend seriousness to the proceedings. For those on the left of the political spectrum, like the Radical deputy Jean Cruppi, the jury was deficient both for lacking high-minded participants *and* for excluding working men who, because dependent on a daily wage, were deemed unable to participate until 1907.

Throughout the period, this conglomeration of *petit bourgeois* men demonstrated their power. Unlike English or American trials, where general verdicts of 'guilty' or 'not guilty' were formulated, they were presented with a sometimes long and complicated list of questions to which they were obliged to answer yes or no. They also decided on the relevance and acceptability of pleas of attenuating or aggravating circumstances. In forming their answers, jurors were not instructed by the judge on the law governing the case on which they were about to decide, but were rather directed to consider only the 'facts'. In addition, the legal definition of what constituted murder was not

30 Cruppi, *La Cour d'assises*, 22.

31 Ibid., 28.

laid out, nor were terms like 'premeditation' or 'lying in wait'—the stipulations for first-degree murder—explained to them. They were asked to consider first if a criminal act had been committed and second if it had been committed with criminal intent. In answering the second question, the jury was asked if the defendant was '*coupable*'.

As is seen, jurors do not only have to say whether Pierre has committed murder, but if he is *guilty* of having committed the crime, which is entirely different, because it is quite possible to have committed a criminal act without being guilty of it, if, as a result of some event or other, the wrongdoer did not understand the implications of his actions. This is the case with children, lunatics, the ignorant, and in a general sense with all those who do wrong without meaning to.[32]

In the jury room, the jurors were notified by a clearly displayed directive to consult their conscience and deliver their 'impression' of the case, a choice of words criticized for the subjectivity it implied. Because no discussion of the legal meaning of criminal intent was provided, throughout the period juries were regularly confronted by *criminels passionnels* who admitted their murders but who were none the less seen as acting in a period of 'temporary insanity' or at the urging of honourable, rather than criminal, motivations. In this way, the juries' interpretation of culpable intention (or its lack) had a vital impact on the outcome of criminal proceedings.

Perhaps even more remarkable was the way in which the jury sometimes attempted to 'bargain' with the President before coming to its decision. The presiding judge was authorized to enter the jury room to address it on any information it required.[33] When he did so, the jurors often asked about his intentions on sentencing, with the judge bound to acknowledge that his independence was limited by his two colleagues on the bench. Acting cautiously, therefore, juries often returned a 'no' answer to all the questions, even after the

32 Anatole Bérard des Glajeux, *Souvenirs d'un président d'assises: Les Passions criminelles, leurs causes et leurs remèdes* (Paris, 1893), ii. 4–5.

33 In 1908, a law was passed which changed this procedure, the President only being able to enter with the attorney of the accused, the prosecutor, and the clerk of the court. See Garner, 'Criminal Procedure in France', 274.

passing of the 1891 law of *sursis*, and simply allowed the defendant to go free.

This tendency towards leniency reached scandalous proportions towards the end of the century and was harshly criticized. At the same time, however, it was also recognized that the jurors' assessment of lack of 'fault' and 'culpability' had something in common with the criminological discourse which was similarly preoccupied with adjusting sentences to individuals, and 'de-penalizing' many offences. If jurors were distressed at the prospect of condemning women or men tainted by hereditary degeneration or damaged by the contaminating effects of the environment, then defence attornies and medico-legists exploited them through a constant diet of deterministic arguments, focusing on the corrupting influence of the social milieu and the fatality of hereditary degeneration.

MEDICO-LEGISTS IN COURT

The vision of criminality and madness the physicians brought with them to the courtroom was shaped by their role in the police and judicial establishment. Psychiatric intervention was not the only function envisaged for medico-legists in the *code d'instruction criminelle*, which laid out provisions for the calling of physicians to aid the detection and solution of crime. The decree of 18 June 1811 specified the conditions of their intervention and fixed their fees, and was primarily directed towards cases of sudden death, poisoning, abortion, infanticide, autopsy, and so on.[34] Such activities were based in the Paris Morgue,[35] which was joined after 1879 by the new Toxicological Laboratory,[36] where important medico-legal teaching sought to instruct students on the practical methods of detecting foul play.

[34] For the history of legal medicine in France see Charles Desmaze, *Histoire de la médecine légale en France* (Paris, 1880).

[35] For a description of the Paris Morgue at the end of the nineteenth century see Ernest Chébuliez, 'La Morgue de Paris', *Revue des deux mondes*, 103 (1891), 344–81. See also Allan Mitchell, 'The Paris Morgue as a Social Institution in the Nineteenth Century', *Francia*, 4 (1973), 581–96.

[36] When Brouardel occupied the chair of legal medicine in 1879, toxicological research was still separate from the Morgue, with investigating magistrates giving

The Morgue was the unquestioned centre of such medico-legal interventions and was headed by Paul Brouardel.[37] From the last days of the Second Empire, Brouardel was an ardent Republican, a supporter of Gambetta and active with several other physicians in the *Ligue Républicaine du VIe arrondissement* during the Commune. He spent his time during the revolutionary upheaval treating the wounded and dying and was even credited with stopping a band of Communards from setting Notre Dame alight. The reminiscences of V. Cornil, a close friend and medical associate, conveyed some sense of the violence, panic, and fear associated with the days when the Communards were massacred by the soldiers of the government of Versailles.

In the next few days, it was no longer possible for us to meet in my laboratory. Bullets whistled through the air and there was fighting in the streets; . . . fires devoured the rue de Lille, the Hôtel de Ville, the Tuileries, and the Palais de Justice.[38]

During these troubled times Brouardel and his associates were preparing their own political and professional futures. The shifting political climate meant, for example, that Brouardel's predecessor, Ambroise Tardieu, lost some of his earlier popularity because of his purported concessions to the demands of the Imperial regime. When the chair of Legal Medicine became vacant in 1879, Brouardel was ready to step in. Indeed, he was the very model of the well-rounded expert envisaged by the founding father of French legal medicine, François Fodéré, whose own work embodied the ideas of medical policing and hygiene at the end of the eighteenth century and during the Empire.[39]

work to specialized laboratories independent of the Paris Medical Faculty. Because of this, a student wishing to deepen his knowledge of toxicology had no means of acquiring this expertise until Brouardel founded the laboratory and gave over its administration to one of his collaborators, M. Ogier. See L. Thoinot, 'La Vie et L'œuvre de Paul Brouardel, 1837–1906', 197–8.

37 Ibid., 193–235.

38 Victor Cornil, 'Souvenirs d'autrefois', *Annales d'hygiène publique et de médecine légale*, 4th ser., 6 (1906), 243.

39 For the early formulation of the field see also François Fodéré, *Les Lois éclairées par les sciences physiques, ou traité de médecine légale et d'hygiène publique*, 3 vols. (Paris, 1799), and his revised *Traité de médecine légale et d'hygiène publique, ou de police de santé adapté aux codes de l'empire français* (Paris, 1813).

Brouardel entirely reformed the education of legal medicine in France with his establishment of the *Institut médico-légal et psychiatrique de l'Université de Paris* which offered its first full-year course in 1903–4[40] and was explicitly designed to create a forensic speciality esteemed by both the profession and the judiciary. He wrote synthetic and authoritative works on medical ethics, professional confidence, medical practice, and charlatanism, as well as on the functions and duties of the medical profession in the twentieth century.[41] Moreover, he compiled comprehensive medico-legal works on sexual assaults, divorce, abortion, traumatic illness (important for the discussion of industrial compensation), as well as more arcane tracts on hanging, poisoning, and the putrefaction of cadavres.[42] He also presided over the important *Comité consultatif d'hygiène* from 1884 to 1903, and was remarkable for the tireless way in which he maintained the links between legal medicine *per se* and the increasingly autonomous area of public hygiene and social medicine.

Although Brouardel was a key medico-legal actor, with the morgue and forensic education his acknowledged fief, there were other, perhaps even more important, places for training psychiatrists to assess the boundaries between criminality and madness. The *Dépôt de la Préfecture de police* received and diagnosed the insane, becoming as a result a key forum for observing the links between madness, poverty and crime. When the Interior Minister created a permanent medical post there in 1845[43] the position was given to one of Esquirol's disciples, Ulysse Trélat (1795–1870). This institutional innovation was prompted by the 1845 decree, appended to the

40 For the list of course offerings see Brouardel, L'Institut médico-légal de l'Université de Paris', *Annales d'hygiène publique et médecine de légale*, 3rd ser., 50 (1903), 297–300.

41 See *La Profession médicale au commencement du XXe siècle* (Paris, 1903); *La Responsabilité médicale; secret médical; déclarations de naissance, inhumations; expertises médico-légales* (Paris, 1898); *Le Secret médical* (Paris, 1887); *L'Exercice de la médecine et du charlatanisme* (Paris, 1899).

42 See *Les Intoxications* (Paris, 1906); *La Mort et la mort subite* (Paris, 1897): *La Pendaison, la strangulation, la suffocation, la submersion* (Paris, 1897); *Le Mariage, nullité, divorce, grossesse, accouchement* (Paris, 1900).

43 Jan Ellen Goldstein, 'French Psychiatry in Social and Political Context: The Formation of a New Profession, 1820–1860', Ph.D. thesis (Univ. of Columbia, 1978), 280.

law of 1838, which removed the power of the Préfet to send the probably insane to asylums on his own authority and required instead the agreement of a doctor.

Located at the *Dépôt* was the *Infirmerie spéciale*, which took on a recognized institutional role from 1872.[44] It was unique both in its policing and administrative function and in the diversity of its clientele. Doctors working there had three primary functions. According to the law of 1838 and the *placement d'office*, they examined individuals picked up by the police and sent them to the famous *service d'admission* at the Asile Ste-Anne where they were examined by its head, Valentin Magnan, or by one of his associates. If not held in the hospital, they were then sent to another Paris asylum such as the Bicêtre or the Salpêtrière. Those whose mental derangement was judged temporary—cases of typhoid, meningitis, or other 'organic affections of the brain'—could be sent for treatment to the Hôtel-Dieu. Finally, a third group were dispatched to a '*hospice*', like Nanterre, which housed those 'afflicted by either congenital or acquired psychological misery and who represent the permanent clientele of the *Assistance publique* . . . '.[45]

The *Infirmerie* received, therefore, 'all the abberant forms of the urban mentality',[46] 'criminals, delinquents, prostitutes, vagrants, invalids, and lunatics'.[47] There were eleven cells for men and seven for women which were equipped to house only twenty people at any given moment. Necessarily, therefore, the physicians who worked there were either esteemed for their quick diagnostic abilities and the unusual range of their clinical experience or decried for the rapid, if not summary, way in which the fate of Paris's poor and destitute was decided. In addition, however, the doctors were equally famous for their research into legal psychiatry. Charles Lasègue was widely hailed for his clinical description of *délire des persécutions* in 1852 which characterized a malady of progressive delirium accompanied, above all, by auditory hallucinations. This was a disorder

[44] Dupré, *L'Œuvre psychiatrique et médico-légale de l'infirmerie spéciale de la préfecture de police (Lasègue, Legrand du Saulle, P. Garnier)* (Paris, 1905), 6.

[45] Ibid., 9.

[46] Dupré, 'Paul Garnier, 1848–1905', *Annales d'hygiène publique et de médecine légale*, 4th ser., 3 (1905), 560.

[47] Id., L'Œuvre psychiatrique et médico-légale, 5.

which was to preoccupy medico-legists and clinicians (Magnan developed the disease category still further and linked it to degeneration), as they sought to uncover the persecutory tendencies which might lead sufferers to violence. Lasègue also wrote important tracts on exhibitionism and kleptomania, thereby extending his interest in impulsive disorders particularly associated with legal psychiatry.[48] He was succeeded by Henri Legrand du Saulle, whose *Traité de médecine légale et de jurisprudence médicale* (1874) became a basic text for the field. Legrand du Saulle also wrote on the medico-legal aspects of hysteria and *délire des persécutions* as well as frequently intervening in criminal cases, sometimes with controversial results.

He in turn gave way to Magnan's disciple Paul Garnier (1848–1905), who supported his *maître*'s emphasis on degeneration and enlarged the system of classification through his medico-legal investigations, particularly on alcoholism, drug addiction, sexual perversions, and the simulation of madness.[49] A leading medical figure in debates at the *Société des prisons*, he was a powerful advocate of measures of social defence against abnormal and dangerous individuals. The clinical course he taught at the *Infirmerie* (see chapter 3) was given in conjunction with another on *médecine légale psychiatrique* at the Paris Medical Faculty in collaboration with Brouardel's *Institut médico-légal*, the combination reflecting the contemporary effort towards the interdisciplinary investigation of criminal management.

Auguste Motet (1832–1909), was also one of the foremost experts in medico-legal work, maintaining strong affiliations with correctional institutions despite spending much of his professional life at the private *maison de santé* in the rue de Charonne.[50] A devotee of Lasèque, he concentrated his scholarly work on legal psychiatry and acted as an expert witness in some of the most famous criminal cases of the era. Other doctors outside the specialist institutions also worked

[48] See *L'Exhibitionnisme* (Paris, 1877) and *Le Vol aux étalages* (Paris, 1880).

[49] See *La Folie à Paris: Étude statistique, clinique et médico-légale* (Paris, 1890). See also *Les Fétichistes, pervertis, et invertis sexuels, observations médico-légales* (Paris, 1896): *Les Perversions sexuelles obsédantes et impulsives* (Paris, 1900).

[50] See Léon Thoinot, 'Auguste Motet', *Annales d'hygiène publique et de médecine légale*, 4th ser., 11 (1909), 358–64.

regularly for the judicial establishment. An authority on aphasia, Gilbert Ballet (1853–1916) developed the treatment of neurasthenia in France—a neurosis associated with extreme mental and physical enervation—and furthered the study of the 'psychoses', deepening the earlier discussions of persecutory delirium by further clinical observations of the 'disintegration' of the personality. He too attended meetings at the *Société des prisons*, became Professor of Mental Illness at the Paris Faculty in 1909, and was active in professional neurological and psychiatric bodies. His ability to unite clinical practice, scientific research, and medico-legal investigation, demonstrated the way in which he and other psychiatrists could happily straddle many different fields at once.[51]

Throughout the period under discussion, these men dominated the Parisian courtroom with their analyses. They were joined by others who, appearing on the official list of skilled experts attached to the *Cour d'appel*, were also obliged to give testimony. They included an older generation closer in temperament to Esquirol and his pioneering ideals, men like Louis Delaisiauve, a specialist in epilepsy and the education of 'backward children', who was a notable liberal republican and parliamentary candidate;[52] and Antoine-Émile Blanche (1820–93), father of the portraitist, Jacques-Émile, who blended literary interests with his psychiatric endeavours. He treated the likes of Guy de Maupassant and Gérard de Nerval in his private asylum and hobnobbed with the intellectual beau monde, meeting Michelet, Pasteur, Turgenev, and Renan.[53] The generation that followed included people like Benjamin Ball (1833–93), who established the widely respected journal *L'Encéphale* in 1888, about a decade after winning the highly coveted Professorship of Mental Illness in Paris. In gaining this position Ball triumphed over his arch-rival Valentin Magnan (1835–1916), who also occasionally put in court appearances and who made important clinical contributions—on alcoholism

51 See his *L'Hygiène neurasthénique* (Paris, 1897) and his important *Psychoses et affections nerveuses* (Paris, 1897).

52 See René Sémélaigne, *La Psychiatrie française* (Paris, 1930), 302–17.

53 Ibid., ii. 69–74; see also Jacques-Émile Blanche, *Pêche aux souvenirs* (Paris, 1949), in which the painter spoke about his father.

and various psychosexual phenomena[54]—which impinged significantly on the medico-legal domain.[55]

This small but eminent group sought to provide a scientific case that would do credit to themselves and their colleagues and keep under wraps any intraprofessional disagreement which might harm their reputation. Exactness in method was to match an appropriate rhetorical style, as Brouardel urged his colleagues to present their material as laconically as possible. One president of the Assises, Bérard des Glajeux, noted the quiet unfolding of the medical case in terminology which the jurors could understand. Perhaps a bit nostalgically, he contrasted Brouardel's style with that of his predecessor, Ambroise Tardieu, who he recalled was 'a marvellous orator and as an artist in words could be compared only to Jules Favre'.[56]

Such efforts were occasionally foiled by contested diagnoses which provoked bitter disputes, sometimes publicly aired in professional periodicals. However, while within the judicial sphere, they loyally tried to work in unison, harmony perhaps enforced by the still difficult role they were obliged to play. At first glance, French legal procedure seemed conducive to the reception of medico-legal expertise. Called at the behest of the investigating magistrate, they presented their reports as servants of the *instruction*. They were thus never faced with the embarrassment of the defence's medico-legist advancing an entirely different interpretation to that of the prosecution's own expert.

Despite this apparent advantage, they none the less had to contend with disbelief and criticism from a variety of different

[54] For the most comprehensive study on Magnan see Paul Sérieux, *V. Magnan: Sa vie et son œuvre* (Paris, 1921); also Théophile Simon, *Un clinicien: Magnan. Un créateur de la psychologie expérimentale* (Paris, 1918); Roger Mignot: 'Magnan et ses études sur l'alcoolisme', *Annales médico-psychologiques*, 15th ser. 1 (1935), 738–47; Charles Vurpas, 'Les Obsessions, les impulsions et les perversions sexuelles dans l'œuvre de Magnan', ibid., 749–59; V. Tuelle, 'L'Œuvre médico-légale de Magnan', ibid., 760–71.

[55] Auguste Voisin (1829–1898) was a key figure in research into hysteria and hypnotism and intervened occasionally in criminal trials. He was joined by a range of other, less well-known experts such as Paul Dubuisson (*c.*1848–*c.*1908), who ultimately headed the Ste-Anne asylum and wrote medico-legal and criminological works. Others were disciples of Brouardel and included Thoinot, Descoust, and Socquet.

[56] A. Bérard des Glajeux, *Souvenirs d'un président d'assises* (Paris, 1893), ii. 149. Jules Favre (1809–1880) was an attorney noted for his eloquence. As Foreign Minister in the government of National Defence after Sedan he signed the armistice with Bismarck; he was elected to Victor Cousin's place in the *Académie française* in 1869.

courtroom actors. Even the defendants would sometimes mock them, as did Jules Mourdedieu when tried for assaulting a neighbour for interfering during a quarrel with his mistress. An unnamed alienist 'declared that Mourdedieu could have acted out of the terror inspired by M. Chauvet's [the neighbour] visit when he came to demand an explanation'. To this line of argument, Mourdedieu replied: 'What a joke!'[57] thereby making short shrift of the medical man's analysis. As late as 1880, Brouardel would complain bitterly of the disparaging remarks made by public prosecutors who, although sometimes obliged to apologize, none the less occasionally unleashed their annoyance.[58] Niggling observations and derisive comments were fairly common. When, for example, a twenty-five-year-old carpenter was accused of killing his brother, the physician Vallon provided what was by psychiatric standards a subtle portrait of abnormality, noting disturbing indications of pathology but concluding that 'Lachéry is not mad but unbalanced'. The president took the opportunity of 'clarifying' Vallon's statement with the following ripostes:

PRESIDENT: Like lots of people.
DR VALLON: Certainly.
PRESIDENT: These unbalanced people even outnumber the rest. [*smiles*]
DR VALLON: I wouldn't go as far as that.[59]

Hence, being a medical expert was not always an enviable occupation. Criticized as inquisitors when they provided what was, in their view, incontrovertible evidence of foul play, and subjected to similar vituperation when they reached conclusions of irresponsibility, they often felt assaulted from both sides. Moreover, while the men called in Paris were highly qualified to testify on medico-legal problems ranging from sudden death to mental alienation, this small élite often felt undermined by the inadequate, and sometimes non-existent, training of provincial colleagues. Their incompetence damaged the reputation of the whole endeavour, a disadvantage which Brouardel claimed led him to promote an advanced diploma in forensic medicine.

[57] *Gazette des tribunaux*, 4 Feb. 1905.
[58] Brouardel, *La Responsabilité médicale*, 242.
[59] Eugène Lachéry, *Gazette des tribunaux*, 1 Mar. 1899.

In addition, they felt undervalued and resented having to do what was frequently a considerable amount of distasteful work for little financial reward. Indeed, until the decree of 21 November 1893, they were obliged to reform complicated operations and mental observations for the niggardly fees prescribed by the 1811 statute. Even the increases they then received were scarcely generous, as the fee for an autopsy in Paris was lifted to only twenty-five francs from the six francs it was previously,[60] while the fee for mental examinations was unchanged at ten francs for a session of approximately three hours.[61]

Perhaps most galling was the way in which they were treated like any other witness, obliged to wait for tedious hours in the *salle des témoins* with 'a different sort of people' who would often ask 'indiscreet and disagreeable questions'. Most of the criminal trials in Paris were of the working poor, and a day spent in close quarters with them was considered irksome, if not downright unpleasant. Occasionally, they were outraged by women who took advantage of their vulnerable position. For example, when called to testify at a trial in Versailles, Charles Lasègue was obliged to speak about a murder attempt in a brothel and found himself 'the only man in the witness room, surrounded for three hours by all the residents of the establishment called as witnesses'.[62]

Despite the irritations and the low remuneration, the complaints of the experts must be put into perspective. These were eminent men who received their incomes from a variety of prestigious sources, as professors, *fonctionnaires*, and physicians at private asylums. Moreover, their medico-legal activities brought fame, if not notoriety, occasional press interviews, fascinating clinical material, and publications in any number of professional journals.

[60] For a discussion of past fees and conditions, changes introduced by the 1893 statute, and proposals for future reform, see the report presented to the *Société de médecine légale* by Vallon, Constant, Chessevant, Masbrenier, Socquet, Thibierge, Thoinot, 'La Réforme des honoraires des médecins en matière d'expertise médico-légale', *Annales d'hygiène publique et de médecine légale*, 4th ser., 13 (1910), 384–404.

[61] Ibid., 389.

[62] Brouardel, *La Responsabilité médicale*, 278.

THE MEDICO-LEGAL REPORT

Although obliged to work under less than ideal circumstances, the power of the medico-legist in the pre-trial investigation was far from negligible. There is, for example, considerable evidence to suggest that jurists and physicians collaborated in removing those deemed incompetent to stand trial from the judicial arena. It is impossible to discover the extent of this practice, although certain clues can be gleaned from published records. Physicians explained how investigating magistrates, in the midst of the *instruction*, would ask for medical intervention, convinced that the accused were thoroughly deranged. Furious epileptics, delirious individuals, those whose intelligence seemed eradicated after their crimes, were all incarcerated under the *placement d'office*.[63] The archival records also show how charges were dropped when greater and lesser criminals—from would-be assassins of politicians to defilers of statues of Gambetta—were described by alienists as hopelessly insane.[64]

Through such instances medico-administrative procedure was substituted for legal due process. The extent of the doctors' power was shown forcefully in the case of Femme C . . ., a former patient at the Salpêtrière who came to the house of Charcot's disciple, Georges Gilles de la Tourette (see next chapter), and shot him three times. She claimed that she had been used as a guinea-pig during research into hypnotism and that this had addled her mind and prevented her from earning a living. She explained that she had asked for compensation and had made the murder attempt when the request was

[63] For scattered evidence of this practice see A. Motet, 'Rapport sur l'état mental d'un individu inculpé d'assassinat et de tentative de meurtre', *Annales d'hygiène et de médecine légale*, 3rd ser., 17 (1887), 445–54; id., Ballet, and Richardière, 'Rapport sur l'état mental de la Femme B . . . inculpée d'assassinat', ibid., 3rd ser., 26 (1891), 40–50.

[64] The D^2U^6 series in the *Archives de la Seine* contains some cases of '*non-lieu*' when defendants were not prosecuted. They include individuals like Pierre M . . . who in 1885 tried to kill the Foreign Minister, de Freycinet, and was described as a '*débile*' by Brouardel, Motet, and Descoust; another, named Octave B . . . in carton 57, who in 1897 struck an unknown passer-by for no apparent motive and who had delirious episodes after; Louis F . . . in carton 44, who in 1893 desecrated Gambetta's statue. Although considered a dangerous lunatic by the intervening physician, Legras, Louis F . . . was set free with a strong warning.

refused.[65] Although the truth of her claims was never clearly established, she was none the less swiftly consigned to a lunatic asylum.

There were other instances in which the alienists sought to adopt a similar approach. One wife and mother, Pauline B . . . , for example, was accused of the attempted murder of her landlord's agent when evicted from her small farming tenancy on the outskirts of Paris. For two years she waged a personal war against the family of the Duc de B . . . and finally succeeded in gaining the public's ear when she made her attack. Convinced that Paul Garnier would be sympathetic, she told him, 'I hope that you are going to write your report in my favour because those scoundrels deserve to be punished',[66] and was dismayed when the doctor described her as a dangerous lunatic suffering from persecutory delirium. She protested her sanity with such vigour that a second group of medico-legists were called who disagreed with Garnier's conclusions; as a result she was tried and gaoled for two years.

Finally, in scattered cases, defendants would collapse in court with their trials postponed pending further medico-legal examination. For example, this was the behaviour of a certain Choquart accused in 1896 of trying to poison his spouse:

> At the moment when his wife appeared at the witness box [*à la barre*], he was overtaken by a nervous trembling soon followed by a violent fit. He struggled and yelled in the arms of the guards who managed, not without difficulty, to take him away.[67]

Others would demonstrate different nervous symptoms, as in the case of Gaby who, at the beginning of his interrogation, 'suddenly collapsed, prey to a violent epileptic fit'.[68] Often taken away for medico-legal examination, such defendants sometimes never reappeared in court, undoubtedly consigned to the administrative authority and hence probably a lunatic asylum.

Such events were none the less exceptions to the normal course of medico-legal intervention, which was conducted and

[65] As she explained, 'Il eût été juste qu'un médecin, M. Gilles de la Tourette ou un autre vînt à mon aide'; see Femme Rose Laurence C . . . D^2U^6 44, *pièce* 18.

[66] Pauline B . . . D^2U^8 241, 12/13 Dec. 1888, *pièce* 29.

[67] *Gazette des tribunaux*, 15/16 May 1896.

[68] Ibid., 26/7 Dec. 1902.

presented according to well-established conventions, the style and nature of which differed markedly from the interrogations of the investigating magistrate. Up to three alienists would visit the detainee in the Paris prisons, often returning several times for further examinations. Defendants were observed from the moment of their incarceration in the *Dépôt*. It was believed that their essential character came to the surface as a result of mixing both with hardened offenders and 'simple mortals, poor innocent folk, obscure wrongdoers' who 'have to suffer the humiliations, the pain, the dangers of promiscuity in the common-room and narrow court-yards which, with their metal bars, resemble cages in a zoo.'[69]

The alienists used their clinical experience to uncover ruses and extort confessions, employing prison guards as tacit assistants to report any abnormalities of behaviour, be they nightmares, fits of screaming, or a refusal to eat. In this way medical and legal forms of interrogation had something in common, as both were based on a one-way movement, with judge or physician asking the questions and defendants able only to answer and defend themselves. All responses, including silence, were possible evidence for reaching a conclusion about the defendant's character and past.

The medico-legists used their bedside manner to establish a sympathetic relationship with the defendants and persuade them to give full and honest answers. The main goal, however, was to elicit any evidence there might be of either insanity or depraved criminal motives. Sometimes the doctors were visibly moved by the tales of woe that emerged and demonstrated their compassion for both female and male *criminels passionnels*, with important implications for the later trials. Mostly, however, they hid well behind an armour of professional strategies used both in the judicial sphere and when executing a *placement d'office*. Wary always of possible accusations of wrongful confinement or of having allowed dangerous lunatics to go free, they advocated the use of quotations to prove, beyond doubt, the reality of the mental derangement during examination, a technique also often used in their medico-legal analyses.[70]

69 Guillot, *Les Prisons du palais de justice (Dépôt de la préfecture: Conciergerie-Sourcière)* (Melun, 1892), 11.

70 Eugène Charpentier, in the discussion following Garnier, 'Internement des aliénés; thérapeutique et législation', *Congrès des médecins aliénistes et neurologistes* (Nancy, 1896), 20.

The use of quotations was only one of the conventions used to describe the subject and construct an argument, the irrefutability of which was the ultimate aim of all the experts. For the alienists the defendants' bodies and behaviour were a source of infinite clues requiring interpretation, their utterances the key to discovering the presence of absence of delusions, and their past histories a virtually limitless field for investigating the precedents responsible for bringing them to their current impasse with the law.

As a literary document, the medico-legal report was a self-consciously crafted essay and varied in length from five to forty handwritten pages. In this respect it was similar to the final judicial indictment read to the court before proceedings began. However, although both regularly included an account of the crime itself and the seeming psychological motivation behind the deed, the medical report was concerned with providing a clinical portrait of pathology ultimately linked to a diseased or disordered body, a concern which did not affect the judiciary.

The reasons for this conventionality lie, in the most superficial sense, in the frequently articulated desire to present a scientific and hence irreproachable case to the judiciary, the reiteration of form and ordered argument serving as rhetorical devices to exemplify and underpin the scientific method. Moreover, these documents were sometimes published in the *Annales d'hygiène publique et de médecine légale*, the *Annales médico-psychologiques*, or the *Archives d'anthropologie criminelle* and were hence subject to scrutiny by colleagues as well. Their similarity is all the more remarkable given the number of authors and their varying aptitudes (some excelling in verbosity, others in concision) and the many types of mental disorders under discussion. As later chapters will show, the content of disease description and psychological analysis did vary crucially according to individual, sex, and class, but this did not generally alter their order or the areas of analysis deemed worthy of emphasis.

The structure of the reports can best be revealed by examining that of Pierre-Laurent-Auguste G . . . , an unemployed seaman accused of trying to murder his mistress in 1891. As the indictment explained: G . . . met Marcelle D . . . and impressed her by maintaining falsely that he was a worker in a linen workshop and earning a good monthly wage. Believing him to be sincere, they 'struck up a relationship [*communauté d'existence*] which deepened as the days went by'.[71] Not long after, however, she began to have suspicions about his earning capacity. He assured her he would be paid at the end of the month. When the day came and he was still penniless, he shot her in the jaw with his revolver as she slept. As she ran to escape, he fired four more times and then tried to kill her with a sword stick before he was disarmed and arrested. First saying he intended to murder her and then kill himself, he furthered this line of defence by asserting that the two had made a suicide compact, a defence which the woman forcefully denied.

As will be seen, such cases—of an unemployed youth trying to kill his mistress and then saying it was a crime of passion or a *suicide à deux*—were far from uncommon in late nineteenth-century Paris. In his report, the alienist Gilbert Ballet first made his contempt for the defendant's self-characterization quite clear and then proceeded to proclaim the objectivity of his medical role by confining himself to the indications of abnormality. Like many of his colleagues, he referred self-consciously to the purpose of psychiatric intervention which was:

> . . . to assess the value of the motives which must have driven G . . ., weigh . . . the responsibility to be imputed to him, study the defendant in detail, trace his personal and hereditary past, and indicate the physical and moral anomalies that observation has revealed.[72]

In line with this general methodological programme, Ballet began the habitual examination of G . . .'s 'cerebral defects', an investigation which in this era almost always centred on the presence or absence of a hereditary predisposition. He found G . . .'s father to be 'a very sober man but who must have been haunted by suicidal ideas and who threw himself in the river Allier in mid-winter with the aim of drowning himself'. A history of childhood illness and traumatic episodes was seen as further depleting a fund of nervous energy already damaged at birth: 'During his infancy G . . . had convulsions and at the

[71] Pierre-Laurent-Auguste G . . . D^2U^8 269, 25 June 1891, Acte d'accusation.

[72] All references to the medico-legal investigation are included ibid., *pièce* 60, which is Ballet's medico-legal report.

age of 11 he contracted a typhoid fever which might have been serious'.

Moving to a different, although related, source of evidence, Ballet then considered G . . .'s physical appearance, finding indications of neurophysiological disequilibrium. 'His face is clearly asymmetrical', with the smaller right side affected by a squint that was so severe he had unsuccessfully sought to have it corrected by surgery. This asymmetrical conformation suggested 'a defective development of certain parts of the encephalon'. Underpinning this was 'an intermittent trembling' of the hands, which made writing difficult and sometimes illegible. In developing further his line of argument, Ballet enunciated one of the underlying precepts of psychiatric theory based on the idea of degeneration: 'Physical stigmata . . . are often associated with individuals who demonstrate a variety of intellectual and moral defects: this is the case with the accused'.

In a characteristic fashion, Ballet continued by shifting attention to the defendant's intellectual attributes, maintaining that, although he seemed to be of average intelligence, further investigation demonstrated that 'this intelligence is partial'. G . . . possessed a clear aptitude for literature, was particularly fond of biographies of famous navigators, and even claimed to like Diderot, Balzac, and Lamartine. But here his intelligence seemed, if not to end, at least to be confined. His incompetence at arithmetic and, even more significantly, his complete inability to spell suggested a distinct disequilibrium of the mental faculties. Such an observation was linked to Ballet's appreciation of cerebral localization: 'This is just how the intelligence of the majority of degenerates is formed: lucid, brilliant even in certain respects, they none the less present surprising gaps which contrast strangely with certain clear, sometimes even remarkable, aptitudes.'

From an analysis of intellectual capacities and defects, Ballet continued with a discussion of G . . .'s affective and moral make-up as well as his 'irregular and disorderly existence'. his expulsion from school because of unruly behaviour, desertion from his regiment at 19—a decision taken, in his own words, 'on the spur of the moment'—and his parasitical existence afterwards, were all cited as evidence of moral incapacity. Arrested and then released, he was ultimately imprisoned for vagabondage, showing an antisocial propensity which Ballet saw as a link in a chain that ended with the murder attempt.

What most repelled the alienist was the defendant's remarkable insouciance: 'when I commit a theft, I forget about it by the next day'. The accused was 'the immoral type', and embodied one of the most common diagnostic categories of the medico-legal domain, that of moral imbecility. Intellectually able to perceive the difference between right and wrong, but unable to experience or feel that difference, G . . . acted with habitual recklessness and acted 'under the influence of one of his sentimental whims, one of the thoughtless and semi-automatic resolutions which even the most degraded minds fall into when they bear the mark of degeneration.' The description was thus of a dangerous electrical machine run riot, his burning head when he fired on his victim a final indication of an irresistible nervous explosion.

Although Ballet was willing to acknowledge that these numerous factors limited G . . .'s responsibility, he none the less stated firmly that society needed to take measures of social defence against such 'a dangerous disabled person'. The verdict of the court reflected the ambiguity of his conclusions. Recognizing that G . . . was dangerous, the court convicted him, but shied away from the prescribed penalty of forced labour for life and gave him only eight years' hard labour. Dangerous but sick, G . . . did not fit neatly into either of the available categories. As in so many of the cases to be examined throughout this book, the alienists' assessment of deterministic disease processes was not equivalent to an evaluation of irresponsibility. G . . . was merely another striking example of the managerial dilemmas that medical expertise introduced into the legal setting.

Ballet's investigation of G . . . demonstrates the characteristic use of evidence, the conventional ordering which habitually appeared in a medico-legal report, as well as the wide array of highly developed medical conceptions employed. Beginning with an account of G . . .'s weakened hereditary capital, Ballet noted his inherent deficiencies as well as the acquisition of other debilitating characteristics resulting from traumatic illness during childhood. Such a destabilized and susceptible physiological economy was observable through a series of physical, intellectual, and moral stigmata: cerebral malformation, neurophysiological symptoms, and reflexive, automatic patterns of antisocial behaviour. In sum the analysis sought to present a coherent and interlinked picture that ran from the legacy of a morose and melancholy father to an unsightly squint and trembling hands, and in turn connect these to an extraordinary love of Balzac, recalcitrance at school, and the attempted murder.

The methods, limitations, and conditions of this form of analysis applied in almost every case in which medico-legal opinion was sought. Their analyses were interwoven into a complex appreciation of moral and social responsibility. Although they investigated each defendant on his or her own merits, their assessments were intimately tied to the construction of typologies of antisocial behaviour in which gender and class loomed large. On some occasions their medico-legal commentary focused on issues which ranged from medical professionalism to highbrow philosophical debate; at other times, their analyses virtually ignored ethical and healing imperatives and concentrated instead on social defence, as in the debates on alcoholism. They focused on sexual relations, notions of personal honour, and, finally, politics, as in the examination of crimes of passion and the anarchist affairs. The way the doctors assessed their subjects, as well as the response of the court to their recommendations, will be examined in the next four chapters.

5

WOMEN, HYSTERIA, AND HYPNOTISM

The Parisian Belle Époque produced several cases involving the issue of hypnotic suggestion in which women in particular were seen as acting unconsciously under the powerful influence of masterful men. Perhaps more than any other, these *affaires* captured the public imagination, filled the pages of the illustrated press, and evoked both widespread derision as well as genuine alarm. While a man who claimed to be a 'seducer without knowing it' when caught in the arms of his employer's wife elicited chuckles of mirth,[1] the lamentations of a young girl whose maidenhood was taken by the abuses of a supposed magnetizer were taken seriously in court. Such cases involved not only considerable lay comment and press coverage, but also commanded professional attention from eminent physicians, lawyers, and social theorists and hence impinged on criminological debate.

One case which excited overwhelming interest in 1890 was that of Gabrielle Bompard,[2] a young woman of respectable middle-class origins who was accused of conspiring to rob and murder a Parisian bailiff. Her defence was that she had acted under the hypnotic suggestion of her older lover, a notorious rake and adventurer named Michel Eyraud, and had executed the most elaborate preparations under his dominating influence. With a delight unusual even for the Parisian press, every detail was served up to the public. The case was,

[1] Robert G. Hillmann, 'A Scientific Study of Mystery; The Role of the Medical and Popular Press in the Nancy-Salpêtrière Controversy on Hypnotism, *Bulletin for the History of Medicine*, 39 (1965), 174, quoted from *La Lanterne*, 'Séducteur sans le savoir', 11 May 1883.

[2] Ruth Harris, 'Murder under Hypnosis in the Case of Gabrielle Bompard: Psychiatry in the Belle Époque Courtroom', in W. F. Bynum, R. Porter, and M. Shepherd (eds.), *The Anatomy of Madness: Essays in the History of Psychiatry* (London, 1985), ii. 197–241.

perhaps, irresistible: her accomplice claimed that she had lured the unsuspecting bailiff, Alexandre Toussaint Gouffé, into her arms, moved him over to a strategically placed *chaise longue*, and tied the cord of her red peignoir around his neck while he kissed her throat. Once these preliminaries were completed, Eyrand pulled hard on the other end of the cord from his position behind a curtain and caught the would-be lover in his snare. As he himself put it, 'Gouffé did not struggle. I would never have believed a hanged man could die so quickly.'[3] In contrast to this picture of willing complicity, however, Bompard asserted that Eyraud had savagely strangled the bailiff with his bare hands, a version of the murder which was never seriously considered by the investigating magistrate.

The purportedly sexual nature of the entrapment was repeatedly referred to and indeed became crucial during the trial when Bompard's character was examined. Was this a woman acting at the behest of an unscrupulous, exploitive mate, or was she rather a vicious coquette, little more than a mendacious prostitute willing to do anything to satisfy her perverse criminal urges? So extreme were the feelings roused that representatives of rival medical schools came to argue their case in court and turned the chamber into a forum for medical debate, with one scholarly disquisition lasting three hours—to the dismay and irritation of the judges on the bench.

The case of Gabrielle Bompard was far from being the only one of this type to arouse such controversy in the 1880s. Other examples demonstrate the tendency to see unconscious suggestion and male domination as in some way present when women behaved in what were considered particularly dangerous or reprehensible ways. Indeed, the more sensational the case, the more likely it was that hypnotism would be proposed as an explanation. Like Gabrielle Bompard, the crime of Gabrielle Fenayrou[4] was seen as sexual entrapment instigated by domineering male suggestion, with a seemingly devoted wife first betraying her husband with one of his students and then conspiring in murder. Influenced by her aggrieved and resentful husband, she lured her unsuspecting lover to a rendezvous

[3] *Archives de la Seine*, $D^{2}U^{8}$ 263, *pièce* 1782.

[4] See for a brief discussion Hippolyte Bernheim, 'Les Suggestions criminelles', *Revue de l'hypnotisme*, 4 (1889–90), 265–6.

where her spouse murdered him. Hypnotic suggestion, not sexual attraction, was also blamed when an upright wife and mother deserted her husband for a poverty-stricken tutor of dubious reputation. Such was the case in the Chambige affair, where the irreproachable Mme Grille was supposed to have been 'fascinated' by the dissolute Chambige, abandoning her home and agreeing to a *suicide à deux* in which she perished but he survived.[5]

In all of these cases, some of the most prestigious medical mandarins and social commentators of the day went to immense lengths to analyse the state of mind of such women, in Mme Grille's case trying to account for her actions by proving that she was deranged.[6] The reason for their interest lies in several distinct but interrelated areas of debate on unconscious suggestion. Hypnotism attracted attention and caused alarm because of the dramatic way in which it demonstrated the reality of unconscious mental activity, explored the recesses of memory, and showed the immense possibilities of manipulating subjects through the imposition of authority.

Although the initial focus of hypnotic investigation centred on medicine,[7] the impact of experimental discoveries became part of more general political and philosophical debate. As a result, men from diverging political and disciplinary positions drew inspiration from the clinical work, with some men undertaking experiments of their own. Alfred Fouillé, for example, justified his notion of *idées forces* through hypnotic experimentation. For Georges Sorel, hypnosis demonstrated how myths of revolutionary consciousness were forged, whereas for Henri Bergson it revealed the nature of unconscious memory. Finally, for Gabriel Tarde, suggestion drove the mechanism of social imitation, which then promoted cultural reproduction, while also explaining the dynamics of crowd behaviour.[8] It is no

[5] See Gaston Lèbre, 'L'Affaire Chambige', in id. (ed.), *Revue des grands procès contemporains* (Paris, 1889), 21–101. The next chapter will discuss the case in more detail.

[6] G. Tarde, 'L'Affaire Chambige', *Archives d'anthropologie criminelle*, 4 (1889), 92–108.

[7] See Dominique Barrucand, *Histoire de l'hypnose en France* (Paris, 1967).

[8] For a discussion of Fouillé's significant interest in hypnotic experimentation see Élisabeth Ganne de Beaucoudry, *La Psychologie et la métaphysique des idées-forces chez Alfred Fouillé* (Paris, 1936), for example, 87. The lesson Fouillé gleaned from hypnosis was

exaggeration to say that hypnosis in the 1880s and early 1890s was at the confluence of almost every major cultural trend, forming an important aspect of the 'revolt against rationalism' and providing experimental proof for the need to revise social and political thinking in line with new discoveries about the human mind.

Such esoteric theorizing was not cut off from the day-to-day sphere of *fin de siècle* cultural life. Indeed, it was often through the vehicle of medico-legal debate that highbrow formulations were clarified and analysed. The 'popular' nature of hypnotic practice—the widespread presence of magnetizing performances, hypnotic healing, and spiritualism—meant that an unusual degree of cultural interchange existed between many different levels of the social and intellectual world, between daily observation and abstract theorizing. Thus, an account of rape under hypnosis that was seemingly sensationalized for popular consumption was at the same time avidly cited in professional criminological and philosophical journals. In each, the centre of attention was the same despite the very different style. All were concerned with discussing the social, moral, and political implications of using hypnotic suggestion to make an individual do something he or she did not want to do or, even worse, of realizing through its use desires which might otherwise have been resisted.

This diffuse alarm represents the pervasive anxiety which underlies the entire medico-legal commentary. Medical concern was doubly aroused by the fact that women seemed particularly susceptible to suggestive influence. It is no exaggeration to say that the physicians considered themselves to be

that 'toute idée tend à devenir un acte', an experimental proof of his own conception of '*idées forces*', so crucial to his elaboration of a reformist, organicist view of Republican social solidarity. Georges Sorel in an article entitled 'Sur les applications de la psycho-physique', in the *Revue philosophique*, 22 (1886), 363–75 examined the role of unconscious suggestion in aesthetic appreciation, an area of inquiry which demonstrated his growing interest in the role of symbols and mythology in animating political activity. Bergson was fascinated by hypnotic experimentation, citing cases of mind reading, observation of books hidden from the subject's eyes, etc. In an astute article entitled, 'De la simulation inconsciente dans l'hypnotisme', ibid., 525–31, he recognized the crucial significance of the *unconscious* rapport between the subject and the operator which meant that both unwittingly accepted an area of shared illusion in order to complete the experiment successfully. Such investigations contributed to his preoccupation with the irrational, intuitive aspects of unconscious mental life.

battling a veritable army of nefarious magnetizers, all eager to destroy the virtue of innocent females, to rape, break contracts, excite vicious passions, and arouse unsavoury thoughts. The enemies of medical—or at least male bourgeois—authority who would abuse hypnosis included a wide variety of potential scoundrels: Jews, working-class men, criminals, magnetizing performers, amateur healers, and household servants.

I intend to examine the layers of ideology and interest which contributed towards the characterization of these groups as embodiments of danger and deceit. At the same time I hope to explain the extreme nature of these medico-legal warnings by examining the clinical and experimental world of hypnotism, to understand the set of authority relationships and interactions between female patients and male physicians which drew strength from an elaborate structure of sexual attraction, theatrical exploitation, and domination. I will suggest that the medico-legal debate in Bompard's case and others focused on the seemingly sensational and explicitly sexual precisely because of the uncomfortable relationship which medical hypnosis engendered between doctor and patient. Alienists often used hypnosis, which demonstrated the dominion of man and science over woman and nature, to reveal the unconscious urgings of the sicker sex and to subject them to rational analysis. This claim, however, is contradicted by the clinical reports and photographic record of the physicians themselves, which chronicle another dimension of medical methods. The medico-legal commentary on hypnosis did not so much confirm the reality of violation by non-medical practitioners as reflect the ambiguous morality and tenuous professional position of the physicians.

The debate on hypnosis was complicated by the existence of two opposing medical schools which competed for interpretive hegemony. The most famous of these centred on the Salpêtrière in Paris where Jean-Martin Charcot conducted his influential studies into hysteria. He and his associates developed an elaborate psycho-physiological interpretation of hypnosis and its relationship to hysteria which helped to fashion their particular therapeutic perspective and medico-legal system. From the early 1880s, however, these views came under unremitting assault from an unsuspected, distant quarter, with Hippolyte Bernheim of the *École de Nancy* systematically attacking Charcot's doctrine and proposing a different conception of hypnosis and its implications for medical treatment and judicial debate.

Although complex, the intricacies of their struggle are important for the light they shed on the argument over the nature of human consciousness, which in turn affected criminological debate. Hypnosis and suggestion were key areas that produced apparently concrete examples of actions taken without conscious understanding or memory. Such unaccountable behaviour consequently demonstrated the failure of classical legal theory to account for such phenomena because of its exclusive reliance on rational calculation and moral assessment. The battle between the two schools is also significant as much for the similarities of their concerns as for their differences. Although coming at the question of hypnotic suggestion from opposing standpoints, the combatants none the less agreed that women were most susceptible to its influence. They thereby jointly raised concern over issues of sexual fidelity and marital constancy which were to spill over and touch upon wider preoccupations with social and political order in general.

Charcot and the Hysteric

Research into hypnosis centred on Paris where several leading practitioners, including A. Dumontpallier at the Charité and J.-B. Luys at the Pitié, sought to share the limelight. Despite their best efforts, however, they were consistently outshone by Charcot, whose personal charisma and authoritative scientific voice earned him an unparalleled reputation as a *Napoléon des névroses*, a physician thaumaturge, and a secular miracle-worker. As a pioneering neurologist, he possessed impeccable credentials to pronounce on the most mysterious of nervous diseases, hysteria, and on hypnosis, which he regarded as a symptom of the illness. Moreover, his acolytes, including men famous in their own right, such as Alfred Binet and Charles Féré, Paul Richer and Georges Gilles de la Tourette, were persistent in disseminating his doctrines.

Charcot's shadow fell over virtually every medico-legal

debate concerning hysteria and hypnotism, and indeed much of the Nancy School's research programme can be seen as an attempt to undermine his authority. Charcot was much more than a scientist. He was an important personality, a man to know in Parisian society, and a representative of a new political order. Cherishing his position in the beau monde, he associated with politicians, conversed with literati, and cut a figure as a commentator on the fine arts at his soirées in the Boulevard St Germain.[9] Because of his background—he was the son of a carriage-maker—Charcot was an emblem of the 'new strata' which the emerging Republic sought to valorize, and gained recognition through his appointment to the special chair in Nervous Diseases in 1882. From this unique position he propounded an impressively influential anticlericalism, a polemical stance which had profound implications for his representation of women.[10]

However, perhaps the more immediate impact on his intellectual development can be traced to his years of stewardship at the Salpêtrière, a notorious Bastille for indigent, insane, and often incurable women. Joining it in 1863, he doggedly established the foundations of his medical empire using the store of feminine pathology in his *musée pathologique vivant*[11] as raw material for his study of nervous diseases. Charcot's standing in this institution was unparalleled. In this faceless mass, patients strained to attract his attention, and it was those with the most sensual, grotesque, or flamboyant symptoms who often succeeded.[12] His remarkable charisma, the subject of much contemporary comment, was responsible for his greatest

9 For Charcot's public life see A. R. G. Owen, *Hysteria, Hypnosis and Healing: The Work of J.-M. Charcot* (London, 1971). 217–34.

10 Jan Ellen Goldstein, 'The Hysteria Diagnosis and the Politics of Anti-Clericalism in Late Nineteenth-Century France', *Journal of Modern History*, 54 (1982), 209–39.

11 J.-M. Charcot, 'Leçons sur les maladies du système nerveux', in *Œuvres complètes*, vol. iii, *Hémorragie et ramollissement du cerveau, métallothérapie et hypnotisme, électrothérapie* (Paris, 1890), 4. For a rather different view of the institutional context see Mark S. Micale, 'The Salpêtrière in the Age of Charcot: An Institutional Perspective on Medical History in the Late Nineteenth Century', *Journal of Contemporary History*, 20 (1985), 703–31.

12 For the most remarkable and enlightening account of Charcot's clinical world see Georges Didi-Huberman, *Invention de l'hystérie: Charcot et l'iconographie photographique de la Salpêtrière* (Paris, 1982); see also Gérard Wajeman, *Le Maître et l'hystérique* (Paris, 1982) and Lucien Israel, *L'Hystérique, le sexe et le médecin*, 5th edn. (Paris, 1983).

therapeutic achievements as well as his most dubious professional practices. Confronted with an intractable hysterical symptom he could exercise his personal power to miraculous effect. For example, his successful order that a nun get up and walk, although she had completely lost the use of her legs, demonstrates the suggestible power of his command.[13]

Such awesome personal authority also had a more dangerous outcome, as it became extremely difficult for his associates to criticize or contradict him. It was only after his death in 1893 that his disciple Babinski felt able to reassess his work on hysteria and dissociate himself from the dramatic and dogmatic portrayal of the disease.[14] Contemporaries regularly commented on Charcot's commanding and intimidating gaze. In his unfinished *chef d'œuvre*, the novelist Roger Martin du Gard summed up the negative response through the critical but humane eyes of his hero, de Maumort:

> His piercing, prying gaze . . . always made me extremly uneasy when it happened to rest on me. He had a tyrannical way of fixing you with his stare which gave me the shivers, as if the mere scientific whim of this man [*caprice d'un clinicien*] could send me to spend the rest of my days in some padded cell in the Salpêtrière.[15]

Charcot catalogued his power in the *Iconographie photographique de la Salpêtrière* in which sexual allurement, demonic contortions, and convulsive attacks were all caught by the probing eye of the camera. The photographs encapsulate the daring ambiguity of a clinical method which sought to be both scientifically irreproachable and artistically compelling. Although the *Iconographie* included records of a variety of patients and their ailments, it gave pride of place to hysterics. As Didi-Huberman has suggested in his brilliant study, Charcot sought to intensify the objectivity and heighten the vivisectional quality of his research by using photography, a seeming mirror-image of nature. Neither a painting nor a drawing, the photograph was more like a microscope, emphasizing and capturing the

[13] Didi-Huberman, *Invention de l'hystérie*, 236, quoting Léon Daudet.

[14] J.-F.-F. Babinski, 'La Définition de l'hystérie', in *Œuvre scientifique, recueil des principaux travaux* (Paris, 1934), 457–64. For other papers in this volume which reinterpret hysteria see 'Ma conception de l'hystérie et de l'hypnotisme', ibid., 465–85 and 'Démembrement de l'hystérie traditionnelle, pithiatisme', ibid., 486–504.

[15] Roger Martin du Gard, *Le Lieutenant-colonel de Maumort*, ed., André Daspre (Paris, 1983), 396–7.

pathological reality, ostensibly without the prejudice of artistic licence.

None the less, like any posed representation, the photographic record provided a remarkable outlet for artistic imagination. Favourite subjects like the youthful and beautiful Augustine were the subjects of tender, even loving portraiture. 'Luckier' than other inmates, she was capable of captivating the attention of the physicians through alluring poses and coquettish positions. These excesses were an integral aspect of her malady but were also the source of her fascination for the physicians who studied her. On the one hand, she was the perfect subject, gratifying scientific curiosity by providing a dramatic vision of the hysterical type; on the other, she was a seductress, exhibiting an explicitly sensual femininity. As Bourneville and Régnard, associates of Charcot, wrote of her charms, Augustine

> is blonde, tall, and strong for her age, appearing quite like any pubescent girl. She is lively, intelligent, affectionate, impressionable, but capricious, loving to be the centre of attention. She is coquettish, pays a great deal of attention to her *toilette*, arranging her thick hair sometimes one way, sometimes another; ribbons, especially brightly coloured ones, are her joy.[16]

> [she is] tall, well developed (with a neck which is a little too thick, voluminous breasts, hairy armpits and pubic region), determined in speech and manner, moody, noisy.[17]

The nature of the psychological bond uniting doctor and subject can be seen from other pictures. Scantily clad, Augustine presents a hysterical contracture in which her contorted arm and leg beckon alluringly. In attacks of *grande hystérie*, her *attitudes passionnelles* present particularly striking positions of *supplication amoureuse* in which her uplifted arms reach out to the attending physician. Other images show her in a state of *érotisme* and finally of *extase* in which the representation of hysterical pathology, sexual orgasm, and religious exaltation are unmistakably interwoven.

Such dramatic representations of women were not confined

16 Désiré-Magloire Bourneville and Paul Régnard, *Iconographie Photographique de la Salpêtrière*, vol. ii (1878), 127–8.

17 Ibid., 125.

to photographs. The theatricality of Charcot's work was emphasized above all by his Tuesday clinical lectures, during which the madwomen's tales of woe, twisted bodies, and extravagant seizures were presented to the bourgeois public. Bouillaud's famous painting of the public presentations show his dramatic method in operation. Speaking to a male audience, Charcot is in the midst of his demonstration with assistants anticipating the inevitable seizure of the woman beside them. Such patients were the great actresses of the medical mise en scène, there to act on cue and demonstrate the validity of his clinical deductions. In the lesson of 7 February 1888, for example, Charcot presented a patient to demonstrate the stages of *grande hystérie*, announcing at the outset that 'this patient will serve to demonstrate what I propose',[18] a conviction of success that was realized when an '*interne* touched the hysterogenous zone situated under the left breast'.[19] After these preliminaries, the attack convincingly began with Charcot commenting on its progress.

Charcot enjoyed a lengthy dominion over the medical community, despite a representation of hysteria which, even by the scientific standards of the day, was far from sober. His early successes in the 1880s were undoubtedly due to his impeccable credentials, which seemed to make him the perfect candidate for clarifying the murky world he probed. His neurological career began with investigations into paralyses, epilepsy, muscular atrophies, aphasias, rheumatism, and spinal affections, areas in which he intended to establish rigorous clinical types exemplifying the inception and development of specific disease processes.[20] When he came to hysteria, he sought to apply the same approach to differentiate it from epilepsy, demonstrate its functional quality, and lay out the guidelines for its evolution.

However, hysteria was less conducive than other ailments to this kind of clinical evaluation since the disorder contained

[18] *Lecons du mardi à la Salpêtrière, Professeur Charcot Policlinique, 1887–1888*, Notes de cours de MM. Blin, Charcot, and Colin (Paris, 1887), 174.

[19] Ibid., 175.

[20] See Charcot's *Œuvres complètes* for the variety of clinical studies undertaken, for example, vol. vii, *Maladies des vieillards, goutte et rhumatisme* (Paris, 1890); vol. iv, *Leçons sur les localisations dans les maladies du cerveau et de la moëlle épinière* (Paris, 1893); and vol. ii, *Leçons sur les maladies du système nerveux* (Paris, 1894).

within it an inescapable paradox which obscured Charcot's clarity of vision from the outset. On the one hand, he conclusively demonstrated that hysterical symptoms were not 'real' in the sense that no organic *siège* could be located to account for them, despite his identification of hysterogenous zones which suggested quite the contrary. On the other, he showed that hysterics were neither malingerers nor simulators, thereby confirming that a 'real' disease *was* in evidence. However, what he did not consider or take into account was the possibility that he himself was unwittingly orchestrating the malady through his suggestive power, commanding its reproduction—quite literally in the photographs and presentations—in the quest for an essential typology. The *metteur en scène* relied upon the dramatic ability of his actresses to sustain his scientific reputation and was therefore dependent on them to verify his findings, a position which left him open to their imaginative manipulation.

The case of *grande hystérie* dramatically illustrates the cycle of reproduction in operation,[21] with a few famous patients duplicating, with minor variations, the law-like course of four stages. Prior to the attack, the subject was afflicted by an *aura hysterica* in which feelings of suffocation, vomiting, and hypersensibility were in evidence. This was succeeded by the true first stage of tonic rigidity which resembled the beginnings of an epileptic fit, with horrible grimaces distorting the face and dramatic movements convulsing the body. In the second period of *grands mouvements*, the subject exploded into a series of gymnastic contortions. As Charles Richer explained: 'It is the period of the *tour de forces* . . .; and it is not without reason that M. Charcot has given it the picturesque name of *clownisme*, calling to mind the muscular feats performed by acrobats.'[22] This was succeeded by *attitudes passionnelles* or *poses plastiques* in which the hysteric expressed a private hallucinatory world, showing successively love, anger, exaltation, gaiety, fear, or sadness. Finally, the attack nearly over, the hysteric often lapsed into a melancholic delirium lamenting her past, recalling unpleasant experiences and expressing mournful emotions.

[21] Paul Richer, *Études cliniques sur l'hystéro-épilepsie ou grande hystérie* (Paris, 1881), 1–146.

[22] Ibid., 73.

The *grandes hystériques* also sometimes gave demonstrations of the neurosis of *grand hypnotisme*, which Charcot likewise intended to subject to proper scientific investigation. Associated with the excesses of Mesmer and rejected by the *Académie de médecine* as a proper sphere for scientific investigation, the history of hypnosis in France was a long and troubled tale of false starts, supposed mysticism, and purported charlatanry.[23] So concerned was Charcot to rehabilitate hypnotism that his disciples compared magnetism to alchemy and hypnotism to chemistry, pointedly drawing out the contrast in method and approach. There were specific methodological reasons for the strong attraction to the subject. His clinical reports were peppered not only with general admonishments to investigate the supposedly dark and mysterious with the light and clarity of science, but also more specific directives to bring clinical observations closer to experimental medicine.

Like his entire generation, Charcot was profoundly influenced and impressed by the Bernardian approach, with hypnotism providing an important opening for experimentation on living subjects.[24] Much of clinical medicine was based on classical techniques of pathological anatomy. In the hospital wards, doctors recorded and observed disease symptoms of the living and then posthumously, and only imprecisely, correlated them to the pathological traces discovered during autopsy. Hypnotism, however, was not hampered by the same difficulties and provided a rare opportunity for what was called psycho-physiological vivisection.

For Charcot and his disciples, *grand hypnotisme* manifested itself in three states—catalepsy, lethargy, and somnambulism. A subject in catalepsy could defy the normal laws of physiology for long periods. While in lethargy, the hysteric's muscles could be mechanically stimulated (neuro-muscular hyperexcitability) with an electric prod to provoke striking contractures.[25] A state of provoked somnambulism produced other,

[23] For the view of the Salpêtrière on the 'prehistory' of hypnotism see Georges Gilles de la Tourette, *L'Hypnotisme et les états analogues* (Paris, 1887), chaps. 1 and 2.

[24] For a most convincing demonstration of this orientation see Didi-Huberman, *Invention de l'hystérie*, in particular, 179–230.

[25] Charcot, 'Études physiologiques sur l'hypnotisme chez les hystériques', in *Œuvres complètes*, iii. 306.

extraordinary physiological reactions such as increased olfaction as well as heightened vision and sensation. Pinching, hitting, probing with metal objects, none of these disturbed the hypnotic tranquillity of highly suggestible subjects who were anaesthesized against pain and unaware of the experimental violence perpetrated on them. The possibility of performing such acts opened up the prospect of experimentation both to discover the bases of hypnotism itself and to use hypnotism as a tool for wider investigation. For example, the neurophysiologist Duchenne de Boulogne conducted pioneering studies on facial muscles and their relationship to emotional expression, using electrodes to evoke grimaces, smiles, and pouts.[26]

Nor did Charcot and his associates try to conceal the parallels they saw between experimental animals and the women under their care. Richet, for example, compared Charcot's inducement of hypnotic sleep with the use of a bright object in an experiment on a chicken. The latter was placed before a Drummond lamp and 'there soon occurred a state that resembled catalepsy'.[27] Similarly, during a clinical lecture in which he hoped to induce an attack of *grande hystérie*, Charcot momentarily acknowledged the possibility of failure due to the lack of co-operation on the part of the subject. Comparing his demonstration to animal vivisection, he maintained that:

> organic processes are not as precise as mechanical ones and I should not be surprised were our experiment not to succeed. It is sometimes said that experiments on animals are not as successful when performed in public as in the laboratory, which is true in this case . . .[28]

Perhaps even more striking than these explicitly physiological experiments was the demonstration of command and control exemplified in provoked somnambulism. In this state, subjects seemed like human marionettes, dancing to the strings of the operator. Necessarily, therefore, the somnambulic

26 'Contribution à l'étude de l'hypnotisme chez les hystériques: du phénomène de l'hyperexcitabilité neuro-musculaire', ibid., in particular, 359–77.

27 'Catalepsie et somnambulisme hystériques provoqués', ibid., 261–2.

28 *Leçons du mardi à la Salpêtrière*, 174.

state became an important aspect of medico-legal debate, as it was in this instance that subjects obeyed commands upon waking without any subsequent memory of them. It was an important, though subtle, aspect of the medico-legal position upheld by Charcot's disciple, Gilles de la Tourette, that a somnambulic subject was indeed an automaton, but was none the less an *automate conscient*. By this qualification he meant that subjects would defy suggestions which went against their inner nature or *moi*, an argument which was to be employed to pronounce responsible those women of perceived bad character whose hypnotic behaviour resembled too well their normal daily activities.

However, the assertion that somehow a unitary *moi* continued to subsist despite the psychic fragmentation induced by hypnosis was contradicted by Charcot's own account of his virtually limitless manipulative powers. While acknowledging that his commands were conducted under experimental condition, he none the less revelled in the 'photographic' (his word) duplication of his will in the brains of his subjects. Talking to the journalists of the *Petit Parisien* and *L'Echo de Paris*, he proudly remarked:

> I have observed some very curious facts about [the workings] of suggestion during . . . *grand hypnotisme*. I have at my clinic particularly sensitive patients who have provided the material for some extremely interesting experiments . . . In effect, once plunged into sleep, the brain of the subject may be considered absolutely blank and incapable of any will of its own. The hypnotist can then . . . imprint on it sensations and pictures as well as generating the will to perform any act. These sensations, pictures, and this will are photographically reproduced . . . without modifications.
>
> For example, if I show a hypnotized subject an imaginary snake or lion on the completely empty floor, the subject will immediately display all the signs of terror; but if I tell her the next instant that it is a humming bird, she will admire and caress it.[29]

These repeated demonstrations of the pathological quality of

[29] A. Pressat, 'Hypnotisme et la presse', *Revue de l'hypnotisme*, 3 (1889–90), 227. In this quotation Charcot used the French word '*le sujet*' to describe the patient, hence employing a masculine form to describe the *grandes hypnotiques*. The French therefore gives a misleading impression, as these experimental subjects were always women. Indeed, a sketch of the experiment shows Charcot demonstrating the humming bird to a female patient.

the women under Charcot's command posed several inescapable professional dilemmas which appeared in veiled and often transmuted form during the medico-legal debates. It may be suggested that the physicians' relationship to the hysterics, particularly during hypnotic experimentation, was fraught with moral and sexual ambiguities which threatened to compromise their integrity. Even by contemporary standards, the theatrical lectures, photographic record, and public experiments raised important ethical issues, stretching to the limit the interpretation of physicians' obligations to patients as dictated by the *secret médical*.

Paul Brouardel was the expert on professional confidence. He wrote learnedly on the ethical attitude to be taken by physicians in guarding the secrets of illness—particularly of venereal disease and hereditary taints—when questions of, for example, prospective marriage contracts or life-insurance premiums were at issue. Clearly, these were areas which required the strictest confidence, as the good name or economic status of middle-class clientele was at stake. However, Brouardel also gave some attention to the issue of hospital admissions where often the inmates' poverty meant they could neither choose their physician nor prevent publications on their illnesses. He none the less maintained that even these people, who depended on the 'hospitality' of the hospital, were entitled to discretion even though there was no exchange of money to seal the contract. All efforts, he maintained, should be made to mask the identity of the subject, even in medical journals.[30]

This, however, was an injunction which Charcot largely ignored. Although initials rather than proper names were used in some of the books, the photographs make no attempt to hide the identity of the subjects. Indeed, the most famous of Charcot's patients became minor celebrities in their own right.[31] Rather than masking the details of hereditary taint and

30 Brouardel, *Le Secret médical* (Paris, 1887), in particular, 114–15.

31 There was a small group of famous hysterics, young women like Augustine discussed above, and others such as Blanche Wittman, whose personal history has attracted some attention. See, for example, Henri F. Ellenberger, *The Discovery of the Unconscious: The History and Evolution of Dynamic Psychiatry* (New York, 1970), 98–9. Mary James investigates in some detail the *grandes hystériques* at the Salpêtrière; see her 'Therapeutic Practices of J.-M. Charcot in their Historical and Social Context' (forthcoming Ph.D. thesis, Univ. of Essex).

personal background, such information was solicited in public and readily provided by the patient. Moreover, women were often photographed naked or only partially clothed and, as already suggested, attracted the camera lens with positions either of sexual allurement or grotesque contortion. The actual and implicit violence of his clinical vision, in which the woes of madwomen were used to regale a curious bourgeois public and further Charcot's scientific and social reputation, may be said to have violated the canons of medical professionalism and the contractual arrangement of confidence that was meant to exist. His work was deemed by some to be an *œuvre de scandale*. Once again, Martin du Gard summed up this attitude when he remarked:

> There was not a glimmer of human pity in that bright and satisfied eye as he paraded smugly—and, in my opinion, with culpable indiscretion and total lack of professional confidence—the mental torments of his clients, not omitting their names, ages, and professions (out of a scientific habit of precision, no doubt). I was horrified at times to hear him smilingly describe a violent and well-defined attack of insanity, which he ingenuously admitted to having knowingly provoked the previous day in order to verify before his pupils the validity of a diagnosis . . .[32]

Charcot's clinical method was the backdrop for the wider medico-legal debate, shading the content of the specific arguments and anxieties presented in it. The drama conducted at the Salpêtrière contributed, perhaps more than anything else, to the generalized fear that hypnotic manipulation induced individuals, and particularly women, to break contracts. Indeed, one of the major concerns voiced by all commentators on the possible abuse of hypnotic manipulation in either immoral or unprofessional hands was that women would be forced to yield up intimate and secret details of their lives, contravene marriage vows, sign over property, and commit crimes, all actions which they had been *encouraged* to perform during experiments conducted at the Salpêtrière.

[32] Martin du Gard, *Le Lieutenant-colonel de Maumort*, 397. Nor was Charcot the only clinician to be attacked for this indiscretion. In 1908 Professor Bouchard recalled the controversy surrounding Magnan's clinical lectures which subjected 'unfortunate lunatics to the frivolous curiosity of students'. Although his lectures were not forbidden, Magnan was obliged to defend himself from these attacks. See the 'Discours' by Professeur Bouchard, in *Jubilé du Docteur Magnan*.

For example, the famous hysteric Blanche W . . . was instructed by Gilles de la Tourette 'to poison' the director of the Théâtre français, Jules Claretie. He informed Blanche that Claretie had murdered René, an *interne* on the ward and obviously a physician whom Blanche revered. Gilles supplied her with a glass of poison and she in turn 'smiled, seeming to forget what she had been told; then slowly, with a charming good grace and an adorably perfidious feminine smile, the poor unconscious woman offered me the glass she believed to be poisoned.' Having drunk from the cup, Claretie was instructed by another physician to feign illness, and promptly cried out in pain. Blanche was accused of the deed and, now terrified, sought to defend herself. As Claretie reported:

> I was watching her through a crack in the door when, with an unforgettable expression of fear, she screamed, repeatedly jabbering in terror, with a bewildered eloquence that even a Sarah Bernhardt could scarcely have matched: 'Ah! it wasn't me! . . . You seem to be accusing me . . ! It wasn't me! . . .,' all the while like a terrified culprit struggling before the investigating magistrate.
>
> Don't tell me this scene was an act. I had proof of the absolute sincerity of the things I observed.[33]

Gilles' experiment dramatically demonstrated that women were susceptible to evil suggestions and, as the official medico-legal spokesmen of Charcot's school, he sought to specify the conditions under which such actions could be perpetrated beyond the walls of the Salpêtrière.[34] What is remarkable about his discussion is the way he and everyone else shied away from the deterministic implications of their hospital practice, maintaining that evil suggestions in the experimental sphere would not necessarily be duplicated in daily life, a position which brought him into sharp confrontation with his opponents at Nancy.

The Medico-legal Debate: The Salpêtrière v. Nancy

Despite his secure position in Paris, where few dared to challenge him, from the 1880s onwards Charcot was audaciously

33 Jules Liégeois, quoting Jules Claretie's article of 11 July 1884, *Le Temps*, in *De la suggestion et du somnambulisme dans leurs rapports avec la jurisprudence* (Paris, 1889), 215.

34 See Gilles de la Tourette, *L'Hypnotisme et les états analogues*, passim.

criticized by the *École de Nancy* under Hippolyte Bernheim, who advanced a view of hypnotism which differed from Charcot's on several key points. Bernheim's attack was supported by a loosely-knit group of sympathizers,[35] men like Ambroise Liébault, a local practitioner-philanthropist; Henri-Étienne Beaunis, a physiologist and forensic expert; and the pugnacious and highly visible professor of administrative law at Nancy, Jules Liégeois, who developed an extended jurisprudential discussion of suggestion and its effects.

The controversy revolved around three intermingling concerns. It began by concentrating on opposing views of the physiological and psychological nature of hypnosis, moved into medical therapeutics, and culminated with differing views on the medico-legal implications. During each debate over a particular medico-legal issue all the diverging levels of discussion would automatically come into play, with the boundaries between medicine and morality, sexual anxiety and concerns over moral responsibility often impossible to determine. The first strand of discussion contrasted ostensibly opposing philosophical perspectives on the mind-body relation which in turn reflected differing interpretations of hypnosis. In early 1891, for example, the philosopher Alfred Fouillé sought to analyse the differences between the two schools for educated laymen in the *Revue des deux mondes*.

From the point of view of philosophical trends, the rivalry between the Paris and Nancy Schools is only an application to a particular case of the great problem concerning the physical and the mental. The Paris school only considers the phenomena of consciousness as indicators of organic movements, without their own action. 'An idea', says M. Binet, for example, 'is nothing but an *appearance*, and behind it hides the energy developed by a previous physical excitation' . . . The Nancy school, on the other hand, attaches much more importance to the mental; it has even contributed to demonstrating the action of ideas in hypnotism, and by extension, in the phenomena of normal life.[36]

The debate was often presented as a struggle between the rival tenets of epiphenomenalism and ideodynamism. The

[35] See Ellenberger, *The Discovery of the Unconscious*, 85–9.

[36] A. Fouillé, 'Le Physique et le mental à propos de l'hypnotisme', *Revue des deux mondes*, 105 (1891), 437.

former represented the 'physicalist' tradition in mental medicine, which opposed metaphysical interpretations of psychic life and grounded its explanations in the neurological, physiological, and evolutionary processes seen to underpin higher mental development. As a challenge to this view of mental disturbance arising from organic and neurological malfunctions, the work of Bernheim and his associates concentrated on the role of *ideas*, on mental suggestions, in transforming physical states. It was not that they rejected the 'physicalist' tradition, as they too cited the importance of, for example, hereditary degeneration in making some subjects more susceptible to nefarious suggestions. However, they sought to emphasize what Bernheim termed 'ideodynamism' primarily because of the optimistic results they were achieving with hypnotherapy. With constant references to his clinical successes in alleviating a variety of painful conditions, Bernheim increasingly came to emphasize the impact of the mental on the physical, rather than the other way round. Far from consisting merely of interpretative differences, therefore, Bernheim's ideas and therapeutic programme constituted a fundamental challenge, promoting a reorientation of psychological analysis and a revision of views of mental processes.

Differing clinical orientations and a divergent perspective on the relationship between morbid and normal mental states played a decisive role in splitting apart the major antagonists. In Charcot's view, hypnotism was indissolubly linked to pathology and was classified as a symptom of hysteria. Such a perspective was undoubtedly partly fostered by the wealth of pathological cases available for study at the Salpêtrière. However, it also represented a more deep-rooted attitude on the nature of mental activity. It is not surprising that Théodule Ribot's work on the maladies of volition, memory, and emotion, discussed earlier, emanated from clinical studies on hysteria carried out at the Salpêtrière. Its inmates seemed to epitomize the validity of his developmental and epiphenominalist perspective which concentrated on the fragility of the higher moral and intellectual faculties and the tendency of the insane to cumulative functional disequilibrium. Quoting the work of Charles Richer, Ribot described the hysterics and their peculiarly mercurial personalities, how 'their characters change like the views of a kaleidoscope'.[37] They seemed to lack the crucial inhibitory mechanism necessary to subordinate emotional excess, sensual urges, and instinctual drives, demonstrating a characteristic mercuriality and lubricity which defined their illness. Hysteria thus provided Ribot with a perfect opportunity to observe the psychophysiological 'dissolution' of the human personality.

For Charcot and his associates, hypnotism reinforced the validity of this general view. A pathological condition similar to a dream, the hypnotic state produced hallucinations and released memories and emotions which the stable, healthy individual could control. Mental images or 'ideas' were certainly useful in understanding the workings of suggestions but they played a subordinate role in the doctors' broader neurophysiological view of human consciousness. For example, in analysing traumatic paralyses, Charcot readily acknowledged that these were the result of ideas 'blocking' normal motor functioning.[38] Despite this seeming similarity to Bernheim's stance, however, Charcot's position none the less contained a fundamental distinction. As Binet and Féré explained in *Le Magnétisme animal* (1887):

> All suggestion consists essentially in acting on a person by means of an *idea*; each suggested effect results from a phenomenon of association of ideas [*phénomène d'idéation*], but it must be added at once that the idea is only an epiphenomenon; taken on its own it is only the superficial sign [*signe indicateur*] of a certain physiological process which alone is capable of producing the material effect.[39]

They went on to explain further by contrasting paralysis 'by physical vibration' with one which was induced by suggestion. Both, in their view, were the result of modifications 'produced in the cortical substance of the brain'. The proper focus of scientific investigation was therefore the 'cerebral reflexes' responsible for determining these different states, not the secondary, although still important, psychological interaction between the subject and the operator.[40]

37 T. Ribot, *Les Maladies de la volonté*, 2nd edn. (Paris, 1884), 113.
38 Charcot, *Œuvres complètes*, iii. 335–7.
39 Alfred Binet and Charles Féré, *Le Magnétisme animal* (Paris, 1887), 128.
40 Ibid. 129.

The emphasis on the physiological aspects of *grande hystérie* and *grand hypnotisme*—neuro-muscular hyperexcitability, cutaneous anaesthesia, the retraction of the visual field, etc.—demonstrates the desire of the Salpêtrière school to subject the disorder to an epiphenomenalist interpretation. In defining hysteria in this fashion, they were following general psychiatric practice, which began with a description of hereditary and neurophysiological defects, but then continued to discuss moral failings and character traits. With hysteria, however, the disjunction between the rhetoric and practice of 'epiphenomenalist' psychiatry was all the more striking because of the obsessive interest the doctors showed in the psychological manifestations of the disease. Charcot may have intended to provide an exacting 'physical' portrait in which physiological stigmata and ultimately disordered cerebral reflexes were unveiled. However, what he contributed was a remarkably dramatic portrayal of female *psychology* in its most pathological form, with a morbid need for attention, foul language, deceit, excessive coquettishness, lying, exaltation, and despondency manifesting themselves in an inexorable and despairing fashion.

By emphasizing the pathological so heavily, this epiphenomenalist orientation negatively coloured the doctors' view of hypnotism's therapeutic value. Because they argued that susceptibility to hypnotism was nothing more than a symptom of illness, Charcot and his associates maintained that it could have only limited effect on a few hysterics, a position which heightened their struggle with the *École de Nancy*. The number of hypnotizable individuals that theatrical demonstrations revealed simply indicated that a high proportion of the population were in fact latent hysterics whose diseased proclivities would be aroused by the widespread use of the technique. The physicians at the Salpêtrière, therefore, saw hypnotism as a dangerous weapon which would incite insanity in people with latent, degenerate susceptibilities, unleashing automatic urges and bestial tendencies that were better kept dormant.

Using this general interpretation, Gilles de la Tourette developed his medico-legal doctrine on hypnosis, demonstrating how the three different stages of *grand hypnotisme* introduced different medico-legal possibilities. For example, the insensibility and rigidity of the cataleptic state made it virtually impossible to perpetrate a criminal action on the subject. Its prolongation would induce a generalized contracture or hysterical fit which would prevent, for example, a rapist from consummating his offence. This was not the case, however, during the lethargic state in which the subject was like 'a corpse before the onset of *rigor mortis*',[41] with a muscular tonicity that invited sexual violation. It was this state that was considered to be the most dangerous for unsuspecting women. The final state of provoked somnambulism, however, had the most important implications. It was in this instance that the subject seemed to obey all the commands of the magnetizer and could execute acts upon waking without any conscious awareness or subsequent memory of them. Nevertheless, despite the striking display of automatism that the subject demonstrated while in a somnambulic trance, the Paris School asserted that deep inside this human marionette a consciousness of 'self' continued to subsist, so that a truly pure hypnotic subject would fail to execute commands that were repugnant to his or her inner nature.

Hypnosis, therefore, could only induce passive acquiescence in crime in the form of rape, not active participation. The reasoning behind this stance was that a simple abolition of female free will could allow sexual violation—an area in which women's control was explicitly represented as being frighteningly unreliable anyway—without any need for the transfer of another's will.[42] The Paris School insisted that to reach any other conclusion led to the medico-legal absurdity of destroying the possibility of punishing any crimes at all by making all offences the result of hypnotic suggestion.

Charcot and his disciples found themselves, therefore, in the rather ironic role of affirming with vehemence the existence of individual liberty and moral choice. This position was completely at odds not only with the performances of the *grandes hypnotiques* —such as Claretie's would-be poisoner, Blanche W . . . , who slavishly obeyed the physician's commands at the expense of her dignity—but also with their scientific ethos that was

[41] Gilles de la Tourette, *L'Hypnotisme et les états analogues*, 91.
[42] Ibid. 321–82.

based almost exclusively on determinist neurophysiological theories and hereditarian ideas. Indeed, the rejection of their own experimental findings on the reality of human automatism under hypnotic influence suggests an indirect acknowledgement of the interplay between power and illusion which constituted the foundation of their clinical experiments. Moreover, it underscores the extreme ambivalence which characterized the attitude of the Salpêtrière when hypnosis was used as a defence in criminal trials.

Charcot's entire system was attacked by Bernheim and the *École de Nancy* after 1882, when the provincial investigators developed their own interpretation of hypnosis. Like most physicians, Bernheim first became acquainted with hypnosis through Charcot's work. Initially, the latter's doctrine, as he wrote in 1906, 'was for me, as for all doctors, a dogma shored up by the authority of a great man'[43] whose value he had not sought to question. Bernheim himself emerged out of a clinical tradition in which mental disorder played an insignificant role. An *agrégé* at the Strasbourg Faculty of Medicine, he moved to Nancy after the Franco-Prussian War when the city replaced the Alsatian capital as a French centre of medical teaching and research. As a general clinician who had done research into pneumonia, typhoid, rheumatism, and heart disease, Bernheim was primarily concerned with medical therapeutics and was acquainted with nervous diseases only through his wide-ranging practice.[44]

His personal interest in hypnotic therapy began when one of his own patients whom he had released from the hospital with an uncured sciatica was successfully treated by a philanthropist–practitioner named Ambroise Liébault, who had been using hypnosis on his impoverished clientele with neither fees nor medical recognition for at least twenty years. After attending some of Liébault's sessions, Bernheim became convinced that this healer, scorned by the medical establishment but who had written a book on his technique as early as 1866,[45] was in fact

[43] Hippolyte Bernheim, *Le Docteur Liébault et la doctrine de la suggestion*, conférence faite sous les auspices de la Société des Amis de l'Université de Nancy, 12 Dec. 1906, 1.

[44] See Pierre Kissel, 'L'École neuro-psychiatrique de Nancy: Le Professeur Bernheim', *Médecine de France*, 68 (1969), 11–13.

[45] Ambroise Liébault, *Du sommeil et des états analogues considérés surtout au point de vue de l'action du moral sur le physique* (Paris, 1866).

the true pioneer and scientific discoverer of hypnosis and its applications.

During the course of his career, Bernheim hypnotized thousands of patients, using the method to treat not only diverse nervous and psychic afflictions, but also conditions such as rheumatism, ulcers, incontinence, neuralgias, and menstrual cramps.[46] Starting from this practical appreciation of hypnotism's therapeutic potential, which was sometimes imbued with an evangelical ardour, the *École de Nancy* developed a theoretical perspective which differed completely from that of Charcot. Rather than seeing hypnotism as necessarily linked to hysteria, they viewed it as a universal and powerful therapeutic tool, and for this reason wished to popularize rather than limit its usage.

Hysteria was in fact perceived as having no bearing on the issue whatsoever, and consequently Bernheim accused Charcot and his followers of having greatly exaggerated the number of hysterics in order to account for the frequency of hypnotic suggestibility. Not only did he maintain that the Salpêtrière had thereby created a completely fictitious hysterical epidemic, he also asserted that the four-stage syndrome of *grande hystérie* was a chimera as well, for nowhere else in France or abroad was it reproduced. Bernheim deduced that its existence in Charcot's hospital was to be attributed to a mutual suggestibility between hypnotizer and hypnotized, rather than to the almost invariable pathological formula that followed the clear-cut lines laid out so dramatically by the *maître*. In sum, he vociferously maintained that Charcot's disease was *une hystérie de culture*, produced by the physician's awesome powers of suggestion on his patients and his self-deluded willingness to be duped by his own authority and doctrine. To underscore this more concretely, Bernheim deployed his own dramatic skills and demonstrated that under hypnosis he could duplicate the same hysterical symptoms in his own subjects.[47]

To counter Charcot's propositions Bernheim developed the

[46] Bernheim, *De la suggestion et ses applications à la thérapeutique*, 2nd ed. (Paris, 1888), 271–568.

[47] Id., *Hypnotisme, suggestion et psychothérapie* (Paris, 1891). For his specific remarks on the illusory nature of Charcot's hysteria and the three stages of hypnotism see pp. 167 and 169.

notion of ideodynamism. He maintained that suggestions administered by the hypnotizer 'activated the brain', causing changes in the organic state of the subject if the disorder was somatic, or provoking a gradual transformation in the emotional state which set off, for example, a hysterical contracture. The state of automatism induced by hypnosis therefore allowed the subject to unleash concentrated energy from the brain, 'to concentrate this force on the organs of animal and vegetable life, to sharpen the senses and faculties, to modify the tissues'.[48] This emphasis on the power of the mental apparatus to transform physical states was in clear contrast to the epiphenomenalist perspective which viewed the mind's faculties as pathologically diminished rather than as heightened and energized during hypnosis.

For the Nancians, the universality of this conception of the power of ideas was such that there was no logical or clinical reason why only the hysteric should be susceptible to it. Consequently, they maintained that anyone could be hypnotized, although certain subjects—for example, soldiers accustomed to the rigours of military discipline or the more docile of the lower orders—were perhaps better suited than others.[49] Accordingly, they concluded that hypnosis was not a neurosis linked to hysteria, but an artificially induced state of sleep. During hypnosis, however, there existed a rapport based on suggestibility between the subject and the hypnotizer which enhanced the patient's receptivity to external ideas. These psychological observations were extended in Bernheim's pamphlet, *De la suggestion dans l'état hypnotique et dans l'état de veille* (1884), a work which put forward the audacious view that a hypnotic state was itself not necessary to procure the effects of suggestion. Later, as his experience with psychotherapeutics grew, Bernheim relied increasingly on this procedure, since unlike hypnosis it sought to involve the conscious side of the patient's personality in order to procure more effective and long-lasting results. If such unconventional procedures increased the wrath of the Salpêtrière School in the 1880s, they were none the less a crucial contribution in developing

[48] Id., *Le docteur Liébault*, 12.
[49] Id., *De la suggestion dans l'état hypnotique et dans l'état de veille* (Paris, 1884), 6.

psychoanalytical therapy, of which Freud was to be the most famous exponent.

In Bernheim's analysis, therefore, mental suggestion held out enormous humanitarian possibilities for the alleviation of pain and stood in sharp contrast to the continuing therapeutic pessimism which characterized Charcot's approach. But despite the optimism which characterized his work, he none the less conceded the possibility that hypnosis and unconscious suggestion could be dangerously abused—to express urges of self-destruction, execute evil designs, and jeopardize moral integrity.

He eloquently expressed this anxiety in his description of the case of Tisza-Eszlár, a Hungarian village where Jews were accused in the 1880s of the ritual slaughter of a fourteen-year-old Christian virgin to use her blood for baking unleavened bread for Passover. Although the mother could not identify a body dragged from the river as her child, charges were none the less brought against thirteen Jews. The key witness was a thirteen-year-old named Moritz, the son of the synagogue's sacristan. After a few hours of interrogation by the police, Moritz said it had been his own father who had entrapped the girl in the synagogue where she was slaughtered and her blood collected 'in two dishes'.[50]

Bernheim was keen to find some explanation for the child's persistence, and was perhaps particularly intrigued because of his own Jewish origins. He was convinced that Moritz was not naturally depraved or deceitful; rather he persisted in his statements because of the overpowering suggestible influence of the police commissioner who convinced him of his people's sinister activities. In sum, the child ultimately accepted the interrogator's belief in Jewish guilt and in all good faith reiterated his father's culpability to the court. As Bernheim explained:

> The child is brought before the investigating magistrate. Humble, depressed, from an impoverished background, he trembles before the imposing figure who represents Force and Justice . . . The words of the worthy official make a deep impression on his untrained mind. . . . Under the power of this strong suggestive influence, the hypnotized

[50] Bernheim, *De la suggestion et ses applications*, 237.

> brain meticulously constructs the scene evoked by the police officer. He has seen it all—the victim prostrate, . . . the person performing the sacrifice plunging his knife in her throat, the blood pouring out. . . . The retroactive hallucination has been created . . . and the memory of the imaginary vision is so vivid that he cannot forget it.[51]

This example of 'false testimony' was significant for Bernheim because of the way in which it illustrated the interaction between individual and social psychology, between the culture of anti-semitism and the internalization of guilt and self-hatred. It was also interesting because it strikingly resembled the kind of experiments which his associate, Jules Liégeois, was practising to demonstrate the reality of criminal suggestion, hence forming the bases of the Nancy School's medico-legal system.

Of the four leading lights in the school, Liégeois was by far the most unconventional, his legal background and occupation as professor of administrative law at Nancy supplying him with no medical preparation for investigating hypnosis and its effects. His interest emerged from his conviction that the practice of hypnotism in unscrupulous hands threatened the bases of a society founded on freedom of contract, a notion resting on mutual and voluntary consent. Liégeois expounded most volubly on the extra-medical realm of hypnosis as early as 1884 when he presented a memoir on its medico-legal implications to the *Académie des sciences morales et politiques* before an audience of philosophers, publicists, social reformers, and medical men. In this statement, Liégeois demonstrated how hypnotism revealed the weak links of genteel society, exposing the chinks in the armour of moral and social absolutes. The cherished objects and ideas most susceptible to manipulation were propriety, property, and the family, with the third category emphasizing in particular what was perceived as the most vulnerable pillar of bourgeois life, sexual fidelity. Indeed, Liégeois maintained that the more extreme the reversal of normal behaviour, the greater the likelihood that hypnotic manipulation had taken place. As he explained: 'Ideas developed spontaneously or acquired through education,

51 Ibid., 238.

sentiments or propensities, sympathy or repulsion, love or hate, prejudices or passions: all of these can in a moment be modified, transposed, upset!'[52]

Under the influence of suggestion, women might contravene their marriage vows or sign over their inheritance to the undeserving, while individuals ran the risk of being punished for crimes they had committed unconsciously under the commands of an evil and rapacious experimenter. His fears were such that he wrote articles accusing hypnotism of imperilling 'national defence and civil society',[53] in which he demonstrated the tenuousness of bourgeois institutions and advocated defensive measures to combat the menace. He elaborated this doctrine replete with prophecies of doom perhaps because of his own extreme reaction to the Commune, on which he wrote earnest polemics demonstrating how socialism and the irrational destruction it produced had undermined and virtually destroyed 'the eternal principles on which societies rest: *Religion, Family, Property, Justice, Liberty*'.[54] The Commune and its revolutionary impulses demonstrated the danger facing society, and Liégeois was dedicated to uprooting these evil influences. In hypnotism and its medico-legal implications he found a perfect vehicle for bringing these views before the wider public.

Despite his sometimes loud and polemical declamations, Liégeois was not a marginal figure in the *École de Nancy* whom Bernheim tolerated out of personal loyalty. Although he did not always agree with the lawyer's tactics in presenting the Nancian case,[55] Bernheim was impressed by Liégeois's medico-legal conclusions and personally drawn to the investigation of judicial errors and their implications, as his examination of the Tisza-Eszlár case testifies. Moreover, it seems that he too was

[52] Jules Liégeois, 'De la suggestion hypnotique dans ses rapports avec le droit civil et le droit criminel', *Séances et travaux de l'académie des sciences morales et politiques*, 120 (1884), 220.

[53] Id., 'L'Hypnotisme, la défense nationale et la société', *Revue de l'hypnotisme*, 6 (1892), 298–304.

[54] Id., *Origines et théories économiques de l'association des travailleurs* (Nancy, 1872), 54.

[55] Unpublished manuscript cited through the permission of Mme Tridon, Nancy: *Les Souvenirs inédits de Henri-Étienne Beaunis*, 424–7. In this excerpt Beaunis explains Bernheim's dismay over Liégeois's tactics in the Bompard case, but never disputes the validity of his conclusions.

1. 'Le Monument élevé à la mémoire du Professeur Brouardel.'

The Third Republic was dedicated to the erection of statues commemorating its 'great men' and their achievements, particularly those of medical men who were lionized as exemplars of civic virtue. Paul Brouardel was so honoured in 1909 with the erection of a bust executed by the sculptor, Denys Puech, and still standing in the 'cour d'honneur' of the Faculty of Medicine. Paid for by subscriptions from his friends and students, the statue displays Brouardel in full academic regalia poised above two, female, allegorical figures, representing 'la Médecine Légale' and 'l'Hygiène,' one of which offers a sheaf of flowers towards the bust. At the ceremony of inauguration, Brouardel's many institutional and academic achievements were vaunted and his stature acknowledged by the presence of the Minister of Public Instruction.

2. 'Hystéro-épilepsie: contracture, *L'Iconographie photographique de la Salpêtrière*, vol. 2, (1878).

The classic photographics of the young hysterical woman, Augustine, illustrate the sexual interplay between the patient and Charcot and his associates. Here Augustine, half-clad and alluringly posed, demonstrates the hysterical contractures affecting her contorted arm and outstretched leg. No attempt is made to hide her identity or to veil her physicality; on the contrary, her sensuality is strongly and unmistakeably conveyed.

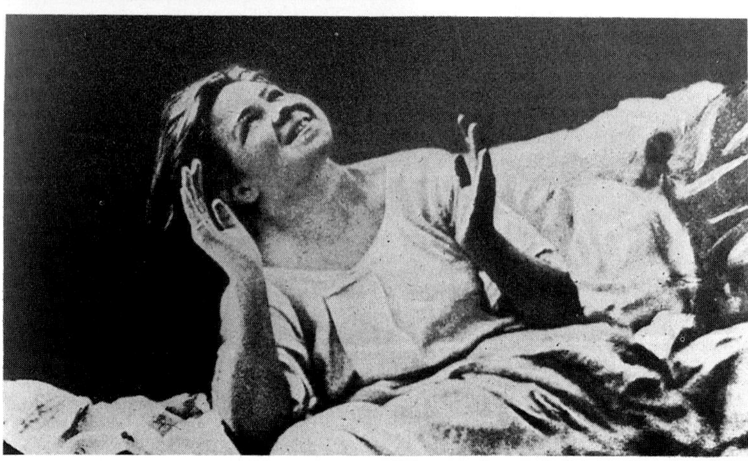

3. 'Attitudes Passionnelles: Extase. *L'Iconographie photographique de la Salpêtrière*, vol. 2 (1878).

The last phase of Charcot's *grande hystérie* was the *attitudes passionnelles* which in the case of Augustine is represented by the expression of ecstasy. In this photograph, Augustine's pose deftly resonates both with religious and physical pleasure, the word *extase* conveying meaningful ambiguity particular to Charcot's construction of the hysterical patient.

4. 'L'hypnotisme—les suggestions provoquées par le docteur Bernheim à Nancy (desseins de M. Vuillier, d'après des photographies) in *Le monde illustré*, 28 November 1885; 1. Elle sommeille les yeux ouverts.—2. Elle croit bercer un enfant—3. Elle est en extase ou en prière—4. Elle sommeille.—A. Il est gentil—B. Il croit voir un éléphant—C. Il croit grimper à un arbre.—D. Il rage.—Il a faim.

Bernheim was as keen as the physicians at the Salpêtrière to demonstrate the power of suggestion. The extremity of the emotion provoked can be seen in the following representations of the unconscious responses of a young woman and a boy, both deemed to be good subjects for experimental manipulation. The most striking aspect of the images is their dramatic, emotional intensity, each described and reinforced by written explanation.

5. 'L'Affaire Gouffé,' in *Le Petit journal, supplément illustré*, 20 December 1890. (detail)

When Gabrielle Bompard was accused of complicity in the murder of the Parisian bailiff, A.-T. Gouffé, the illustrated press had a field day. Throughout the weeks of the pre-trial investigation, much was made of her lover's account of the murder in which he claimed that Gabrielle Bompard entrapped the unsuspecting bailiff in her sexual snare, allowing Eyraud to hang him with the aid of a rope and pulley. It was precisely these sensationalist details (hotly denied by Bompard who claimed that Eyraud had strangled Gouffé with his bare hands) which increased public interest in the trial and ensured a wider audience for the more esoteric debate over hypnosis and its medico-legal implications.

6. 'Après l'acquittement,' *Paris illustré*, 1 November 1884

This detail of an illustrator's two-page representation of the moment after acquittal captures the melodramatic feeling surrounding the trial of a young, pretty and elegantly-dressed woman. She is shown here holding a handkerchief and looking winsomely over her shoulder at the commotion created by the verdict.

7. 'Assassinat de sa femme et de ses enfants Perrecy-les-Forges (Saône-et-Loire) in *Le Petit Parisien*, 1 October 1899.

The *Petit Parisien* provides a portrait of domestic horror in which a husband beat his victimized wife, with a stunned daughter at her feet and a terrified son quavering on the bed. The scissors ultimately used to slit the childrens' throats are displayed menacingly in the foreground. The protagonist, a tailor named Serry, is described as a man possessed by crises of jealous rage, which lead to the destruction of his family and his own suicide by hanging. In this illustration, as in many others, a picture of masculine brutality is heightened by the martyrization of innocent women and children. Despite the dismay provoked by this and other similar crimes, neighbours suggested that the only possible explanation for Serrey's deed was a 'coup de folie'.

8. 'Un Drame parisien. Le double suicide du faubourg Saint-Honoré,' *Le Petit Journal*, 7 July 1895

The illustrated weeklies revelled in crimes considered to be particularly 'Parisian' in inspiration and execution, that is, especially lurid and often involving personages of elevated social stature. In this instance of double suicide, an honourable lawyer, M. Carré, kills himself while his wife takes up the smoking pistol to murder herself in turn. An imputation of adultery is put forward to explain the husband's suicide, although the extremity of the deed and his wife's response suggest to the more suspicious that perhaps darker motives were at work.

9. 'Le Duel Déroulède-Clemenceau,' *Le Petit Journal*, 7 January 1893.

After an exchange of insults, in which the arch-patriot Paul Déroulède impugned Clemenceau's national feeling, a site was arranged and pistols chosen as a weapon. What is remarkable is that two elected deputies were publicly engaged in illegal activity, assisted by a massive crowd which the police did not disturb. Neither protagonist seriously aimed at the other and neither suffered legal repercussions. The illustration concentrates on the formality of the encounter, with the attending seconds watching in top hats, the pistol box opened at their feet. Indeed, the only indication of disarray among the participants is a discarded overcoat and a toppled hat.

deeply affected by the apparent threat unconscious suggestion posed for the liberal order, a feeling perhaps intensified by his own forced move to Nancy and the growth of vocal anti-semitism. Indeed, his accounts of suggestion in individual crimes are peppered with references to contemporary political and religious extremism and its dangers, a discussion which was particularly important for criminological debate. As he expressed it on one occasion:

> Nihilists, anarchists, socialists, revolutionaries—all kinds of political and religious fanatics—don't they become . . . criminals by the force of suggestion? On days of popular agitation, the crowd—composed of many decent folk each taken on his own—turns fierce and blood-thirsty on a poor inoffensive devil exposed to public condemnation by a spiteful denunciation. Does this not demonstrate the power of collective suggestion? An idea, a simple word—spy, traitor, exploiter of the people!—spreads through the crowd. Tempers flare! . . . The masses are blinded by passion. The beast is unleashed.[56]

Liégeois's medico-legal system was thus an integral rather than an incidental aspect of the Nancian approach and linked a therapeutic doctrine to a wider social philosophy. In accordance with Bernheim's view that all individuals were susceptible to hypnotic suggestion, Liégeois maintained that any criminal act, even murder, could be successfully induced in any individual hypnotized by someone with criminal aims. Necessarily, therefore, it was this doubly iniquitous evil-doer who should be held responsible for the crime, rather than his subject, who should be considered no more guilty than the pistol used by a murderer to shoot his victim.

So convinced was he of the validity of his system that he appeared as a witness in the case of Gabrielle Bompard. During a three-hour presentation, he argued that Eyraud had hypnotized her into an extended *état second* and had compelled her to act as his accomplice. It was during this state, he maintained, that she had been induced to rent the flat as well as buy the necessary accoutrements of clothing and accessories to facilitate Gouffé's murder. Not only did Liégeois supply this extended account of her mental state, he also provided a long-winded explanation of his own experiments and a

56 Bernheim, 'Les Suggestions criminelles', *Revue de l'hypnotisme*, 4 (1890), 265.

historical account of judicial error due to the prejudiced inability to consider the possibility of murder under hypnosis.[57]

Although his arguments were ridiculed by exponents of Charcot's doctrine such as Brouardel, Liégeois's performance none the less strikingly brought the Nancian view to public attention. During the trial, the opposing schools discussed the role of suggestion in human behaviour, both arguing for its omnipresent influence, but each drawing different conclusions about how best to manage the likes of Gabrielle Bompard. For Liégeois, who came to her defence, the role of suggestion greatly attenuated her moral responsibility.[58] For Charcot's associates, in contrast, it merely demonstrated the extent to which such vicious degenerates were the dangerous victims of their ill-formed psycho-biological natures and proved how important it was to eliminate them.

Despite these divergencies, however, all agreed that the notion of 'free will' used in judicial analysis was inadequate in accounting for the reality of unconscious suggestion, an attitude which was fundamental to the development of the criminological approach. Even after Liégeois's valiant efforts, the jury basically agreed with Brouardel, focused on Bompard's unsavoury character and past history, and awarded her a penalty of twenty years in prison. Although suffering considerable embarrassment by his flamboyant defence of a less-than-satisfactory person, Liégeois none the less steadfastly clung to his views. Indeed, he hypnotized Bompard on her early release in 1903 and reportedly had the satisfaction of seeing her relive Gouffé's murder with paroxysms of fear and loathing worthy indeed of the time and trouble the lawyer had invested in her cause.[59]

The ideas Liégeois developed were based primarily on the laboratory experiments conducted at the Nancy clinics. During the experiments he induced false confessions, made people

[57] *Affaire Gouffé: Procès Eyraud-Bompard* published in Paris by the *Gazette des tribunaux* (1890), 96–135; these pages contain most of the medico-legal debate between Liégeois and his Parisian opponents, Brouardel, Motet, and Ballet.

[58] For Bernheim's seconding of Liégeois's general case see his, 'Discussions et polémique: Épilogue d'un procès célèbre', *Revue de l'hypnotisme*, 5 (1891), 270–3.

[59] 'Les Drames vécus, la confession de Gabrielle Bompard', *Le Journal*, 8 Dec. 1903.

commit murder, and generally enjoyed the pleasure of watching his commands minutely executed by suggestible subjects of impeccable reputation, several of whom were magistrates. Indeed, the experiments were of the same dramatic quality as those conducted at the Salpêtrière, and Liégeois even cited the case of Claretie's fictitious murder as another example proving the validity of his position.[60]

Bernheim and Liégeois did not, however, apply the same standards of criticism towards their own experiments as they did towards Charcot's clinical studies. At one moment they could perspicaciously condemn Charcot's evocation of hysteria as a debased chimera, but at another justify their own medico-legal experiments as irreproachable. They maintained this position despite their similar dramatic quality and the presence of an audience, which Liégeois regularly entertained in a fashion reminiscent of Charcot's lectures. Indeed, the workers at the Salpêtrière concentrated their attack on the poorly controlled nature of Liégeois's experiments and the unscientific approach of this amateur who, in their view, practised on undiagnosed hysterics. For them, the trials were mere illusions that did not reflect actions taken outside the Nancy laboratory where moral choices were experienced more dramatically.

Despite these mutual accusations of dubious scientific procedure, the fact remains that both schools were convinced that, at some level, unconscious suggestion could be dangerous. The willingness to perceive this danger, and to elaborate opposing medico-legal systems to demonstrate its operation, suggests the extent and persistence of the anxiety, the nature of which will be probed more carefully by examining first issues relating to women's sexuality, the family, and bourgeois values in general.

Women, Seduction, and the Family

Although Liégeois's bold assertions were far from winning universal acceptance, there was none the less agreement about

60 See, for example, Liégeois, *De la suggestion et du somnambulisme*, 130–41.

the seriousness of his warnings on the possibility of involuntary and, moreover, unconscious seduction under hypnosis—an anxiety which concerned medico-legists and moralists of all affiliations. Discussion revolved around the notion of female suggestibility—since women were acknowledged in both the lay and medical discourse as weak-willed and fickle—and also centred on the exposure of a female population that needed protection from rapacious and unscrupulous sexual violators. As a parallel to this concern, it focused on groups seen to pose particular dangers to genteel womanhood, concentrating on such male seducers as household servants, Jews, and lovers of otherwise dutiful wives. Indeed, a wide range of candidates were nominated, except the physicians and experimenters themselves, who were held up to be the only individuals pure enough to use such a dangerous tool as hypnotism safely.

Such a discussion operated on several levels. It demonstrated explicit concern over the mysterious and uncontrollable nature of women's sexual feelings and the threat these were believed to pose to bourgeois order. The debate also revealed areas of unease and tension within the bourgeois household, focusing on strained class relations in which servants were accused of making unwarranted sexual approaches to their social superiors. Finally, the nature of the fears expressed perhaps denotes a process of unconscious projection, with the 'experts' manifesting their unease with the moral, professional, and sexual dilemmas that hypnotic manipulation created by accusing others of desires which they themselves experienced.

One striking example of the possibility of rape under hypnosis had been investigated by Paul Brouardel as early as 1878 in a case tried in Rouen. The *affaire* was conducted around a series of familiar conventions, sometimes stressing the evil Jew preying upon the Christian virgin, at other times emphasizing the wily woman, perhaps with her mother in league, stalking the hapless wanderer. The prosecution maintained that the itinerant dentist, Paul Lévy, had cynically and violently abused an innocent young woman who had come to him for treatment. The details of the encounter were even more outlandish than the charge, since the woman asserted that the sexual encounter had taken place in the presence of her mother while the girl was nearly horizontal in the dentist's chair. At first denying the accusations, Lévy later admitted to having had sexual relations with Mlle Braquehais, but maintained that this had been with her full consent and, in his opinion, in order to force a marriage. In his view, only when they found out that he already had a wife and two children did the mother and daughter stop coming and complain to the police.[61]

Berthe's account of sexual violation was given credence by the court. Of apparently impeccable character, she had previously lived quietly *en famille* and gone regularly to confession. All men who visited the household were rigorously inspected by the mother and father and two marriage candidates had already been dismissed for trifling inadequacies, circumstances which suggested the unlikelihood of Lévy's charge that the women were in league in an unscrupulous husband-hunt. Because of her supposed flightiness and purported naïvety, as well as her unprepossessing appearance, the court found Lévy's claim that she had seduced him with provocative *allures* hard to believe. She insisted instead that she had been violated in a state of torpor without any conscious knowledge of it. Her suspicions were aroused by pains in her lower back and genitals and confirmed by a visit to the doctor.[62]

The first explanation for her state of mind was that she had been abused when Lévy had given her a dose of chloroform. The medical ethics on anaesthetics had long been contentious,[63] not only because improper usage might result in death, but also as the state of submission they produced might tempt an unscrupulous practitioner to abuse his power. Lévy was particularly vulnerable to such an accusation, as there was indeed the possibility that he did profit sexually both from his female bourgeois clients as well as from his women servants. Unfortunately for the investigating magistrate who put forward this hypothesis, no anaesthetics of any strength were

61 *Archives de la Seine inférieure*, Cour d'assises, Ull, *pièces* 61, 63, 64.

62 Ibid., *passim*.

63 For an enlightening account of comparable debates in England see Mary Poovey, '"Scenes of an Indelicate Character": The Medical "Treatment" of Victorian Women', *Representations*, 14 (1986), 137–68. For another example of the problem of professional ethics posed by anaesthesia in France see Dr Lutard, 'Peut-on violer une femme pendant l'anesthésie?', *Revue de psychiatrie, de neurologie et d'hypnologie*, 5 (1901), 77–80.

found in his pharmacopœia, and it was Brouardel who ultimately suggested the possibility of hypnosis in facilitating the crime. After an examination of the woman, the professor's lengthy report concluded that Berthe Braquehais's undeniably hysterical and susceptible disposition had left her open to the possible manipulation of Lévy's magnetizing talents, although there was nothing in his past to suggest he had ever practised such arts. After a trial conducted *huis clos*, which thereby prevented the legal arguments in court ever coming to light, Lévy was condemned to ten years' imprisonment.[64]

Brouardel's careful elaboration of his hypothetical case against Lévy reveals the Salpêtrière's early confidence in such a possibility, since the expert's apparently impartial intervention as an academic dignitary from the capital seemed vital to the trial's final outcome. His contribution had the effect of blending a native anti-semitism with the possibility of sexual violation. The fact that Lévy was a Jew and to some extent a social outcast served to place him under suspicion from the outset, underscoring the difference between him and more responsible practitioners who could be trusted *not* to exploit their professional capacity. The question remains whether or not Mlle Braquehais's just anger would have found such an attentive ear if the violator had been a more obviously respectable physician. For men like Brouardel, such an affair emphasized the necessity of protecting pure and genteel femininity from such enterprising mountebanks and established one of the fundamental similarities between the partisans of the Salpêtrière and others championing the cause of the Nancy school.

For example, later on, Liégeois would discuss the sexual havoc which hypnotism might produce: 'In a state of induced or spontaneous somnambulism, or in a *secondary state*, women or young girls could be raped without knowing or feeling it, having only the slightest memory of what had happened upon waking.'[65]

[64] Brouardel, 'Accusation de viol accompli pendant le sommeil', *Annales d'hygiène publique et de médecine légale*, 3rd ser., 1 (1879), 39–57; for details of the trial see *Journal de Rouen*, 20 Aug. 1878, 1–2.

[65] Liégeois, 'L'Hypnotisme et les suggestions criminelles', in Dr Croz *fils* (ed.), *Congrès international de neurologie, de psychiatrie, d'électricité médicale et d'hypnologie* (Paris, 1898), 208.

In his view, such disastrous results could occur with frightening ease because of the unhappy fact of women's suggestibility. He went so far as to suggest that women should neither travel alone nor stare at strangers, reasoning that extended eye-contact with a predatory male would be sufficient to lead her astray. The following interchange characterizing his general view of the feeble nature of female will occurred during the Bompard trial:

THE PROSECUTING ATTORNEY: Doesn't the Nancy school go so far as to advise nervous women never to travel alone since a man, simply through mental suggestion . . .

M. LIÉGEOIS: [*sharply*] Simply through mental suggestion . . . no, but from a steady gaze, yes.[66]

To guard against such dangers, Liégeois advocated the implantation of suitable moral qualities by men of irreproachable character, thereby helping the female mind to cope appropriately with all eventualities. In 1892, for example, he suggested a practical programme of giving every nervous woman a 'moral vaccination'.[67] This meant that each would be hypnotized by a competent and trustworthy practitioner who would insert a permanent suggestion into her unconscious to thwart the aims of any nefarious magnetizer.

This shared anxiety about the purity of womanhood was directly linked to fears about the lower orders and the threat they posed to the sanctity of the family. These sexual interlopers were portrayed as insidious agents, lurking about and preying upon the *foyer familial* from within. No household, be it 'rich, opulent, princely, royal even' would be 'out of danger, because there is no place where women and young girls are not sometimes exposed to the occasionally prolonged contact or presence of people of doubtful morality: servants, *valets de chambre*, coachmen, etc.'[68] As the hypnotic state eradicated consciousness, it enabled these plebeian and bestial schemers to infiltrate the minds and violate the bodies of refined womanhood, creating evil inclinations which, once seeded, could be

66 *Affaire Gouffé*, 128.

67 Liégeois, 'Hypnotisme et criminalité', *Revue philosophique*, 33 (1892), 233–72; see, in particular, 272–3.

68 Id., *Congrès international de neurologie*, 208.

difficult to uproot. Moreover, because of the amnesia he could induce in his victim, it would be virtually impossible to find and punish the culprit. Consequently, a gentleman could do little to protect his treasured family circle from the working-class hypnotizer-rapist who could potentially transform every loving and devoted wife into an unknowing adultress and mother of bastard children.

Hypnosis was thus seen as promoting the possible spiritual and physical proletarianization of bourgeois women. Not only would their minds be degraded by contact with the working-class male, but also their bodies would become the vessels of a debilitated heredity of which they were perhaps unaware. What was under discussion here was the supposed hidden strength of the working-class sexual urge and its perceived power to overwhelm and unleash female sexual feeling which the bourgeois male—with his refinement and civilized restraint—could not arouse.[69] As Léon Blum suggested, in his work on love and marriage,[70] respectable wives and mothers might be tempted into infidelity with undesirables in the search for sexual pleasure which the marriage-bed did not offer. As he explained, men who made love to virginal wives disregarded and even outraged their sexual feelings. Accustomed to the deceptive flattery of mistresses and prostitutes who needed their custom, respectable husbands neglected their spouses who then sometimes betrayed them in the search for love and romance.

The commentary not only exposed the clear anxiety about sexual inadequacy among bourgeois men, but also perhaps reflected unease about a more fundamental double standard in sexual interactions between middle-class men and their female social inferiors. The entire bourgeois culture which placed such

[69] Robert Nye in his work on male sexuality in nineteenth- and twentieth-century France has shown how the chief concern of medical prescriptive literature, intended for a middle-class public, was the possibility of masculine 'impuissance', demonstrating a widespread concern with the possibility of the loss of masculine force; paper delivered in *Symposium on Medicine and Society in Late Nineteenth-century Europe*, Wellcome Institute for the History of Medicine, London (June 1986). For more on the working-class character, its base urges, and life-style from the 'scientific' perspective see Jean Borie, *Mythologies de l'hérédité au XIXe siècle* (Paris, 1981).

[70] See his *Du Mariage* (Paris, 1907). For more on the sexual feelings of middle-class women see Peter Gay, *The Bourgeois Experience: Victoria to Freud, Education of the Senses* (New York, 1984).

a high premium on the virginity of the woman as the ultimate seal of the marriage contract necessarily impelled future husbands to look elsewhere for their pleasure.[71] It is not particularly surprising that the fears concerning rape under hypnosis concentrated on servants, that large class of underpaid domestics who had the privileged position of observing at close proximity the supposed ideal of the bourgeois *foyer*.[72]

The vehemence and pervasiveness of these warnings may perhaps be attributed to a projection on to these underlings of the clear historical reality of the sexual exploitation of female servants by male masters. Indeed, the judicial records are full of instances in which bourgeois men used their position of authority to proposition domestics who felt obliged to comply for fear of dismissal and subsequent penury. Gabrielle Bompard's father and Lévy the dentist, to name just two, enjoyed the sexual favours of female employees. Occasionally, an abused maidservant would come before the *Cour d'assises* for attempting to murder a master who had taken advantage of her, made her his mistress, and then later evicted her. Such cases of desertion not only occurred within the *foyer* but also more frequently on its periphery, when a working-class mistress in her own *quartier* was abandoned when the man married. The two supposedly separate spheres of working-class and bourgeois life were intermingled through the latter's sexual predations. Recognizing that such incursions took place, and indeed often tacitly encouraging them as a means of preserving the purity of middle-class women, bourgeois commentators perhaps also worried lest the sexual contacts ceased to flow only in one direction.

Equally, the interposition of the physician into the marital relationship created new possibilities for sexual tension. Popular and medical writing from the middle of the nineteenth century onwards stressed the expanding domain that medical men were carving out for themselves within the bourgeois *foyer*,

[71] For an impressive account of the illicit world of prostitution, its bourgeois justification, and regulation, see Alain Corbin, *Les Filles de noces: Misère sexuelle au dix-neuvième siècle* (Paris, 1978).

[72] For the idea of servants as having a pernicious effect on the respectability, health, and sanctity of the *foyer familial* in the eighteenth century, see Jacques Donzelot, *The Policing of Families: Welfare v. the State*, trans. Robert Hurley (London, 1979), 9–20.

sometimes superseding the priest as a secular confessor privy to the intimacies of women.[73] The doctors trod a thin line between reinforcing patriarchal authority through their medical knowledge, which confirmed the innate inferiority of women, and trying to enhance their own status as the privileged confidant, whose learned statements on childbirth, child-rearing, and women's health solidified an alliance with the wife. This intimacy was widely criticized—even though it was accompanied by the discretion of the *secret professionnel* in cases of middle-class clients—as it seemed possible that women might confess secrets of conjugal life injurious to the husband's reputation and honour.[74]

The issue of medical hypnosis therefore added another dimension to this discussion. Because of their own ambiguous status with regard to female sexuality, physicians were highly sensitive to the issue of seduction and rape. Occasionally they would sometimes directly acknowledge their sexual feelings when dealing with aristocratic or middle-class women, an attraction either denied or expressed in veiled terms when discussing working-class hysterics. In one often-cited case, for example, Bernheim and others acknowledged that an unnamed physician had carried on a passionate romance with his beautiful, aristocratic—but unfortunately married—patient during prolonged somnambulic trances, in which she declared her undying love for him. However, she ardently denied the illicit love-making in her conscious state, so that when she became pregnant she went insane, lost her baby, and spent the rest of her life in an asylum. Unlike Lévy, who was locked up for years, the unnamed doctor was not prosecuted, although the ensuing scandal irretrievably damaged his reputation and obliged him to emigrate.[75]

This long and tragic story warned practitioners of the consequences of such lustful but, in Bernheim's view, completely understandable proceedings and also demonstrated the temptation that hypnotic therapy presented. An example of the

[73] Donzelot, ibid., repeatedly refers to this characterization of medical power. See also Ludmilla Jordanova's tangential discussion of similar concerns in 'Romantic Science? Michelet, Morals and Nature', *British Journal for the History of Science*, 13 (1980), 44–50.

[74] See Angus McLaren, *Sexuality and Social Order: The Debate over the Fertility of Women and Workers in France, 1770–1920* (New York, 1983), 44–64.

[75] Augustin-René Bellanger, *Le Magnétisme: Vérités et chimères de cette science occulte; un drame dans le somnambulisme, épisode historique, les tables tournantes, etc.* (Paris, 1852), 207–90; the date of this event is not cited.

projection that such an awareness could produce when it went unacknowledged is provided by Brouardel's advice on precautions needed when administering chloroform to women. Unlike many who saw anaesthetics as a way for the unscrupulous practitioner to rape the patient, Brouardel reversed the argument and insisted that the danger lay in the possibility that the woman's state of unconsciousness might lead her to leap off the table and seduce the physician.[76]

The preoccupation with women's mysterious sexual feelings also provoked a search for scientific explanations why respectable wives broke their marriage vows to pursue brutal lovers. In one of his lectures, for example, Charcot described the case of a thirty-eight-year-old woman who, because of her degenerate susceptibilities, craved to be hypnotized by a popular magnetizer during the 1887 festival in Aubervilliers. Not daring to volunteer in the presence of her husband, she later returned unaccompanied and after the treatment 'was tormented by the desire to leave her home and find the one whom she considered to be her master'.[77] Subjugated in this way, she vanished and was only retrieved by her husband with the aid of a police order. Her condition did not improve, however, despite the salutary influence of her spouse's presence and, by the time she was put under Charcot's care, she was in a state of complete mutism. Thus silenced by the shame of her deed, she was subjected to the prying eyes of Charcot's audience and presented as an example of the danger facing society. Although more humble than Mme Grille, who also deserted husband and home in quest of a disreputable mate, she joined her social superior in a category which, as the next chapter will show, aroused medical, criminological, and lay commentary.

Spiritualism, Magnetism, and Medical Authority

The criticisms of Charcot's method and discoveries were more than scientific rebuke, since any attack called into question not

[76] Brouardel, 'Une Femme peut-elle avoir des rapports inconscients pendant le sommeil?', *Annales d'hygiène publique et de médecine légale*, 43 (1900), 46–7.

[77] Charcot, 'Accidents hystériques graves survenus chez une femme à la suite d'hypnotisations pratiquées par un magnétiseur dans une baraque de fête', *Revue de l'hypnotisme*, 4 (1890), 8.

only his work but also the ideological and political position he embodied. The elaboration of hysteria was more than a scientific project; it was also a demonstration of the way science would supersede religious explanation and reign triumphant as the ultimate social arbiter under the Third Republic. Second, it emphasized the rational exploitation of hypnosis by the medical profession and formed part of a campaign to bar the amateur healers, performers, and spiritualists who had staked a prior claim to its use. Hence, his work was an attack on other sources of ideological, religious, and spiritual authority, aiming to establish medicine as the sole and ultimate arbiter of nervous and psychic conditions.

Such a campaign was necessary because the profession's position remained precarious despite great gains. In a sense, historians have taken the medical rhetoric of triumph over 'superstition' and 'mysticism' too much at face value, not recognizing the extent to which it was still permeated by uncertainty. Above all, physicians were engaged in an important professional struggle associated with the 1892 law on medical professionalization and were keen to guard against the threat of competing practitioners.[78] There were also deeper intellectual reasons for this anxiety. Charcot and his associates felt obliged to separate themselves from the 'popular' origins of suggestive or magnetic healing, to which they were deeply, if embarrassingly, indebted.[79] Precisely because hypnotherapy contained the possibility that the panoply of scientific medicine—the laboratory, the clinic, the operating theatre—were less than absolutely essential, it implied that anyone with healing power and suggestive influence might succeed as well as, or better than, the practitioners of orthodox medicine. This concern perhaps explains why Charcot's school seemed so keen to regard hypnosis as a neurosis that unleashed disease and disorder and which, like a dangerous drug, needed to be administered with scientific precision.

[78] For the background to this law and its significance see Jacques Léonard, *La Médecine entre les pouvoirs et les savoirs: Histoire intellectuelle et politique de la médecine francaise au XIXe siècle* (Paris, 1981), 275–302.

[79] Anne Harrington has described the complicated world of *fin de siècle* hypnotism in which the philosophical and practical boundaries between neo-mesmerism, popular spiritualism, and 'establishment' medicine were blurred; see her forthcoming 'Hysteria, Hypnosis and the Lure of the Invisible: The Rise of Neo-mesmerism in fin de siècle medicine', in Bynum, Porter, and Shepherd, *The Anatomy of Madness*, vol. iii.

On another level, Charcot was also fighting against insidious influences within the intellectual community. Bernheim's view of the healing powers of hypnosis and emphasis on ideodynamism coincided with a variety of other idealist trends in contemporary social philosophy, fitting in with a new stress on varieties of religious experience and anti-rationalist, intuitive explanations of psychophysical relations.[80] At the very moment that Charcot was seeking to elevate hypnosis to a scientifically untouchable level, other practitioners, often not medically trained and with a different outlook, were openly building contacts with the world of popular magnetism and spiritualism. These included men like Bergson, Liégeois, and Delbœuf, a Belgian philosopher-philanthropist who wrote extensively on the moral, social, and political implications of hypnosis.[81]

Nineteenth-century scientists had not previously been isolated from the apparently highly successful French spiritualist movement.[82] However, it was in this period that the phenomenon of spiritualism became a *legitimate* area of philosophical and scientific enquiry, becoming annexed to positivism and altering the epistemological perspective of many previously 'materialist' practitioners.[83] For many years,

80 The literature surrounding this general trend in late nineteenth-century European thought is enormous. See, however, the helpful H. Stuart Hughes, *Consciousness and Society: The Reorientation of European Social Thought, 1890–1930* (London, 1959). For a more contemporary discussion see Antonia Aliotta, *The Idealistic Reaction against Science*, trans. Agnes McCaskill (London, 1914).

81 Joseph Delbœuf was a Belgian mathematician, philosopher, and philanthropist who practised hypnosis as a lay healer, learnt his trade from popular magnetizers, and wrote extensively on all aspects of hypnosis. He was an extremely important figure in contemporary polemics on the subject.

82 The most famous spiritualist of the nineteenth century in France was Hippolyte Rivail, who wrote under the pseudonym of Allan Kardec. His *Livre des esprits, contenant les principes de la doctrine spirite* (Paris, 1857) sold literally in hundreds of thousands and went into many editions.

83 'Experimental' spiritualism in France took its lead from the London Psychical Society and the pioneering work of men like Myers. For a history of their work and its implications see J. Perry William, 'Psychical Research and Psychiatry in Late Victorian Britain: Trance as Ecstasy or Trance as Insanity', in Bynum, Porter, and Shepherd (eds.), *The Anatomy of Madness*, i. 233–54; see also his 'The Making of Victorian Psychical Research: An Intellectual Élite's Approach to the Spiritual World', Ph.D. thesis (Univ. of Cambridge, 1984). The English influence can be seen most strongly in the *Annales des sciences psychiques* which sought to ascertain the veracity of various psychic phenomena. Notable Frenchmen interested in this work included the famous physiologist Charles Richet, Théodule Ribot, Bernheim, Beaunis, Liégeois, Liébault, and the young Pierre Janet.

Charcot held out against seriously addressing the question of spiritual experience or non-scientific and 'popular' expressions of faith. However, in the last year of his life, he wrote on 'faith-healing' when one of his patients afflicted by a tumor returned cured from Lourdes.[84] He acknowledged the practical benefit of her pilgrimage, ascribing the cure to suggestion, but denying the role of divine intervention. Despite his late willingness to discuss her experience as a pragmatic therapeutic option, through most of his career he was a vital figure in a campaign to outlaw non-medical forms of healing, especially those espoused by popular magnetizers articulating a variety of spiritualist messages and doctrines.

The accusations made against the amateurs focused on their lack of scientific method, imputation of dangerous sexual exploitation, and the provocation of mass hysteria among degenerate and susceptible audiences. The Nancians were also criticized during this campaign because of Bernheim's applause for men like Liébault who had advanced the cause despite the derision of the medical establishment. When Brouardel spoke of his school's research, he linked its work with spiritualists, mediums, and mystics who believed in turning tables and talking hats.[85] Liégeois was equally unashamed of his affiliation with the world of poplar magnetism and acknowledged that his experimental career was possible because of their *laissez faire* attitude. Indeed, he even praised a popular magnetizer of considerable contemporary fame named Hansen who had helped him with his technique, calling him a 'man of good faith and absolute integrity who did not pronounce a single word which in any way at all could be accused of charlatanism'.[86] In this respect, however, it was the Nancians rather than the Parisians who were isolated in their attitude. In Switzerland, Austria, Italy, Belgium, Germany, and Denmark it was the views of Charcot and his disciples which were duplicated by like-minded medical practitioners, with the result that, by 1890, hypnotic performances were legally banned in several parts of the continent.[87]

[84] Charcot, *La Foi qui guérit* (Paris, 1897).

[85] *Affaire Gouffé*, 130.

[86] Delbœuf citing Liégeois, *Magnétiseurs et médecins* (Paris, 1880), 16.

[87] Pressat, 'L'Hypnotisme et la presse', 226.

Parisian disapproval of the magnetizers was ostensibly based on the harmful effects theatrical presentations were supposed to have on a suggestible and gullible public. At the level of the individual, this concern was once more imbued with the question of sexuality. The rapport between the magnetizer and his usually female subject was frequently described in sexual terminology as a relationship between a prostitute and her pimp, and once more gave rise to alarm over the possibilities of rape that this opened up. Gilles de la Tourette, as the loyal disciple to Charcot and Brouardel, was the main advocate of banning the performances and spoke in his expert capacity as alienist, medico-legist, and mental hygienist. In a book devoted to the issue, he concentrated on the seamier side of *spiritisme*, describing at length how young girls were lured into seances by the blandishments of the operator and by the applause of a vulgar and stupid audience.[88]

The doctors were alarmed at the possible consequences such performances might have for audiences which, in their view, threw caution to the winds in the foolish search for titillation by dabbling in the supposedly supernatural. French physicians who agreed with Charcot joined in the call that such popular entertainments be banned and cited blood-curdling examples of magnetizing's deleterious effects.[89] For example, an accident which occurred when a circus passed through Béziers was blamed on amateur abuse of the practice. A young girl, magnetized into a cataleptic trance, was introduced into the lion cage, where the wild beasts tore her thigh to shreds. In another case, the physician Edgar Bérillon accused a performing magnetizer of suggesting to his audience that a fire was rapidly spreading through the theatre, with the result that they stampeded out of the building, treading women and children mercilessly underfoot in a blind panic.[90] Such Zolaesque images of savage violence were stressed in order to waken the public to the dangers facing them, and to imply by contrast how doctors with their standards of professional ethics would not be found taking similar advantage.

[88] Gilles de la Tourette, *L'Hypnotisme et les états analogues*, 298–383 and, in particular, 383–450. For Charcot's position see *Œuvres complètes*, ix. 479–80.

[89] Pressat, 'L'Hypnotisme et la presse', 225.

[90] Edgar Bérillon, 'Hypnotisme utile et hypnotisme dangereux', *Revue de l'hypnotisme*, 3 (1888), 2.

Such an attitude towards popular performances was a natural consequence of the Parisians' view that hypnotism was an *agent révélateur* of latent hysterical and pathological symptoms which destroyed the capacity for proper moral and intellectual activity. In the hands of enterprising mountebanks this danger was increased, with hypnotism promising to trigger off mass explosions of hysteria in a susceptible, often degenerate, public. The fact that the crowds who came to these shows were composed of the popular classes and, it was claimed, of adolescents attracted by the miraculous claims of the performers, meant that the danger of psychic accidents was enhanced. One physician from Bordeaux, for example, where the performances were outlawed in 1888, described in undoubtedly exaggerated terms the immoral scenes which occurred in the city after a performance by Alfred D'hont, called Donato, the most renowned magnetizer of the day:

> Disorder and profound trouble result from hypnotic procedures falling into unqualified hands. Pimps put girls to sleep in brothels; tradesmen, rakes, and dandies of every sort were hypnotizing their mistresses. It had become an absolute mania, and I approved of the measures taken by the municipality of Bordeaux to forbid the continuation of Donato's performances, because I believe . . . that it is not good to store dangerous poisons and arms in everyone's hands.[91]

Those physicians who accepted Charcot's pronouncements on the subject denounced unequivocally not only this 'unwholesome curiosity of an idle and impudent public, to put it mildly',[92] but also the emotionally charged attitude of the audience which 'recalls from the past . . . the great mental epidemics of the middle ages with their convulsionaries, their sorcerers, and their superstitions.'[93] The Swiss physician Ladame, tireless in his warnings against theatrical presentations, described the debasement of the subject on the stage in the following way:

> The hypnotized subject, made a spectacle of to the crowd bubbling up with unwholesome emotion, publicly held up to ridicule, brutally

[91] 'Correspondance et chronique: Les Dangers de l'hypnotisme—une lettre de A. Pitres de Bordeaux', *Revue de l'hypnotisme*, 3 (1888), 65.

[92] Dr Guermonprez, *Congrès international de l'hypnotisme expérimental et thérapeutique, tenu à Paris du 8 au 12 août 1889* (Lille, 1889), 16.

[93] *Premier congrès international de l'hypnotisme 8–12 août* (Paris, 1889), 'Rapport de M. le docteur Ladame', 30.

held in thrall, made to hallucinate to the point of raging madness, reduced to the last extremity by the hideous criminal suggestions the magnetizer orders him to perform . . . the hypnotized subject of public performances is truly a victim.[94]

In the name of social order, mental hygiene and human dignity, the Parisian School and its followers called for an end to this public outrage. This apparently humanitarian campaign was part and parcel, however, of a broader movement to monopolize the practise of hypnotism, to annex it permanently to scientific medicine. 'The law', wrote Ladame, 'is very severe when it comes to the sale of a few drops of Laudanum, while allowing somnambulists and magnetizers to practise with impunity'.[95] His views were overwhelmingly endorsed by the 1889 conference held in Paris on hypnotism and attended chiefly by physicians.[96] Here also they called for the outlawing of theatrical performances after an undignified session during which the few supporters of the magnetizers were shouted down by a clique allegedly led by Gilles de la Tourette.[97]

The vituperative nature of this campaign, in which often questionable evidence of crime and madness was used to strengthen their case,[98] suggests that other interests were at stake. The physicians were in fact responding to the assaults made by the amateurs who hurled similar accusations of charlatanry against the medical establishment. The most powerful demonstration of the unity of the opposition took place during the 1889 Congress of Human Magnetism,[99] held at virtually the same time as the scientific gathering mentioned above.

The portrait of sinister, money-grubbing sensationalists hardly seems confirmed by the magnetizers themselves, many

94 Ibid.

95 Gilles de la Tourette, citing Ladame, *L'Hypnotisme et les états analogues*, 450.

96 *Premier congrès international de l'hypnotisme 8–12 août*, 44.

97 Delbœuf, *Magnétiseurs et médecins*, 31.

98 One of the most extensively cited cases was of a supposed rape in Switzerland after a mesmeric performance; see 'La Névrose hypnotique devant la médecine légale. Du viol pendant le sommeil hypnotique', *Annales d'hygiène publique et de médecine légale*, 3rd ser., 7 (1882), 518–33.

99 *Congrès international de 1889: Le Magnétisme humain appliqué au soulagement et à la guérison des maladies: Rapport général d'après le compte rendu des séances du congrès* (Paris, 1890).

of whom were pastors, retired army officers, or itinerant healers who sometimes practised their art free of charge. Although they disagreed among themselves about the theories on hypnosis and their relationship to healing—some attributing it to a mesmeric fluid or animal electricity, others to an unspecified *force neurique rayonnante* or suggestion—they were unanimous in decrying Charcot's coupling of hysteria and hypnosis and the consequent implication that the latter had only limited therapeutic applications. Many vehemently opposed his practice of producing somnambulistic trances and cataleptic states since their own techniques did not rely on the inducement of artificial sleep which, they maintained, produced hysteria or mental congestion and resulted in madness or debility. Moreover, there was general agreement over the pitiful and deplorable nature of the *maître*'s extravagant demonstrations, which they asserted were more pernicious and socially destructive than their own presentations that informed the masses of powers official medicine wished to keep hidden. Charcot's entire system—the four stages of hystero-epilepsy which erupted so conveniently, the way in which madwomen's woes were used to entertain the public, the theatrical use of bright objects, loud noises, and gestures to induce hypnotic sleep—was condemned as a sadistic game devised by a devil in the name of official science.[100]

One of the more interesting figures in this 'fringe' community was Donato, whose travels throughout Europe had earned him an extensive reputation. Unlike many of his colleagues, Donato employed techniques very similar to those introduced to the medical world by the *École de Nancy*, with suggestion rather than manipulation of magnetic fluid providing a theoretical basis for his therapeutic and theatrical practice.[101] His impact on the academic world was substantial, with Enrico Morselli of Turin dedicating a chapter in his *Magnetismo animale* to his techniques and accusing official

[100] For an example of the kind of tirade fired at Charcot's School see Jean Rouxel (pseudonym: Auguste Leroux), *Rapports du magnétisme et du spiritisme* (Paris, 1892), 257–313.

[101] See Edouard Cavilhon, *Le Fascinateur magnétique* (Paris, 1882), with a preface by Prof. Donato; Donato, *Cours pratique d'hypnotisme et de magnétisme* (Paris, n.d.). For the best summary of Donato's theory and technique see 'Discours de Donato', in *Congrès international de 1889*, 427–42.

science of plagiarizing the amateur's discoveries.[102] Donato was supposed to have introduced Ladame himself to the wonders of hypnosis and claimed to have been profoundly hurt by the Swiss physician's relentless attacks later on. Joseph Delbœuf never tired of praising Donato's knowledge and candour and defended all amateurs with a vigour that matched the venom of Gilles de la Tourette's assaults.[103]

One of the undoubted reasons for the attack mounted against Donato was his early, unrestrained, and perceptive criticism of Charcot. Anticipating Bernheim's assessment of the Parisian psychiatrist's work, Donato claimed in 1882 that Charcot had unwittingly suggested the hysterical crises in his patients who allowed their fits to conform 'to his ingenious predictions'.[104] Strongly criticizing the errors of medical traditionalism which forced students to accept and promote the fallacious doctrines of the *maîtres* to assure professional advancement, Donato championed the masses as the ultimate arbiter in determining scientific truth:

> But the humble magnetizers, professional hypnotizers, tired of being repulsed by the academics, appealed to the crowds, showing them that the official scholars were denying the evidence. The crowd acclaimed the independent apostles of a misunderstood truth and forced the princes of official science to bow before the irrefutable facts.[105]

His assertion that 'the academies too often hinder [*émasculent*] progress'[106] was seconded by sympathetic journalists in the popular press who reported on the 1889 magnetizing conference, one remarking that 'without doubt, this scarcely tallies with the academic dogmas under which the mandarins of scientific orthopaedics claim to discipline all new ideas under threat of heresy'.[107]

In accordance with their criticism of the nature and structure of official science, Donato and other 'experimental spiritualists' called for the end to medical professionalism, maintaining

102 Enrico Morselli, *Il Magnetismo animale: La Fascinazione e gli ipnotici* (Turin, 1886).

103 See Delbœuf, *Magnétiseurs et médecins* passim.

104 Cavilhon, *Le Fascinateur magnétique*, p. xxxii.

105 'Discours de Donato', 431.

106 Ibid., 432.

107 Gautier, 'Chronique', *Le Figaro*, 5 Sept. 1889.

that if the doors of the dissecting chamber and the clinic were flung open, a revolution in therapeutic procedures would be quickly accomplished by plebian practitioners. They claimed that the amateur healers, concerned only with the alleviation of suffering and uncompromised by state subsidies and official dogma, would not be duped by the type of fraud and trickery that Charcot's system contained. *Doctoralisme*, as one indignant spiritualist called medical power, 'is a hundred times more intolerant, more monopolistic, more despotic than clericalism and militarism [*caporalisme*] combined'.[108]

In the end, the bid for medical monopoly was relatively successful and, although Brouardel was unable to have strict provisions against magnetizers inserted in the 1892 law, some were successfully prosecuted for practising after that date.[109] Despite the growing institutional and legal power of the medical profession, however, the ideas which magnetizers and spiritualists advanced did infiltrate 'official' science on all the levels already described above. In many respects, Charcot's interpretation of hypnosis represented a rearguard action, increasingly superseded by other accounts. Indeed, hypnotism was to become less significant within the medical community, as men like Freud discarded it in favour of other means of psychological analysis. Perhaps, as Forrester has suggested, the ambiguous professional relationship which resulted from the hypnotic rapport, and demonstrated so vividly at Charcot's clinic, was ill-adapted to the proprieties of medical consultation in which middle-class women were involved. Although Freud slowly rid himself of hypnosis from his therapeutic repertoire, he none the less retained and deepened his understanding of the role of the doctor-patient relationship for facilitating a cure. The notion of transference, of 'contracting the disease of love', was to remain a cardinal feature of the psychoanalysis, the origin of which can be traced to the recognition of the

[108] Rouxel, *Rapports de magnétisme*, 297. The word *doctoralisme* pertains both to an academic degree and the attitude of pomposity assumed to go with it.

[109] Brouardel explained how the proposal to outlaw magnetizers jeopardized the passage of the 30 Nov. 1892 law on medical practice so that, in the end, the article on amateur hypnotic healing was left purposely vague. Their right to heal was later upheld in Angers, but in 1892 magnetizers were successfully prosecuted in Lille and Paris. See Brouardel, *La Profession médicale au commencement du XXe siècle*.

psychological bond created between hypnotized subject and operator.[110]

Responsibility and the Pathologization of Women

As a unified field of social and intellectual struggle, the debate over hysteria and hypnotism had profound significance for the wider contemporary discussion of free will and moral responsibility. The very scope of the debate, which ranged freely between medical factions, plebeian practitioners, journalists and philosophers, suggests the extent to which hypnosis focused any number of sexual, social, and political anxieties, providing a dramatic and easily grasped demonstration of the 'unconscious' at work which cut across fundamental social and intellectual divisions.

Throughout this wide-ranging polemic it is impossible to escape the obsession with women which permeated the discussion. It was not that Charcot, for example, did not have male subjects; indeed he was also famous for emphasizing the frequency of male hysteria.[111] Despite this, his writings and, more particularly, the popular perception of hysteria almost always concentrated on women's passive or manipulative qualities and the ability of men to overpower and control them. Why this concentration? I would suggest that the debate which exploded during the Third Republic represents a refined stage in the medical 'pathologization' of women, a process accelerated by the anticlericalist struggle which Charcot championed. This emphasis was perhaps heightened because of the rising strength of the secular Republican ideology emerging in the late 1870s and early 1880s which stressed universal suffrage, political equality and civic education. On one level, the regime, including such close personal associates of Charcot as

[110] John Forrester, 'Contracting the Disease of Love: Authority and Freedom in the Origins of Psychoanalysis', in Bynum, Porter, and Shepherd (eds.), *The Anatomy of Madness*, i. 255–70.

[111] Charcot, *Œuvres complètes*, iii. 253–398, 422–40. For a larger discussion see Mark S. Micale, 'Diagnostic Discriminations: Jean-Martin Charcot and the Nineteenth-century Idea of Masculine Hysterical Neurosis', Ph.D. thesis (Univ. of Yale, 1982).

Paul Bert, regarded itself as the emancipator of French womanhood, delivering it from the obscurantism of the Church through Republican education. At another, women's presumed dedication to Catholic dogma and ritual was continually invoked as one important and inescapable reason for denying them equal participation in professional, civic, and political life.[112] The intensification of the scientific data adduced to demonstrate the 'natural' inferiority of women and their inherent pathology is perhaps an indirect indication of this tension. The portrait which Charcot helped to paint was remarkable for equalling Catholicism in stressing female incapacity at the same time that it undermined the divine and spiritual qualities which the Church had reserved for women.

As mentioned at the outset, Charcot's entire clinical project was inspired by his rabid anticlericalism, the significance of which demands one final detour here. On one level, Charcot's efforts in the late 1870s were a mere continuation of a longer psychiatric campaign. Alienists had sought to understand religious enthusiasm as a pathological monomania or demonopathy as early as the July Monarchy and had provided extensively argued scientific treatises on such historical phenomena as, for example, the late eighteenth-century convulsionaries of St Médard.[113] Their role in controlling religious excess was extended when, in the late 1850s and early 1860s, the alienist Louis-Florentin Calmeil intervened with the aid of government against the villagers of Morzine, in the extreme south-east of France, whose religious 'hysteria' ultimately led them to insane asylums.[114]

Despite such precedents, however, Charcot's assault

[112] For further discussions see Steven C. Hause (with Anne R. Kenny), *Women's Suffrage and Social Politics in the French Third Republic* (Princeton, 1984) and Patrick Kay Bidelman, *Pariahs Stand Up! The Founding of the Liberal Feminist Movement in France, 1858–1889* (Westport, Conn. and London, 1982).

[113] Catherine Laurence Maire, *Les Convulsionnaires de Saint-Médard: Miracles, convulsions et prophéties à Paris au XVIIIe siècle* (Paris, 1985); for a discussion of the ideas surrounding 'hysterical' epidemics in the first half of the nineteenth century see Goldstein, 'Moral Contagion': A Professional Ideology of Medicine and Psychiatry in Eighteenth and Nineteenth Century France', in Gerald L. Geison (ed.), *Professions and the French State, 1700–1900* (Philadelphia, 1984), 181–222.

[114] For the disturbances at Morzine and psychiatry's reaction to them see Goldstein, 'Moral Contagion', and Gérard Wajeman, *Le Maître et l'hystérique* (Paris, 1982), 35–78.

represented a qualitative change. His anticlerical demonstrations were masterminded with visual flair, complementing the photographic record and clinical presentations with art-historical analysis and 'retrospective' diagnosis. With Richer's help, Charcot examined *Les Démoniaques dans l'art*, using old masterpieces to demonstrate that hysteria was not the *invention* of a doctor, but rather a disease of the ages which France's premier physician could now penetrate and understand. To show the similarity between the paintings of the convulsionaries of St Médard and the '*démoniques d'aujourd-hui*', he juxtaposed them against the classic drawings of *grande hystérie* first published by Richer in 1882.[115] It is no exaggeration to say that the specific symptoms and dramatic stages were moulded to some degree by this religious iconography. The *attitudes passionnelles* in particular showed the kinship between religious symbolism and female pathology, with women poised in positions of religious supplication, ecstasy and even crucifixion. Indeed, it can be argued that rather than liberating women from the stereotypes of Christian symbolism, the representations of the hysterics at the Salpêtrière pathologized both the religious meaning and the women who expressed them.[116]

Nor was the assault limited to the past. One way Charcot and his associate Bourneville took up the struggle against Catholicism involved the case of Louise Lateau, a Belgian girl from the region around Mons et Charleroi, around whom a medical polemic whirled. In 1868, this simple, pious villager began to have periods of religious exaltation, succeeded by stigmata which erupted every Friday for almost five years. She demonstrated not only the major stigmatic points on feet, hands, and chest, but even bled occasionally from a crown of thorns. Medical commissions were sent to investigate the phenomenon, and Lateau became the focus of conflicting scientific opinion. Her major defender was a Catholic doctor named Imbert-Gourbeyre, who conducted physiological experiments to ascertain whether or not she was simulating, trials

115 Charcot, *Les Démoniaques dans l'art* (Paris, 1897), 78–106.

116 For further commentary on the subject see the postface by Georges Didi-Huberman of Charcot's *'Les Démoniaques dans l'art', suivi de: 'La Foi qui guérit'* (Paris, 1984), 125–82.

117 Antoine Imbert-Gourbeyre, *Les Stigmatisées* (Paris, 1873), 198.

which would have even satisfied the fastidious Charcot: she 'allowed herself be pinched, pricked, cauterized, burned, electrified, without demonstrating the least sensibility'.[117] Lateau demonstrated remarkable spiritual and intellectual accomplishment during these ecstasies. Not only could she identify blessed objects unknown to her, she was also able to speak in refined French, a remarkable achievement for a woman of humble and uneducated origin.

Anticlerical and Catholic physicians agreed on the incontestability of the phenomena observed, but were opposed when they came to interpret their nature and meaning. The two sides spoke in incompatible terms, the former regarding the visions as evidence of hysterical pathology, the latter believing fervently in the spiritual quality of Lateau's mysterious enunciations. Charcot's associate Bourneville expressed himself in disdainful and coldly rational terms,[118] while Imbert-Gourbeyre wrote in the respectful language of religious awe. Unwilling to acquiesce in the designation of religious ecstasy as a pathology, he considered the hysterics at the Salpêtrière to be sensuous demons, diabolically possessed, and was shocked by and critical of the way in which their sad lives were displayed in public. As he remarked:

> What exactly are these ecstasies at the Salpêtrière? M. Richer's own description gives the entire picture. . . . During the stages of the *attitudes passionnelles* (the stage of the so-called esctasies), the patients are subject to sad, happy, erotic, or terrifying hallucinations . . . Under this influence they stage an exact pantomime of the scenes in which they were either the victims or the guilty protagonists. Sometimes they fight and struggle against the seducer who comes to life again in their imagination; sometimes they contemplate their lover with an attentiveness mixed with joy. . . . *Past embraces and scenes are repeated and portrayed in rapidly changing poses, the cynicism of which defies description* [arrête le crayon] . . . *Words escaping their lips tell what is happening . . . Lewd scenes are interspersed with dances and songs . . . From time to time a religious memory strikes a contrast. The hysteric rapidly murmurs an edifying prayer but soon she returns to her lewd talk and the attitudes passionnelles reappear.*

[117] Antoine Imbert-Gourbeyre, *Les Stigmatisées* (Paris, 1873), 198.

[118] See D.-M. Bourneville, *Science et miracle: Louise Lateau ou la stigmatisée belge* (Paris, 1875); for examples of his 'retrospective' diagnosis see *La Possession de Jeanne Fery: Religieuse professe du couvent des sœurs noires de la ville de Mons* (Paris, 1886).

In short, lust and fury, that is the picture of the so-called estasies at the Salpêtrière.[119]

Such hideous exhibitions, he maintained, had no relationship to Louise Lateau, whose modesty, heightened intelligence, and intense spirituality contrasted sharply with the harsh sensuality, moral debasement, and disequilibrium of the hysterics. But it was precisely this distinction between demonology and ecstasy that Charcot wished to break down. Writing about St Catherine of Sienna, he acknowledged the inspired qualities of paintings such as Sodoma's *Sainte Catherine en extase*, while at the same time asserting that artistic licence had encouraged the painter to omit 'all appearance of violence, every convulsive phenomenon'. Science, however, revealed a harsher reality in which 'all the characteristics of ecstasy are found in hysteria; these rigidities and contractures are of an eminently hysterical appearance'.[120]

In effect, by attempting to strip away the Christian underpinning for women's subjugation, his secular account of their inferiority tended to direct all descriptions towards a unifying pathologization:

> . . . One felt that in all the talk of this terrifying man, he barely distinguished between society ladies and the 'hysterics' he was treating in his ward and that if it had been up to him he would have placed the whole of society behind the bars of his institution . . . [121]

As the Third Republic continued expanding amounts of scientific explanation would be adduced to demonstrate this inferiority, with evidence ranging from the embryological and anthropological to the anatomical and physiological.[122] In this developing system Charcot's psychiatric descriptions would hold a place of priority, with less flamboyant varieties of hysteria seen to contaminate the nervous systems of virtually all women. This psychiatric analysis would infiltrate into many other aspects of medico-legal debate and will be shown to explain, at least in partial form, why women were almost always deemed irresponsible for their acts.

119 Imbert-Gourbeyre, *La Stigmatisation* (Clermont-Ferrand/Paris, 1894), ii. 448–9; see chap. 25 in general, 433–65.

120 Charcot, *Les Démoniaques dans l'art*, 108.

121 Martin du Gard, *Le Lieutenant-colonel de Maumort*, 398.

122 For an outline see Yvonne Kniebhler and Catherine Fouquet, *La Femme et les médecins: Analyse historique* (Paris, 1983). For more on women's physiology and 'nature' see Thérèse Moreau, *Le Sang de l'histoire: Michelet, l'histoire et l'idée de la Femme au XIXe siècle* (Paris, 1982); and Stéphane Michaud, 'Science, droit, religion: Trois contes sur les deux natures', *Romantisme*, 13 (1976), 23–40.

6

FEMALE CRIMES OF PASSION

In 1880, the actress Marie Br . . ., stage name Béraldi, dressed herself in a large hat and lorgnon and stalked her old lover and his new mistress in the streets of Paris. Ultimately, she walked up behind him, shot him in the back and then, satisfied with the deed, voluntarily gave herself up to the police. Despite her obvious premeditation and the open way in which she acted, Br . . . was acquitted by the jury at her trial.[1] In a similar fashion, literally hundreds of other murderesses between 1880 and 1910 committed crimes of passion against erring, irresponsible, or brutal mates and were almost invariably exonerated by the court.

While the previous analysis of hysteria and hypnotism focused chiefly on the medical characterization of womanly susceptibility to suggestive influence, this chapter will examine the various representations of feminine motive and responsibility in cases of crimes of passion. Above all, I will investigate the reasons for the clemency meted out by exclusively male *petit-bourgeois* juries. At the same time I hope to provide some account of the more hidden dimensions of manipulation and exchange that characterized the interaction between, on the one hand, the official masculine world of psychiatric assessment and judicial analysis and, on the other, the feminine arena of dramatic and righteous self-presentation and retrospective rationalization.

The varying interpretations of women's nature, sexuality, and psychology which resulted provided a range of sometimes competing, but more often overlapping, views of female responsibility. From the legal point of view, women were, like all defendants, ostensibly judged by a judicial morality based on notions of free will and moral responsibility. Although the women demonstrated a keen awareness of their circumstances,

[1] For the case of Marie Br . . . see D2U8 92, 23 Mar. 1880.

generally admitting their offence and even describing their sometimes elaborate preparations, investigating magistrates none the less tended to treat them as irresponsible agents. On the medical side, psychiatrists brought to bear a clinical, scientific vision, professedly based on determinist theories of neurophysiological disinhibition and hereditarian degeneration, which almost always stressed some aspect of the hysterical disorder and linked a portrait of irresponsibility to a wider account of women's biological life cycle.

These two specialists' viewpoints were supplemented by other characterizations. Besides their autobiographical statements made under interrogation, their personal world was opened up to the magistrates through such things as love-letters and sometimes diaries, all of which were used to assess motive. More importantly, perhaps, these documents were important personal accounts of the experience of despair, jealousy, and anger which the defendants referred to in order to justify the moment of 'temporary insanity' that was, in their view, the cause of the violence.

Despite the strength of the representations of womanly incapacity in both the legal and medical realms, however, the defendants responded with a canny combination of resistance and compliance. On the one hand they expressed a highly refined sense of female honour and, on the other, represented themselves through a particular melodramatic rhetorical style. As I will hope to show, their self-portraits were crucial in contributing to the acquittals they received.

Before proceeding, I must make one crucial proviso. In this welter of texts and statements, documents and proclamations, the deep tragedy affecting the women becomes necessarily diluted by the process of reconstruction which followed the deeds themselves. Indeed, the same warning must be administered for the succeeding chapters dealing with male offenders. Unfortunately, in attempting a historical analysis, there can be no recourse simply to social explanation or the self-explanatory statements to account properly for the undeniable despair, perhaps even dementedness, that clearly overcame many of these people before and during the committal of the crimes. It is necessary to acknowledge that, in these various forms of reportage, the realm of desire, fantasy, and conflict are largely inaccessible to us. Indeed, even the most personal documents—the love-letters and poems—are historical constructions marked by conventions of rhetoric and style which contributed crucially to a characterization of feminine nature that promoted a vision of womanly irresponsibility.

Crimes of Passion

Hundreds of defendants of both sexes who came before the *Cour d'assises* between 1880 and 1910 claimed to be *criminels passionnels*.[2] What is significant is that although men outnumbered women in using the crime of passion as a defence, the proportion of female crime associated with passion was much higher.[3] Indeed, the only legal justification for the crime was article 324, line 2 of the Penal Code, which stated that a husband who murdered his wife or her lover when he caught them in *flagrante delicto* had committed excusable murder,[4] although men were in fact acquitted for killing under conditions which were much less straightforward (see chapter 8). A woman, on the other hand, was not similarly entitled and could only have her husband fined if she surprised him in the same compromising position, and even then the discovery had to be made in their home to justify legal action.

Despite this lack of judicial sanction, however, women used murder as a response to a variety of male injuries and were

[2] For a slightly earlier period (1870–80) see Joëlle Guillais, *La Chair de l'autre: Le Crime passionnel au XIXe siècle* (Paris, 1986).

[3] The number of crimes of passion rose steadily in the period along with the number of murders. In 1880 there were six committed, five by men, out of a year's total of thirty. By 1905 this had risen to thirty-four out of ninety-six and to thirty-five out of 100 by 1910. While male crimes of passion never rose above a third of male murders, it was the dominant form for women: five out of six female murders in 1881, five out of eight in 1895, nine out of eleven in 1905, while all fourteen murders by women in 1910 were crimes of passion. The acquittal for women was almost customary. Of the five in 1895, three women were acquitted, one received a year in gaol, while the fate of the third is unknown. In 1905 there were seven acquittals, one unknown, and one penalty of three years. In 1910 sentences were harsher, with one life sentence and three gaol sentences of six, two, and three years; none the less in that year there were still nine acquittals and one unknown. The archival series used to determine the penalties is D[1]U[8] at the *Archives de la Seine*.

[4] James McMillan, *Housewife or Harlot: The Place of Women in French Society, 1870–1914* (London, 1981), 17–18.

regularly acquitted. The crimes were committed in a repetitive, even ritualized, fashion. *Criminelles passionnelles* often recalled the long periods of anguish, which were occasionally written down, and sometimes presaged the assault with public recriminations or attempts at reconciliation. The attacks themselves were usually executed in the street with either revolvers or vitriol—both, as will be seen, weapons suggestive in symbolic meaning. The acts were social dramas which involved passers-by as audience and also as participants, attempting to disarm the assailant, attending to the wounded, and calling for the police. An indication of the general commotion which sometimes accompanied such incidents can be seen most vividly and perhaps tragically in the case of Amicie Lépée G . . . who had decided to murder her husband for failing to provide for her and their children. Walking near the *Palais Royal*, she assaulted her target with a revolver and received unusual assistance from passers-by who pinned him down in the belief that it was she who was under attack. In the resultant scuffle she fired and killed the man, only to find that she had made a mistake and he was not her husband at all.[5]

After such attacks, the offender was taken away to the police, generally admitted premeditation, showed occasional bouts of confusion and remorse, and explained her motives. For example, in 1882, the linen-maid Eulalie Louise Chevalet J . . . shot at her husband after they had parted and he refused to have her back. She exemplified a common characterization of emotions which preceded and followed such crimes when she remarked to the investigating magistrate:

> When the revolver was loaded, I lay in wait for my husband, having seen him leave his room; I followed him along the Blvd de Grenelle; I asked him again to take me back . . .
>
> At that moment I wanted to hit him . . . it was only two or three hours later that I began to regret what I had done.
>
> It was really his fault that all of this happened; if only he hadn't rejected me; he should have spoken to me gently, not scorned me and treated me like a stranger.[6]

After such preliminaries, the arduous months of pre-trial

[5] Amicie-Lépée G . . . D^2U^8 149, 12 Nov. 1883, Acte d'accusation.
[6] Eulalie Louise Chevalet J . . . D^2U^8 134, 14 Nov. 1882, *pièce* 12.

investigation began. What had started for many as an inescapable emotional necessity often became a period of intense depression and isolation. Generally women of an otherwise law-abiding nature, they were closeted with the petty thieves and prostitutes in the walls of St Lazare, and experienced conditions which undermined both their morale and health. If their lovers or husbands had survived the attacks, they were obliged to submit to confrontations in the investigating magistrate's office, and press their case before an often angry and dismissive opponent. Occasionally, they were forced to witness the result of their deeds by viewing the corpses. The widow Eugénie Pathier B . . ., a woman who vitriolized her lover to death, was made to confront her victim's cadaver and was questioned in this manner by an indignant investigating magistrate:

> 'Here is your work; do you recognize C . . . [?]' Without answering us the accused began to cry and wanted to throw herself on C . . .'s body; she said, 'Your honour, let me kiss him.' We held her back and steered her immediately into another room.[7]

Such an exercise was meant to strike at the core of emotion and, as can be seen from this quotation, the interchange was solemnly logged by the secretary to establish the emotional and moral state of the defendant, to see if she had repented of her crime. The women's state of mind before, during, and after the deed was therefore probed by a variety of means and a characterization was built up through testimony, judicial interrogation, and medico-legal examination.

The same sense of drama accompanied the *criminelle passionnelle* into the courtroom. Already a symbolic setting, the *Cour d'assises* took on an even more theatrical aspect during the trials. Society ladies arrived to view the proceedings in their finest *toilettes* and were admiringly described by the attendant journalists. As Jean Cruppi described them: 'To imagine the Assize, let us choose a day when a *crime célèbre* is being tried; on such days, when the Parisian Court session is invaded by the public, the dominant note . . . is gaiety.'[8]

[7] Eugénie Pathier B . . . D2U8 217, 25/26 July 1887, *pièce* 53.
[8] Jean Cruppi, *La Cour d'assises* (Paris, 1898), 43.

Largely because of these elaborate preparations, the crime of passion was a universally recognized cultural phenomenon in which the outcome was, to a large extent, pre-ordained by the style and form of execution and presentation. As I shall show, it was these stylized aspects which not only defined the deed, but also assured exoneration and enabled women especially to express their emotions within the boundaries of a particular melodramatic mode.

Motive and Melodrama in the Crime of Passion

There were a variety of motives which impelled women to commit crimes of passion. Although various forms of abandonment and infidelity counted for the majority, they also killed simply to avenge their reputation. These murderesses tended to be society ladies who, dissatisfied with recognized judicial channels against libel and defamation, resorted to violence in much the same spirit as men engaging in a duel. Such ritualized male violence, illegal but often extolled during this period,[9] was off-limits to women wounded by slurs on their character. The most famous in this category were women like Mme Caillaux, the second wife of the controversial premier, who in 1914 shot and killed Gaston Calmette, the editor of *Le Figaro*, for printing the intimate love-letters she and the politician had written each other before their marriage. The resulting trial was so absorbing it was said that even the government neglected the more urgent matter of military preparations, waiting expectantly for the acquittal.[10]

An earlier crime which enlivened the public was that of Jeanne Royannez Clovis-Hughes, the wife of a Radical deputy, who had been falsely charged with fornication. Despite the

[9] Robert Nye of the University of Oklahoma at Norman is now beginning work on male duelling in the *fin de siècle* as part of a larger project on male sexuality and social roles in nineteenth- and twentieth-century France; Edward Berenson at the University of California at Los Angeles is completing a work on the Caillaux Affair which will also discuss male duelling.

[10] For another analysis of middle- and upper-middle-class murderesses see Mary Hartmann, *Victorian Murderesses: A True History of Thirteen Respectable French and English Women Accused of Unspeakable Crimes* (New York, 1977).

fact that the private investigator responsible for the attacks on her virtue was sentenced to prison for defamation in 1884, Mme Clovis-Hughes's sense of justice was not assuaged and she revenged herself more completely by shooting him six times as he was leaving the Palais de Justice. Her husband, himself the veteran of a duel, congratulated her on her success and she, in turn, proudly proclaimed her premeditation to the investigating magistrate and was duly acquitted by the jury.[11] The reactions to her crime were intensely ambivalent. Admired for her resolution, she was also seen as a peculiarly brutal and vengeful murderess, one who stooped so low as to shoot a man in the back. Her forcefulness aroused fear which even crept into the criminological commentary. In discussing her case, for example, Cesare Lombroso cited her slightly abnormal jutting jaw as an indication of unbecoming masculine determination.[12] However, this very combination of characteristics aroused sexual excitement, with a generous sample of the anonymous letters sent to the couple demonstrating the fantasies of desire woven around her: 'Your wife is just a vulgar whore . . . I myself have held Mlle Royannez [her maiden name] in my arms palpitating in an erotic spasm . . .'.[13]

These women were important exceptions in an otherwise more common selection of *petit bourgeois* women and *femmes du peuple* who murdered for reasons of abandonment, jealousy, or infidelity. Their notion of honour was also highly developed, but shaped out of a different set of claims which were easily recognized by contemporaries. They concentrated their complaints not on a defamatory third party but rather against the men directly responsible for their damaged marital and domestic prospects. There was, for example, the tapestry worker Amélie-Marie-Augustine S . . ., who threw vitriol into her husband's face, sentencing him to death for abandoning her when pregnant;[14] the domestic servant Marie-Françoise-Léontine F . . ., who tried to murder her lover, the father of

[11] Jeanne Royannez Clovis-Hughes D2U8 169, 8 Jan. 1885.

[12] Cesare Lombroso and Guglielmo Ferrero, *The Female Offender*, introd. by W. Douglas Morrison (London, 1895), 245.

[13] Jeanne Royannez Clovis-Hughes D2U8 169, 8 Jan. 1885, *pièce* 172.

[14] Amélie-Marie-Augustine S . . . D2U8 151, 25 Jan. 1884.

her unborn child, who deserted his familial responsibilities;[15] Désirée Zéphirine V . . ., who attempted to murder her former lover and the father of her child and also assaulted the wife who had supplanted her.[16]

All these women believed that their honour had been abused, and their explanations to the investigating magistrate set out an unwritten code that even official representatives of the law rarely disputed. For example, Désirée V . . . explained that, even after many years of separation, she could not forgive her ex-lover for leaving her: 'I only wanted to leave him a memory of me. He had taken my honour . . . He took me when I was chaste [*Il m'a pris sage (sic)*] and stole my honour . . . He wrecked my standing for ten years'.[17] Marie-Françoise-Léontine F . . . readily acknowledged her desire to kill her lover who had promised her marriage: '. . . I wanted to kill him. He wanted to abandon me after making me pregnant . . . He dishonoured me and dishonoured my family.'[18] Indeed, her lover made the court's task of acquittal simple when he cynically admitted: 'I promised her as one does with all young women; she was a novice, and it was the only way to get anywhere; otherwise she would not have given in to me.'[19] Finally, the *vitrioleuse* Amélie-Marie-Augustine S . . . considered her situation to have been made worse by the fact that her lover had sold the furniture and left with the proceeds. Speaking of her loss of honour, she said, 'he had lost my household',[20] an act which, like pawning jewels and other valuables, was an indication of damaged marital status within the community and hence a recognizable motive for a crime of passion.

In all these and numerous other cases, the motivation of the women involved coincided exactly with the moral outlook of the judges and intervening psychiatrists. When, for example, a woman had not been promised marriage or did give birth to a child, her claims to honourability were distinctly more difficult to prove. Moreover, when they admitted that they

15 Marie-Françoise-Léontine F . . . D2U8 156, 9 May 1884.

16 Désirée Zéphirine V . . . D2U8 147, 21 Sept. 1883.

17 Ibid., *pièce* 10.

18 Marie-Françoise-Léontine F . . . D2U8 156, 11 Jan. 1884, 1st interrogation.

19 Ibid., *pièce* 27.

20 Amélie-Marie-Augustine S . . . D2U8 151, 25 Jan. 1884, *pièce* 109.

wished to please themselves in love or, even worse, gave indications of sexual desire, the reaction was harsher. For example, in 1883 Edmée-Rose G . . . attempted to kill her lover P . . . when he tried to leave her after two years of living together. The son of a perfume manufacturer, P . . . was only able to pay off his gambling debts with his father's help and then only on condition that he break with her. Although she was an erstwhile waitress in a brasserie, and hence under suspicion of prostitution, he admitted that G . . . had served and cared for him devotedly despite his giving her a venereal disease. However, she repeatedly acknowledged that he never promised marriage and that she had not wanted it, and this admission immediately cast doubt on the validity of her motives. Her eccentric views on marriage brought on the following exchange in the *cabinet du juge d'instruction*:

> [Q] When a woman wants to be protected against desertion she finds a means of doing so through marriage; but if you had wanted to do so, you would have been obliged to marry a man of your own class and work to live; . . .
> [A] I never had a taste for marriage. I would have wanted to marry someone I could love, without worrying if he was rich or poor.[21]

In fact, because she refused the compensation which his family offered in return for a quiet, untroubled rupture, she was doubly criticized. The acceptance of the money on both sides represented a contract of silence, and her recalcitrance suggested that she wished to destroy the reputation of a bourgeois family. The investigating magistrate thus made a rigid distinction between her and the women cited above, remarking: '. . . your situation cannot be compared to those women whose adventures impress public sensibility; here there is no question of betrayed promises, seduction, cowardly abandonment, or disowned paternity.'[22]

Although she was decidedly outside the 'code of honour', and was denied the status of a *criminelle passionnelle* because tainted with the possibility of an avaricious motive, G . . . was none the less acquitted. Lenient treatment seemed appropriate

[21] Edmée-Rose G . . . D^2U^8 139, 29 Mar. 1883, *pièce* 41.
[22] Ibid.

because she was hardly even aiming at her intended victim when she pulled the trigger and also because, having committed the crime under unique and probably unrepeatable psychological circumstances, G . . . was not regarded as a 'criminal personality' and hence posed no future threat to society. Moreover, there was clearly some residual sympathy for a young, female outcast who had corrupted, and who was herself corrupted further by, the dissolute son of a bourgeois family.

A broken marriage promise, an unrecognized child, a virgin abandoned after giving in to the amorous and duplicitous advances of a dishonourable man, all of these were acts which not only offended the dignity of 'virtuous' women but also practically undermined their marital prospects and, with unmarried mothers, meant that a crucial means of financial support was lost. These cries of genuine distress were not a novel phenomenon. Such complaints were a common part of the interplay between family obligations and sexuality in earlier periods and in various cultures. However, one of the distinguishing characteristics of the *fin de siècle* crime of passion was its solitary nature, with the women taking matters into their own hands as the only means of 'resolving' their situation.

Remarkably absent from the scene are brothers or fathers, mothers or sisters, who occasionally testified before the judges but who were neither told of the murder plans nor were participants in their execution. All of the women cited above were born in the provinces, which at first sight suggests that the family network was unavailable to provide necessary support and unable to impose sanctions. However, there was also an equally large proportion of native *parisiennes* who adopted similar strategies of self-defence despite their family's proximity. In all these cases, and in many others, the women stood alone with revolver or vitriol in hand, waiting to inflict the damage.

Indeed, it was perhaps because these women were seemingly unprotected that they habitually received such sympathy. Certainly their fate is in marked contrast to that meted out in the rare examples in Paris of Italian families whose male members organized to protect the honour of their women. Marie

Antoinette El G . . . claimed to have been raped by her fiancé Esposito D . . ., who in turn denied any sexual advances and then refused to go ahead with the wedding plans. Faced with Esposito's denial and refusal, the girl's father and uncle killed him and at their trial in 1891 were rewarded with sentences of twenty and ten years' hard labour respectively. Such male lawlessness was unceremoniously condemned by judge and jury alike, the family's rights to protect its female members rejected.[23] It seems clear that their Italian origin and the fear of a bloody vendetta, perceived as a primitive sociological phenomenon endemic to 'inferior' southern 'races', contributed significantly to the harsh judicial assessment. Had Marie Antoinette herself committed the crime, she might have very well received a far more indulgent sentence, with her deed qualifying as a crime of passion.

Motive and style of execution were necessarily intertwined in determining the responses of the magistrates who prepared the cases for public examination. The perception of female violence was inseparable from the ritual texture of the scenario enacted—the period of emotional disturbance, the public execution of the deed, the pre-trial judicial interrogation, and the trial itself—during all of which the women presented a retrospective account of their feelings of despair, anger, and sometimes regret to the officials and to the public gallery. The characterization of public honour—based on damaged marital, financial, and social prospects—was generally accompanied by, and indeed perhaps inseparable from, an account of the psychological distress experienced by romantic disappointment. Indeed, no matter how humble, almost all referred to the dangerous and debilitating consequences of 'love sickness', to feelings of victimization and betrayal, and sometimes provided extended accounts of the 'illness' through letters, diaries, and sworn statements. As will be seen, the particular manner of this self-representation was crucial in arousing genuine compassion while at the same time rendering a portrait of female irresponsibility.

The case of Marie Magdeleine B . . ., which began this chapter, exemplifies many of the features of this particular

[23] Victor D . . . and Carmine D . . . D^2U^8 263, 2/3, Jan. 1891.

mode of feminine self-representation. Although ordinary enough in its outlines, the case was none the less unusual for the amount of written testimony which it left behind—an entire correspondence from an *homme galant* to his *petit bourgeois* mistress and her diary of 'love sickness'. These were carefully transcribed by the judicial officials, with her commentary inserted as marginalia in the manuscript. Like directions in a play, these recount her perception of the changes in their relationship, as well as her reconstruction of the emotional confrontations between them.

B . . . was a woman of modest origins who had won some success as a lyric singer. She characterized herself as an honourable woman who had, through some forcefulness of character, resisted the predations of men in the theatrical world until, during a tour to Biarritz, she met and fell in love with a rich *rentier* named Robert G. . . . The letters they wrote each other record the progress of their relationship. He wooed her gently prior to her 'fall', writing: 'You are, with no flattery at all, the most adorable woman that I have ever met.'[24] In return, she gave way to him without extracting either promise of marriage or guarantees for the future. She was none the less convinced that he would care for her forever, as he explained: 'I assume all responsibility, word [*foi*] of a gentleman [*galant homme*].'[25] However, he soon cooled towards her when he learnt she was pregnant and encouraged her to go to an abortionist, instructing her to burn the correspondence lest his family hear of these 'ennuis'.

She insisted on having the child despite his protests while he, in return, disavowed paternity and even refused to look at the child. Her letters to him expressed the anger and shame of her position, as she explained:

> If you knew the torture which you subject me to when you don't come to see me for two days, you would shed tears of shame and regret, because you are not as bad as you would like to appear.
>
> The torments of hell are nothing compared to those that I endure, and I must be strong indeed to continue living.
>
> Don't push me too far, Robert: I am capable of anything, even of killing myself, to make you feel remorse and to disturb you in your pleasures.

[24] Marie Magdeleine B . . . D2U8 92, 23 Mar. 1880, letter 4.

[25] Ibid., letter 5.

Of what rock is your heart fashioned?

I blush to have your child: it will have no love in its heart [aucun bon sentiment] and will curse its mother.

Listen! Tell me that you will never change: I will get rid of the two of us at the same time; it is better to finish everything right away because it would be cowardly to live the life you make me lead.

Mercy, Robert! Have pity; let me live because, I swear that I feel myself dying; I am at your feet; I weep; I implore you! Return, love me![26]

So despairing was she at his change of heart and refusal to see the child, she acquired a revolver and attempted suicide at his feet. In response, he threatened never to see her again and sought to avoid her. When the child died, he refused to go to the funeral, preferring instead to amuse himself with friends. After this incident she began to plan her vengeance, because of the wound inflicted on her as a grieving mother. In a journal entitled '*Impressions, douleurs, tortures*', she recorded her emotions, wrote poems, and stated her refusal to accept such treatment:

My daughter has been buried for seven months and it is four months since I have seen Robert.

He sends me money and imagines that I can live that sort of life!!!

No! a thousand times no!

I have vowed to die because he does not love me and because all hope of becoming a mother again is lost.

[26] Marie Magdeleine B . . . D^2U^8 92, 23 Mar. 1880, letter 34; she phrased the French as follows:

Si vous connaissiez les tortures que vous me faites subir, lorsque vous êtes deux jours sans venir me voir, vous verseriez des larmes de honte et de regret, car vous n'êtes pas aussi méchant que vous voulez paraître.

Les supplices de l'enfer ne sont rien, comparés à ceux que j'endure, et il faut que je sois vraiment forte pour exister encore . . .

Ne comblez pas la mesure, Robert: je suis capable de tout, même de me tuer, pour vous donner des remords et vous troubler dans vos plaisirs.

Mais de quel roc est donc sorti votre cœur?

Je rougis d'avoir un enfant de vous: il n'aura aucun bon sentiment et maudira sa mère.

Ecoute! dis-moi que tu ne changeras jamais: je te débarrasse des deux en même temps; il vaut mieux en finir tout de suite car il y aurait lâcheté à vivre de la vie que vous me faites.

Grâce, Robert! pitié, laissez-moi vivre, car, je vous jure, je me sens mourir, je suis à vos genoux, je pleure, je t'implore! reviens, aime-moi! . . .

But since I don't want another woman to be the mother of his children, I must kill him![27]

Other details, similar in content and various in form, could be produced almost endlessly from the texts of Marie B . . .'s case as well as from a range of other, more modest cases in which women of humble origin and modest occupation similarly expressed themselves in language reminiscent of a romantic heroine. For example, the domestic servant Agathe G . . . preceded her murder attempt against her soldier-lover for a broken marriage promise by suicidal letters and threats. In order to make him think of her suffering, she wrote: 'When you discover these few lines you will be rid of she who bothers you . . . You are therefore . . . free to walk on my corpse without fear . . .'.[28] Like her social superiors, she prepared her crime by writing poetry, verses used by the investigating magistrate to demonstrate her state of mind when she went into action:

> My heart is cold, my head is livid
> I am sad and don't know why . . .
> Always, like a spectre livid,
> Tedium stands before my eyes . . .[29]

The case of Marie B . . . was hence just one of several examples which demonstrate the romantic disappointment that resulted when male testimonials of love were followed by harsh words, disenchantment, abandonment, and finally emotional coldness. Through the marginalia to the text, and within the love-letters themselves, B . . . contrasted her self-appraisal of passionate devotion—proven by the deep feeling which prompted the suicide attempt and murder threat—with her

[27] In 'Impressions, douleurs, tortures', entry for 10 Nov. 1879. The French is: Il y a sept mois que ma fille est en terre, et voilà quatre mois que je n'ai vu Robert. Il m'envoie quelque argent et s'imagine que je peux vivre de cette vie-là! ! ! !. Non! mille fois non! J'ai résolu de mourir, puisqu'il ne m'aime pas et que tout espoir d'être encore mère est perdu. Mais je ne veux pas qu'une autre femme soit la mère de ses enfants à lui, et, pour cela, il faut que je le tue!

[28] Agathe G . . . D^2U^8 130, 28 June 1882, *pièce* 8e.

[29] Ibid., *pièce* 2; the French is:

> Mon cœur est froid, ma tête est livide,
> Je suis triste, et je ne sais pourquoi . . .
> Toujours, comme un spectre livide,
> L'ennui se dresse devant moi . . .

lover's contempt for her feelings, callousness towards the child, and mocking 'gallantry' that, in her view, sought to turn her into little more than a prostitute.

Once again it is difficult, if not impossible, to provide a deeper account of the complexity of emotional conflict. Instead, we are left only with these stylized self-representations, the structure and nature of which may provide some insight into the more limited historical problem of why this method of feminine expression prior to the crime itself and during the process of judicial evaluation proved so persistent and attractive. In trying to understand this set of linguistic expressions, I was struck by the homology with the style of the romantic heroine in the theatre as well as in a range of other texts—be they the *faits divers*, the *feuilleton*, or even the novel. The critical analysis of melodrama, a rhetorical mode which pervades these literary forms, may provide some insight into the nature of the language employed and the emotional effects it was often successful in producing.

As Brooks[30] and others have demonstrated, melodrama emerged from pantomime during the Revolutionary years and was refined as a popular form which drew all classes to the theatre. It was constantly re-adapted, reshaped, and transmuted throughout the century, with even the 'bourgeois' and 'social' theatre and novel which emerged in later periods partaking of the style in modified form, albeit with a concentration on altered themes.[31] As Brooks has explained, melodrama's major characteristic is hyperbole, an emphasis on ideal oppositions and a plasticity of representation which leaves little to the audience's imagination. In melodrama, participants give vent to their innermost thoughts, leaving no one guessing as to the intentions underlying their actions. Indeed, there is no psychology *per se*, only a constant restatement and

[30] Peter Brooks, *The Melodramatic Imagination: Balzac, Henry James, Melodrama and the Mode of Excess* (New Haven, 1976).

[31] Melodramatic theatre had its heyday during the first few decades of the nineteenth century; see, for example, Maurice Albert, *Les Théâtres des Boulevards, 1789–1848* (Paris, 1902); the continuation of melodramatic language and plots, with increasing psychological complexity, can be observed throughout the nineteenth-century theatre in its romantic and realist guises; see Michel Lioure, *Le Drame de Diderot à Ionesco* (Paris, 1973); also Armand Kahn, *Le Théatre social en France de 1870 à nos jours* (Paris, 1907).

continual clarification of virtue and the attempt by the forces of evil to undermine and deride it.

In romantic melodrama, as opposed to other subjects which focus on brigands, monstrous crimes, or other kinds of catastrophes such as tempests, famines, fires, shipwrecks, etc.,[32] the 'good'[33] heroine figures as the incarnation of virtue, an '*ange pur*'. The dramatic tension of the plot revolves around her plight, generally made desperate by the insensitivity, deceitfulness, or even villainy of men. Indeed, such literature provides a powerful, if stylized representation of animosity between the sexes, one which bears a striking analogical relationship to that contained in the self-representations of *criminelles passionnelles*.[34]

In writing of the conventional traits of the romantic heroine, Ihring has focused on her characterization in which 'purity and innocence, dishonour and shame are the aspects most stressed'.[35] Such protagonists are both made for love and destined to be tortured by it. They wept, fainted, and trembled in reaction to fear and dishonour and were prone to rhetorical flights in which they described their plight and the (generally) masculine forces of evil which put obstacles in the way of romantic union. They were convinced that they were made for

32 The spectacular theatre grew more sumptuous as the century drew to a close and seemed to attract ever larger audiences; see Eugen Weber, *France: fin de siècle* (Cambridge, Mass., 1986), 166; for an analysis of similar developments in England see M. R. Booth, *Victorian Spectacular Theatre, 1850–1910* (London, 1981). The other literary genre devoted to the same melodramatic presentation was the *faits divers*; see *Le Fait divers* (Musée national des arts et traditions populaires, Paris, 19 Nov.–18 Apr. 1983), catalogue edited by Alain Monestier; and *Les Canards illustrés du 19e siècle: Fascination du fait divers* (Musée-galerie de la Séita, Paris, 9 Nov. 1982–30 Jan. 1983), catalogue edited by Jean-Pierre Seguin.

33 There was an equal number of 'evil' heroines in both literature and in the melodramatic portrayal of famous women offenders; one of the most notorious was Marguerite Steinheil, who, in 1908, was accused of murdering both her husband and her mother. As Elisa D. Gelfand has explained: 'Women like Steinheil were viewed as villains in the popular social melodramas of the time: she was the "tragic widow", the "whimsical actress", and her trial was a "Shakespearean drama" with "clowns" and "traitors", a "theatre the night of a grand opening".' See Gelfand's *Imagination in Confinement: Women's Writing from French Prisons* (Ithaca, 1983), 180. After a year in preventive incarceration Mme Steinheil was acquitted.

34 For further reflections of the romantic heroine throughout the nineteenth century and the changes of style in her representation see Jules Bertaut, *La Jeune Fille dans la littérature française* (Paris, 1910).

35 Grace Pauline Ihrig, *Heroines in French Drama of the Romantic Period, 1829–1848* (New York, 1950), 9.

misfortune, and at moments were inclined to pray for death as a release from the consequences of this deceitful life. For example, the heroine of Bourgeois and Francis's *Jeannette*, published in 1831, expressed herself in a manner similar to that of Marie B . . .: 'Ah . . . Death! For me, it would be a blessing [*indulgence*], pity, forgiveness perhaps . . . Ah! to die, to die, that is my only wish, my only desire . . . Heaven inspires me . . . Yes . . . shame ends in the tomb.'[36]

Romantic heroines came in a variety of stylized forms, representations which had in common an atmosphere of intrigue and seduction of which they were the unconscious victims. Sometimes they were virtuous, solitary mothers obliged to protect their offspring in a hostile world. Without protectors, they were often the subject of masculine predations and were hence forced to make promises which compromised their virtue. Others were *ingénues*, sentimental hearts filled with dreams of romantic love and unschooled in the duplicitous wiles of men. They gave themselves generously at the first indication of masculine passion and were naïvely predisposed to take male promises in good faith. Sometimes, indeed, the romantic heroine was even a 'fallen woman' who is scorned by society while her seducer goes unpunished, a recognition of the social condition of women who were uncompensated and unprotected by the law. Such virtuous characters were not limited to the upper ranks of society. Women of the poorer classes, innocent servants, clerks, artists, and the unemployed also figure prominently as innocent maidens ready to believe the avowals of love made by corrupt social superiors who, having triumphed in seduction, immediately tire of their feminine playthings. As one hero remarked to his distraught mistress: 'Get out of my sight, coward who believes that the honour of a woman and her love can pay for themselves. Go, I despise you as much as I abhor you.'[37]

Clearly, the crime of passion was not a play. Indeed, one of the greatest distinctions between dramas and these crimes was the way in which, rather than turning to other masculine protectors to 'solve' their predicament or relieve their distress, the 'real-life' heroines became violent agents, avenging their

[36] Ihrig, op. cit. 12.

[37] Ibid., 138, quoted in Frédéric Soulié's *La Closerie des Genêts* (Paris, 1846).

honour in a way not generally associated with the 'gentler sex'. Despite this important disjunction, the similarity between melodrama and the crime of passion rested on the coincidence of rhetorical form and style of execution. This was particularly striking in the case of Marie B . . ., who was herself an actress, put on a disguise to stalk her lover, and described her emotions in theatrical terms.

The romantic distress in both the literary and legal records demonstrates a similar predilection towards an emotionally transparent self-representation and the use of ideal oppositions to explain issues of immense psychological complexity. The extremes provided by both play and trial offered, at least for audiences, an opportunity for ritualistic catharsis and an affirmation of shared values. Sometimes the affecting nature of a case would literally reduce the public gallery to tears almost in the same way that a stage performance pulled the heart-strings of an attentive audience. In 1901, for example, Eugénie Danciot came before the court to answer for the murder of her lover who had promised her marriage, was the father of her child, and then sought to marry someone else when his parents discovered their intimate correspondence. Her extreme youth, sincere love for the young man, as well as her desire for the child, whom he encouraged her first to abort and then to deposit at the *Assistance publique*, all aroused the sympathy of the largely female public in attendance. As the journalist for the *Gazette des tribunaux* remarked: 'Today, at the Assizes there were tears amongst the elegant female audience crowded into the chamber. Even those that could restrain their tears were unable to shield themselves against strong feeling.'[38]

While *criminelles passionnelles* were often greeted with sympathy and sadness, they also had to contend with another range of emotional responses, including derision and sarcasm. It was this second set of reactions, as intimately related to melodrama as the first, which may explain why women and their deeds were often met by a characteristic lack of respect. In the end, melodrama differs essentially from tragedy. If the latter is meant to reaffirm universal values which no one dare mock, then melodrama evokes very different responses. In contrast to

38 *Gazette des tribunaux*, 5 Apr. 1901.

the tragic heroine, the romantic protagonist has no tragic flaw which can be held responsible for her demise. On the contrary, her virtuous innocence emphasizes female helplessness and contributes to a portrait of victimization so transparent that it militates against sustained interest.

In melodrama the play's success depends on its ability to absorb the audience's sympathy by revealing the dastardly doings of the heroine's enemies and contrasting them to the 'pure' qualities and commendable aspirations of the heroine. The narrative of injustice which the *criminelle passionnelle* presented in court was subject to the same standards of judgement. Sometimes the sympathetic appraisal of female crimes of passion was lost in a commentary which mockingly focused on the repetitive style of the deeds, an inference which suggested that their innocence was not total.

There was, therefore, an implicit accusation of contrivance, reinforced by the fact that many of the attackers seemed almost determined to miss their targets. When explaining themselves to the police they insisted on their premeditation, thereby assuring an appearance in the *Cour d'assises*, which alone was judicially competent to try cases of premeditated, first-degree murder. It seems possible that the women knew that if they answered a charge of simple assault their cases would be 'correctionalized', sent to the *Tribunal correctionnel*, where a panel of three judges and no jury determined penalties. Were they 'playing the odds', angling for an acquittal by addressing the jury and the occasion to embarrass their ex-mates while emerging from their ordeal with no penal record? In some cases, certainly, the unhurt victims asked the *juge d'instruction* to drop charges, expressly because they did not want their mistresses to be prosecuted, but perhaps also because they wished to avoid the damage to their reputations which a courtroom trial would bring.[39]

Moreover, the way in which some left behind grief-stricken poems and notes of homicidal intent reminiscent of the convention of leaving farewell missives prior to suicide, suggests a possible recognition of the appropriateness of certain forms.

[39] See, for example, the case of Edmée G . . . D^2U^8 139, 29 Mar. 1883, whose lover Monsieur P . . . wished that the whole matter be dropped.

One student of female crime, Camille Granier, actually referred to the ostensible lack of originality which marked women's deeds.

It isn't surprising that she succeeds in making people believe in the uniqueness of each crime. The female delinquent undoubtedly premeditates her attack and embellishes it more readily than does a man. But she fails to avoid repetition and to conceal the poverty of her invention.[40]

Women's 'embellishment' of their acts—their stylized discourse of betrayal—is seen by Granier as merely unimaginative self-dramatization. His assessment points to the central dilemma. In seeking to provide a coherent explanation for their acts both to themselves and to their putative audience, their melodramatic mode of presentation—from the committal of the crime right through public trial—had a deeply ambiguous effect. It promoted celebrity and evoked genuine compassion, while at the same time undermining any real comprehension of the painful and complex motives behind women's criminal acts. It often produced acquittal, but at the cost of appearing to collude in a generalized judgement of women as emotionally histrionic and irresponsible. The novelist Paul Bourget put it clearly in his satirical view of the reactions of an abandoned woman:

When you want to break with a woman, . . . simply take the train without making a song and dance [*sans tambour ni trompette*] and allow twenty-four hours for her to get over wanting to shoot you. During these forty-eight hours [*sic*] she shrieks, she storms, she buys laudanum, she poisons herself, she makes a mess of it. As in all things, she doubles the dose, but when you return, you have been replaced.[41]

Such mockery was based on an acknowledgement of a familiar style which, being universally recognizable, was less threatening. The texture of the ritual scenario provided a framework in which women were simultaneously excused and dismissed. As suggested, the instruments contributing to this assessment were a language which characterized the reality of love and its loss, the representation of the ordeal of abandonment

40 Camille Granier, *La Femme criminelle* (Paris, 1906), pp. vi–vii.
41 Quoted in Léon Rabinovitch, *Les Crimes passionnels* (Paris, 1931), 138–9.

and a particular form of execution in which the deed was committed publicly, without shame and with a willingness to be caught immediately afterwards.

Hysteria, Suggestion, and the Crime of Passion

The exaggerated emotional state of women was an important feature of a view which regarded them as hysterical, a characterization which was regularly used in the courtroom to describe women's ostensibly unaccountable behaviour. As has been seen, in Charcot's clinic, hysteria represented a very specific conception of bodily illness linked to a wide array of psychological and behavioural abnormalities. In lay parlance, however, it was used to denote any common form of excess emotion. Physicians and jurists used the term in both ways, sometimes referring to particular physical or neurosphysiological symptoms and/or a technical appreciation of deranged emotions, while at other times calling a woman hysterical when making general statements on women's volatility, infantilism, unpredictability, and suggestibility. The way in which these two strands of characterization interpenetrated—and indeed how women's self-representations were used to enrich this portrait of irresponsibility—will now be discussed.

When women came under the physicians' gaze during their pre-trial detention, it was generally to determine whether or not they were afflicted by hysteria. Although rarely adjudged entirely insane (no female defendant in this era was ever identified as suffering from *grande hystérie*), they were equally rarely given a clean bill of health. On the contrary, their excessively emotional nature was generally linked to bodily symptoms and familial history. Degenerative taints were searched for, peculiarities of development—particularly the onset of menstruation—were noted, and any evidence of *petite hystérie* minutely described.

In examining these women, physicians were placed in a peculiarly difficult position. As always, they were obliged to draw boundaries between passion and illness, to determine the difference between exalted sentiments on the one hand and morbid impulsions on the other, even though both necessarily affected judgement, will-power, and character. As in many other instances in which their expertise was called for, alienists had the effect of excusing the crime but condemning the perpetrator with the taint of abnormality. A touch of hysteria—a tendency to sobbing, unwillingness to eat, or a mercurial character—could explain away seemingly unwholesome motives and at the same time imply that the individual was not seriously dangerous or deserving of punishment.[42] There were those who demonstrated some 'classic' hysterical symptoms such as retraction of the visual field, hemianesthesia (loss of sensibility on one half of the body), or susceptibility to hypnosis.[43] Still others evidenced minor hysterical fits with '*mouvements expansifs*' while in prison.[44] While acknowledging these deviations from the norm, however, the doctors decided that none of these women was irresponsible. As will be seen, however, they were eager to lend their expert support to a wider view of female irresponsibility, and regarded these defendants sympathetically as *femmes passionnées* rather than *malades*.

Occasionally, however, they found women both repellent and dangerous, and reflected their reactions in the medical reports. The hysterical dispositions of such women would be linked to instinctual disorder and mental defects, as in the case of Louise C . . ., who became the object of medical scorn and even undisguised anger. The servant-mistress of a medical colleague, she made accusations which were the nightmare of the profession, asserting that her *maître* had infected her with a venereal disease and given her an abortion. After having been 'demoted' to the kitchen when her employer's brother came to Paris, she pursued the physician with vitriol and menaced him in the streets. Ultimately, she rented an apartment in the Rue de Dunkerque, hired a lady's maid to complete the effect, and,

[42] Edmée Rose G . . . D2U8 139, 29 Mar. 1883, medico-legal report by Paul Brouardel.

[43] Blanche Augustine D . . . D2U8 283, 23 Mar. 1892, medico-legal report by Gilbert Ballet.

[44] Marie Françoise Léontine F . . . D2U8 156, 9 May 1884, medico-legal report by Benjamin Ball.

posing as a respectable married woman who had fallen ill, charged her servant to send for him. In the struggle that ensued after he arrived she managed to wound him in the eyelid and thigh.

When examining her, Dr Bouchereau recounted with disgust her high spirits, the fact that after several months she recounted her exploits with an 'obvious joy' and was particularly satisfied about the shame which must have befallen the doctor and his family. Moreover, she showed no need to explain her vengeful deeds, nor to repent of them. For the psychiatrist she was an obvious degenerate, combining a hysterical disposition—exaggerated emotions and a characteristic tendency towards lying—with what he termed *débilité mentale*. Her feeble-mindedness was evidenced, not by any derangement of the mental faculties, but by her insistence that she, a mere servant-girl without any pretence to virtue, had the right to punish her employer. He described her as having

> . . . a deficiency of balance in all her being: her inferior functions are developed at the expense of her higher ones: everything that makes up animal life dominates her brain; . . . like all degenerate beings, she slavishly obeys her instincts . . . dissembling natures like hers never tell the truth . . . in her responses it is difficult to separate truth from falsehood . . . She showed herself to be whimsical, fickle, irritable, lazy . . . There is no doubt that Louise C . . . is a hysterical woman, presenting the exaggerations, the perversions of character and feeling so commonly found among those impaired by this neurosis.[45]

Despite these condemnatory remarks, not so dissimilar to the medical characterization of male degenerates afflicted by moral imbecility, Bouchereau and his colleagues hesitated in affirming her irresponsibility.[46] Psychiatrists generally reserved a diagnosis of degeneration for those whom they wished to see condemned as both mentally unstable and socially dangerous. In such cases their role as the humane guardians of the insane clashed with their other position as medical policemen and social hygienists, the first dedicated to treating the unfortunate,

[45] Louise C . . . D²U⁸ 195, 28 Apr. 1886, first medico-legal report by Dr Bouchereau.

[46] Ibid., second medico-legal report by Dr Bouchereau, Motet, and Ballet.

the second to containing the dangerous excesses of pathological individuals. In their view Louise C . . . fell into the second category and ought to have been punished with the full weight of the law. This is one of the few cases in which a negative medical characterization of a vicious degenerate was not reinforced by the court, which decided to acquit the vengeful servant. Indeed, it seems that her claims to have contracted venereal disease from her employer, as well as the allegations about the abortion, allowed her to receive judicial indulgence despite her obvious defects of character.

The physicians' attitude to Louise C . . . was somewhat unusual because she herself and the way in which she committed her crime were also slightly extraordinary. Faced with the habitual run of depression, anguish, and remorse which most *criminelles passionnelles* displayed, the alienists were inclined to concentrate on their woes and forget the victims. In case after case, they pointed to extreme behavioural characteristics, but avoided the harsher medical vocabulary of degeneration. They cited 'strange behaviour', 'wild natures' (*natures emportées*), 'nervous crises', or 'excited passions', but ruled out other terms such as 'delirium' and 'morbid impulsion', which would have required a conclusion of insanity and hence irresponsibility.

Moreover, in most of these cases, the women's self-representation of their mental state reflected, in lay terms, the psychological portrait painted by the psychiatrists. Using language which signified a state of temporary madness before and during the crime, they maintained that they had acted in a 'blind impulse of jealousy and rage', in a moment of 'panic', 'excitation', or 'madness', all passions that were attributed to the moral outrage they had suffered. The nature of the medical sympathy towards these women can be seen from Paul Garnier's assessment of Marie Velsch P . . ., an abandoned wife who unsuccessfully tried to murder her husband and new mistress. In reporting on the case, the alienist wrote:

> Femme P . . . could not tolerate a situation which was in reality distressing and painful. A deep resentment, the pride of an outraged wife, armed her, rather than delirium . . . passion is not madness. However, when the will is subdued by a state of passion, penal responsibility can be diminished, but such an evaluation falls within the orbit of a moralist rather than of a physician.[47]

[47] Marie Velsch P . . . D2U8 212, 24 Mar. 1887, medico-legal report by Paul Garnier.

Garnier was thus unwilling to 'medicalize' her deed, but continued by stating that her responsibility was attenuated by nervous exasperation and exaltation. Femme P . . . was acquitted by the jury.

Nor was he alone in expressing himself compassionately. Motet, for example, in examining Désirée V . . ., who tried to kill her old lover for abandoning her, was visibly moved by the woman's sorrowful remembrance of her dead baby and acknowledged the enormous financial sacrifice she made to buy it a burial plot. Knowing that she made her living as a seamstress, he remarked: 'she underwent hardship in order to amass the necessary amount; in this respect, she appeared to us to be an unhappy woman worthy of pity'.[48] Moreover, he demonstrated an appreciation of emotional complexity, recognizing that she had taken a casual lover to become pregnant again but refusing to judge her for her moral irregularity. In fact, he suggested that her pregnancy was an extenuating circumstance, one which contributed to her current emotional instability. At the same time, he resolutely refused to acknowledge any serious mental defect.

The role of the psychiatrists in such cases was, therefore, decidedly ambiguous. On the one hand, there was an acknowledged need for medical expertise to determine a specific technical issue—the impact of hysteria, with the possible complication of a delirious or impulsive complication. But in all the instances in which the physiological signs of hysteria were cited, the psychiatrists none the less asserted that these alone were insufficient to warrant a medical evaluation of insanity. However, when hysteria was not in evidence, they provided a portrait of deranged emotions and passions which was, in behavioural and descriptive terms, virtually indistinguishable from the medical portrait of the disease. In fact, they were merely underscoring a strong element of medical thinking on the subject of hysteria which saw little difference between normal and hysterical women. Hysteria was 'one of the expressions, one of the conditions of the feminine character'.[49] What seemed, therefore, like an exercise in

[48] Désirée Zéphirine V . . . D2U8 147, 21 Sept. 1883, medico-legal report by Motet.

[49] The physician Henri Huchard, quoted in Gérard Wajeman, *Le Maître et l'hystérique* (Paris, 1982), 131.

distinction and categorization tended to assimilate all women under an umbrella of uncontrollable impulsion, irritation, fickleness, and excitation. The only major distinction they did seek to make was between hysterics who were morally corrupt—those like Louise C . . .—and others who were merely prisoners of their neurotic natures, volatile but not malicious, and frequently worthy of genuine compassion.

But while there was a grudging acknowledgement of the motives and temporary madnesses of seduced and abandoned women, there were other instances in which women's accusations and actions were considered too threatening. For example, Mlle Gélo, a young Russian medical student, tried to kill a philosophy professor at the Collège de France, implying that the aged and ostensibily irreproachable scholar had sexually abused her. Her deed was made all the more terrible in that she missed her target and inadvertently killed her best friend who was trying to disarm her. The judge clearly had difficulty in accepting her version of the event and sought to find some medical reason for her apparent hallucination, asking Garnier the following question: 'Wasn't there in this instance a kind of auto-suggestion?' The psychiatrist replied: 'This phenomenon is not rare. Notably, after a dream, the hysteric can in good faith imagine an event that never existed. Very often, too, the hysteric lies.'[50] In this instance, a medical view of mental disturbance was deemed to explain the woman's apparent misapprehension. This view was automatically, indeed indissolubly, linked to the professed opinion of the presiding judge: he not only confirmed Mlle Gélo's neuropathic state but also focused on female irrationality in the abstract, a position which he maintained was proven by her refusal to relate the details of the compromising encounter. The implication was that women let their imaginations carry them away, were prone to fabricate stories, and in good faith believe themselves to be victims of male violation when nothing had actually occurred. In such a case, the attempted murder was seen as a wasteful if not derisory gesture, an opinion substantiated both by the medical view of deranged nature and the legal assertion of simple irrationality, two pronouncements on her state of mind

[50] *Gazette des tribunaux*, 20 Apr. 1901.

which were so mutually reinforcing as to be virtually indistinguishable. She was acquitted and returned to Russia.

The tendency to excuse women for their crimes was promoted by the view that they were not quite adults and therefore not fully responsible for themselves. Their inferior intellectual development meant that they were often described as minors, a social and biological state which destined them to childbearing and rearing roles. So, when discussing the apparent cruelty of their acts, reference was made to their particular stage of evolutionary development in which their childish viciousness suggested an inherent savagery. It was maintained that biological demands of maternity were so great that this impaired their sense of judgement, of 'intellectual synthesis', and made them more callous, intractable, and inured to moralization and repentance than men. One medical commentator expressed this sentiment concisely in 1910:

> If women commit fewer crimes, they are . . . more cruel, more obstinate . . . less likely to repent than men . . . The great and miraculous function of maternity, the necessity of maintaining the species, condemns the reproducing woman [*la créatrice*] to an inferior degree of individual evolution and, . . . by her lesser capacity for mental synthesis and her impulsiveness, places her . . . between the adolescent and the adult.[51]

At the same time, their childish side meant that they were more easily suggestible and prone to reflexive, imitative behaviour which, by and large, was foolish rather than savage. Hence, crimes of passion, and the way in which they were regarded as rituals to be repeated by any number of disgruntled females, were seen as infantile, hysterical, and an eminently feminine means of attracting attention.

In this period, medical men and jurists involved in criminological debate sought to understand the mechanism of mental contagion which generated particular fashions for violence. The physician Paul Aubry concerned himself particularly with psychic degeneration and the role women played as suggestible recipients for 'contagious' ideas. He described the process in 1890 as 'a mixture, a combination of four

[51] Quoted in Hélie Courtis, *Étude médico-légale des crimes passionnels*, DM thesis (Toulouse, 1910), 10.

terms: suggestion, imitation, heredity, and contagion'.[52] He maintained that this psycho-biological coincidence explained mental epidemics in general and the crime of passion in particular.

Like many others working in the criminological domain, Aubry associated himself with the advances of Pasteurian microbiology through the use of a system of germ/culture metaphors, and described the growth of murder as the 'morbid element' in a '*terrain préparé*'. In his view, the unhealthy soil was the French population which having little judgement, and even less fortitude, was susceptible to the unseemly delights of public exhibitionism that the crime of passion offered. Women were particularly prone to such behaviour, and were irresponsibly urged on by the journalistic world that flattered the stupid vanity of the female mind. As he explained,

> . . . the newspapers recount at length all of the details of the trial; they describe the charms of the defendant, her *toilette*, her previous life; they reproduce some of their letters; some even go so far as to give to their subscribers a portrait of this interesting person. What more is needed to excite the imagination of a woman who is often not very intelligent? It is easy to throw vitriol at someone; one is certain to be acquitted and to be gossiped about for forty-eight hours.[53]

In describing the *criminelles passionnelles* in this fashion, Aubry referred to the common variety of female offender. There were, however, extraordinary cases which created more anxiety and once again raised the issue of unconscious suggestion and its dangerous implications for moral and social order. For example, cases of previously respectable women, who ran off with unsuitable men and preferred a *suicide à deux* to their 'natural' position, were posthumously analysed to understand the pathological mental state which had prompted them to take such deviant action. In cases of passionate romance, couples were bound together by 'rapture', either through a kind of mutual suggestibility which operated on both of them, or through the domination of one partner over the other. In the latter instance, commentators stressed the domineering effect the man had on his 'enchanted' mistress in an attempt to neutralize the implied criticism of bourgeois norms that

52 Paul Aubry, *La Contagion du meutre: Etude d'anthropologie criminelle* (Paris, 1896), 1.
53 Ibid., 107.

women's sometimes 'scandalous' behaviour offered. Such a discussion surrounded the celebrated and ambiguous Chambige affair of 1888 in which Mme Grille, a thirty-year-old English protestant wife and mother, of impeccable character, was found naked and dead in a villa in Sidi-Mabrouck, Algeria, beside the twenty-two-year-old Henri Chambige.[54]

Rather than disowning his wife, M. Grille, a prominent colonial notable, maintained that she had been 'fascinated' by Chambige, who had lured her to the isolated villa in order to rape and murder her. In contrast to the prosecution's case, Chambige asserted that the highly strung wife had herself proposed the double suicide, unable to reconcile her passionate love for the younger man with the cruel abandonment of her adored children. The case was further complicated by the fact that Chambige was a promising new member of the decadent school of literature who had written an article on 'the Goncourt brothers and exoticism' and whose perverted propensity for such nihilistic work, the prosecution maintained, had 'suggested' the idea of murder in order to desecrate the values of duty and honour that this 'model family'[55] represented. It cannot be known whether love or literature was in fact the ultimate cause of the crime, but the suggestible power of both was used as a means of explaining the murder and of underscoring the destructive excesses which such passions produced.

For contributors to the *Archives d'anthropologie criminelle*, the Chambige Affair typified 'the eternal legend of the dove fascinated by the vulture and ensnared [*venant se jeter*] in its talons.'[56] They were unwilling to countenance the possibility that Mme Grille had participated in her fate. Gabriel Tarde was so disturbed by the implications of her death that he carefully developed a case for her temporary insanity:

> For me when Mme G[rille] was taken away with Chambige in the carriage to the Villa Sidi-Mabrouck, it was not her, but rather a semi-lunatic that went, and I judge her almost completely irresponsible. I see the proof of this in what preceded and in what followed; in the abrupt way she forgot her children upon leaving and, sub-

[54] For an account of the trial see Gaston Lèbre (ed.), 'L'Affaire Chambige', in *Revue des grands procès contemporains* (Paris, 1889), 21–101.

[55] Ibid., 22.

[56] Émile Laurent, 'Les Suggestions criminelles', *Archives d'anthropologie criminelle*, 5 (1890), 631.

sequently, in the horror of their memory which took the form of regret for not having brought them, in the suddenness of her terrible decision, and in the unheard of indecency of the crime's execution. This zealous Christian wanted to die like a pagan, and the deep and sudden collapse of her Christianity suggests that the crime cannot be explained away as a mere sign of the times but is rather a manifest symptom of her madness.[57]

With such explanations, Mme Grille's behaviour was rationalized while Chambige was condemned as a reprobate, not only for the values he embodied but also for having survived his mate, a fact which put at risk his claim that she had wished to die. He was punished with a penalty of seven years' imprisonment and the case itself came to embody anxieties about a whole range of other moral, sexual, and social-psychological problems. The specialist commentary surrounding the *affaire* reveals the links made between marital infidelity, cultural decadence, and harmful suggestibility which could produce temporary insanity and, in a moment, sweep away treasured values, social boundaries, and even the instinct for self-preservation. This set of sentiments was perhaps most eloquently expressed in Paul Bourget's preface to his novel *Le Disciple*, a fictionalized account of a not too dissimilar crime which counselled young men to resist the temptations of *fin de siècle* materialism in favour of traditional values. While an enormous commentary surrounded the examination of female passivity in such instances, an equally anxious and rich analysis of educated, masculine middle-class decadence pervaded an accompanying analysis of male responsibility.

Theories of suggestion, contagion, or enticement emphasized the childish and passive side of female 'nature'. However, other aspects of the crime of passion generated more worry. Unwilling to tolerate philandering, women seemed to be showing an unbecoming 'masculine' determination, demonstrated most forcefully by the unladylike habit of carrying firearms and throwing vitriol. The majority of *criminelles passionnelles* were *revolvériennes*, the widespread use of guns generating a degree of sexual equality in murder if in nothing else, and allowing the physically weaker female to inflict as much harm as men. Mme

57 Tarde, 'L'Affaire Chambige', *Archives d'anthropologie criminelle*, 4 (1889), 101.

Clovis-Hughes, for example, was an excellent shot, had been given a small revolver by her husband, and was known to regard it 'like a jewel'.[58] Moreover, the small hand-gun seemed particularly suited to female needs. Not only was it easily hidden in a handbag, it also, unlike the knife, dagger, or sword-stick employed more frequently by men, allowed the offender a greater distance from her victim and hence from the attack's horrifying outcome.

On the other hand, the fact that women were frequently bad shots, missed their targets, and often seemed glad to do so, made them at the same time the butt of jokes about female incompetence. These reassuring failures, the fact that they were often appalled by the actual killing, and keen not to view the bloody results, were all seen as evidence of their fundamental frailty and sensibility and the ultimately inconsequential nature of their violence. Hence, the discussion of women carrying firearms demonstrated a persistent tendency to swing uneasily between the perception of dangerous potency and harmless impotence, the phallic symbolism of the weapons raising anxieties which could be at least partially offset by the perception of female ineptitude and emotionalism.

This range of reactions was expressed even more vehemently in the case of the *vitrioleuses*, whose acts of disfigurement produced horrified and frightened responses. The male commentary on these offences emphasized what they perceived as loathsome cruelty which, by blurring and burning the victim's features, meted out a fate which to some was worse even than death. Vitriol-throwing was the annihilation of individuality, robbing the victim of his distinctive human traits through burning and obliteration. Perhaps even more significantly, it condemned the victim to a life in which his appearance could only evoke repulsion or pity, with the intent to deprive him or her of the possibility of further amorous or sexual activity. In fact, this was often the stated goal of the vitriol-thrower, who aimed as frequently at female rivals as against disloyal mates.

In defending themselves, the *vitrioleuses* referred not only to the loss of love and loyalty, but more grandly to a loss of social

[58] Jeanne Royannez Clovis-Hughes D2U8 169, 8 Jan. 1885, *pièce* 8. As she remarked, '. . . Besides, I thought of this revolver more like a jewel than a real weapon.'

position, a theme which recurs no matter what class they came from. The stated aim was therefore to produce the same effect on the victim and confer a state of sexual and social impotence, an almost literal 'loss of face', which was considered to be an appropriate vengeance for the wrongs they had caused. This can be seen in the case of the Comtesse de Létil, whose crime was said to have started off the vogue for vitriol-throwing. A thirty-year-old aristocrat, known for her intelligence and affection for her four children, she had the misfortune to have an adulterous and indiscreet husband. Describing her elevated motives for throwing vitriol at her upstart rival, the countess told the court in 1880: 'I wanted to mark this girl's face . . . not because she was my husband's mistress, not even because she covered the name of my family with dishonour, but because she could have become the mother of my children after my death.'[59]

Having laid her unimpeachable motives before the jury, the Comtesse was duly acquitted. The trial provided a precedent for clemency which Parisian lawyers were keen to exploit when pleading for less elevated clients. For example, in December of the same year, Mme Tarpeau vitriolized her husband's mistress, and in pleading her case the defence attorney reminded the court that: 'Your predecessors have acquitted de Létil, a lady of distinction; you have before you an honourable working woman who was as unhappy as she. Will you condemn her?'[60] So, despite the universal horror with which vitriol-throwing was greeted, the ethos of the crime of passion none the less triumphed in rendering even this deed somehow acceptable. Although perceived as a premeditated act of brutality and cruelty, the familiar representation of honourable motives meant that even the *vitrioleuse* was often acquitted.

The *criminelle passionnelle* was a solitary figure who acted openly and eloquently before the world, insisting that society take account of her honourable intentions. The leniency afforded her was no doubt in large part due to the way in which she was compared and contrasted with other exemplars of female crime within the criminological literature of the era. The indulgent

[59] Gustave Macé, *La Police parisienne, femmes criminelles* (Paris, 1904), 21.
[60] Ibid., 24.

verdicts meted out to her were similarly bestowed on the infanticidal mother, if as a young innocent she was seduced by rapacious employers and sought to hide her offence by killing her baby.[61] She too was considered to be acting out of honour and a sense of shame and, although her deed was condemned, her motives were readily deemed 'understandable' by medicolegists and judges.

Such offenders were often contrasted favourably with another set of 'evil' or 'bad' women. Abortionists, for example, were seen as acting in stealth through a network of female complicity from which they sought to profit.[62] Domestic cruelty was also condemned, and women who beat their children through a programme of seemingly relentless torture often received the highest penalties of the era.[63] Finally, on the spectrum of female criminality, the *criminelle passionnelle* was

[61] See Paul Brouardel, *Le Mariage, nullité, divorce, grossesse, accouchement* (Paris, 1900), 285–6.

[62] For images of the abortionist see Angus McLaren, *Sexuality and Social Order: The Debate over the Fertility of Women and Workers in France, 1770–1920* (New York, 1983), 136–153; the harsh treatment meted out to a suspected abortionist can be seen from the case of Eugénie Pathier B . . . D2U8 217, 25/26 July 1887. She threw vitriol at her lover and succeeded in killing him. Although she represented herself as a *criminelle passionnelle*, deserted by her lover and left with a child, she was none the less sentenced to forced labour for life. The fact that she was a midwife, living in a neighbourhood ostensibly frequented by women needing abortions, suggested that she would have been able to rid herself of an unwanted pregnancy. Moreover, there was no one who could testify to having seen her with child. When it was discovered that she had tried to bribe one of her co-detainees into committing perjury and attesting to the birth of the baby, the investigating magistrate insisted that she had fabricated a story of the child's existence to extort money from her former bourgeois lover.

[63] Women who burned, maimed and beat their children to an early death, sometimes with the encouragement or consent of a husband or lover, were given the harshest penalties of the era. Femme S . . . and Femme N . . . both appeared in *Cour d'assises* in 1889 and 1890 respectively, and were condemned to forced labour for life. In fact, the sad history of such children was taken as evidence of the need for laws to protect them against the ill-treatment and immorality of their parents. See, for example, Bernard Schnapper, 'La Correction paternelle et le mouvement des idées au dix-neuvième siècle, 1789–1935', *Revue historique*, 263 (1980), 319–50. On p. 340 Schnapper explains that discussions of similar beatings in the 1860s produced no noticeable public response, but, by the 1890s, cases similar to those of Femmes S . . . and N . . . were cited in Béranger's senatorial report to underpin the law of 19 Apr. 1898 which forbid the mistreatment of children. This movement was also part of a more long-term process which contributed to the establishment of a juvenile court system in France in 1912. For this general history see Philippe Meyer, *The Child and the State: The Intervention of the State in French Family Life*, trans. Judith Ennew and Janet Lloyd (Cambridge, 1983) and Donzelot, *The Policing of Families: Welfare v. the State*.

placed at the opposite end from the prostitute.[64] While the former was distinguished by her honourable intentions—her desire for marriage and legitimate children—the prostitute was characterized as the female 'born criminal', innately predisposed to a dishonourable existence.

The *criminelle passionnelle* was acquitted because her stated motives seemed to reinforce a portrait of the feminine which was neither socially dangerous nor morally deviant. Despite her 'masculine' willingness to take up arms, she reassuringly presented the distinguishing features of her sex through melodramatic self-representation and symptoms of psycho-physiological disequilibrium, aspects of the *criminelle passionnelle* which led many a commentator to underscore the inconsequentiality of female violence.

And yet, the long disquisitions surrounding female violence were replete with ambivalence and laced with fear, reactions which were perhaps all the more remarkable given that it was universally acknowledged that women were far less prone to break the law than were men. It may be suggested that the construction of a typology of female criminality was more than an exercise in 'objective' social-scientific study. In the same way that Charcot's view of hysteria in the 1870s and 1880s was linked to his particular vision of the pathological association between religion and female neuroses, so criminological attitudes towards women were influenced by the perception of a transition in relations between the sexes, manifested, above all, by the growing and pervasive concern over the 'women's question' during the Third Republic.[65] When, for example, mothers such as Mme Grille seemed to prefer romantic immolation to familial obligation, then masculine commentators readily assembled a range of 'scientific' arguments to find some 'rational' explanation for seemingly irrational behaviour.

Moreover, criminologists were vividly aware of the advent of *féminisme* on to the stage of Third Republican political and social debate. The dread of a possible change in the sexual

64 See Lombroso and Ferrero, *La Femme criminelle et la prostituée*.

65 For the most illuminating introduction to the 'woman's question' in France and its political, social, and biological complexities, see Karen Offen, 'Depopulation, Nationalism and Feminism in Fin de Siècle France', *American Historical Review*, 89 (1984), 648–75.

division of labour can be detected behind the scientific phraseology which dissected female 'nature'. For example, in a preface to de Ryckère's *La Femme en Prison* (1898), the premier criminologist from Lyons, Alexandre Lacassagne, praised his colleague for investigating women's crime as part of an important aspect of contemporary *féminisme*. In assessing the claims of women to a fuller role in society, he recognized the importance of more knowledge, '*des clartés de tout*', to understand the feminine state and prescribe her future social role. At one moment praising the strides women had made in entering the professions and demonstrating their aptitudes, the next Lacassagne maintained that such accomplishments were due to perseverance, even stubbornness, rather than native talent.[66] His musings were seconded by Cesare Lombroso, who, in his work on prostitution, felt obliged to credit the women scientists who had aided his research, but who then furnished several hundred pages of 'evidence' proving women's inferiority.[67] No causal connection can be drawn between the commentary surrounding violent women on the one hand and the wider, but still minority, movement for the emancipation of women on the other.[68] However, as the conclusion will show, criminological discourse was inflected by the very real fears which *féminisme* aroused, anxieties which perhaps explain the pervasive fascination with womanly violence.

[66] Alexandre Lacassagne, preface to Raymond de Ryckère's, *La Femme en prison et devant la mort: Étude de criminologie* (Lyons, 1898), p. viii.

[67] Lombroso and Ferrero, *La Femme criminelle et la prostituée*. For remarks on feminism see p. xv.

[68] There has been a range of new works on the history of feminism, suffragism, and women and socialism in France. See Offen, 'Depopulation, Nationalism and Feminism', which has a thorough bibliographical inventory in the footnotes. See also her ' "First Wave" Feminism in France: New Work and Resources', *Women's Studies International Forum*, 5 (1982), 685–9. Other major works include Charles Sowerwine, *Sisters or Citizens? Women and Socialism in France since 1876* (Cambridge, 1982); Hause/Kenny, *Women's Suffrage and Social Politics in the French Third Republic*.

7

ALCOHOLISM AND THE WORKING-CLASS MAN

If the courtroom discussion of hysteria focused on women, then the analysis of alcoholism and drunken violence concentrated on men. Between 1880 and 1910, approximately 25 per cent of Paris cases of actual or attempted murders were committed by those who either cited alcohol as an excuse, had a drinking habit, or had been drinking before the crime.[1] These deeds were committed by men from all strata of the working classes, from casual day labourers to skilled craftsmen, and included a significant number of white-collar '*employés*' whose relationship to working-class life in Paris during this period remained close if ambiguous.[2]

This is not to suggest, however, that the issue of female alcoholism was never raised. Raymond de Ryckère, for example, asserted that 'genteel' middle-class alcoholism was on the rise.[3] He argued that women in the upper ranks drank on the sly, experiencing both self-disgust and impulsive need, and were stricken by a semi-conscious recognition that their vice was likely to deform or destroy their offspring. Working women, however, were deemed to have no such delicacy. When they became alcoholics, their most brutal and repulsive penchants came to the surface. Indeed, as this and the next chapter will demonstrate, men who killed inebriated wives or mistresses were treated with extreme leniency. When Antony Tellier strangled his wife, his explanation that he was crazy with rage when he came home to find her dead drunk was

[1] In 1885, around 27 per cent of the total of fifty-seven cases in Paris were related in some way to alcohol. This figure rose to about 35 per cent in 1895, out of a total of sixty-seven cases, and dropped back to around 15 per cent, of a total of ninety-five cases, by 1905.

[2] See Leonard R. Berlanstein, *The Working People of Paris, 1871–1914* (Baltimore, 1984), 111–21.

[3] Raymond de Ryckère, 'L'Alcoolisme féminin', *Archives d'anthropologie criminelle*, 14 (1899). 205–6.

sufficient to excuse him. While a 'chorus of praise' from neighbours and employers testified to his upright and diligent disposition, in contrast, the victim was 'depicted as a bad housewife and incorrigible drunk'. Except for her mother's defence, the consensus view was that the wife somehow deserved her fate.[4]

Although drunken working women only rarely committed a crime, the few that did were treated with exceptional harshness. For example, Femme Carminati[5] murdered her brutal and equally drunken husband with a hatchet after years of mistreatment and abuse. Although identified as an incorrigible alcoholic by the physicians who examined her, she was none the less gaoled for six years, a severity that suggests that her drinking acted as an aggravating circumstance and placed her crime outside the usual boundaries of the crime of passion. Her case, and those of other women in similar situations,[6] demonstrates the condemnatory attitude taken towards drunken female violence, a stance which sometimes contrasted sharply with the perception of similar, more numerous male assaults.

Because alcohol and violence were so often associated, drink preoccupied officials who investigated male defendants, engaging both jurists and alienists on the question of how to deal with individuals who were manifestly dangerous but often apparently irresponsible. Drunken comportment demonstrated most strikingly the way in which human beings could act automatically and unconsciously, hence raising issues as to how to manage men who put society and themselves at risk through their intemperate habits.

Although interest in alcoholism reached a climax in this period, medical preoccupation with the subject was well established. Over-indulgence had long been associated with gout, and early nineteenth-century anatomical investigations minutely described the pathological effects of drinking in cirrhosis of the liver. The term *delirium tremens* was widely used

[4] *Gazette des tribunaux*, 17 Apr. 1907.

[5] Ibid., 9–10 Feb. 1903.

[6] See also the case of Femme Routaboul, ibid., 25 Nov. 1893. She received a penalty of twenty years' hard labour for killing her son after successive attacks of brutality. Recognized as an alcoholic who had already attempted suicide, she was none the less condemned with the full weight of the law. It must be admitted, however, that her penalty would probably have been equally harsh for a similar crime if she had been sober. See above, chap. 6, n. 67.

from around 1810 and certain nervous conditions associated with impulsive drinking were already identified, with the alienist Rayer coining the term *œnomanie* in 1819 to describe the monomaniacal need to drink wine.[7] The term 'alcoholism' itself was invented in 1852 by the Swedish physician Magnus Huss. His 'discovery' was greeted somewhat complacently by the French medical community,[8] which made the distinction between '*ivrognerie*'—or the old-fashioned vice of drunkenness—and the harsher disease condition of alcoholism that suggested an almost uneradicable addiction. None the less, the social and biological consequences of excess drinking were gaining increased attention, with hygienists like Louis-René Villermé linking it to industrialization and poverty.[9] Such connections were strengthened by men like Morel, who, in his *Traité des dégénérescences*, cited drink as a crucial factor behind racial debilitation.

But while alcoholism concerned the medical world before 1870, the subject engrossed it afterwards. The Commune was a watershed in the bourgeois perception of drink, a shift remarkable for the key role the medical profession played in promoting the picture of riotous and dangerous disinhibition.[10] As Barrows has shown, medical language and ideas had an important role in constructing images of drunken violence linked to revolutionary chaos. In the *Annales médico-psychologiques*,[11] for example, distinguished psychiatrists joined in a general cry of bourgeois anguish by describing Parisian workers as debauched drunks, as violent, absinthe-drinking maniacs. The political meaning of the revolutionary upheaval was explained away as a produce of pathological excess, 'a

7 See Jean-Charles Sournia, *Histoire de l'alcoolisme* (Paris, 1986), 55–60 and William F. Bynum, 'Chronic Alcoholism in the First Half of the Nineteenth Century', *Bulletin of the History of Medicine*, 42 (1968), 160–85.

8 See Michael Marrus, 'Social Drinking in the Belle Époque', *Journal of Social History*, 7 (1974), 117.

9 For more on Villermé's studies on working-class life see William Coleman, *Death is a Social Disease, Public Health and Political Economy in Early Industrial France* (Madison, 1982).

10 Susannah Barrows, 'After the Commune, Alcoholism, Temperance and Literature in the Early Third Republic', in John Merriman (ed.), *Class Experience in Nineteenth-Century Europe* (New York, 1979), 205–18.

11 For a full discussion of this see *ibid.*, as well as articles by Lunier, Bouchereau, Magnan, and Laborde in *Annales médico-psychologiques*, 5th ser., 7 and 8 (1872), and by Dr Lunier, ibid., 9 (1873).

monstrous attack of acute alcoholism'[12] that was underpinned by statistical tables and hundreds of clinical observations which sought a cool and sober scientific explanation for seemingly irrational events.

If the political anxiety about the Commune shaped the conditions and terms in which the exaggerated and polemical discourse on drink was fashioned, the discussion also reflected an inescapable social reality. The French in this period were indeed drinking more than ever before, consuming novel and more potent beverages and doing so in an expanding number of public drinking places. The number of cafés in Paris grew from 5,000 in 1789 to 22,000 in 1870, soaring to 40,000 in the mid-1880s, receding again to 25,000 in 1890, and levelling off at 30,000 in 1900.[13] The cafés were de-regulated in 1880 in accordance with *laissez faire* economic principles, a measure which no doubt encouraged the boom.[14] In the capital their numbers were greatest in *arrondissements* where there was the highest percentage of working-class people, with some streets having one in every building block.[15]

Partly because of this, consumption also sky-rocketed. That of wine rose rapidly from 61 litres per head in 1790 to 75 in 1850 and a massive 113 litres in 1890. Even more dramatic was the fourfold rise in the annual consumption of spirits to 4.35 litres a head.[16] Such inexpensive and potent drinks, particularly absinthe, became popular after the phylloxera epidemics devastated the vineyards of the Midi during the 1870s and 1880s. Workers also began to drink them, although to what extent is not clear. It was suggested that they were emulating a bourgeois and bohemian habit—'*l'heure de l'apéritif*'—which seems to have become popular around the 1860s.[17]

[12] Jules Bergeron, 'Rapport sur la répression de l'alcoolisme', *Annales d'hygiène publique et de médecine légale*, 38 (1872), 6.

[13] W. Scott Haine, '"I go to the café to create my relations": Sociability and Strategy in Parisian Working-Class Cafés, 1870–1890', Ph.D. thesis (Univ. of Wisconsin-Madison, 1984), 16–17.

[14] Barrows, *Distorting Mirrors: Visions of the Crowd in Late Nineteenth-Century France* (New Haven, 1981), 67.

[15] Haine, 'I go to the café', 17. For more on the numbers of cafés and their social role in France around the turn of the century, see Jacqueline Lalouette, 'Le Débit de boissons urbain entre 1880–1914', *Ethnologie française*, 12 (1982), 131–6.

[16] M. Marrus, 'Social Drinking in the Belle Époque', *Journal of Social History*, 7 (1974), 117.

[17] For a condemnatory picture of bohemian Paris painted by Henri Legrand du Saulle in the 1860s see his *La Folie devant les tribunaux* (Paris, 1864), 540. In this

Moreover, perhaps inexperience with the effects of such beverages led many to mix them, producing what might very well have been novel and often explosive behaviour. When, for example, Claude-Marie F . . . shot and killed his son in an alcoholic fury, much was made in the medical report of the variety and quantity of drink he consumed: 'Every day he drank around 2½ litres of wine, cognac after every meal, several glasses of vermouth, and often some absinthe as well.'[18] This mixing seemed to exacerbate his chronic alcoholism, defects of character, and dangerous 'abnormal over-excitement'.

From the 1870s onward a series of reformist campaigns and political measures sought to tackle the drink problem, each stage in the struggle reflecting changing political concerns and managerial strategies. The 3 February 1872 law on public drunkenness was passed in the wake of the Commune, sponsored by the physician and liberal reformer, Théophile Roussel.[19] It laid down procedures for incarcerating or fining individuals found drunk in public and even made *marchands de vin* liable for selling alcohol to those already drunk. The measure effectively instituted an unprecedented level of surveillance of working-class cafés, producing regular confrontations between police and clients.[20] In the same era, the *Société de tempérance*[21] was established and attempted to award medals to working men for sobriety, diligence, and regularity. Although this organization's programme of moralization gained few adherents, the temperance campaign in general grew in strength in the 1890s, becoming finally organized in the *Ligue nationale contre l'alcoolisme*, which brought together a range of disparate reformist groups in 1903.[22] Their efforts were

description Legrand du Saulle emphasizes the way young men drank absinthe because it was deemed to encourage artistic creation.

[18] Claude-Marie F . . . D[2]U[8] 259, 10 Sept. 1890, *pièce* 51*a*, medico-legal report by Socquet.

[19] See Haine, 'The Regulation of Taverns, Cabarets and Cafés in France from the Old Regime to 1880', Masters thesis (Univ. of Wisconsin, 1980), chap. 4.

[20] Id., 'I go to the café', 240–84.

[21] Barrows, 'After the Commune', 211–12.

[22] See Jacques Borel, *Du concept de dégénérescence à la notion d'alcoolisme dans la médecine contemporaine: Les Campagnes anti-alcooliques de 1865 à 1965* (Montpellier, 1968), 51–79. For more on temperance see P. E. Prestwich, 'Temperance in France: The Curious Case of Absinthe', *Historical Reflections/Réflexions Historiques* (1979), 301–19, and her 'French Workers and the Temperance Movement', *International Review of Social History*, 25 (1980), 35–52.

bolstered by the research of prominent alienists, men such as Paul-Maurice Legrain and Valentin Magnan, whose focus on the moral, biological, and social dimensions of drink had an enduring impact on the courtroom perception of alcoholic violence. Although the campaign never captured a wide and enthusiastic following, alcoholism none the less entered the national consciousness as a recognized social pathology.[23]

The orientation of the later campaign was more strongly shaped by social-hygienic and degenerationist concerns, placing the alcoholic 'scourge' at the centre of a wealth of interrelated social ills. Psychiatrists in particular assumed many roles in these campaigns. As hygienists, they were leading figures in temperance societies, while as physicians in asylums they were obliged to treat alcoholics and lobbied for special institutions. As medico-legists, they also attempted to determine the responsibility of drunken murderers and hence sought to establish when drink excused crime and violence. As will be seen, these varying roles sometimes clashed and, in each instance, their position on the subject varied significantly.

In all these cases, as well as when contributing to popular journals and serving on governmental commissions, they helped construct a chain which linked the individual drunk to general conceptions of abnormality, social dangerousness, and national degeneration. Legrain's research into alcoholism was indicative of this approach. When chronicling the hereditary history of 215 families he found that 168 of them were afflicted by one form or another of '*folie morale*', induced in his view by alcoholic excess:

> Included among the things we have listed under the heading of '*folie morale*' are bad instincts and vices of all types: lying, insubordination, precocious prostitution, debauchery, adultery, confirmed drunkenness, sexual perversions (self and mutual masturbation, exhibitionism, pederasty), exploitation of women, theft, fraud, habitual vagrancy. Corresponding to each of these morbid activities is a more or less extensive number of convictions which puts [*fait émerger*] our

[23] An indication of the concern is demonstrated by several legislative projects aimed to limit the number of *débits de boisson* and eliminate the *bouilleurs de cru*. Although these bills came to nought, a vocal anti-alcoholism lobby none the less generated considerable publicity for the crusade. See, for an example of this polemical literature, Joseph Reinach, *Contre l'alcoolisme* (Paris, 1911).

hereditary drinkers into the category of official and repressed criminality.[24]

As if this chronicle of afflictions was not enough, Magnan and Fillassier drove home the point by maintaining that at the asile Ste-Anne 75 per cent of the disorders were due to alcoholism.[25] Nor were the effects of the disorder—biological, social, or economic—confined to the affected individual. When Brouardel discussed the problem at the 1889 *Congrès international d'hygiène publique*, he employed the arguments of political economy and cited the range of 'hidden' costs which the alcoholic caused society. He needed to be maintained in an asylum or a prison, contaminated others through example, and, finally, his 'epileptic, scrofulous, and idiot children' would drain the public purse because of their inability to support themselves.[26] The mental and physical debility caused by drink also meant that alcoholics were useless as military recruits. Undisciplined, often struck down by liver complaints, afflicted by various deformities which made them difficult to clothe and care for, such working-class men were described as moral and physical traitors.[27]

Finally, alcoholism was considered one of the key reasons behind the increase in *crimes de sang*, particularly unpremeditated murders, which, the statistics suggested, had been on the rise since the 1880s. Between 1830 and 1880 the levels of murders in France remained steady, around 180 or 190 a year; by 1904 the figure was as high as 289, with the first significant increase having come with the 217 cases recorded in 1881. During a discussion of the *Société générale des prisons*, Joseph Reinach linked this increase to the deregulation of the cafés:

Now we come to 1880. 1880 was, if you think about it, one of

[24] Paul-Maurice Legrain, *Hygiène et prophylaxie: Dégénérescence sociale et alcoolisme* (Paris, 1895), 6.

[25] Valentin Magnan and Alfred Fillassier, 'L'Alcool et la folie à l'asile Ste-Anne', *Archives d'anthropologie criminelle*, 28 (1913), 159–60.

[26] Brouardel, 'Discours prononcé à la séance générale d'ouverture'; *Le Congrès international d'hygiène publique*, compiled by Dr Reuss (Paris, 1889), 14.

[27] J. Lalouette, 'Le Discours bourgeois sur les débits de boisson aux alentours de 1900', *Recherches: L'Haleine des faubourgs*, 29 (1977), 322–4.

this country's most inauspicious years: it was in fact in 1880 that the law was passed which allowed the opening of bars [*débits de boisson*] from then on without prior authorization. From that moment there was an outburst of alcoholism, and since then we have seen the number of murders, suicides, and cases of madness grow . . . (applause)[28].

While his senatorial colleague, Béranger, suggested that strikes were as much responsible for these events as alcohol—giving vent to another common anxiety often reiterated at such meetings—Reinach none the less insisted that drink, while not the sole cause of criminality, was the 'dominant cause'.

This representation of the alcohol problem—its perceived affiliation with dangerous political adventures, disease, working-class disorderliness, and crime—all affected the portraits of violent drunkards who came before the courts. But while the general picture of alcoholic excess seems unequivocably condemnatory, the commentary on drunken killers in actual trials was more complex. Held up as an exemplary *moral* failing, drunkenness could also indicate irresponsibility. Sometimes seen as an aggravating circumstance, more often it tended to reduce the ultimate penalty. As with women, the judges, psychiatrists, and journalists represented the drunken killer in an ambivalent fashion, with the defendant's own accounts of temporary amnesia and insanity proving important for explaining their seemingly uncontrollable and antisocial behaviour.

Once again, a characterization of a particular biological and social 'nature' was at stake, in which various competing stereotypes of the working-class man—of habitual brutality and occasional uncontrollability, inveterate laziness and periodic irregularity, sexual deviance and intermittent marital infidelity—were all assessed to generate a conclusion of either punishment or absolution. My aim here will be to place these representations of male violence in context by concentrating on the discussions of work, family, politics, and play to which medical and legal characterizations of drunken comportment and violence were attached.

[28] Reinach, 'Sur le projet relatif à la suppression de la peine de mort et à son remplacement par un internement perpétuel', *Revue pénitentiaire*, 3 (1907), 307.

ALCOHOLISM AND DISEASE

Although medico-legists had a catalogue of clinical disease entities which should have made the job of distinguishing between ordinary drunkenness and alcoholic illness straightforward, these classifications rarely surfaced in pre-trial reports. Part of the difficulty lay in the fact that, like Charcot's *grande hystérie*, the dramatic and alarming clinical stages of alcoholic illness afflicted only a small minority of patients. Magnan's award-winning *De l'alcoolisme* (1874) laid out these qualities of explosiveness and violence, with attacks of absinthe fury likened to epileptic fits during which the sufferer went through a series of uncontrollable symptoms: '. . . violent electrical jerks . . . tossing and turning, babbling, incoherence, hallucinations'.[29] Indeed, the discussion of alcoholic delirium provided as much a picture of war and revolution in progress as a portrait of disease, with the content of alcoholic hallucinations full of Prussians, spies, Communards, and national guardsmen.[30]

The most extreme version of the illness was dipsomania, which would intermittently strike and force sufferers to commit acts they found abhorrent. A volitional malady tied to degeneration, dipsomania was a rare alcoholic condition to which otherwise virtuous—and often middle-class—women sometimes succumbed, although men were the more common victims. Dipsomaniacs would murder, steal, starve their families, or prostitute themselves to obtain drink. It was 'a morbid need, irresistible, independent of the will'. The afflicted individual would fight desperately to regain self-control, even introducing petrol, rhubarb, or fæcal matter to make the alcohol undrinkable.[31] None of these expedients would

29 V. Magnan, *De l'alcoolisme, des diverses formes du délire alcoolique et de leur traitement* (Paris, 1874), 86. For a comprehensive look at Magnan's study of alcoholism see Mignot, 'Magnan et ses études sur l'alcoolisme', *Annales médico-psychologiques*, 15th ser., I (1935), 738–47.

30 For Magnan's description see Victor Vétault, *Étude médico-légale sur l'alcoolisme: Des conditions de la responsabilité au point de vue pénal chez les alcoolisés* (Paris, 1887), 128.

31 Magnan, *Lecons cliniques sur la dipsomanie faites à l'asile Sainte-Anne*, ed. Marcel Brian (Paris, 1884), 139. For an analysis of Magnan's preoccupation with obsessional disorders see Charles Vurpas, 'Les Obsessions, les impulsions et les perversions sexuelles dans l'œuvre de Magnan', *Annales médico-psychologiques*, 15th ser., I (1935), 748–59.

prevail, however, because the underlying degeneration would propel the sufferers to other misdeeds.[32] Even if they could be cured of dipsomania, there was no guarantee that the degeneration would not surface in another form, rearing its head as a sexual perversion, pyromania, or some other impulsive behaviour.

A special medical response was reserved for *absinthisme*, or absinthe fury, which particularly affected those with latent degenerative propensities. So terrible was the *fureur alcoolique*, that a glass or two of the drink could induce a man to commit murder under its influence. Absinthe in fact had a special symbolism for the debates on alcoholism, representing the shift from wine and cider, *boissons hygiéniques* associated with agriculture and familiar drinking rituals, to manufactured spirits whose artificiality and potency were dangerously 'modern'.[33] This important strand of temperance rhetoric was promoted most vigorously by vineyard-owners eager to re-establish their clientele after the phylloxera. A physician from Bordeaux, a region most concerned with the fortunes of the vine, exemplified this attitude when he contrasted 'absinthe, bitters, vermouth and all the poisons of the industrial distillery'[34] with wine, the 'natural' and 'healthy' patrimony of the French.

> After a period of jeopardy, the prosperity of the vine is set to recover the splendours of the past. This return of fortune is a happy portent for the future of wine and a precious symbol of the great reawakening of the French soul whose aspiration and destiny—through the genius of her diplomats, poets, artists, scholars, and philosophers—are intermingled with those of all mankind.[35]

Repeated efforts to outlaw absinthe were unsuccessful until 1915 when national emergency and fear of disorder in the trenches finally overwhelmed the substantial power of the spirits lobby. For all the medical warnings—to drive home

[32] See Bynum, 'Alcoholism and Degeneration in Nineteenth-Century European Medicine and Psychiatry', *British Journal of Addiction*, 79 (1984), 59–70.
[33] See Prestwich, 'Temperance in France: The Curious Case of Absinthe', 301–19.
[34] F. Cayla, *Le Vin, le buveur de vin et le buveur d'alcool* (Bordeaux, 1901), 6.
[35] Ibid., 10.

their point, doctors injected dogs and rabbits with massive doses of the drink, concluding that the animals' rapid and miserable death was proof of its dangerous properties—absinthe remained a favoured beverage throughout the period. It was a tantalizing drink, the 'green fairy', whose aroma and inebriating qualities were praised as an aid to artistic creativity and an enhancer of sociability. A wide variety of daily objects were produced to further its consumption and heighten its attraction: luxurious bottles and labels, special absinthe glasses, ashtrays, matchholders, and elegant spoons advertising particular brands.[36] Against this image of delightful escape and heady excitement, medical and judicial officials provided another picture, concentrating on the dark and poisonous effects of the drink and the violent behaviour it produced.

Other examples of the effects of alcohol were found in *folie alcoolique* or *delirium tremens*, the disease Zola immortalized in his description of Coupeau's agitated fury in *L'Assommoir*. In this state the patient might converse with imaginary beings who insulted and threatened him, or be frightened by hallucinations of animals—rats, insects, dogs, and snakes—that crowded him and prevented him from sleeping. It also occurred in a less acute form that was typified by severe depression and accompanied by hallucinations and ideas of persecution. Finally, chronic alcoholism could equally reduce a man to physical and emotional incapacity, addling his faculties and destabilizing his physiological economy, a condition which could produce trembling hands, mumbling and stammering, liver spots on the skin, cramps in the shins, as well as morning sickness.[37]

All these instances implied irresponsibility, at least theoretically, and reinforced the medical view of drink as a key agent allowing lower reflexive and instinctive urges to run riot, nullifying the power of the volitional and intellectual faculties, and making motor co-ordination virtually impossible. Rarely, however, did alienists enter such descriptions into their legal reports and in the three decades under examination, no defendant

[36] See the exhibition catalogue edited by Marie-Claude Delahaye, *L'Absinthe: Histoire de la fée verte* (Paris, 1983).

[37] Magnan, *De l'alcoolisme*, 166–255.

accused of murder was identified as a dipsomaniac. In the case of Félix B . . . in 1885, Motet entertained the idea that this dissipated agricultural labourer known for his alcoholic binges was afflicted, but the possibility was dismissed after his immoral and irregular past was investigated. B . . ., it appeared, drank only when he had the money, a pattern of behaviour which demonstrated that he was not driven by an irresistible impulse but rather indulged his vice.[38]

Absinthisme was very occasionally accepted as a medical excuse. When examining the case of Alphonse C . . . in 1886, for example, Motet was convinced that this carpentry worker —once struck by a typhoid fever and hence possibly debilitated by its long-lasting effects—had been driven to beat his mistress to death by the poisonous effects of two glasses of absinthe, and likened his fury to that of an epileptic fit: 'Individuals suddenly struck with alcoholic fury nearly always act in this fashion. Their manner of hitting out and their relentlessness towards their victims recalls the fury of epileptics . . .'[39] The jurors, however, were less than entirely convinced by this argument and C . . . was gaoled for five years.

While Motet's description demonstrates the seriousness with which the alienists regarded the demonic power of the beverage, physicians, judges, and juries generally saw absinthe-drinking as an aggravating rather than extenuating circumstance. Defendants were treated harshly when they used it as a basis for a plea of amnesia for particularly brutal deeds. In November 1902, for example, Elie Lassie tried to murder and rob the owner of his building. When he came before the court he remarked: 'I had been drinking absinthe . . . and acted in a bout of madness. I remember nothing and know nothing . . .'.[40] None the less, he was sentenced to forced labour for life.

Chronic alcoholics also benefited only rarely from medical indulgence. Claude-Marie F . . ., mentioned earlier, was an alcoholic policeman who aimed at his wife but accidentally murdered his son. The medico-legist Soquet readily acknowledged that F . . . had been inebriated, was susceptible

[38] Félix B . . . D2U8 170, 24 Jan. 1885.
[39] Alphonse C . . . D2U8 194, 22 Mar. 1886, medico-legal report.
[40] Elie Lassie, *Gazette des tribunaux*, 10–11 Nov. 1902.

to fits of rage when drunk, and that his mental faculties were weakened and his body impaired by the corrosive effects of alcohol. Despite the convincing portrait of disease which the physician painted, he remarked, 'Must we conclude from the preceding that the defendant is irresponsible? We do not hesitate to reply in the negative.'[41] Soquet maintained instead that F . . . was responsible for his deeds because he had induced his malady, a conclusion with which the jury agreed, evidenced by the penalty of twelve years' hard labour.

A preliminary glance at court cases demonstrates, therefore, that medical classifications of alcoholism are not necessarily a useful guide to medico-legal conclusions. Although at first glance psychiatric knowledge seemed to transform vice into illness and immorality into pathology, alienists' disease descriptions were more ambivalent, pervaded by a condemnatory moral vision which was particularly apparent in the discussion of alcohol. They too perceived excessive drinking as a vice and condemned those whose habits ultimately caused a full-blown psychophysiological disease. In this way alcoholism was often perceived even by medical men as a culpable offence. Unlike general paralysis, it was a disease the sufferer 'chose' to have through his decision to drink. They accordingly felt most indulgent towards the dipsomaniac, often a degenerate from birth, who was at least repelled by his vicious passion, and were less merciful towards the chronic alcoholic who seemed the author of his own degradation.

Moreover, as suggested in chapter 2, the alienists' perspective, despite their deterministic rhetoric, was delicately balanced through a combination of mechanistic and voluntaristic perspectives. Heredity predisposed individuals to disease, but habits, milieu, and education could prevent or encourage its appearance. Human thought, behaviour, and emotion were the product of underlying neurophysiological and evolutionary processes and the central nervous system a finely tuned hierarchy of reflex activity. However, those who disturbed its delicate functioning through excess alcohol consumption and neglected the moral and medical injunctions against excess were thus responsible to some extent for their deeds.

[41] Claude-Marie F . . . D^2U^8 259, 10 Sept. 1890, medico-legal report.

'Partial Responsibility', Social Defence, and the Medical Management of Alcohol

Alienists were embarrassed by their ambivalence towards alcoholism in numerous ways, especially as they often operated within a legal system which also failed to apply clear-cut guidelines. Only in one area were the legal provisions precise: drunkenness could not constitute a legal excuse. The code of 3 Brumaire year IV maintained

> that drunkenness is a reprehensible and voluntary state and can never constitute an excuse that law and morality will allow; that in consequence the jury cannot be asked to consider the question of whether the accused was in a drunken state at the moment of the offence in order to make this a motive in law.[42]

The 1810 penal code contained the same provision, and hence questions posed to the jury could not refer to the matter.

However, as mentioned before, jurors were asked to assess whether or not the defendant was guilty not only of the unlawful act but also of criminal intent. They were instructed to consult their own consciences when confronted by a defendant who had committed a crime while drunk and, like judges in lower courts, often handed out lesser sentences. There were specific instances in which jurists recommended leniency for those who drank unknowingly (when they were tricked into getting drunk, for example) and increased severity for others who drank to give themselves courage to commit a crime.[43] But between these two poles was the great number of defendants who had drunk knowingly but not maliciously, and in each case a judgement depended on an assessment of the individual. While such a state of affairs promoted flexibility, it also emphasized the irreconcilable conflict between a moralistic condemnation of drunkenness and a deterministic appraisal of the irresponsible behaviour alcohol caused. As one confused medico-legist said—reiterating legal argument but qualifying it with medical experience—alcoholism is a 'voluntary and reprehensible state and can never constitute an excuse that

[42] V. Vétault, *Étude médico-légale sur l'alcoolisme: Des conditions de la responsabilité au point de vue pénal chez les alcoolisés* (Paris, 1887), 33–4.

[43] See Gustave Poittevin in the preface to Codsi Goubran, *L'Influence de l'ivresse sur la responsabilité pénale: Étude de la doctrine et de la jurisprudence française* (Paris, 1925), 8.

morality and law will allow . . . but, on the other hand, a moral being cannot respond to the acts of a machine.'[44]

The alienists' position in court on alcohol was complicated by a range of intraprofessional disagreements. Starting as a debate over 'partial responsibility' which had bedevilled medical and legal relations since the 1820s (see chapter 2), the discussion on drunken killers ended by involving participants in a searching debate over the alienists' social role and political allegiances after the Commune. The discussion on the 'supposed irresponsibility of alcoholics' in the *Société médico-psychologique* in 1879 and 1880 exploded when Eugéne Dally, a physician, anthropologist, and one of the few self-professed Darwinian ideologues in France, expressed his irritation at the nature of medical intervention in cases of drunken violence.[45]

His chief target was what he considered his colleagues' tendency to add alcoholism to the other assorted 'isolated' deliriums and obsessions which led to conclusions of partial responsibility and encouraged jurors to lighten sentences. For him, the attenuation of penalties for alcoholism was evidence of psychiatrists falling prey to a dangerous sentimentality which had already led to the excesses of the Commune. His own position was a strident manifestation of the philosophy of social defence. Most of his contemporaries at the 1879–80 meetings, however, still recoiled from such a severe approach. For example, Legrand du Saulle and Delaisiauve felt conspicuously uneasy with the idea of a new system of crime control based exclusively on social defence, despite their adherence to science and its deterministic precepts.

Dally's remarks at the conference were hence received with indignation by Delaisiauve, an eminent Republican whose political career had reached its apogee in the early days of the 1848 Revolution.[46] He rejected the anti-democratic implications of Dally's position and, as a result, drew apposite

[44] Henri Legrand du Saulle, Georges Berryer, Gabriel Pouchet, *et al.*, *Traité de médecine légale, de jurisprudence médicale et de toxicologie* (Paris, 1886), 711–12.

[45] Eugène Dally, 'La Responsabilité morale et la responsabilité sociale', *Annales médico-psychologiques*, 6th ser., 5 (1881), 96–112.

[46] Louis Delaisiauve, ibid., 6th ser., 5 (1881), 110–12, 286–98; see also his 'De la prétendue irresponsabilité des alcooliques criminels', ibid., 6th ser., 4 (1880), 83–107. For another perspective on the problem see Legrand du Saulle, 'Sur la prétendue irresponsabilité des alcooliques', ibid., 6th ser., 3 (1880), 118–30.

parallels between the latter's views and Bismarckian authoritarianism, portraying both as riding roughshod over individual rights and the workings of justice. Legrand du Saulle, on the other hand, countered with arguments which remained within more narrow professional boundaries. He pointed to the disjunction between the obvious danger posed by the violent alcoholic and the clinical fact that some of these offenders were indeed irresponsible. Dally's opponents, therefore, advocated the maintenance of current medico-legal methods of analysis which took into account the alcoholic's personal, moral, biological, and social history to determine his responsibility. In so concluding, the humanitarian rationale for psychiatric intervention was upheld: those who were sick were to be acquitted and treated, and only alienists were qualified to make the distinction between vice and illness.

This reluctance to abandon what Dally would have considered 'outmoded' thinking had its roots in the history of psychiatric practice, which oscillated uneasily between the imperatives of healing and policing, voluntarism and determinism, that were outlined earlier. The growing acceptance of notions of 'social defence' after 1880, however, meant that alienists became far less concerned with the civil rights and moral responsibility of alcoholic murderers. The change in attitude was bound up with several developments in professional practice. The alienists were involved in a broader campaign to reform the law of 1838 (see chapter 2) and with it the nature and number of institutions available for separate categories of the mentally ill. The problem of alcoholism featured significantly in this movement, and psychiatrists were keen to classify drunkards according to criteria of curability. These assessments affected not only their therapeutic vision, but also their evaluation of drunken offenders and their potential for rehabilitation.

Their increasing severity becomes more understandable when the drudgery as well as the frustrations such people caused is examined. For the alienists, incorrigible alcoholics not only took up space in their hospitals, but also exposed them to decisions which compromised their professional standing.[47]

[47] See Marandon de Montyel, 'Des entraves que le traitement de l'alcoolisme peut apporter à la liberté individuelle', *Revue de psychiatrie, de neurologie et d'hypnologie*, 3rd ser., 1 (1896), 72–81.

An indication of their difficulties can be gleaned from the not atypical case of Pierre-Marie Hervé, an alcoholic who was confined on four occasions for alcoholic delirium, but who had to be released each time he came to his senses, thus preventing any effective longer-term therapy. On the fourth occasion, however, his wife begged the physician, Marandon de Montyel, to keep him inside a few months longer as she was afraid of the consequences of his inevitable return to the bottle. Despite the fact that he had no legal right to do so, Marandon kept Hervé inside until his recovery and exemplary behaviour forced his release two months later. Within thirty hours, Hervé got drunk and killed his wife, accusing her of trying to keep him in the asylum in order to carry on an affair. As a consequence, the alienist was pilloried by the press, which maintained that psychiatrists 'confine reasonable people but are keen to free homicidal maniacs . . .'.[48]

Under attack both for having kept Hervé inside illegally and for having let him out, Marandon found that not even his colleagues stood by him. Paul Garnier diagnosed persecutory delirium during the subsequent pre-trial investigation, citing as evidence the defendant's belief in his wife's infidelity, which he stated was manifestly absurd as the woman was so ugly no one could possibly have had an affair with her. As Marandon had published cases of patients who had simulated insanity when they were in fact sane, he was not surprisingly distressed at the idea that he might himself have fallen victim to the same mistake.

Because of Garnier's assessment, Hervé was never brought to trial, but was again locked up under the care of a third alienist who reached a still different conclusion. Dr Charpentier not only decided that Hervé was sane, but also that he was a violent wretch who deserved severe punishment. However, his attempts to bring the man to justice met with little success, as the impressive record of apparent mental disorder Hervé had accumulated meant that charges were not pressed. In a final twist, four years later Hervé tried to murder Charpentier as well, maintaining that he had not been mad for years and was thus entitled to his freedom. As Marandon remarked:

48 Marandon de Montyel, 'Le cas de Pierre-Marie Hervé', *Archives d'anthropologie criminelle*, 14 (1899), 121.

. . . in Paris, drunks are sent to our wards as madmen for the least alcoholic delirium. Their internment generally works in their favour afterwards by virtually confirming their madness. They know it, the scoundrels, and profit greatly from it! Once they have been locked up as madmen they do not hesitate to repeat shamelessly anything they can get away with in our asylums.[49]

Hervé's case demonstrates the managerial dilemmas alcoholics posed. Intraprofessional disagreement caused by the unclear distinction between vice and illness, and the recurrence of alcoholic violence which alienists were supposed to prevent, both conspired to undermine medical prestige. Caught between the law of 1838 with its protection of individual rights on the one hand, and their own dissonant perceptions on the other, it is perhaps not surprising that confusion and sometimes bitterness resulted. Physicians such as Marandon and Charpentier sincerely regretted psychiatry's naïve eagerness to list drunkards among the insane and were dismayed that perhaps they were somehow helping murderers avoid just punishment. Equally, they were angered even more by the personal risk they ran from inmates seen as the incarnation of working-class aggression and brutality.

The alienists' understandable distress at such a situation did not mean, however, that they categorized all alcoholics as irredeemably dangerous. On the contrary, increasing experience with rehabilitation meant that by the end of the century they had a clear idea of who could be treated effectively. Moreover, this emerging approach impinged signficantly on their notion of a 'cure', difficult to define in many branches of medicine, but particularly so in psychiatry. Degeneration made for less than optimistic prognoses and led to the fear that, even if one set of symptoms could be eradicated, another would assert itself.[50] What is particularly significant is that the concepts and language surrounding the treatment and 'cure' of alcoholism were often interchangeable with those of criminology. The idea of a cure was bound up with early treatment and a speedy

[49] Marandon de Montyel, 'Le cas de Pierre-Marie Hervé', *Archives d'anthropologie criminelle*, 14 (1899), 144–5.

[50] For an introduction to the problem see the work of Hubert Aviat, *La Question des établissements spéciaux pour la cure de l'alcoolisme: Maisons de convalescence, d'abstinence et de travail* (Arcis-sur-Aube, 1900), 13–17.

return to temperate habits. 'Recidivism' in either the criminal or alcoholic context tended to be seen as incorrigibility.

Such considerations came out of the experience of a clinical world which was at odds with a much-sought-after ideal. The doctors envisaged rest-homes where alcohol was forbidden, where patients were fed on nourishing food and occupied by useful outdoor work in summer and workshops in winter. They acknowledged that in this respect they lagged far behind northern European countries. Approval for the construction of a special hospital for alcoholics was voted in 1894 by the *Conseil supérieur de l'assistance publique*. By 1900, however, there existed only three specialized facilities at the asylums of Ville-Évrard, Ste-Anne, and Villejuif, and even these were plagued by a variety of problems which often doomed the physicians' therapeutic plans from the outset.

Moreover, the attempt to enforce a regime of *total* abstinence was regularly foiled by the other patients and the asylum work-force, often alluded to as difficult and unruly. Not only could the personnel not be counted on to act as paragons of temperance, they were also known to bring drink in for alcoholic patients. Equally, life in the asylum for 'treatable' alcoholics was acknowledged to be demoralizing. If alcoholics were 'mad' during their drunken states, afflicted by hallucinations, and debilitated in both mind and body, a moderate period of abstinence brought rationality, if not calm. To be obliged to live with often long-term inmates was necessarily a therapeutic drawback which physicians continually condemned.

A look at printed case records demonstrates the nature of alienists' distinction between worthy and unworthy cases, as well as their appreciation of the link between alcoholism and the working-class way of life [*manière de vivre*]. Those who could be cured were categorized as *alcooliques simples* who, when unemployed, in bad health, or subjected to peer pressure, had episodes of intense drinking, found themselves in asylums, and needed to stay there only to 'dry out'. Unfortunately, such types were relatively rare. Most became *buveurs d'habitude* (habitual drinkers), *ivrognes*, who were the true victims of working-class existence. Alienists became social observers in examining such men, condemning their daily routine and the way they drank, socialized, and worked:

The great unifier for the factory is the *cabaret*; the morning snifter, the four o'clock drink . . ., stirrup-cup, alone or with others, the dreadful habit of taking Monday off, standing your round, these are all precedents the worker avoids only with difficulty. Business in the market takes place glass in hand. On nearly all building sites and shop floors it is normal to go at certain times to the closest *cabaret* and drink wine, hard liquor, or maybe even absinthe in varying amounts depending on the occasion. In some trades (carters, delivery boys, etc.) the workers don't even get a tip, but accept instead a 'wee drop' . . .[51]

Paul-Maurice Legrain's clinical observations demonstrate indulgence towards those that were 'dragged along' by harmful example. The hairdresser Isidore M . . ., for example, voluntarily admitted himself to Ville-Évrard in 1899 for his addiction to absinthe. Aged 37, he confessed to having drunk his first drop at 22, ceding to the teasing of his mates and becoming addicted. When he finally came to the asylum he was a physical and emotional wreck, incapacitated by trembling and terrified by hallucinations. He demonstrated his willingness to be cured by asking to stay on in the asylum to avoid any possibility of relapse.[52]

Such fortunate examples were contrasted with instances of the incurable patient, men such as the pedlar Adolphe H . . ., who entered Ville-Évrard in 1899 for the fourth time. The son of an alcoholic father, H . . . was particularly prone to the disorder, a tendency made worse by his trade which gave him many opportunities for drinking and chatting. His favourite brew was rum, drunk only occasionally, but invariably resulting in violence against his children and wife. In his worst attacks he was no more than an animal, and this, it seemed, was above all what marked him as incurable: 'During the attack, he loses all notion of human dignity and feeling. "He was not a man any more, he was an animal," said his wife. He relieved himself wherever he was, sometimes even in his pants.'[53]

Such distinctions were important to the alienists' vision of their therapeutic mission. They were decreasingly concerned with the likes of H . . ., who, in their view, represented the incurable degenerate requiring custodial care and security measures to protect both his family and society. H . . . was a

[51] Aviat, op cit., 20–1.
[52] Ibid., 21–4.
[53] Ibid., 36.

piece of social detritus which they literally wished to sweep away. As Legrain put it: 'The systematic rooting out of those who exploit our asylums cannot fail to have a beneficial effect. There is always relief from the staff and a sigh of satisfaction from the good patients every time I have this sort of cleaning out operation.'[54] H . . . demonstrated all the more forcefully the need to treat alcoholics in the earlier stages of their illness so that such 'recidivism' could be prevented.

Drink and Courtroom Evaluation

The descriptions of alcoholic violence provided a special opportunity to reflect upon the anthropological separateness of some working-class men, emphasizing a set of bodily weaknesses and incapacities as well as aesthetic irregularities. The commentaries contained two opposing strands of analysis which made up the paradoxical attitude held by both the judges and the psychiatrists on working-class life. On the one hand, much was made of the repulsive or pathetic characteristics of men corrupted by alcohol and driven to violence; on the other, these taints gave an indication of the chronic sickness, harsh circumstances, and debilitation against which the defendants struggled. In every analysis these two elements battled with one another, the first expressing an irrepressible disgust, the second reluctant pity.

A third and even more difficult element was the subjects' own participation in constructing this portrait of physiological difference. Time and time again, they eagerly provided details of familial and personal illness—aided often by wives and mothers who spoke at length about strange incapacities to convince the authorities of their menfolk's *bizarreries* and hence irresponsibility. Both judges and alienists were in the difficult position of having to decide when to take these accounts into consideration; whether they believed or rejected them was a very good index of the official attitude. For example, in 1899 the defendant Schneider was condemned for murdering and robbing his employer's wife. It appears that Schneider sought

[54] Quoted ibid., 71–2.

to limit the severity of his punishment by recounting his hereditarian taints, illnesses, suicidal and alcoholic tendencies. The president, however, made short shrift of this line of defence, implying throughout that the man was guilty of contrivance:

Q. You have testified, as has your mother, that there is some madness, a certain hereditary taint in your case. Your father was not mad . . . Your mother is very rational, and your brothers and sisters are all well-behaved and well-balanced. You have said that in Alsace you had a grandmother who was a little bit deranged and relations known as 'the nutty Schneiders'. You apparently suffered from fevers in the Tunisian penitentiary and tried to commit suicide. A doctor who examined you decided you were clearly responsible for your acts. In 1896 you tried to suffocate yourself. But was this genuine? You admitted having drunk a considerable amount of rum and from then on had the beginning of a paralysis confirmed at the St-Antoine hospital. Later, in the Boulevard St-Martin, you fired a revolver into the air and at that moment had a type of epileptic attack which was due only to having drunk a large amount of absinthe.[55]

Schneider was condemned to death, a penalty commuted to forced labour for life.

Although in this case both the judges and alienists were unimpressed by actual and self-professed indications of pathology, in most other instances they seemed eager to ferret out physical and mental signs of disorder. Alphonse C . . ., for example, the carpentry-worker mentioned earlier who drank two glasses of absinthe and then beat his mistress to death, had an epileptic mother suggestive of a tainted blood-line, which was further debilitated by typhoid in 1872. For the examining alienist, Motet, the illness was a key factor in leaving the man 'good only for work'. Not only was he unable to imbibe the early 'morning drop' (*goutte du matin*), his intelligence was also diminished to the extent of making reading and simple arithmetic difficult.[56]

Another defendant, the Alsatian Joseph H . . ., who killed his mistress in 1890, was also 'very imperfectly endowed' with intelligence (he could hardly speak French after many years in Paris), a fact which contrasted strikingly with his robust frame

[55] *Gazette des tribunaux*, 6–7 Feb., 1899.
[56] Alphonse C . . . D^2U^8 194, 22 Mar. 1886, medico-legal report.

and Herculean strength. Obviously fascinated by this combination, Benjamin Ball went on to examine other physical peculiarities to assess his heightened susceptibility to alcohol and discover the driving force behind the premeditated murder. Ball therefore stuck needles into his tongue and under his fingernails, but found these produced no visible signs of pain, and concluded that such defects entitled H . . . to some indulgence.[57] Nor were these the only kind of disorders cited. Evidence of deformed genitals, neurological and anatomical malformation, and a variety of unpleasant skin conditions were all catalogued to demonstrate the biological substratum of weakness and disease which supported a tendency to alcoholic violence.

Evidence of physiological abnormality could operate either for or against the defendant in court. The theory of degeneration provided an infinitely flexible model which was used contingently either as a means of reinforcing judicial condemnation with a psycho-biological portrait of amorality and dangerousness, or as a way of promoting clemency by demonstrating the gigantic social and hereditarian pressures against which the defendant struggled. While the alienists often decided that a subject was only partially responsible for his deeds, there were also instances in which the portrait of racial separateness led alienists to conclude that the subject was irretrievably savage.

Some cases, however, were so extreme that the physicians knowingly ignored humanitarian and healing imperatives and emphasized instead their policing and defensive function. With Lesteven in 1894 they were even prepared to forget the question of moral responsibility which the judicial system asked them to answer. A habitual drinker who asked prostitutes to perform 'acts against nature', Lesteven was brought to court for throwing his victim out of a window after a sexual encounter. During the trial his other crippled and scarred victims were paraded before the court, each testifying to his perverted tastes, drunken habits, and violence. The *Gazette des tribunaux* described him as having 'an enormous head in proportion to his body; his forehead bulges terribly . . . when he stares at a witness,

[57] Joseph H . . . D^2U^8 259, 18 Sept. 1890.

his gaze seems singularly hard, almost ferocious,'[58] a sketch illustrating the popular vision of thorough criminality and degeneration incarnate. Lesteven was thus portrayed as an avatar of arrested evolutionary development, his ferocious countenance more reminiscent of the savage tribesmen of the primitive past than the civilized inhabitants of contemporary Paris.

The alienists' analyses were in line with such perceptions. While Vallon, Ballet, and Motet noted that his mother had died in a lunatic asylum and that he himself might have passed through the Asile Ste-Anne for a temporary alcoholic delirium, they were none the less unwilling to countenance any evaluation of diminished responsibility. Motet explicitly stated his reasoning: 'When I talk about responsibility, I don't mean the continual changes to which it is occasionally subject according to circumstance, environment, or state of health.' He implied that the defendant's moral liberty was not entirely intact but none the less concluded that 'society must defend itself against those like Lesteven who endanger it . . .'.[59] In the psychiatrist's view, whether or not Lesteven was responsible was irrelevant since his dangerousness overrode humanitarian considerations. The '*Espagnol de Montmartre*' was accordingly sentenced to death, a fate he escaped by jumping out of a window of the Petite Roquette prison and committing suicide.[60]

An equally forceful description of degenerate proclivities could, however, have an opposite effect, as is demonstrated by the case of Francois-Hippolyte-Alexandre L . . ., who murdered his mistress in 1888 when she refused to cook him a meal. During the pre-trial proceedings, L . . .'s mother intervened energetically by casting aspersions on the dead woman for her domineering character.[61] She also happily supplied information on her son's history of infantile convulsions, typhoid fever, and St Vitus's dance, maladies which exempted him from military service and perhaps proved his weakened ability to resist the effect of alcohol. The fact that he had murdered the woman after only one small glass of wine—which

[58] *Gazette des tribunaux*, 15 Feb. 1894.
[59] Ibid.
[60] Ibid., 28 Feb.
[61] D2U8 232, 29 Mar. 1888.

he maintained had given him a headache and caused him to lose his temper—meant to Paul Garnier that he was a degenerate who fell into the category of *alcoolisable*, that is having an 'excessive susceptibility to spirits'.[62] Convinced that even a small quantity of drink could produce violence in such a man, Garnier was manifestly sympathetic even though he refrained from concluding that L . . . was entirely irresponsible. Such factors as L . . .'s extreme repentance when told his mistress was dead—'he fell on the floor crying'[63]—solicitude for their little girl, good work habits, and the fact that the victim was seen as imperious and neglectful of her duties, all contributed to the verdict of not guilty.

In sum, the alienists' medico-legal reports provided highly sophisticated causal sequences of antisocial behaviour which offered no single scientific account of human action.[64] In the cases of Lesteven and L . . . they provided two equally deterministic portrayals which led to entirely opposite conclusions and verdicts. Both defendants were described in mechanistic terms, but only the latter was exonerated, the divergence demonstrating that deterministic explanations were not always equivalent to an assumption of irresponsibility.

THE ALCOHOLIC, THE FAMILY, AND THE CAFÉ

Consideration of irretrievable degeneration and social dangerousness competed in courtroom trials with other conceptions of working-class waywardness which could be reformed, treated, and somehow excused. Drunken murders generally occurred during a domestic quarrel, an argument in or near a café, or at work. Each of these examples will be considered in turn, since they provided a set of prescribed and recognizable *loci* associated with working-class life and drunken comportment.

62 Ibid., medico-legal report by Paul Garnier.

63 Ibid., *pièce* 4.

64 For a discussion of the nature of the alienists' narrative of disease and social incapacity in relation to medico-legal analysis see Roger Smith, 'Expertise and Causal Attribution in Deciding between Crime and Mental Disorder', *Social Studies of Science*, 15 (1985), 67–98.

Bourgeois alcoholics virtually never came to court to answer for drunken, violent crimes. In contrast, drunken working-class men were considered eminently able to destroy their families through particularly vile acts against spouses and off-spring. Many were thought of as degenerate social misfits afflicted by 'morbid jealousy', a term borrowed from the novelist Paul Bourget's *Physiologie de l'amour moderne* (1890). The jealousy was delusional and inexorable, but so powerful that it left an honourable wife in terror. For one medical student of the subject this 'insane' jealousy resulted from the disgust of wives when men demonstrated their animalistic tendencies: 'The husband, his genital organs excited initially by the alcohol, is brutal, demanding, and vicious; sometimes he sees his wife refuse intercourse because she is disgusted by his vices or drunkenness.'[65] Coupled with the eventual sexual lassitude and even impotence that alcoholism ultimately produced, such behaviour, it was argued, could exacerbate an already fraught domestic situation.

In his thesis on the 'alcoholic personality' dedicated to the notable anti-alcohol campaigner and physician Jouffroy, one Dr Escoube dwelt on the characteristics demonstrated by such individuals. One sixty-three-year-old *employé de commerce* of Prosper S . . . was described in this way:

> He gets fuddled [*gris*] almost every day.
>
> He borrows money without telling his wife to satisfy his passion for alcohol.
>
> He has always been very jealous . . . He searches through every corner of the apartment to assure himself that no lover of his wife has been there . . .
>
> For the past eighteen months (since October 1892) he has gone on frequent binges.
>
> He left his home to wander, drinking whenever he had the chance, sleeping on benches. He went away for a week or a fortnight without anyone having news of him.[66]

Perpetually drunk and supported by his wife, eternally and unjustifiably jealous, a vagabond and a self-imposed outcast, the likes of Prosper S . . . were a menace both to themselves and their families.

[65] J. Escoube, *La Jalousie morbide des alcooliques* (Paris, n.d.), 52.
[66] Ibid., 11–12.

When similar men came before the *Cour d'assises* they were treated with considerable harshness.[67] An indication of medical attitudes can be gleaned from a report on Alfred Émile H . . ., an unemployed and violent drinker who maltreated and left his wife, threatened to disfigure her, and sought to live off her wages. He later attempted to kill the woman, and did actually slaughter his daughter and mother-in-law. H . . . thus not only stood accused of two actual and one attempted murders, but also of striking at one of the most fundamental and precious of human relationships, that between father and child.

H . . . was analysed in the context of these perceptions, with the alienists seeing his actions—which were preceded by long sojourns in the café—not as the medical condition of *fureur alcoolique*, which implied a degree of irresponsibility, but as an *accès de colère*, a moral assessment that demanded condemnation.[68] The report, indeed, describes his actions in the terms and language of a temperance tract. The analysis reconstructed him as a perfect demonstration of the need to control the working-class male alcoholic. His uncontrollable temper, subjugation to his mother-in-law, inability to take decisions, and the failure to provide for his family, all became proof of his wilful moral and biological self-destruction, as well as the physical destruction of his family. The medical view not only coincided with that of the judiciary, it was also in sympathy with the jury, and H . . . received a penalty of forced labour for life.

Men like H . . . provided evidence of the need for greater protection of women and children. Indeed, an important aspect of contemporary temperance writing focused on the working-man's preference for the café to the home which, it

[67] Not infrequently men would come before the *Cour d'assises* to answer for similar deeds. Seignot, for example, was an inveterate drunkard who beat and reproached his wife for unjustifiable jealousy. In the middle of the night he got up and finally strangled her to death in front of their children; see *Gazette des tribunaux*, 13 Mar. 1896. Although Pierre Eugène N . . . was not jealous of another man, he was accused of living off his wife in order to feed his addiction and of killing her when she left him to live with her mother: 'Elle m'a exaspéré en me quittant, en me laissant sans ressources; elle a suivi les conseils de sa mère, qui aurait voulu se débarrasser de moi et me mettre sur le pavé . . .' (see D²U⁸ 96, 19 July 1880, *pièce* 15). He received a penalty of forced labour for life.

[68] Alfred Émile H . . . D²U⁸ 278, 27 Oct. 1891, medico-legal report submitted by Motet and Ballet.

was implied, would keep him out of trouble. One manual directed at working-class women explained that the 'rich man has a thousand ways of filling his leisure hours. The working man [*homme du peuple*] has only two: either he stays at home or he goes to the *cabaret*.'[69] Such a statement not only placed the burden of providing homely comforts on the wife, but also concentrated attention on women's role in pacifying and domesticating male urges. The enormous quantity of literature on temperance and the family continually emphasized the importance of a private *foyer* as the best available social distraction from the company of male comrades.

A key aspect of the working-class ne'er-do-well was his tendency to frequent drinking places where the civilizing influence of female companionship was lacking, an impression which was in fact far from accurate.[70] Disapproval of the café was reinforced because it was thought to compete not only with the *foyer* but also with the workplace. It was also seen as encouraging disorderliness and vice, presided over by a Machiavellian *marchand de vins* who spoon-fed his clients eau-de-vie and turned a blind eye to the presence of casual prostitution. Indeed, after the 1890s, even the socialist leadership expressed concern over alcoholism. For them, excessive drinking was an outcome of capitalist exploitation, and efforts were made to remove working-class men from the 'contaminating' influence of the café to the more politically minded *bourses de travail*, *maisons du peuple*, and co-operative societies.[71]

Despite this alarm, the café remained the major focus of working-class sociability throughout the period. It provided the opportunity to read the newspaper, discuss politics, eat, and drink without interference, and sometimes even supplied a *pension* for married couples and their children. As one bourgeois

[69] Parent (pseudonym), *Le Rôle de la femme dans la lutte contre l'alcoolisme* (Brussels, 1890), 13.

[70] An investigation of judicial records demonstrates that women frequently attended the café. While some were of dubious reputation (women, for example, who served there as waitresses were sometimes suspected of prostitution), the majority came in with friends and companions. Indeed, it seems clear that some working-class families took *pensions* at the local *débit de vins*, with women, men, and children jointly eating and drinking there.

[71] For a discussion of the socialist appreciation of drink and the working classes see Lalouette, 'Le Débit de boisson en France, 1871–1919', Ph.D. thesis, 2 vols. (Univ. of Paris I, 1979), 119–34, in particular, 121.

commentator admitted, 'the *cabaret* is the working man's parlour [*salon*]'.[72] Indeed, it sometimes also functioned as an informal labour exchange, and the *marchand de vins* had an important role in the local community, often acting as a witness to marriage ceremonies.[73]

In ideal terms, the working-class vision of the café matched and opposed the bourgeois reformer's view. Neither, however, sufficiently expressed the mixture of violence *and* pleasure, disorderliness and relaxation which comprised café life. Cafés did tolerate some habitual drunkards and were sometimes used by women as places to solicit. Parisian *bals* were occasionally the scene of drunken brawls[74] and many unpremeditated murders occurred in or near them because of disagreements over women, cards, a demand for an extra drink, or a light for a cigarette.[75] Attempts to keep the café 'respectable' could also end in violence. When, in one instance, a customer made some possibly provocative observations on a woman's hair, the woman, her chaperone, and their interlocutor were all thrown out, with the violence taking place immediately outside.[76] The café owner would often act as a kind of umpire when disputes arose, and those wishing to keep their establishments relatively peaceful were occasionally attacked. The *marchand de vins* L . . ., who refused to serve an already drunk L . . ., ended up in a fight in which his son-in-law was killed.[77]

[72] Henri Roberts's preface, in Louis Moison, *Le Péril alcoolique* (Paris, 1911), 7.

[73] See the unpublished paper by Haine, 'From Shopkeeper to Social Entrepreneur: The Parisian Wine Merchant, 1870–1890'. Paper presented to the Social Science History Association, Toronto, Oct. 1984.

[74] For one of the many examples of such struggles see the case of Ernest Adrien R . . . who accidentally killed a man who stepped on his foot in a dance hall (D^2U^8 175, 1 Apr. 1885); R . . . was acquitted. For more on popular entertainments in the period including *bals*, *cafés-concerts*, etc. see Charles Rearick, *Pleasures of the Belle Époque: Entertainment and Festivity in Turn-of-the-century France* (New Haven, 1985), *passim*.

[75] Cases of this nature are virtually limitless. See, for example, Louis M . . . D^2U^8 258, 6 Aug. 1890, which chronicles a murderous fight that began after some remarks were made over M . . .'s wife. For a fight involving a woman see Paul B . . . D^2U^8 246, 10 Sept. 1889. Englebert G . . . D^2U^8 244, 10 Apr. 1889, asked for a light from another customer, took his cigarette away, was thrown out by the *marchand de vins*, and ultimately killed the man who had offered him the light.

[76] See the case of D . . . D^2U^8 255, 5 July 1890. In another instance a *marchand de vins* sought to eject a prostitute from his establishment, and a few minutes later she and her lover assaulted him. See Ernest D . . . D^2U^8 225, 9 Nov. 1887.

[77] See the case of Gilbert L . . . D^2U^8 251, 5 Sept. 1889.

Despite the complexities of café life revealed by the judicial records, middle-class commentators almost always stressed aspects associated with male debauchery and disorderliness. In the struggle against these, they sought to establish a 'natural' alliance with working-class women, emphasizing the way masculine dissipation brought on domestic ruin. As the *Gazette des tribunaux* summed up this recurring theme in 1893:

> Here is another crime we can put down to alcohol. Vermeinen, a young, thirty-year-old housepainter, earns high wages. His wife is hard-working, economical, and the household could be perfectly happy . . . but Vermeinen drinks. He has a passion for absinthe and drinks most of his pay in the bar; . . . as a result there are frequent scenes between husband and wife.[78]

The view was constantly reinforced that the man was at best a wayward child and at worst a moral and biological culprit whose drunkenness and brutality risked isolating him from his family. Rather than the husband or herself, it was 'the child that the woman ought to defend, the child who might still be saved, despite the tremendous power of the model'.[79] Working-class women, otherwise often described as instinctual, superstitious, badly conducted creatures, were transformed in such commentaries into angels of the hearth, protecting the culture of domesticity against brute male force:

> Without a doubt there are some admirable parents, above all those mothers who sacrifice their lives in an obscure, silent, and therefore more truly impressive fashion, through continuous and unceasing devotion. [She is] desperate to sustain, through work, patience, economy, and example, the physical and moral health of all those dear—although often ungrateful—beings who populate her poor home![80]

There were in fact dramatic examples of women whose children were put at risk by drunken husbands and who blamed themselves for not leaving to protect their offspring. Investigating magistrates would sometimes arrange quite remarkable confrontations between husband and wife when a

[78] *Gazette des tribunaux*, 7 Jan. 1893.

[79] Brada (pseudonym), *La Femme et l'alcoolisme* (Paris, 1913), 167.

[80] Georges Bonjean, *Enfants révoltés et parents coupables. Études sur la désorganisation de la famille et ses conséquences sociales* (Paris, 1895), 106–7.

child was killed by an inebriated father, presenting a melodramatic representation of family tragedy precipitated by alcoholism. In the case of Claude F . . ., the policeman who drunkenly killed his son, the magistrate came with the defendant and the attending medico-legist, Socquet, whose presence was required because the distraught mother refused to give up the body:

We found the defendant's wife there. The woman is in a state of violent despair which seems momentarily to impair her reason. She comes out with incoherent sentences, recalling the merits of her son, his enthusiasm for work, all the qualities that made him passionately loved by her and his father . . .

The characterization of her distress was deepened by the even sadder dialogue between the two bereaved parents:

DAME F . . .: You killed your little boy! His last words were of forgiveness for you. If he could he would tell you again, 'Daddy, I forgive you!'

DEFENDANT: He said, 'You've killed me, Daddy!'

DAME F . . .: He said to me, 'Mummy, I'm gone, he's killed me'; . . . poor little thing, poor little angel. You will never shed enough tears! What do I have left now? You gave me a son and have taken him away again!

DEFENDANT: Shut up. I'm as miserable as you are!

DAME F . . .: I did everything in my power to get rid of your wretched weakness; even now that my son is dead, I ask myself if I did everything I should have done. What a miserable fate we have. May God send you mad so that you can suffer less. I think they will let you embrace our child one last time.

DEFENDANT: I ask for nothing more.[81]

Such cases were seen as proof of the 'disintegration of the family' and the inadequacies of working-class men as fathers. The emphasis on this paternal incapacity was an important feature of the analysis of juvenile delinquency by men such as Henri Joly, Adolphe Guillot, Georges Bonjean, and Alfred Rollet, all avid campaigners for a juvenile court system.[82] Most of all, the father seemed unable to command

[81] Claude-Marie F . . . D^2U^8 259, 10 Sept. 1890, *pièce* 8.

[82] For more on the campaign against juvenile delinquency and the movement for new corrective procedures for the young see above, chap. 3, nn. 103 and 104.

respect, not only because of the loosening of social restraints which urban life encouraged, but also because of the irresponsible, brutal behaviour which led his children, particularly the sons, to disregard him:

In how many families does the worker's son regularly see his father coming home in a most disgraceful state. It no longer affects him so normal does the spectacle seem. He listens to his coarse remarks and witnesses his violence and vileness. Should we really be surprised that the head of the family loses all moral authority?[83]

Georges Bonjean continued in this vein by maintaining that in such situations the beneficial effect of the family was destroyed and children developed 'bad instincts, the savage envy held by the lower ranks against the higher, the spirit of revolt, antisocial hatreds, suspicion of all laws, rules, and morality, ferocious appetites and burning ambitions . . .'.[84]

An official attack on parental neglect and maltreatment was enshrined in the 1889 law on paternal authority. The measure allowed children to be taken away from their parents if they encouraged them in criminal acts or debauchery.[85] It also empowered judges to deny paternal rights to those convicted of public drunkenness, a feature recognizably directed against men rather than women. For Maurice Legrain, this was to be one of the more potent weapons in the anti-alcohol campaigner's arsenal, and he chastised judges who refused to apply the law because it seemed too harsh. In his view their indulgence did not save the family but only promoted its further destruction.[86]

Despite the apparently deep and pervasive opprobrium heaped on the working-class male, there was a second element of argument which tended to *excuse* men for their attacks on women, if less frequently for those on children. Drunken assaults were often seen as male crimes of passion, provoked by

[83] Bonjean quoting A. Guillot, *Enfants révoltés et parents coupables*, 97–8.

[84] Ibid., 98.

[85] For more on the history of paternal authority, see Henri Pascaud, *De l'autorité paternelle sur la personne et sur les biens des enfants légitimes ou naturels* (Paris, 1893), 61–84; for the specific provisions of the law of 1889, see 71–4; see also B. Schnapper, 'La Correction paternelle et le mouvement des idées au dix-neuvième siècle, 1789–1935', *Revue historique*, 263 (1980), 319–50.

[86] Legrain, *Hygiène et prophylaxie*, 188–9.

women who deserved their fate because of neglected duties. When L . . ., mentioned earlier, killed his mistress after a glass of wine, the feeling was that her character was responsible for exacerbating his already excitable nature. Moreover, the way she had refused to cook him dinner was considered to be a particularly condemnable misdeed. Food was considered an important counterbalance to the effects of alcohol and the inability or refusal of a *ménagère* to provide it at home was often regarded as sufficient to drive a man both to the café and intemperance.[87]

In a range of other cases also, men were acquitted for killing women suspected of bad conduct that might range from a flirtatious or coquettish manner to actual infidelity (see chapter 8). Even the Herculean H . . ., whose epidermal insensibility fascinated the intervening medico-legist, was acquitted despite his manifest premeditation. The jury undoubtedly ruled in his favour because they believed his view of the dead woman's character: H . . . had asked her to marry him, she turned him down to marry someone else but suggested they continue as lovers. Disgusted by such double-dealing, he stabbed her several times with a sharpened pair of scissors.[88]

DRUNKEN MEN, POLITICS, AND WORK

Although brawls and attacks on women made up the lion's share of alcoholic violence, a connection was occasionally forged between drink, politics, and a working-class way of life associated with agitation in the café and fractiousness at work.[89] When working men came before the *Cour d'assises*,

87 Lalouette, 'Le Discours bourgeois sur les débits de boisson'; for the emphasis on domestic science and the importance of good nutrition in counteracting alcoholism see 325–31.

88 Joseph H . . . D2U8 259, 18 Sept. 1890.

89 This set of concerns were articulated clearly in Denis Poulot's *Le Sublime*, an account of a Parisian entrepreneur's trials and tribulations with his artisan workforce at the end of the Second Empire. The 'sublimes' were skilled craftsmen who were still indispensable in the workplace but who rigorously and ostentatiously ignored authority, cohabited rather than married, religiously taking days off—in particular, 'Saint Lundi'—and espousing political views which were equally contemptuous of the bourgeois work ethic. See the introduction by Alain Cottereau to his edition of Denis Poulot's *Le Sublime* (Paris, 1981) (7–130). The extent of the continuation of this kind of 'sublimisme' in the early Third Republic is more difficult to determine.

two central issues were probed to determine whether they deserved indulgence. A good and diligent work record, for example, was almost always noted by the investigating magistrate and often mentioned by the President during his interrogation. On the other hand, evidence of past unemployment, arrests for begging or vagrancy, insults to the police, or a bad word from the boss in the workshop, was often sufficient to prejudice the outcome of the case.

Workers who attacked employers or foremen when dismissed were generally treated severely. In several cases—some involving alcohol and others not—embittered workers would plan the murder of those they considered their enemies.[90] By and large these were not crimes with explicit political meaning, but occasionally they were surrounded by revolutionary rhetoric, as in the 1906 case of the mechanic Victor Pivitot, who was dismissed after taking time off work when his mother fell ill. He came back to the factory to shoot the foreman and, while beating the dead body, proclaimed 'Long live revolt! Down with foremen, the executioners of the workers!' The killing was the second time he had shot at a superior, a previous trial ending in acquittal because of his lack of success. It was considered remarkable that despite his revolutionary utterances, he was considered a gentle man, a very good worker, and an esteemed member of the community. Indeed, his neighbours came out in force to defend him, the *concierge* telling how he had generously paid for her son's funeral, fed penniless workers, and bought little presents for the local children. In sum, they maintained that Pivitot was 'a most perfectly honourable man, good in every respect'. Despite these recommendations, he was none the less sentenced to ten years' imprisonment.[91]

Pivitot was considered an exceptional case, a good man embittered by his own and others' poverty. Other political activists, however, were generally regarded less sympathetically, as intelligent trouble-makers uninterested in honest labour and prone to drink and agitation. Time and time again, left-wing

[90] See, for example, the case of François Spano (*Gazette des tribunaux*, 29 Jan. 1904), an Italian worker accused of killing the foreman, who had discharged him. He was given the death penalty, a punishment commuted to forced labour for life and reduced once again, in 1932, to twenty years' hard labour.

[91] Ibid., 10 Jan. 1905.

activism was a major plank in the prosecution's case against working men with political affiliations—even those without violent anarchist sympathies. For example, when the baker's boy Joseph Garesio was accused of killing a drinking companion after a stay in a café, the *Gazette des tribunaux* described him 'as one of those people, more assiduous at political meetings than in the bakery, who try and drag diligent workers into strikes for no reason'.[92]

Although such men were clearly regarded as self-consciously subversive, the nature of the link between alcohol and political protest was more diffuse and is correspondingly harder to pin down. Other kinds of judicial records, especially those of the Correctional Tribunal, demonstrate the way drink enabled workers to resist authority. Haine's analysis of cases of 'insults against police' (*outrages aux agents*), often uttered in the café and later attenuated with the words, 'I was drunk', demonstrate the persistence of revolutionary ardour well after the Commune. It seems that the police were keen to prosecute such insults to their authority, as the number of such crimes leaped from an average of just under 800 a year during the 1860s to over 3,000 for the decade between 1870 and 1880. Repeatedly, working men laced their insults against the police with threats of revenge for a massacre of the Communards.[93] With such explicitly political catcalls as *assassin de Versailles*, interspersed with more derogatory and obscene epithets such as *canaille*, *fainéant*, *coquin*, *voleur*, *vache*, and *cochon*, Parisian workers made their feelings about the police clear.

There was occasionally a case that seemed to epitomize the connections between café agitation, drink, and rebellion against authority. In October 1889, Pierre D . . . shot his boss in the leg and grazed his ear after he got drunk in a café. The son of a stone-cutter, D . . . had moved up the ranks at the Chemin de fer du Nord through his intelligence and alacrity, but was transferred, without notice, to work at a lower position so that he could be watched more closely, a move that was due to his reputation for being a drinker, prickly, and politically unreliable. At first an ardent supporter of Clemenceau, he

92 Ibid., 6 Jan. 1904. Despite all attempts to make the charge stick, Garesio was acquitted, denying persistently that he was the author of the crime.

93 See Haine, 'I go to the café to create', 251; Susannah Barrows of the History Department at the University of California at Berkeley is pursuing a full-length study of alcoholism, the café, and politics in the early Third Republic.

later attached himself to the left wing of the Boulangist movement and was politically active in the eighteenth *arrondissement*. He was known to expatiate on his views to the working-class clientele in the *débit de vins* where he ate and drank, and this habit persuaded the police to take a dark view of him:

> Very much a braggart and gossip, his comments would often set off tumultuous arguments in M. S . . .'s establishment where he took his meals. This latter wanted to get rid of such a coarse and embarrassing boarder . . . He seems to have had a good basic education and, as he is gifted with a certain eloquence, he easily shone amongst his table companions. . . .[94]

The alienists who examined him declared that he was a '*névropathe*' whose tainted heredity and general emotional disequilibrium made him particularly susceptible not only to the ravages of alcohol but also to left-wing politics. Their description was similar to the rapid changes of mood, vanity, and impulsiveness of female hysterics and was corroborated by such organic symptoms as hyperanaesthesia in the left mammary region, the summit of the head, and by his excessively sensitive testicles.[95] The jury agreed with Motet's assessment of D . . .'s dangerousness and gaoled him for five years, followed by two years' exile from Paris. The punishment was extremely severe for a crime that had caused so little damage because it was affected by the exacerbating connections with politics.

Drink and the Vision of the Working-class Man

In certain instances, psychiatrists seemed particularly eager to advocate harsh measures to protect society against abnormal and dangerous individuals who drank. In the eyes of contemporaries, the prostitute murderer, Lesteven, was a pervert, H . . . unnaturally destroyed his family, and D . . . was a subversive. Such men seemed to confirm the extreme picture of moral, social, and biological disintegration found in the writings of temperance organizers, jurists, and physicians when they wished to draw attention to the wide-reaching implications of alcoholism for the nation and moral fabric of society.

[94] Pierre Eugène D . . . D^2U^8 254, 5 June 1890, *pièce* 106.
[95] Ibid., medico-legal report.

Despite the insistence on imminent racial and social destruction, however, the official world that examined working-class men *generally* came up with a less severe characterization. Although there were frequent indications of moral laxity and biological abnormality, the physicians, judges, and jurors were often sympathetic, provided the drunken outbursts coincided with a good record at work, a decent family life—even if this meant cohabitation—or if the deed could somehow be classed as a crime of passion.

In effect, while the *Cour d'assises* condemned the working-class life-style in general for its violence and irregularity, the working man himself was often viewed with patronizing indulgence. These lenient verdicts, the speeches of the defence attornies and the testimony of offenders' families, implied that the murderer was basically irresponsible, sometimes violent perhaps, but none the less not a thorough and irredeemable brute. An example of this attempt to use the stereotype of the working-class drunk to lessen the offence can be seen in the case of Joseph A . . ., who in 1881 murdered a *marchand de vins* over a disputed card game. When called to testify, his wife repeatedly remarked that he was a good husband and how as a result she treated him leniently when he drank. For her, he was 'like a child' who only strayed into alcoholic excess when life 'got on his nerves'. Insisting that he was more gently eccentric than viciously deranged or brutal, she remarked judiciously: 'He's not a drunkard. He only gets drunk about once a month . . . He has a sober, thoughtful character, if a bit odd. For myself, I've thought for a long time he was a bit wrong in the head.'[96] Although his eccentricity had never been noticed before, particularly by his boss, who commended him as a good and diligent worker, his wife's testimony that he had a fundamentally gentle nature and was not morally responsible for his acts was accepted by the jurors, who acquitted him.

This image of the child was often coupled with that of the irrepressible savage, both states regarded as a lower level of nervous and evolutionary development on which proper education and restraint had not yet made an impact. As children could not be held responsible and punished for their acts like adults,

[96] Joseph A . . . D^2U^8 93, 8 Apr. 1880, *pièce* 21.

so drunken working-class killers were deemed to merit a lesser punishment to that meted out to the truly normal and respons. ible. Medical and legal writing tended to sway back and forth between the two images. with the former receiving lighter penalties, and the latter harsh ones.

Indeed, a look at the cases where drunkenness was involved shows a relatively standard response in terms of sentences. Defendants received penalties of less than two to three years when involved in a fight in which no premeditation was evident or when they killed mistresses or wives deemed in some way unworthy. Those who were the cause of aggression in a public brawl—thrown out of cafés and coming back with friends to cause trouble, for example—generally received five to eight years; while those involved in particularly heinous murders received penalties that stretched from ten years to forced labour for life.

Drunken killers themselves sought to shore up the stereotypical image of irresponsibility, with the majority telling investigators that they were *pris de boisson* when they committed their crimes. When, for example, Lucien Auguste C . . . knifed a comrade at the *marchand de vins* during a drinking session after a funeral the indictment expressed irritation over this line of defence: 'the only excuse he gave to lessen the gravity of his acts was that he was drunk and did not know what he was doing.'[97] Although considered a paltry excuse, the three-year sentence indicates a certain degree of indulgence which was demonstrated repeatedly and even more unequivocally when the defendant was deemed to have an otherwise inoffensive character. The most famous criminal advocate of the day, Henri Robert, whose familiarity with such defendants was probably unsurpassed, captured the general attitude of parental exasperation in such cases:

Most common murderers act not because of hatred, greed, love or revenge. Those who kill for the pleasure of killing are intoxicated and give way to an unthinking anger due to the stimulation of alcohol, and particularly absinthe.

Once the crime has been committed, the victim lying on the ground never to rise again, they weep floods of tears and do not even

[97] Lucien Auguste C . . . D2U8 255, 27 June 1890.

remember what they've done . . . they acted under the influence of murderous drunkenness. I often have to go into a murderer's cell to ask him why he killed, and receive the heart-breaking reply: 'I don't remember, I had been drinking, I was drunk . . .'[98]

Not only did working men themselves regularly agree with the doctors about their drunkenness, they sometimes even embellished the reports as a means of convincing the psychiatrists of their irresponsibility. This was certainly the case in the example of a butcher's boy named Billiet, a handsome habitual drinker who was unhappily married to a wife characterized as surly and unattractive.[99] He regularly drank wine, eau-de-vie, and liqueurs but was never over-excited by them, maintaining a sobriety which surprised himself as much as his café friends. However, it was claimed that his drinking led to idleness and increased his disenchantment with his wife, who also purportedly started to drink in an attempt to persuade him to stay at home. On the night of 12 May 1879, he claimed to have been attacked by persistent insomnia and terrifying hallucinations of mice and other animals. When asked the next morning by his wife to go to the abattoir, he refused, murdered her in a violent fury, and gave himself up to the police.

The intervening psychiatrist, Legrand du Saulle, concluded that Billiet had been struck by a *folie alcoolique* and hence could not be considered responsible. As a result, Billiet was acquitted and Legrand du Saulle was pilloried by colleagues not only for appearing to give medical sanction to the murder but also for being excessively naïve. Dally, for example, asserted that Legrand du Saulle had been duped and was too willing to believe the defendant's tales of visions and sensations of being 'strangled by blood' (*étranglé par le sang*).[100] What is interesting in Billiet's case, as well as in that of Hervé, is that the doctors were perceived of as incompetent, outsmarted by the dissembling qualities of depraved men. In contrast, when dealing with female hysterics, alienists were virtually never accused of being duped. Womanly contrivance was assumed, regarded as a part of female nature, and automatically identified as a symptom of illness.

98 Moison, *Le Péril alcoolique*, 6–7, pref. by Henri Robert.

99 *Gazette des tribunaux*, 24 Sept. 1879.

100 Dally, 'La Responsabilité morale et la responsabilité sociale', 114–15.

A set of social prescriptions seems to have governed the assessment of drunken violence with extreme cases, such as Lesteven, H . . . and D . . ., falling outside the sphere in which drunkenness could confer absolution. These examples were seen as incorrigibles who had broken the bonds governing human relationships—between men and women, between father and family, between employer and employee. Occasionally the experts would give self-conscious expression to the perceived boundaries operating in such cases. Dr Dubuisson, for example, when speaking to the court in 1898 in the case of Senftleben, a lazy drunkard who knifed his daughter in the stomach, summed up the general perspective on the difference between the irresponsible *malade*, the alcoholic monster, and the ordinary working man whose degenerate state and unhealthy milieu led him irresistibly, but not maliciously, to drink. The first and last were to be excused, the second could be condemned with a clear conscience:

Nothing is more reasonable and just than to consider the unconscious madman, demented person, idiot, or epileptic irresponsible . . . as none of these are the authors of the evil which pushes them and makes them act. Is it the same with alcoholics? Evidently not. He is, perhaps, no more aware at the moment when he commits a crime under the influence of drink, but he is at the moment when he starts drinking and from then on he is responsible for everything that might result from his excesses.

There are, it must be said, excusable alcoholics. One couldn't hold it against a man who is surprised by drunkenness for the first time; or a hereditary degenerate [*déséquilibré héréditaire*] sent on a binge by a thimble of wine; or a worker who, when drinking is part of his profession . . . gets fatally dragged into some debauch. But nothing excuses Senftleben.[101]

The picture of medical intervention in cases of alcoholism, perhaps more than any other type of violent crime, seems to give the impression of merely reinforcing appraisals that the court might have reached on its own. The alienists appeared to be in the position of rubber-stamping with scientific approval the lay moral condemnation of excess drinking. However, a closer look at the role they played demonstrates that they did

[101] *Gazette des tribunaux*, 3 Dec. 1898.

not cynically condemn those they despised and exonerate those they liked. As in all other cases, they took a clear moral position in their reports on alcoholism; but at the same time, the scientific method of investigation and description they employed weakened the system of classical jurisprudence and the reliance on free will, even while appearing to be in agreement with it. Like their legal colleagues they were keen to impute blame, but they did so by identifying ostensibly neutral social-scientific factors in causing antisocial behaviour.

The individual in such an analysis was fragmented into many elements and a seemingly causal chain of explanation was constructed, an assessment which necessarily undermined the significance of the notion of moral agency. It would, then, be too simplistic to see the general degree of agreement that existed in court between alienists and jurists as evidence of psychiatrists falling into line with the judiciary's wishes. By the turn of the century the influence flowed as much in the opposite direction, as was evident in the writings of progressive jurists who advocated strong measures of social defence against drunken killers. The importance of medical discussions of alcoholism in this context lay, therefore, in the obvious way in which it joined morality and science so inextricably together, forging a combination which was crucial in helping to create a common ground between like-minded jurists and physicians contained within the more general programme of criminological investigation.

Thus, the representation of drunken men in court can be seen to contain several important strands of analysis. Almost always, the commentary emphasized the incapacity of working-class men to take on the duties of fatherhood and citizenship. For example, in the discj ssion of their relationship to children, the working man was seen as a moral and biological culprit, passing on both a dangerous heredity and equally reprehensible habits and values. The attack on paternal authority implied a transferral of rights and obligations from the father to the state which would act *in loco parentis* in the upbringing of children. The state/paternity analogy is too clear to be belaboured, but none the less underscored an important trend in legal and medical management strategies.

Similarly, the portrayal of drunken men—fractious at work,

politically unreliable, and dangerous to their families—strengthened doubts about the wisdom of entrusting political sovereignty to such people. When, for example, working-class men were portrayed as an undifferentiated bloc during the Commune, commentators expressed fears about giving such unreflective masses a say in the political process. Although the Commune may have represented an extreme, and unique, manifestation of the dangers of mass political participation, the lesson it imparted was reiterated in succeeding decades, especially during recurring periods of instability. The formation of trade unions, organized socialist parties, and a demonstrated willingness on the part of many workers to work peacefully for reform did not reassure many of the bourgeois commentators who prided themselves on their keen observations of the working-class mentality. What they perceived was the 'spirit of revolt', still very much alive and revealed through the class struggle and the polarization of democratic politics.

8

MEN, HONOUR, AND CRIMES OF PASSION

Men claimed passion as the motive for the killing of wives, lovers, or rivals in almost half the murder cases during the era. In deciding whether or not to condemn them, the court probed deeply into their attitudes towards marital duties and sexual behaviour, searching for credentials which proved honourable intent, loyalty, devotion, or sometimes merely evidence of romantic attachment. Professing such motivations was often sufficient in itself to warrant an acquittal, although significant exceptions to this rule abounded. As important to the final verdict as the characterization of men's behaviour and feelings was an analysis of the comportment and attitude of the female victim, her infidelity or incompetence forming a key aspect of pre-trial investigation and courtroom trial. The assessment of male responsibility was therefore based on a broad social and psychological assessment of correct or justifiable motive, one which explored the dimensions of intimate sexual relationships. This evaluation gave full reign to a far-ranging discussion of appropriate and inappropriate forms of male honour and emotion, a discourse as replete with ambiguities and ambivalences as that which surrounded the discussion of *criminelles passionnelles*.

Here I will examine visions of masculinity and analyse the different means by which attributes of gender were constructed during investigation and trial. In order to accomplish this task, I will concentrate on the sometimes similar, but more often contrasting, means of preparation, execution, and justification which typfied male and female crimes of passion. The concepts of male honour, despair, and outrage were often couched in very different terms from those which women used, and the kinds of language employed impinged importantly on the more wide-reaching discussion of moral responsibility.

While the chapter will focus on representations of masculinity which attracted leniency, I will also examine a range of character and behaviour considered to be 'dishonourable'. Through the hostile questioning and commentary, it is possible to sketch out the boundaries of unacceptable male action and identify those men seen as especially dangerous social types. Perhaps the most significant was the figure of the male 'decadent', a youthful, middle-class nihilist who represented the most 'dishonourable' and hence reprehensible of so-called *criminels passionnels*.

Visions of Masculinity and the Crime of Passion

When defending their motives for killing women, men often referred to the need to defend their honour against disloyalty. But the notion of honour, and the frequent recourse to the concept as a means of self-justification, conveyed many different meanings. It was often implied that action sprang from the fact that witnesses, the representatives of public opinion, had observed and acknowledged an insult. If such a public affront was given through an assault on reputation or via a physical insult such as a slap, then the offended party often felt obliged to restore his reputation with a duel.

This form of male confrontation, which seems to have had a certain renaissance in the *fin de siècle*, brought the issue of male honour very much to the fore. Although women were sometimes the cause of a duel, confrontations were more often based on insults between men, and frequently involved people of considerable political note. For example, some of the most famous duels resulted from the Dreyfus Affair. Thus, in 1898, Colonel Picquart—who was credited with breaking up the army 'conspiracy' against the Jewish captain—fought Henry, the man who ultimately killed himself in his cell. Similarly, Clemenceau, the ardent Dreyfusard. fought the anti-Semitic ideologue Drumont.[1] The motivations for duelling were, however, as numerous as the clashes, ranging from men who

[1] See Douglas Johnson, *The Dreyfus Affair* (New York, 1966), 129.

gallantly defended the artistic reputations of female protegées against insulting remarks,[2] to much more lowbrow affairs involving political invective in the press.[3]

The duel was unusual for the way in which it formalized a means of satisfying wounded pride and emotion, the need for violence justified in the name of honour and executed with the ritual precision of the military exercise from which it borrowed much of its style. It was generally rationalized by the view that only private justice could avenge private wrongs, that the public domain of litigation was incompetent to judge such matters. It thus demonstrated the intractable conflict between legality and honour, the first demanding due process, the second immediate satisfaction. For the 'man of honour', legality was a meddlesome affair that imposed its dilatory and compensatory processes and increased the humiliation as it did so. In contrast, codes of honour—and the willingness to die or go to prison for them—embodied social attitudes which no legal system could properly represent. In this way duelling in the *fin de siècle* continued to embody an 'aristocratic' mentality: by defying the law, participants demanded the personal right to justice, and refused to become the object of state arbitration.[4]

The formality of the duel presupposed premeditation, with protagonists engaging seconds, choosing weapons and appropriate sites, as well as often negotiating extensively prior to the encounter. The entire procedure was governed by the application of 'gentlemanly' forms, the demonstration of fairness and the assertion of the unavoidability of conflict. Although the most personal of grievances were at issue, the ritual tended to empty the conflict of all that was personal. Indeed, the elaborate conventions were designed to suppress the expression of anger and emotion, with the reparation of honour—and hence of social integrity—taking first place over the satisfaction of wounded feelings. The confrontation reconstituted the

[2] See, for example, Eugène Louis H . . . , Jean-François B . . ., Pierre Marcel F . . . , Émile Tanneguy de W . . . , Jean Louis Marie S . . . D2U8 234, 25/26 June 1888.

[3] See Henri Alexis C . . ., Antoine P . . ., Charles Marie A . . ., Ferdinand Gustave P . . ., Eugène B.-G . . . D2U8 136, 26 Dec. 1882.

[4] For an anthropological view of masculine honour see Julian Pitt-Rivers, *The Fate of Shechem or the Politics of Sex: Essays in the Anthropology of the Mediterranean* (Cambridge, 1977), in particular, 1–17.

winner's honour and also, by implication, delivered justice. Indeed, it was not even necessary to win: to have taken the *risk* of combat was frequently sufficient to heal wounded pride and restore an aura of honourability. In most cases there was no need at all for the opponent to die or be injured, which is why much of the time the bullets flew wide of their mark and so many combatants lived to fight another day.

Although duels occurred relatively infrequently and were largely confined to the political, artistic, and social élite, they stimulated an extended commentary. Unlike lower-class violence, however, they rarely became the topic of criminological discussion, an absence which perhaps merely confirms the general appraisal of the duel as a private matter, a traditional form of masculine confrontation in which the managerial strategies and psychologizing tendencies of the criminological experts had little or no role to play. The juries, when called to try such cases, fell in with the consensus of leniency by responding with an acquittal.

The masculine crime of passion sometimes showed similar characteristics. As with the duel, the murderer asserted that honour underpinned his action, admitted premeditation, and took pains to have his deed publicly known. Both the duellist and the *criminel passionnel* in this context portrayed themselves as men of action, inexorably bent on fulfilling their duty and satisfying their honour. This was especially the case when *criminels passionnels* killed rivals, whom they portrayed as mere thiefs, criminals who stole their wives and disrupted the harmony of their *foyer*. When, for example, Ferdinand Brunet discovered that his beloved wife was sleeping with the foreman in the factory where she worked, he shot the man six times, miraculously not killing him. Although clearly despairing and furious at the moment of the crime, Brunet justified himself afterwards not by claiming temporary insanity, but rather by stressing his premeditation and the need to defend his honour: 'He acknowledged that he wanted to kill Fay and regretted that he hadn't succeeded. But he added that in avenging his honour publicly and with *éclat*, today he considers himself satisfied.'[5] Although a worker in a toy factory, Brunet expressed himself

[5] *Gazette des tribunaux*, 11 Oct. 1905.

with a self-possession, even coolness, reminiscent of duellists. Like them, he showed no regret and made no attempt to deny rational calculation, implying thereby that his murderous act had a judicial character.

The extent to which public knowledge of dishonour could provoke a crime of passion is perhaps best illustrated by the case of the *marchand de vins*, Régis M . . ., who suspected his wife of infidelity and was obliged through community pressure to show his mettle. Despite a distaste for violence, M . . . felt the need for some public action to restore his social position when an anonymous mischief-maker sent him a lamb's head crowned with stag horns. As a result he shot, unsuccessfully, at the suspected lover. The jury at the subsequent trial took its habitually clement stance.[6]

Although assaulting a rival was fairly common, men usually chose instead to execute the women whose disloyalty had become public knowledge and had thus dishonoured them. In law at least, men could feel justified in killing their wives, as the murder of adulterous spouses caught *in flagrante delicto* was excusable under the penal code. Such straightforward examples were relatively rare, however. In practice, local gossip, 'proof' of adultery found in love-letters, or the detection of suspicious meetings, were generally sufficient to produce an acquittal, a judgement seen to fulfil the spirit of the law if not its letter.

Occasionally, voices against such violence would be raised. In 1872, for example, a man called Duborg was acquitted for the murder of his adulterous wife. When the newspaper *Le Soir* suggested that perhaps the woman's punishment had been too severe, the dramatist Alexandre Dumas *fils* responded by a self-righteous and famous tract entitled, *Tue-la*, which demanded feminine fidelity on pain of death.[7] In fact, Dumas *fils* did not believe in a double standard of morality. As an illegitimate child himself, he condemned lax sexual morality in either sex and indeed supported Marie Magdaleine B . . . in 1880 because of her status as a betrayed mother. None the less, his *Tue-la* was seen as the summation of the unforgiving male point

6 Régis M . . . D2U8 156, 26 Xpr. 1884.

7 Patrick Kay Bidelman, *Pariahs Stand Up! The Founding of the Liberal Feminist Movement in France, 1858–1889* (Westport, Conn. and London, 1982).

of view, a mentality regularly expressed by *criminels passionnels* when they defended themselves in court.

The strength of the consensus about female infidelity can be seen during the prosecution of these cases, which were often pervaded by gentle questioning, sympathetic agreement, and a generally commiserating tone. Even during the pre-trial investigation, the concern to demonstrate the man's righteousness could creep into the text of the official indictment, despite the object of building up a case for the prosecution. For example, this was the somewhat inverted way the prosecution presented the cases against Joseph M . . ., a policeman who murdered his wife: 'M . . .'s wife engaged almost openly in prostitution and the numerous scandals she caused contrasted with the irreproachable attitude of her husband, who appeared to suffer cruelly from the situation.'[8] With such a presentation of the wife, acquittal was once again virtually guaranteed.

To suggest that all defendants and officials felt comfortable with the killing of women would greatly overstate the case. On the contrary, men often demonstrated confusion, mental anguish, and remorse before, during, and after a crime of passion. Indeed, in some instances the question of honour was not even raised and instead a discussion of manly despair as heart-rending as any which women produced was presented to the court. A good example of this reaction was demonstrated by Méry de Contades, a middle-aged man with a fatigued appearance, drooping moustache, and pince-nez. Very different in physical appearance and emotional style to the unrepentant man of action, de Contades explained how his wife had betrayed him after many years of happy marriage and the birth of a daughter.

The case was made all the sadder by the fact that the marriage had been a love-match repudiated by his aristocratic parents who demanded a woman of higher social standing. None the less, determined to win her, de Contades had made his own fortune as an electrical engineer, waiting many years to ask for her hand. With such a background of sentimental attachment, he was horrified to discover that her lover was a friend of the

[8] Joseph M . . . D^2U^8 168, 6 Dec. 1884, *Acte d'accusation.*

family, a physician who regularly attended their daughter. So distraught was he at her infidelity, he became convinced that she was 'prey to a nervous illness that made her irresponsible; he attributed the power exercised over her by Dr du Bouchet to the effect of hypnotic manœuvres . . .'. Unable to deal with the situation any longer, de Contades shot, but did not kill, du Bouchet.

In almost every way, de Contades differed from the other examples cited above. However, his presentation of confusion, hesitation, and despair—even seeking to excuse his wife and to find pathological justifications for her actions—was as readily accepted by the jurors as was the more common and more aggressively male stance of vengeance. If the defendant did not reinforce a portrait of uncompromising, self-righteous masculinity, he was none the less a figure of sympathy, particularly for the female audience who flooded the gallery during his trial in 1903. Even the male journalist of the *Gazette des tribunaux*, although convinced that de Contades deluded himself in his diagnosis, was none the less sympathetic: 'Mme de Contades, whose husband thinks she is afflicted by a nervous illness, never had anything but an "illness of the moral sense".'[9]

By far the most usual representation of the *criminel passionnel* combined the defence of honour with an equally compelling portrait of emotional disturbance. In this way, the male self-presentation was similar to that of female perpetrators (see chapter 6). Typical of this kind of offender was Luna de San Pedro, a Malay artist, who in 1893 murdered his wife and attempted to murder his mother-in-law and brother-in-law. Through the description of domestic detail, the painter built up a common picture of conjugal disintegration and female duplicity, the first signs of which were his wife's refusal to wear mourning garb after the death of their little girl. Indications of infidelity were followed by her confession, his unsuccessful attempts first to reconcile and then reform his wife, and finally, a bout of temporary insanity—'I went mad . . . mad . . .'—which led him to the crime.

Unlike the unrepentant Brunet mentioned earlier, Luna

9 *Gazette des tribunaux*, 11/12 May 1903.

repeatedly reiterated his regret: 'I loved that woman very, very much. And now I have nothing left. How unhappy I am.' In an interrogation unabashedly favouring him, the president suggested that the painter had been mistreated by the dead woman's family who, being of mixed Spanish and Indian origin, believed themselves to be superior. The sympathetic reaction to Luna was based on the view that he had been abused by a prejudiced and unworthy family. Such a response can only be understood within the broader racialist terms in which his case was discussed. Luna's defence included the reading of an expert report by a friend and associate who suggested that similar attacks of personal violence were not uncommon in his culture. The defendant successfully won an acquittal by reinforcing racial prejudice with an account of his exotic 'hot-bloodedness', at the same time that he used the rhetorical flourishes of French *criminels passionnels* to play on the heart-strings of the jury.[10]

All these cases demonstrate the representations of masculinity which were acceptable in the eyes of the court. However, the execution of women aroused far more ambiguous emotions than these seemingly straightfoward acquittals would suggest. Certainly, there was no 'conspiracy' within the judicial establishment to 'let the man get away with it'. Indeed, the extent to which men were punished with a wide range of sentences for violence against women suggests that there were very strict notions of what constituted an excusable crime of passion.[11] The implication was that male social superiority carried concomitant responsibilities, and judges were determined to lay down the parameters for sympathetic treatment. The masculine 'complicity' surrounding these cases was subtle and required an intense scrutiny of past behaviour and character. The establishment of motive was all the more necessary because assaults on the 'weaker' sex carried an

[10] *Gazette des tribunaux*, 9/10 Feb. 1793.

[11] In 1900, for example, sixty-one murder trials took place in Paris, of which twenty-two were *crimes de sang* perpetrated by men against women. Eleven were acquitted for their attempted and successful murders; one received a penalty of one year; four were awarded two-year sentences; one, a three-year punishment; one, five years' imprisonment; one, seven years' hard labour9 another, eight years' hard labour; still another ten years'. Finally, there was a father who tried to kill his daughter, a crime of passion of a very special variety, who was sentenced to twenty years' hard labour.

implication of brute domination and lack of chivalry. While violence against women sometimes restored male honour by punishing errant wives, it could also have the opposite effect, allowing dishonourable men to take advantage of female weakness.

Hence, offenders who saw themselves as *criminels passionnels* attempted to establish the purity of their motives through certain styles of execution. For example, they were as likely as their female counterparts to act in public, preceding their deeds with statements of grievance and afterwards giving themselves up to the police. However, in contrast to the female crime of passion, men not infrequently attempted suicide after the assault, with the subsequent defence often resting on whether this self-destructive urge was genuine. A convincing attempt at self-murder was seen as proof of temporary insanity, an indication of some passing psychopathic propensity and hence irresponsibility.[12] Men who followed this course represented themselves as despairing lovers who longed for romantic union in death. In contrast, a feigned suicide attempt was seen as evidence of a dangerous criminal personality and a wish to hide vicious or depraved motives. Women, in contrast, chose this tactic only rarely. When it was adopted by Vena Guillou in 1904, the medico-legists maintained that her wounds suggested that she had not really intended to kill herself and that her defence was a sham.[13]

Men also often killed mistresses as part of the era's frequent suicide pacts. As in the combination of murder and suicide, assessment rested entirely on establishing the man's sincerity in those cases where he survived. In its report on Armand Joly, the *Gazette des tribunaux* clearly laid out the two alternative possibilities. A 'lover and poet', Joly murdered his seventeen-year-old fiancée and then shot himself, a deed which provoked the following musings: 'Was he carried away by his romantic imagination? Or was he following a coldly conceived plan?' These questions were answered by an acquittal when the jury took into account the near fatality of the two bullets which seriously wounded him in the head.[14]

12 This kind of double death was associated with the growth of suicide in general and with self-murder for romantic reasons in particular. For a discussion of this see Louis Proal, *Le Crime et le suicide passionnel* (Paris, 1900), chap. 2.

13 *Gazette des tribunaux*, 16 Feb. 1904.

14 Ibid., 21 June 1905.

The discussion surrounding the style of execution concentrated attention on the impact of the masculine body on the feminine form. Although the revolver was the most popular weapon for both men and women, the former were more ready to use sword-sticks, daggers, or even umbrellas with hidden blades.[15] These implements presupposed a certain degree of physical strength, and required a close and often bloody final confrontation with the victim. Other means of murder, notable for their brutality and implying conscious criminality, were also employed, however. When men shot their wives or mistresses in bed, or strangled them in *hôtels garnis*, the judicial response was generally harsher. Such methods were considered cowardly and, often committed in private and hence with a possible intent to conceal the crime, required extensive explanation to win the status of crimes of passion. Not infrequently, such defendants were unsuccessful in their pleas if they were shown to have been wife-beaters, drunks, or out of work prior to the murder.

However, the court did often condone masculine brutality when otherwise 'honourable' men, with no record of previous violence or misconduct, claimed to have been driven to murder. In such instances, men beat women to death with furniture or strangled them in a rage. In court, they repented of their crimes and presented a picture of temporary insanity, maintaining that an irresistible explosion had led them to violence.

Men in general appear to have been much more prone than women to resort to physical brutality and were more likely to be exonerated for it. Although women used revolvers and vitriol, they were almost never accused of long-standing programmes of abuse against their menfolk. As has been suggested, the representation of the cruel, vengeful woman focused primarily on mothers who employed sustained physical violence against children.[16] The rare exceptions of 'husband-beating' produced horrified reactions from investigating magistrate, judge, jury and neighbours, a universal condemnation which suggests that some fundamental norm, almost a taboo, had been transgressed.

[15] Joseph Henri Eudoxe de V . . . D^2U^8 197, 28 May 1886.
[16] See above, chap. 6, n. 63.

Thus, when Anastasie Deulot S . . . was tried in 1892 for murdering her husband by dousing him with gasoline and setting him alight, the neighbours and the prosecution portrayed the victim as a docile, sweet-tempered man, his drunken habits dismissed as an indication of his unhappy existence. Although she violently denied the charge of murder and claimed it had all been an accident, testimony of previous verbal and physical violence sealed her fate, and Anastasie S . . . received a penalty of forced labour for life.[17] She was the only woman of this period to be accused of sustained abuse against a husband which ended in murder. She was also one of the very few to have received such an extremely severe punishment.

Divergent styles of male and female execution were matched by similar disparities in their self-representations. While jealousy, abandonment, and, above all, infidelity dominated the list of reasons given by both sexes, the way the grievances were expressed differed markedly. Men, for example, rarely accused women of seduction or broken marriage promises, an accusation which was effectively open only to women. This is not to suggest that men were unaffected by abandonment, however. On the contrary, they too lamented their fate and referred to emotional despair, lack of sexual intimacy, and sometimes even shortage of funds after the loss of a wife or companion. Both men and women frequently cited dereliction of duty within the family and household as a motive. However, the emphasis in such complaints differed once more. Women accused men of callousness, brutality, drunkenness, and profligacy at the café, while men tended to stress the abandonment of housewifely tasks, with an occasional condemnatory reference made to female drunkenness.

Such a listing, however, gives little sense of the varied forms of narrative depicting female inadequacy. What is clear is that *all* men, no matter what class, were acquitted if their wives were disloyal. But, in justifying their acts to themselves and to the world, the killers went beyond this statement of fact to give a more detailed picture of female perfidy. Indeed, their recitations provided a keen sense of the relationship of sexual role to class position. The treatment accorded these accounts suggests

[17] Anastasie Deulot S . . . D^2U^8 286, 10 Aug. 1892.

strongly that the assessment of a man's responsibility was to a large extent based on how much the female victim was considered to have lived up to her social and familial obligations. The trial was thus as much an investigation of the victim as it was of the defendant.

A good example of an exasperated bourgeois husband was Joseph K . . ., a lamp manufacturer who had the misfortune to have a wife who slept with his employees, a sin worsened by her wish to enjoy a gayer, less private life. Her behaviour was so scandalous that he successfully won a divorce suit and kept custody of the children. None the less, he decided to avenge his honour as well. Catching her with friends at a local fair, he ran her through with a sword-stick, declaring, 'She's trash [*saleté*]. She left me and abandoned her three children.'[18] In K . . .'s stated opinion, his wife embodied all the faults most heinous to the bourgeois household: impropriety with employees, public immorality, and desertion of children.

Henri R . . . , a prosperous *petit-bourgeois* brazier with his own workshop, also had an unfaithful wife who slept with one of his business competitors. Unlike K . . .'s wife, who seemed unimpressed by her middle-class duties, R . . .'s spouse wanted enjoyment beyond her station. The ultimate disintegration of his business and *ménage*—so intimately tied together—were blamed on her illicit relations and the frivolous tastes which she had developed under his rival's influence: 'She loved to dress up [*aimait la toilette*], had aspirations that were above mine and our station in life, neglected the housework, gave herself over to reading, talked about going dancing and riding and treated me with irony and suspicion.' To undergo such personal and professional humiliation was too much for him and he decided to kill her lover: 'I wanted to kill him. . . . I was justified in what I did and don't feel sorry about it. If I could have another chance I'd do the same again.' This presentation of the wife's faults as well as his categorical attempts to restore his honour, won him a ready acquittal from the jury.[19]

Even the poorest, and often less reputable, working man successfully sought the protection of the crime of passion to

[18] Joseph K . . . D2U8 226, 22 Dec. 1887, *Acte d'accusation*.
[19] Henri R . . . D2U8 141, 26 May 1883, *pièce* 54.

establish his right to violence. Jean-Alphonse L . . ., who threw his wife to her death out the window, was particularly gifted at contrasting his ideal of a working-class *ménagère* with the actual performance of his wife. In a plaintive autobiographic account, which revealingly commenced with the remark, 'this is the sad life of my wife', L . . . laid out a lengthy catalogue of her faults:

> . . . I saw irregularity in her conduct. She started drinking and neglected her work and home . . . nothing pleased her but working outside. She often came back drunk . . . The concierges noticed it; many times they picked her up in the corridors . . . she often slept elsewhere and was no wife to me.

L . . . thus depicted his wife as a prime example of working-class waywardness which he juxtaposed with his own exemplary behaviour: 'In my case, I came quietly home from work. I never went out without her and brought back my wages to her.'[20] With such a testimonial, L . . . was acquitted by the jury.

But women were killed for lesser crimes than infidelity. Henri T. . .,[21] for example, tried to kill his wife for selling the assets of the butcher's shop she was running, accusing her of ruining their children. His crime was excused by virtue of the man's perceived right to control property. Henri W . . .[22] was acquitted for murdering his spouse merely for having intemperate habits and 'provocative airs', behaviour which ruined his standing in the community. Others killed their wives for drunkenness and were excused even when the women's alcoholism could be traced to some identifiable grief. Although both the husband and local witnesses agreed that the wife had acquired her habit because of a child's death, her husband[23] was none the less acquitted for beating her head in when he found her in a drunken stupor on the floor.

However, despite the repeated references to female culpability, there was another class of crimes against women which *were* punished, sometimes quite severely. These demonstrate the accepted boundaries of the male crime of passion by

20 Jean Alphonse L . . . D2U8 148, 22 Oct. 1883, *pièce* 40.

21 See Henri T . . . D2U8 120, 21 Nov. 1881.

22 Henri W . . . D2U8 134, 11 Nov. 1882.

23 Joseph T . . . D2U8 159, 26 June 1884.

showing which murderers were seen to be beyond the pale of absolution. The most commonly punished were husbands or lovers who led their mates a 'martyr's life', with repeated drunkenness and beating prior to a final, and often successful, murder attempt. In such cases women were portrayed as suffering victims, attempting to remain loyal and devoted under intolerable circumstances, with the reference to martyrdom conjuring up a vision of saintly sacrifice (see chapter 7). Other men were punished when their mistresses left them and were murdered after they were frightened into coming back.[24] Pimps who killed prostitutes after they tried to escape were generally given extremely stiff sentences,[25] while husbands who murdered wives who had won a legal separation were also treated harshly.[26] Those who wounded pregnant women were less likely to be acquitted unless it was suspected that the child they were bearing was the fruit of an illicit love affair.[27] 'Indecent' proposals were also scorned, as in the case of Octave Gabriel D . . . who fell in love with a fourteen-year-old girl and shot her in the back five times when she rejected his advances. Employees who sought to take advantage of a woman employer in straitened circumstances were also condemned, as in the case of Pierre L . . .[28] who tried to seduce the widow he worked for and, on her refusal, killed her with a hatchet.

[24] There were many varieties of this kind of crime. Some women postponed leaving, fearful of vengeance, only to be executed when they finally did depart. Others, like Rachel D . . . succeeded in leaving her lover Pierre S . . . but had sex with him after the separation and was killed; Pierre S . . . received a penalty of forced labour for life: see D2U8 204, 30 Oct. 1886. For another case of a woman who left her lover only to return, leave again and finally be killed by him see Antoine Alexandre S . . . D2U8 129, 25 May 1882; S . . . received a penalty of ten years' hard labour.

[25] For one of several examples see Prosper Gevrey, *Gazette des tribunaux*, 7 Feb. 1896, who killed the wife who tried to liberate herself from him. He received a penalty of forced labour for life.

[26] There were scattered instances of this kind of murder and attempted murder. For example, Jacques Francois P . . . tormented his wife even after legal separation, ultimately grazing her in the arm and scapula, without serious injury. He received a penalty of four years' imprisonment, a relatively harsh punishment considering the minor nature of her wounds. See D2U8 146, 27 Aug. 1883.

[27] See, for example, Pierre-Marie G . . . who delivered such a blow to his wife's abdomen that the child's feet were visible; see D2U8 224, 22 Nov. 1887; he received a penalty of twenty years' hard labour and twenty years' exile from Paris.

[28] D2U8 133, 19 Oct. 1882. He received a penalty of forced labour for life.

Real outrage greeted men who seemed to abuse the ritual scenario of the crime of passion to further 'dishonourable' aims. When in 1897 Alfred Michecopin shot and murdered his former fiancée in the Place du Carousel and then attempted suicide, the judicial inquiry revealed what were considered to be the defendant's iniquitous motives. An *agent d'affaires* who had already been divorced for 'notorious misbehaviour', he had fallen in love with an employee at the Crédit Foncier, Léontine Duviguet, proposed, and was accepted until she and her mother discovered more about his background. After the engagement was cancelled, Michecopin tried to woo her back and, when this failed, to compel her to return with threats.

The elaborate murder was regarded as a villainous means of trying to dupe the court, the suicide attempt a contrivance to pass off his vengeful deed as a justified crime of passion. Indeed, Michecopin seems to have badly miscalculated the response to his crime. Although he appeared in a state of pitiable emotional collapse, the court remained hostile. He was suspected on several accounts, first for lying to an honest family about his past and second for claiming that the woman had been his mistress when the autopsy confirmed her virginity. The fact that her hymen was intact meant that he was seen as having no rights over his victim. The outraged judge summed up the prevailing attitude of condemnation when he remarked, 'Do you really think that someone who has grossly deceived a family as you have, has the right to kill in this way a perfectly upright and honest girl when found out?'[29] Michecopin received a penalty of hard labour for life.

If the likes of Michecopin aroused disgust and anger, then other dissolute bourgeois were also condemned. While working-class men who beat and maimed their wives were sometimes condemned, violence was often seen as indicative of a particular *manière de vivre*—regrettable, sometimes punishable, but not altogether unusual. In contrast, those who had benefited from the privileges of education and familial affection, but who repudiated their background and descended into debauchery, were regarded with extreme hostility. Profligate sons of good families appeared often enough in court to arouse considerable

[29] *Gazette des tribunaux*, 31 Jan. 1897.

attention. Their descent into a position of social danger symbolized the nightmare of the respectable: rather than deserving their privileges, they were shown to have abused them and were thus considered especially dishonourable. The interrogation and reporting of such trials were often pervaded by a didactic, moralistic tone, as if to demonstrate the need to maintain strict standards of restraint in the face of dissolute tendencies.

Perhaps the best example of this type was George Deslerbe, who was tried in 1905 for the murder of his mistress. A privileged graduate of the famous Lycée Louis-le-Grand, Deslerbe had sought entrance to the École Polytechnique but was obliged to settle for a position at the Banque de France in Nancy. Forced to resign because of his excesses—he lived illicitly with a mistress, spent all his money, and even threatened her with a revolver—Deslerbe moved to Paris and took a modest position in another bank. It was here that he took on the role of a playboy:

> Very vain and always obsessed by the wish to keep up appearances, he took the name of a viscount, Georges de la Reclerte. He passed himself off as a son of an [important] family, spending substantial sums of money he was given by a sister while waiting to fall heir to a great fortune. He kept up a gentleman's carriage, frequented fashionable restaurants and pleasure spots, took up motoring and sport, and poured his money down the drain.

Such a life of pleasure and extravagance came to an abrupt end when his embezzlements were discovered and he was obliged to flee the capital. Returning, he asked his new Parisian mistress for support and shot her dead when she refused to help him.

Seeing him as a despicable man, the presiding judge summed up his view of the case in the opening interrogation: 'The murder of your mistress has been the culmination of your life of debauchery and embezzlement', an interpretation which Deslerbe's weak protests failed to alter. Indeed, the judicial attitude illustrates the rigid boundaries between dishonourable and honourable masculinity. This view was supported by the attending psychiatrist who saw in the defendant a 'lack of harmony between his faculties' which none the less fully entailed his moral responsibility. Deslerbe was sentenced to ten years in gaol.[30]

Responsibility and the Crime of Passion

After their deeds, many *criminels passionnels* spoke in a language of uncontrollability which was taken to indicate temporary insanity. A man committed such deeds 'dominated by a passion he cannot master';[31] 'under the control of a fit of anger which makes him lose his head';[32] or when 'jealousy and anger make him unaware of his acts'.[33] Jean Alphonse L . . ., who flung his wife out the window, described his experience in this way: 'A cloud passed over my eyes: I was no longer a man; I cannot tell you what was going on inside me . . .'.[34] The description implied that his state caused a loss of humanity, turning him into a raging beast or murderous machine that was, by implication, devoid of moral awareness. Sometimes even those who obviously premeditated their acts by buying a weapon and lying in wait for their victim none the less asserted that the appearance of the woman or rival touched off a kind of irrepressible explosion leading them to commit their crimes.

The phrases employed and the emotions described differed little between the sexes. Women too used the same extreme, sometimes ferocious, terms and both provided a portrait of unaccountability. However, while women were often tainted by a pathological diagnosis of hysteria, bona fide *criminels passionnels* generally escaped such description. Not only were women more likely to be investigated by psychiatrists, their bodies were also more often the focus of discussion in court, with reference made by judges and attornies to menstruation, pregnancy, and lactation.

This is not to suggest that men who claimed passion as a motive were never examined by physicians. On the contrary, the likes of Deslerbe were often described as *déséquilibrés*, but

30 Ibid., 15 May 1905.
31 Antoine Mathieu C . . . D2U8 114, 22 Aug. 1881, *Acte d'accusation.*
32 Jean V . . . Roch D2U8 183, 20 Aug. 1885, *Acte d'accusation.*
33 Joseph Henri Eudoxe de V . . . D2U8 197, 28 May 1886, *Acte d'accusation.*
34 Jean Alphonse L . . . D2U8 148, 22 Oct. 1883, *pièce* 40.

such conclusions generally meant that they were not to be acquitted, that their depraved or degenerate characteristics made them a real social danger. Michecopin's exalted emotions and '*trouble moral*' thus made him a possible candidate for a conclusion of extenuating circumstances. However, for Garnier and Vibert he was nothing more than a 'nervy, easily emotional person', unstable perhaps, but 'sound in mind' (*sain d'esprit*) and therefore responsible for his crime.[35] In such cases, psychiatric intervention had the effect of placing the offender outside the honourable category, an evaluation which led to a hefty penalty. In contrast, women who were deemed hysterical were regarded as irresponsible. Their extravagant emotions, pathological tendencies and violence were *not* seen as particularly dangerous to society, a conclusion which, as has been shown, invariably resulted in an acquittal even if the hysterical woman was also sometimes placed outside the bounds of honour.

Some tentative conclusions can be drawn from the differential treatment. When they committed crimes of passion, both men and women characterized themselves as being in a state of temporary insanity, an excuse which judges, jurors, and psychiatrists largely accepted. However, women's seizures of uncontrollability were somehow more closely tied up with perceived underlying pathology of female nature. In contrast, male irresponsibility in such cases was described as a bout of madness similar to a moment of rage, passing off with the crisis of emotional intensity. The 'temporary insanity' of such men was contrasted to the moral depravity and more fundamental disequilibrium of men like Deslerbe and Michecopin. Except for a passing moment, therefore, the *criminels passionnels* were considered to be normal, a condition which the opposing perception of women's inherent instability generally did not allow. Buch an assessment of male normality was clearly stated by Enrico Ferri:

[35] *Gazette des tribunaux*, 31 Jan. 1897. Interestingly, however, Garnier did call him a '*criminel passionnel*', a description which in this context was used to make the distinction between a veritable *malade* and one whose excess passions had led him to break the law. In this instance, therefore, the term was used in a pejorative sense, implying that the defendant's account of his romantic infatuation was nothing more than a transparent veil attempting to hide the crime of unbridled vengeance and brutality that lay underneath.

There is almost nothing abnormal in the man who kills for love—*above all when he tries to kill himself immediately afterwards*— . . . or in legitimate jealousy pushed to the point of killing. [Equally there is nothing wrong] in open revolt against a society which indulges rich rogues and cares nothing for the unsung martyrs of daily work; in the man who avenges his family's honour or horribly wronged filial love. A small disturbance is sufficient to produce these crimes, a *sensitivity*, an undue impulsiveness arising from an excessive *irritability* of the nervous system. Because a truly stable man is only brought to fratricidal violence by the inevitable need to defend himself. Such a man may be a pseudo-criminal, but never a real one.[36]

By and large, participants in criminological debate agreed with Ferri that the motives of such people were entirely comprehensible and defensible. According to this perspective, the *criminel passionnel*—driven as he was by love, despair, or an assault on his honour—could not be considered to have a 'criminal personality'. At best he was upholding 'decent' values in an 'indecent' society too willing to tolerate lax moral standards; at worst he had an 'excessive irritability', being innocently impulsive and unable to control his temper. In recognizing the essentially harmless nature of the one-time offender, both jury and criminologist accepted that the *criminel passionnel* committed his crime under unique and unrepeatable psychological circumstances and should hardly be the primary focus for an analysis of inveterate criminality. This dichotomy between the passionate and the cold-blooded—the one-time offender and the habitual criminal—operated forcefully in the judicial and medical appraisal of social dangerousness central to criminological discussion.[37]

Perhaps most importantly, particularly for theorists like Raymond Saleilles, the treatment of the crime of passion

36 Quoted in Hélie Courtis, *Étude médico-légale des crimes passionnels*, DM thesis (Toulouse, 1910), 54–5. In this quotation Ferri included in the 'normal' category women who committed infanticide after having been abandoned by a seducer. They were deemed to have killed their children out of a sense of honour and were generally regarded sympathetically by jurors and medico-legists alike. Their motivations were largely considered 'comprehensible', as, in general, no hysteria or even temporary insanity was associated with these women whose crimes were classifiable with those cases of masculine crimes of passion cited above.

37 The *criminel passionnel* did ultimately become the subject of psychiatric intervention and analysis, in the 1930s finally becoming a '*fou dangereux*'. For this interesting evolution see Joëlle Guillais, *La Chair de l'autre: Le Crime passionnel au XIXe siècle* (Paris, 1986), 281–6.

offered a perfect example of the individualization of penalties in action. Although extremely suspicious of the exaggerated and inexpert reactions of Paris juries, he still saw their tendency to acquit in such cases as indicative of the transformation of social *mœurs* and hence of a modified *conscience collective*, sentiments which needed to be incorporated into the movement for penal reform (see chapter 3). Saleilles maintained that the jury, in rendering an acquittal in cases of crimes of passion, went 'beyond the law . . . it is simultaneously a display of instinctive conscience as well as principle: they act to make the notion of the individual dominate that of the facts'.[38]

THE ROMANTIC HERO

If the psychiatric profession expended little time and energy in 'pathologizing' the mental state of *criminels passionnels*, this is not to suggest that they were uninterested in the plight of the male lover and the psychological characteristics accompanying his bout of temporary insanity. Indeed, on occasion, their interest was almost transformed into obsession, with physicians actively praising and sympathizing with men they regarded as the victims of romantic disappointment.

The most extraordinary example of the complicity between a defendant and medical experts involved Julien-Vital M . . ., a house-painter accused of murdering his mistress in 1884 by hitting her over the head with a file and then strangling her with a towel when he discovered that she was leaving him for another man. After several interrogations, M . . . was submitted to psychiatric examination because of his excessive emotivity, particularly his constant sobbing. The most remarkable feature of the interaction between defendant and the doctors, Motet and Blanche, was the unusually lengthy forty-page medico-legal document which resulted, approximately twenty of which were ostensibly a quotation from the defendant.

In their reconstruction, M . . . came across as both meditative and confessional in tone. Indeed, the voice of the

[38] Raymond Saleilles, *L'Individualisation de la peine* (Paris, 1898), 14.

experts and that of the defendant were so intertwined as to be virtually indistinguishable, with the alienists' prefatory remarks flowing seamlessly into the accused's own account. It seems extremely likely that the defendant's recitation was reconstructed and reworked by the experts, with the form of the report differing significantly from the usual conventions. Presented in immaculate handwriting, as if copied out by a professional clerk, it was unapologetically psychological and rhetorical in tone, neglecting the usual physiological and anthropological reflections. Rather than limiting themselves to a positivistic terminology, the physicians seemed keen both to lay out the originality of the subject and to demonstrate their own cultivation and expository talents.

That they chose M . . . as the object of their admiration and compassion is perhaps in itself slightly strange. In many respects, M . . .'s claim to be a *criminel passionnel* was not especially good. There was, for example, considerable evidence of a less than spotless character. As stated in the indictment: 'he was not a very good worker . . . and preferred amusement to work. On top of this, he had a very violent character. In 1876, he was prosecuted for threatening to kill [*menaces de mort*] his father; and in 1879 he was sent to prison . . . for insulting behaviour [*outrages*].'[39] Not only was his past besmirched by such offences, the crime had also been executed in such a way as to cast doubt on his motives. Although M . . . continually reiterated his love for the victim, Nathalie D . . ., he had none the less left the scene of the crime without trying to revive her. Rather than turning himself in immediately to the police, he wandered around Paris, purportedly meditating suicide and jumping into the Seine. The only actual evidence of this intent, however, came from a self-serving source—the defendant himself—who, in a piteous note, wrote: 'I prayed, cried, everyone was without pity.—For myself, I regret my crime and I will surely try to kill myself.'[40]

Despite these dubious factors, the physicians none the less portrayed M . . . as an autodidactic and introspective working man whose higher principles could not be understood by the

[39] Julien-Vital M . . . D2U8 164, 25 Sept. 1884, *Acte d'accusation.*

[40] Ibid., medico-legal report, 27.

women he adored. Their characterization gave him many of the conventional attributes of the male romantic hero who, like his female counterpart, came in a variety of stylized forms. The representation of M . . . owed much to the sympathetic type, in which a man out of joint with the social world and its hypocrisies is punished for his sensibilities and higher aspirations.

In general, the romantic hero was very different from the man of action who unself-consciously knows his rights, privileges, and duties and proceeds accordingly. In contrast, such characters were moody and solitary, prone to introspection with tendencies towards melancholia and despair. All romantic heroes, however, were distinguished by a painful awareness of the fundamental differences between themselves and the common herd, their lineage traceable from Goethe's Werther to Châteaubriand's René, through the weary *enfant du siècle* of Musset. Sometimes they were personally involved in momentous moral and philosophical questions, probed their own and others' motivations, and rebelled against authoritarianism and injustice. In sum, they were seekers of new values, spiritual urges which often resulted in excessive, if not morbid, emotivity.[41]

Many of these elements combined in the physician's portrait of M . . . From the outset, his external, physical demeanour—'a short man . . . pale . . . with a delicate appearance'—indicated spiritual qualities. Like many romantics, M . . . depicted his own past as 'melancholic to the point of hypochondria', a condition intensified by his solitude and his inability or unwillingness to 'take part in the games of his age'. In sum, the medical interest in the subject was due to their recognition of him (and M . . .'s self-representation) as a man very different from, and moreover above, those of his own class: 'Sincerity and Honesty are in fact the very basis of his nature . . . From our first interview with M . . . we noticed how much he differed from the other defendants we are asked to examine

[41] For an introduction see Lloyd Bishop, *The Romantic Hero and his Heirs in French Literature* (New York, 1984); Bishop's bibliography gives a general summary of the literature. For a seminal work on the continuity of the romantic tradition from the early nineteenth century to the 'decadent' era of the 1890s see Mario Praz, *The Romantic Agony*, trans. Angus Davidson (London, 1933).

every day.'[42] Perhaps most importantly, M . . .'s distinction was made all the more apparent by his intellectual sophistication, through his readings of the '. . . *Confessions of Saint Augustine*, *Funeral Orations of de Boussuet*, *Thoughts of Pascal*, writers like Montaigne, Rabelais, La bruyère, Corneille, Racine, Molière, Voltaire, Jean-Jacques Rousseau, Châteaubriand, Lamartine, Victor Hugo, Alfred de Musset, Michelet, and many others besides'.[43]

He was also unusual for his artistic sensibilities. When he first came to Paris from Brussels, M . . . had strolled along the quaysides of the Seine where 'he spent hours looking at the old engravings, books, manuscripts [*autographes*], and portraits'.[44] Most of all, his idealism directed him to identify with the oppressed. He wandered about the Tuileries admiring the statues, particularly one by Ugolin representing Hunger. One of his favoured spots was the Musée du Luxembourg, where 'he stood in contemplation in front of the Volon's Antiquarian, the Miners' Strike, the Infanticide, the Worker and his Children. These were his favourite paintings.'[45] Like many romantic heroes, he showed his rebellious tendencies and their humanitarian inspiration, avidly following political debates, admitting his flirtation with Blanquist ideas, and describing his abhorrence for Malthusian concepts, believing in the rights of the poorest people to be fruitful and multiply and satisfy their material needs.

As interesting to the physicians as his refined tastes and political sentiments was his analysis of his family situation and its relationship to his overwhelming concern—both personal and political—with women, the 'woman's question', love and marriage. He expounded on his father's brutality, and his rebellion against domineering masculinity. His mother, in contrast, was a paragon of gentle, Christian domesticity. He summarized the development of his own views concerning women who fell into the category of either *Le Bon Ange* or *Le Démon du foyer*, explaining the important role of the 'feminine element' in shaping his view of the world. Once again, the political and

42 Julien-Vital M . . . , medico-legal report, 2–3.
43 Ibid., 4.
44 Ibid., 9.
45 Ibid.

personal were bound to each other in the narrative of M . . .'s past. He described his regret at the condition of working-class women who, like his sister, had gone into the factory and who 'did not delay long in showing, through her manner and language, that she was succumbing to the distressing influence of the new environment in which she lived. . . .'[46]

This reformist outlook was applied to his relationship with his mistress, for M . . . was, above all, a romantic hero in love. The physicians reported how he despised marriages of convenience based on social position, fortune, or mere vanity. Instead he exalted the power of love, an affectionate union between two consenting individuals, an ideal which he had almost given up until his meeting with Nathalie D . . . . He claimed to have adored her as the perfect image of a working-class wife: 'Her conversation was marked by good sense; she was thrifty, sober, never inactive, a very good housewife; her gaze and bearing were modest. She worked every day to calm me. . . .'[47] His passion was infused by the desire to bind her to him in loving monogomy. He claimed that his affection was so great that he had forgiven her constant infidelities, the fact that she had had a child out of wedlock, and been infected by a venereal disease, explaining her waywardness as the result of 'physical causes for which she was not responsible',[48] an assessment that the medical men might well have endorsed.

The aspect of M . . .'s testimony which most impressed the alienists and was taken as the ultimate proof of his sanity was his apparent willingness to take responsibility for his deed: 'He is clear in his mind that he never gave way to any base passion or self-interested feeling. . . . He does not seek to absolve himself, but insists that . . . he be judged according to the truth.'[49] His desire to incur blame rather than to evade it, as others in his class often seemed inclined to do, was seen as an indication of his higher moral nature. Indeed, M . . . was shown as deliberately distancing himself from the unrepentant man of action by asserting that husbands had no real right to kill disloyal wives, maintaining throughout—and in spite of his own behaviour—that love should triumph over brute male force.

[46] Julien-Vital , M . . . medico-legal report, 6.
[47] Ibid., 14.
[48] Ibid., 13.
[49] Ibid., 37–8.

Fascinating on its own account, the romantic representation of M . . . reveals important themes about the relationship of particular kinds of story-telling to the assessment of responsibility. Above all, the medico-legal document was an *histoire d'amour*,[50] the tribute society expected from the wayward lover to explain and legitimize his behaviour. M . . .'s tale fell into this category and was one which the physicians, for example, used to evoke sympathy and spark off recognition. On one level, M . . .'s story differed little from the range of other tales told by men with less erudition and less rhetorical flair; at another, his *histoire d'amour* was distinctive because it self-consciously employed a range of literary and artistic references, using the romantic hero, his sensibilities, and tastes as points of orientation. During his days in preventive incarceration, M . . . showed his deepening religiosity by reading St Augustine and other Christian classics. Moreover, he even was said to have punctuated his explanation to the doctors with citations from books, suggesting parallels between the predicaments of fictional characters and his own situation.

M . . .'s story was, therefore, evocative in the extreme, perhaps all the more so once sifted through the literary sieve of the attending alienists. We enter into a familiar world of solitary childhoods and romantic readings; dreams of a better life and political engagement; dichotomized characters filled with severe fathers and gentle mothers; a world in which young men quest for the ideal woman, only to be betrayed by her.

The most important accompaniment to the narrative was M . . .'s tears, repeatedly referred to by the magistrate and the doctors and the stated reason for a medico-legal intervention. Considerable attention was paid to the lachrymose effusions of women during their interrogations and trials, their tears seen as integral to femininity, a symbol of grief as well as a weapon that the weak used as emotional blackmail. But while *all* women were prone to tears, men like M . . . who cried were considered to have romantic temperaments and wept because of this special sensibility. Far from being a sign of effeminacy, the trait was well within the boundaries of acceptable masculinity.

[50] See Susan Sontag (ed.), *Barthes: Selected Writings* (Oxford, 1982), 426–57. For an illuminating interpretation of the *histoire d'amour* in understanding Julien Sorel's 'crime of passion' see Ann Jefferson, *Reading Realism in Stendhal* (Cambridge, 1988), 45–90.

As Barthes has suggested in his analysis of the *histoire d'amour*, the lover cries as much for himself as because he is a romantic. This is not to suggest that the pain is contrived, but rather that the way the heartbreak is talked about is enmeshed in a series of shared associations and recognizable signs. When the lover cries he does so for an audience, even if this audience is his own romantic sensibility. When M . . . cried, he did so for many different audiences (himself, the magistrate, physician, judge, jury, and gallery), which were called upon to judge his story and to decide his guilt or innocence. Indeed, it would not be an exaggeration to suggest that when M . . . cried he told his story all the more forcefully, living his grief and reconstructing its mythical qualities. Crying was very much a part of this process, making his story 'truer' than words: 'Words, what are they? One tear will say more than all of them.'[51]

But, for all that M . . . was represented by himself and others as a romantic, the circumstances surrounding the murder aroused doubt. From the description of romantic attachment, M . . . continued with a much less savoury portrait of a disintegrating relationship, of Nathalie's betrayal, his contracting her venereal disease, and her ultimate, mocking abandonment. The murder itself lacked any of the established forms for the crime of passion and indeed its method of execution worried the investigating magistrate. Much time and trouble was spent trying to ascertain whether or not M . . . had actually tried to commit suicide, an action seen as the appropriate course for a romantic lover. Ultimately, a wet *porte-monnaie* was taken to suggest that he had jumped into the Seine, with M . . . himself maintaining that only an instinctive urge of survival brought him back to the river's surface.

In confirming his romantic masculinity, M . . . and the doctors who examined him were also engaged in condemning Nathalie D . . . Indeed, at no stage do the doctors show any sympathy for the victim, agreeing throughout that his desire to improve her moral stature through fidelity and mutual affection was perfectly proper even though the woman herself did not want to be reformed. Beside M . . .'s description of the

[51] Sontag, *Barthes*, 428; in this instance, Barthes is quoting Schubert.

perfect working-class *ménagère*, there emerged another portrait of a woman bent on independence. Although a domestic earning low wages, D . . . was neither desirous of marriage nor a 'martyr' to her lover's demands. Even when he offered marriage she turned him down, preferring instead to carry on a liaison with him while also, it was suggested, taking money from lovers as she required.

The judicial records contain references to any number of *ouvrières* who enjoyed a large amount of personal and sexual freedom, choosing lovers, then leaving them if they were beaten, or if they found a richer or more agreeable companion. The cases frequently describe women who had lived in more than one *ménage* and had children from several relationships. Although their wages were meagre, they earned steadily and their income from work at home, in small workshops, or cafés contributed essentially to the household budget. When they walked out, consequently, the man they left behind was hurt both emotionally and financially.

This picture of relative autonomy and strength—to a certain extent forced upon them by economic circumstances—must be contrasted with other women tortured by brutal, drunken husbands and with the *criminelles passionnelles*, who struggled to have promises of marriage fulfilled and their children legitimized. While the last two categories of women were generally the object of compassion, the likes of Nathalie D . . . were either condemned or regarded suspiciously by the judiciary and the physicians. It is perhaps not surprising therefore that M . . .'s characterization of his own motivation, and the indirect expression of the many shortcomings of his mate, met with a sympathetic response and an acquittal in 1884.

Both men and women who committed crimes of passion portrayed themselves, and were indeed represented by others, in a manner suggestive of romantic literature. As protagonists in the ordeal of love, abandonment, and loss, both sexes sought to communicate the intensity of their feelings, and the moment of temporary insanity it brought on, through highly emotive, even transparent terms. But there are several key differences between both the literary and the courtroom attributes of the male and female protagonists. While men *could* be introspective and intellectual, angry at the world and separate from it, women were depicted as being almost entirely emotional, pouring forth their feelings without analysing them. In addition, not once in the period did a woman seek to provide evidence of her literary interests or cultivated tastes in order to justify her crime—or if one did,. there is no record of it. While intellectualism in the likes of M . . . was seen as an absorbing exception to the brutish qualities of other working-class men, similar tendencies on the part of the domestics and seamstresses who killed their lovers would have seemed decidedly idiosyncratic if not pathologically eccentric. Finally, while M . . . could refer to his hostility towards a domineering father, to the hypocrisy of society, and even to marriage, *criminelles passionnelles* never represented themselves as rebels. On the contrary, their defence almost always rested on their desire (if not their right) for men to live up to social norms, and for 'wronged' women like themselves to find a respectable, honourable place within society.

THE ANTI-HERO: *FIN DE SIÈCLE* DECADENCE AND THE DEBATE OVER RESPONSIBILITY

The positive accounts of the *criminel passionnel* portrayed him as man of honour, heartbroken victim, or romantic hero, indeed, as someone often combining any number of these qualities. However, despite all the time and effort spent on representing the *criminel passionnel* in a positive and sympathetic light, there were still those who saw him and his actions only negatively, as portents of moral and social collapse. On the most basic level, crimes of passion were seen as demonstrating a disrespect for the law founded on selfishness and unbridled passions, particularly unseemly sexual appetites. The philosopher and critic Ferdinand Brunetière—in reviewing a book on the subject for the *Revue des deux mondes*—regarded the crime of passion as a kind of social regression and saw the failure to punish such deeds as an indication not of an advanced '*conscience collective*' but as a return to barbarism: 'a negation of the law while all other crimes are only violations. . . . The fact that we do not see this, do not care any more, seems to me the most foreboding aspect of the indulgence towards crimes of passion which grows day by day.'[52]

Indeed, it seemed that both the state of barbarism and of excessive civilization produced an inability to perceive the difference between right and wrong. This view was most commonly expressed when describing the frequent suicide pacts of the era in which often young, unmarried couples seemed to use death as a means of 'resolving' their impossible situation. It was acknowledged that despairing lovers killed themselves to escape the injustices of avaricious or snobbish parents who refused marital consent.[53] While such individuals were often pitied, they were also regarded as somehow lacking in energy and will-power, too eager to succumb to romantic despair. Above all, they were condemned for rejecting the values of family, honour, country, and religion, and for placing their own individualistic urges for happiness above social requirements.[54]

Indeed, the death rites surrounding the *suicide à deux*—for example, the extravagant dining and drinking of champagne as a prelude to the act—suggested an insouciance which often irritated commentators. Significantly, it was the man who was primarily responsible for organizing the death scene, arranging the hotel room, ordering the food and drink, buying the weapon, and actually killing his mistress first. These deeds were considered to be his role, the murder a manly act designed to spare the woman. Moreover, it was often suggested that the woman lacked sufficient courage and physical strength to kill her mate and then herself, even though she was occasionally seen as the emotional inspiration of the crime.

By killing the women first, however, men who survived were necessarily suspected. The most famous example of such a case

52 Ferdinand Brunétiere, in 'Savants et moralistes', *Revue des deux mondes*, 108 (1891), 212.

53 See Proal, *Le Crime et le suicide passionnel* (Paris, 1900), chap. 2, 'Le Double Suicide passionnel'. This was an old theme which featured prominently as part of the critique of marriages of convenience engineered by avaricious or insensitive parents: even in this period, consent was essential for men wanting to marry until the age of twenty-five and women up till age twenty-one by art. 148, l. 1 of the Civil Code.

54 For an expression of this point of view by a judge see A. Bérard des Glajeux, *Souvenirs de la cour d'assises*, ii. 68.

was the notorious Chambige affair, the later investigations of which focused on the motivations of the young 'decadent' as well as on the mental state of his 'passive' victim (see chapter 6). Indeed, the case produced a sensation in the literary, philosophical, and criminological world, a tremor strengthened by the publication of Paul Bourget's *Le Disciple* in 1889, which, despite the author's heated denial, was widely considered to be a fictionalized account of the crime.[55] Both the book and investigation of the case strikingly concentrated on a cynical seduction of an otherwise honourable woman, the women's 'purity' providing an important counterpoint to the 'decadence' of the real and fictionalized 'anti-heroes'. These men were particularly dishonourable for exploiting their intelligence, education, and personal power for morally destructive ends. Moreover, as the heirs to bourgeois ethics of self-denial and effort, they were seen as traitors to the energy and enterprise of their fathers.

The representation of Chambige gives some indication of the fear and disgust which the young man aroused. His boyhood history was portrayed as a study in excessive *amour-propre*, isolated reverie, and excessive abstraction. Although he was not accused of being a homosexual, Gabriel Tarde suggested that Chambige had been reared in an excessively 'platonic' atmosphere, an implication of effeminacy which was often seen as the decadent's distinguishing trait. This atmosphere of artificial self-obsession—engendered at school and fostered by student life in the Latin Quarter—was thought to have led Chambige into crime. When confronted with Mme Grille, he thought only of their union, without considering her 'children, husband, family, duty, honour'. Rather than being ashamed, Chambige sought to portray the double suicide as a martyrdom to the ideal of love which he extolled as more important than social duty. Even though he recognized that his ideal was an

[55] See Albert Autin, *'Le Disciple' de Paul Bourget* (Paris, 1930), 38. Autin suggests that Bourget was inspired by a case concerning a certain Lebiez, who justified a murder by reference to Darwin's thesis of the 'struggle for life'. Despite Bourget's repeated denials, the proximity of the publication of his volume and the Chambige affair (as well as the double suicide of the Austrian emperor's son with his mistress, Marie Vetsera) meant that *Le Disciple* was widely interpreted as a commentary on such cases.

illusion, a momentary enchantment, he none the less insisted that its evanescent beauty was worth dying for.[56]

In the many analyses of the case, Chambige was portrayed as being decidedly effete, entirely lacking in positive energy and resolve except for his ill-conceived criminal enterprise. His case demonstrated romantic imagination in an almost entirely negative light. Like M . . . he was self-conscious, rebellious, and melancholic, but here the comparison ended, as Chambige's mentality was seen as deeply and irredeemably pathological, particularly in its social consequences.

By calling Chambige a 'decadent', commentators used the term in both a general and a technical sense, the former referring to the collapse of moral values and the decay of civilization, the latter specifying a particular imaginary sensibility which reached its peak between 1880 and 1900.[57] Through his own association with the decadent movement and his writings on the subject, Chambige naturally became a means of discussing the moral implications of its doctrines. A wide range of associations were aroused by *décadentisme*, immediately conjuring up Baudelaire, Schopenhauer, Wagner, and Oscar Wilde, a constellation of artists whose ideas were seen as key to the movement's growth.

In France, the decadent movement bore several distinguishing features. The spiritual and aesthetic proclivities—the love of the occult, use of drugs, and fascination with dream states—all reflected the exploration and valorization of the unconscious mind and the inner 'self'. Others explored the limits of aestheticism, their novels reflecting a search after ever more exquisite sensations, a tendency which, in the case of Huysmans, for example, sometimes led to Catholic ritual. The love of the fantastic, the creation of artificial paradises in painting and literature, the obsession with eroticism, all featured prominently as themes.[58] Above all there was a concentration on pessimism

56 For Tarde's description of the young man, his youth and schooling, see 'L'Affaire Chambige', 92–9.

57 For an illuminating introduction see Jean Pierrot, *The Decadent Imagination, 1880–1900*, trans. Derek Coltman (Chicago, 1981).

58 See Alfred Edward Carter, *The Idea of Decadence in French Literature* (Toronto, 1958) and Praz, *The Romantic Agony*, 187–412. For the pervasive influence of Schopenhauer in the early 1880s see Guy Michaud, *Message poétique du symbolisme* (Paris, 1947), 210–14; for the monumental, if evanescent, impact of Wagner on

and the futility of human existence, feelings which the decadent tried to counteract through the world of fantasy, introspection, and sensation.

Paul Bourget was one of the key theorists of the movement and in his early critical work, *Essais de psychologie contemporaine* (1883), laid out a view of the psychology of the decadent, particularly his inability to reconcile the world of reality with his higher aspirations. The decadent's tastes led him to search out ever more refined sensations, making it difficult, if not impossible, to enjoy simple pleasures. The futile search for the ideal brought on nervous exhaustion and volitional incapacity, tendencies accentuated by scientific inquiry which, having demystified the natural world, denied the consoling effects of religion.[59] As will be seen, however, for all that the decadents rejected positivism—the world of cause and effect, of hypothesis testing, and quantifiable relations—they absorbed much of contemporary psychological theorizing about the 'unconscious' mind.[60] Indeed, it was the abstract appreciation of mental operations in *Le Disciple* which encouraged the young protagonist to excuse his own immoral acts as the result of ineluctable necessity.

Bourget was thus in the ironic position of using the literary techniques associated wtih the decadent sensibility to warn against the dangerous moral effects which this method of psychological dissection produced. His novels became famous for their psychological pointillism,[61] the careful, almost obsessive, way

French arts and letters see Claude Digeon, *La Crise allemande de la pensée française* (Paris, 1959), 394–6; for the relationship of Catholic revivalism to the decadent movement at the end of the century see Richard Griffiths, *The Reactionary Revolution: The Catholic Revival in French Literature, 1870–1914* (New York, 1965), 69–224; see also Jerrold Siegel, *Bohemian Paris: Culture, Politics and Boundaries of Bourgeois Life, 1830–1930* (New York and Harmondsworth, 1986), in particular, 242–94; for an illuminating account of the impact of the decadent movement in art and literature which emphasizes its pervasive misogyny see Bram Dijkstra, *Idols of Perversity: Fantasies of Feminine Evil in Fin de Siècle Culture* (New York, 1986).

59 Pierrot, *The Decadent Imagination*, 11–16.

60 For the importance of scientific ideas to Bourget's work, see Jules Grasset, *L'Idée médicale dans les romans de Paul Bourget* (Montpellier, 1904); for more on *Le Disciple* see Albert Feuillerat, *Paul Bourget: Histoire d'un esprit sous la Troisième République* (Paris, 1937), 135–48.

61 This was a term used by William Johnston in private discussion. For more on his understanding of the negative connotations surrounding the term 'intellectuel'—and hence young men like the misguided Chambige—in late nineteenth-century political and cultural discussion see 'The Origin of the Term "Intellectuals" in French Novels and Essays of the 1890s', *Journal of European Studies*, 4 (1974), 43–56, in particular, 48–9.

they examined the mental processes of the protagonists. In *Le Disciple*, he concentrated on the mental connection between a philosopher and his disciple, Adrien Sixte, a figure widely believed to have been modelled on Hippolyte Taine. Sixte is portrayed as a desiccated materialist who sees no relation between his philosophical theories and the moral behaviour of his readers. He is only shocked out of complacency by the death of a young aristocratic girl, Charlotte de Jussat, whose seduction was coldly planned by a self-professed disciple, Robert Greslou.

Greslou sends Sixte the narrative of his exploits, in which he uses his master's philosophical precepts to account for his past and explain the motivation behind the seduction of Charlotte, a pure, frail young woman whom he has been employed to tutor. The novel concentrates on the opposition between the cerebral, puny Greslou and Charlotte's brother, André, a soldier whose physical vitality is likened to that of a thoroughbred horse, his psychological virility revealed through his equally strong sense of honour, will-power, and strength. Always alive to his inner mental and emotional workings, Greslou analyses his mixture of admiration and envy of André, an ambivalence which he virtually admits suggests the idea of seducing the sister. Besides the psychological tensions, the novel is also riven with class antagonisms. The educated bourgeois is merely a servant in an aristocratic household which survives, not through its achievements, but on its patrimony. As with his connection with Sixte, Greslou is mostly preoccupied with his esteem for and emotional impact on the man he admires. Charlotte, in contrast, is a mere cypher for the greater struggle between himself and André, with all the homo-eroticism that this deep attraction implied.

With the seduction itself, Bourget sought to exemplify the decadent's mentality. Unconcerned with the moral implications of his act, Greslou systematically destroys Charlotte's resistance through a series of well-timed suggestions, cultivating her pity during his own bouts of melancholy, and completing her sentimental education through the reading of romantic authors. Having thus prepared his prey, he declares his love, cold-bloodedly noticing that he himself is overwhelmed by the romantic illusion he has so painstakingly created. After much resistance, they consummate their love, Charlotte succumbing on the sole condition that they then commit suicide together. Having possessed her, however, he finds the idea of mutual immolation less attractive. Dishonoured and recognizing how abused she has been, Charlotte kills herself.

The rest of the novel centres on the struggle between two incompatible philosophies of life, competing views of male behaviour and the crime of passion. Greslou is implicated in Charlotte's death and is even brought to trial. While André, always faithful to the truth, exculpates him in court of physical responsibility for her death, he none the less asserts Greslou's *moral* culpability and later shoots him in the street, uttering the words, 'Justice has been done'. Like the true aristocrat, André proclaims his right to go beyond the law, and suggests that his murder has a judicial character. In thus lauding the aristocratic sensibility, Bourget—a famous dandy well known for his love of English upper-class life—inverted the bourgeois perception of the aristocrat as a figure of decadence, portraying him instead as the uncompromising bearer of traditional moral values.

Although now almost forgotten, *Le Disciple* caused a great stir at the time. Taine published a letter of self-justification; the arch-rationalist Anatole France expressed his hostility to its implications; and Ferdinand Brunetière, editor of the *Revue des deux mondes*, endorsed the novel as the dawn of a new age.[62] He and others since him maintained that *Le Disciple* came as a thunderbolt, heralding the beginning of the end of naturalism and accelerating the critique of Zola's experimental novel.

More importantly, however, it raised the vexed question of the relationship of science to morality, suggesting that there was an irremediable opposition between the two. By suggesting that scientific knowledge could be used for morally reprehensible ends, the novel was seen as a direct attack upon the ideology of mainstream anticlericalism which had underpinned the social and educational programme of the early Third Republic. The blow was felt all the more forcefully because Bourget had once regarded the likes of Taine as secular prophets. The shifting perspective of science as morally subver-

62 Autin, *'Le Disciple' de Paul Bourget*, 67–118.

sive, perhaps even evil, was one which was increasingly voiced by a new generation who sneered at Renan and rejected Zola. When in 1895 Brunetière publicly announced his belief in the 'bankruptcy of science', he was expressing a more far-reaching reaction which even touched some practising scientists. This view made considerable headway in the literary and philosophical world, particularly among the younger generation, who made their way increasingly towards Bergsonianism and often Catholicism.[63]

Perhaps even more importantly, the discussion surrounding *Le Disciple* suggests the extent to which the debate over moral responsibility—ostensibly largely devoted to the examination of the 'dangerous classes, working classes'—also impinged vitally on nagging questions of moral doubt within bourgeois culture. It was not only the degenerate masses who seemed prone to moral blindness, but also the well educated, the civilized, and the most refined. The poor and the ignorant, the privileged and the well bred, both were tainted by the reigning amorality, the 'born' criminal and the 'cultivated' criminal representing the janus-faced nature of the debate over moral responsibility.

Indeed, in writing the novel, Bourget made his concerns explicit, distinguishing two types of the *jeune homme de 1889*. The first was the famous 'struggle-for-lifer' christened by Léon Daudet, who was nothing more than a 'civilized barbarian . . . a calculating-machine servicing a pleasure-machine'.[64] Although objectionable and very much a product of the same 'demoralizing' trend, this type was less dangerous than the 'refined and intellectual epicurean . . . this delicate nihilist', whose critical spirit was so sharpened by contemporary philosophical argument that 'good and bad, beauty and ugliness, vice and virtue, appear to him objects of mere curiosity'.[65] This is the manner in which the nation's bourgeois youth is condemned. Filled with sophisticated ideas, but no longer able to comprehend eternal moral values, they are inevitably a danger to themselves and to society.

63 Harry W. Paul, 'The Debate Over the Bankruptcy of Science in 1895', *French Historical Studies*, 5 (1967–8), 299–327.

64 Bourget, *Le Disciple*, 3rd edn. (Paris, 1901), 11.

65 Ibid., 12.

Clearly, the likes of Chambige and Greslou were fitted into the latter category and, as examplars of the state of middle-class culture, suggested the continuing decay of the nation's youth and sensibilities. Indeed, *Le Disciple* may be read as a tale about France, its opposing personalities contained within the two masculine guises of André and Greslou. One was aristocratic, active, forceful, honourable, and, above all, manly; the other was bourgeois, puny, decadent, and, above all, effeminate. These two types warred against one another, each battling for supremacy. While women were generally considered to be suggestible, *Le Disciple* implied that the most susceptible to deleterious influences were young men with effeminate casts of mind. In this way, the cultural association between femininity and suggestibility was maintained, only to be perverted even further by young men whose excessive intellectualism was a source of extreme cultural debilitation. While Charlotte was, in the end, easy prey, she was at least portrayed as an innocent victim; Greslou, in contrast, was somehow wilfully perverse. At the same time that he was cold and calculating, he was also passive, accepting without critical judgement the doctrines of his master. As a vision of dangerous manhood, the decadent was the one which aroused considerable concern, merging a view of decaying values with the debate over moral responsibility.

9

CONCLUSION

This book has delineated the way various forms of discourse about crime and madness overlapped with issues of class, gender, and politics in *fin de siècle* Paris. The debate was so pervasive and so acerbic that it inspired an attempt to revise penal law, to bring the process of trial and condemnation more into line with scientific developments. Although the discipline of criminology was not crowned by a major revision of the penal code, the discussion associated with its emergence none the less ushered in new and significant reinterpretations of the relationship between the individual and society, the nature of social interaction, and the means by which society could cope with the demands of 'modern civilization'.

Central to this discussion were the opposing arguments of law and psychiatry. Psychiatry in the nineteenth century was often conceived of as a scientific, deterministic discipline that left little room for free will and moral responsibility. In contrast, the law was portrayed as a system which took free will as its essential axiom. Such categorical appraisals fuelled the struggle between the two professions and promoted a powerful myth of philosophical incompatibility which overshadowed their common elements.[1] This study has used the discussion about the relationship between crime and madness to show the disjunction between medical and legal self-characterizations on the one hand and the intricate reality of their approach to criminality on the other. This does not mean that the two systems of analysis were identical—far from it—but rather that the historical relations between the professions were more complex and complementary than rhetorical utterances would immediately suggest.

Like physicians, lawyers and investigating magistrates possessed a keen sense of causation in human behaviour and

[1] See Michael Moore, *Law, and Psychiatry: Rethinking the Relationship* (Cambridge, 1984), esp. chap. 1.

used a variety of psychological concepts such as intention, desire, motivation, and mental state to assess whether a defendant deserved punishment. Although the dictates of the penal code demanded irrevocable penalties for particular crimes, the interrogatory process, as well as the determination of motive and character during courtroom trials, none the less allowed notions of psychological causation to play a crucial, if implicit, role in legal appraisal. At the same time, psychiatrists were as obsessed by the question of moral agency as jurists. For all that they relied on the elaborate theory of hereditarian degeneration and neurophysiological automatism, they also continued to emphasize the individual's obligation to struggle against nature and circumstance. The frequently voiced belief that habits of mind and irregular impulses could and should be controlled suggested the extent to which psychiatrists believed in the possibility of promoting the autonomy of the individual.

Still, alienists were often disappointed men, seeking, but frequently failing, to impose their own exacting standards on working-class patients. The cult of self-restraint is often associated with England and a Victorian ethic of repression, but in France, at least among doctors, these tendencies were just as evident. The fact that alienists were often self-made men who had laboured long and hard with the forces of political and institutional reaction meant that they placed a high premium on strength of will. Under the hostile political climate of the Second Empire they had worked and waited, and tended to exhort patients and the defendants they examined to do the same.

It is perhaps for this reason that whilst French physicians were fascinated with the psychological symptoms of mental disorder—fantasies, dreams, and extreme emotions—they still regarded these manifestations as indications of disease, not as clues to new therapeutic strategies. Indeed, in many instances, evidence of fantasy among hysterical women was taken to indicate mental impoverishment and psychic exhaustion, a perspective which even Pierre Janet, with his innovative work in psychological analysis, upheld to a certain extent with such terms as '*insuffisance psychique*' and his preoccupation with asthenic syndromes.[2] Such analyses emphasized deficit and

[2] H. F. Ellenberger, *The Discovery of the Unconscious: The History and Evolution of Dynamic Psychiatry* (New York, 1970), 364–86.

conflict which diminished rather than enriched the individual. This stress marks a clear contrast between the French alienists and Freud and Breuer, whose *Studies on Hysteria* disagreed with Charcot in concentrating, not on deficit, but on an *excess* of moral feeling in the patients.[3] Indeed, in their view, it was precisely this surfeit of wilfulness and rectitude which put the female patients into conflict with social roles they were obliged to play.

Despite the mechanistic rhetoric of French psychiatrists in court, however, an account of biological disorder did not irrevocably lead to an assessment of irresponsibility. As much as the judges and jurors, the alienists were attempting to determine the degree to which an offender was socially incapacitated.[4] Precise criteria upon which that assessment was based often varied between individual physicians and between professional groups, but all were searching for a judgement which was essentially social in nature. The clearest example of the lack of an equation between determinism and irresponsibility can be seen in the case of alcoholism. Like all others who assessed the drunken working man, the physicians were trapped within a language which stressed polarities, in this instance, those of control v. disinhibition, head v. hand, dangerousness v. harmlessness. These polarities provided a means for thinking about human action along a series of sliding scales which entailed both a moral judgement *and* a scientific assessment.

This is not to suggest that medical appraisals were identical with those made by other observers. In essence, several judgements were effectively made in each individual case and, from the conjunction of these, the court attempted to determine how a defendant could best be managed. The disintegration

[3] See Josef Breuer and Sigmund Freud, *Case Studies in Hysteria*, trans. James Strachey (New York, 1987), 103–4. For example, in discussing the case of Emma von N., Freud noted that she 'gave us an example of how hysteria is compatible with an unblemished character and a well-governed mode of life. The woman we came to know was an admirable one . . . To describe such a woman as a "degenerate" would be to distort the meaning of that word out of all recognition . . . I must confess, too, that I can see no sign in Frau von N.'s history of the "psychical inefficiency" to which Janet attributes the genesis of hysteria. . . . I am inclined to believe, then, that all this involved a considerable *excess* of efficiency . . .'.

[4] R. Smith, 'Expertise and Causal Attribution in Deciding between Crime and Mental Disorder', *Social Studies of Science*, 15 (1985), 67–98.

of rigid guidelines that accompanied the multiplication of analysis was indicative not only of the fragmentation of standards of judgement, but also of the growing numbers of evaluations to which defendants were subjected. As the amount of information required went far beyond the determination of motive and the search for whether or not the defendant was the author of the crime, the process of examination and adjudication became more rigorous and onerous, both for the court and for the individual on trial.

Classifications of mental functioning and disturbance were all on some level associated with gender. In particular, the polarities which were proposed to describe the mind and central nervous system—higher and lower, culture and nature, control and disinhibition—were linked through a series of correspondences to masculine and feminine properties. Such polarized descriptions were important both because they sought to make sense of the connections between the moral, biological, and social realms and because they implied a series of prescriptive ideals. However, the subtlety of the analysis was limited by contemporaries forcing complicated phenomena into such reductionist categories. In both medical diagnosis and in courtroom assessment, participants were often aware of this difficulty, and sought some way of lessening the difference between the complexity of lived experience and the rigidity of the available classifications. But rather than jettisoning the oppositions entirely or forging a new set of theoretical propositions, they tended instead to invert them, supplying new variations and remoulding them to suit various arguments. For example, when working-class men were accused of killing women in a drunken fury, the usual association was often reversed. Men in such cases were portrayed as degenerate and deranged 'nature' while their wives took up the role as civilizing agents, guarding the 'culture' of domesticity against base male instincts.

Even in medical diagnosis the trend was similar. Throughout this work, I have demonstrated the extent to which hysteria was a feminine malady. However, the gender associations of the disorder were in fact becoming far more complicated, as Charcot designated certain men as hysterical in his scientific crusade against a uterine interpretation of the disease.[5] It is important to note that hysteria was associated not with the aesthete or decadent male, but with artisans who had suffered unusual episodes of traumatic shock such as 'railway spine'. Although these men were not considered effeminate, they none the less suffered a variety of symptoms—sensitive zones on the head or genitalia, suffocation in the chest—similar to those that afflicted women.

This transfer of an essentially female malady to a small proportion of the working male population reinforces my conclusions about parallel developments in courtroom evaluation. Working men were perceived as being less responsible than their middle-class counterparts, inclined to respond to the pressures of modern existence like women by unleashing instinctive urges and becoming uncontrollable. In the few cases when male hysteria was discussed in court—as in the example of Pierre Eugène D . . ., the political activist fired from his job, or Adrien Virgile Legrand, the hairdresser's assistant who slashed his child's throat—doctors tended to present a portrait of degeneracy and dangerousness. Even though hysterical, these defendants were less likely to benefit from the medical or judicial indulgences offered to a similar class of women. The same can be seen in the relatively rare cases of alcoholic women, who, like hysterical men, were viewed as having moved outside the boundaries of acceptable and understandable gender-determined behaviour; as a result, they too tended to be treated more harshly.

Medical analysis also reinforced the drawing of conclusions about the links between bodily function and necessary social role, strengthening, among other things, the view that menstruation, lactation, and the bearing of children inevitably consigned women to the domestic sphere. Women were to be associated with biological rather than cultural reproduction, a tidy division of labour congruent with the ideology of separate spheres. Nineteenth-century culture—as well as our own—blurred the distinction between biological events and the cultural meaning ascribed to them. Contemporaries failed to

[5] See Mark S. Micale, 'Gender, Science and Psychiatric Diagnostics: Jean-Martin Charcot and the Nineteenth-Century Idea of Masculine Hysterical Neurosis', unpub. paper circulated from the Wellcome Institute for the History of Medicine (London, 1987).

see that it was not biological difference, but rather the subjective, cultural interpretation of its social consequences that was under discussion.[6]

The judicial records help to tell a story about the problem of moral responsibility and the emergence of criminology. They also indicate the way the debate over crime and madness intersected with contemporary cultural perceptions of gender and social role. The history of the evaluation of moral responsibility, therefore, cannot be analysed in isolation from the history of sexual antagonism or from the dynamics of the family, work, and community.

The depositions examined here suggest a complex ambivalence towards perceived roles and expectations. Working men were expected by middle-class observers to be *pères de famille*, to command respect and authority among dependants and in society at large. Women, in contrast, were increasingly idealized as obedient wives and mothers, looking after their children and husbands from their base in the *foyer*. Such an attitude towards the sexual division of labour was far from being confined to the middle and upper classes, as socialist leaders also joined in a chorus of praise for the working-class *ménagère* supported by a working man able to provide a liveable family wage.

This position ignored the reality of working-class life, in which men were often unemployed and women obliged to work. In addition, it may have increased the potential sphere for sexual antagonism, since only rarely could couples live up to the prescribed ideal. Although women seemed unwilling to work only infrequently, they did often refuse to tolerate men who drank or were financially irresponsible or violent. The more badly brutalized led a life of horrific victimization, often taking refuge at the homes of families and friends. An even larger number, however, demonstrated that they had not learned the attitudes of deference to masculine authority so prized by the middle classes.[7] These women were often

[6] For a feminist refutation of these arguments see Michele Rosaldo, 'The Use and Abuse of Anthropology: Reflections on Feminism and Cross-Cultural Understanding', *Signs*, 5 (1980), 389–417.

[7] For more on sexual antagonism and the working-class family see Ellen Ross, ' "Fierce Questions and Taunts": Married Life in Working-Class London, 1870–1914', *Feminist Studies*, 8 (1982), 575–602.

unafraid to unleash violent reproaches or to threaten their mates with eviction.

The system of temporary alliances struck up during interrogation was extremely fragile, with the magistrates' ambivalence revealing the contradictory attitudes towards gender roles. They were placed in an awkward position when confronting assertive wives and violent husbands. The officials showed a pronounced tendency to censure women for their allegedly strident tone at the same time that they exhorted husbands to demonstrate appropriate protective behaviour. In some instances, magistrates characterized assertive women as nagging shrews and were inclined to sympathize with the husband's 'right' to exert 'discipline'. In other cases, they sought to protect feminine 'martyrs' from masculine brutality, thereby suggesting that working men were somehow responsible for the disarray of their households.

Differences in class also related to assessments of manliness and hence of responsibility. For example, in discussing the violence of working-class men in the streets of Paris, the police and judiciary rarely considered the similarity between these encounters and upper-class duels. While sometimes street violence erupted spontaneously, just as often it was as ritualized as those in which challenges were sent and seconds chosen. Working-class men were as concerned as their social superiors both with retaining their honour within the neighbourhood and with avoiding official channels. Where the bourgeois commentator saw only disorderliness and unthinking violence in such cases, the working man saw highly structured methods for restoring his honour.

The typologies designating honourable and dishonourable masculinity were highly class-specific. For example, the 'decadent' was thoroughly middle-class or aristocratic, as such a condition depended on the prior existence of a certain level of refinement, education, and sophistication. In contrast, the working-class man was thought to be unable to raise himself above an unreflective, spontaneous level. The most dangerous were described as savages, utterly barbaric in personality, appearance, and deeds, a 'sub-species' which seemed to validate Lombroso's notion of the born criminal. The image of savagery was applied most consistently to the urban *apaches*, whose 'tribal' ritual underscored a sense of group ferocity and menace. They were described as wandering bands, the line between vagabondage and more dangerous criminality becoming blurred as specialists projected the course from unemployment and idleness to violent antisocial behaviour.

The fact that such people were unemployed, without fixed domicile, and with neither skill nor trade, all contributed to the perception of them as urban riffraff who, quite literally, could not be domesticated. Bourgeois mythology about them focused on the infested quarters of the city, particularly Montmartre and the areas around the *barrières*, where prostitution, vice, crime, and violence were rampant and civilized existence seemed to be ebbing away.[8] This association of crime with certain geographical locations heightened the sense of a city sectioned into zones of light and dark, with certain areas off-limits to the respectable. While late nineteenth-century campaigns against crime and vice were partly guided by a desire to reform and improve the lot of the poor, they were usually aimed at containing their contaminating effects and preventing them from taking over the 'civilized' quarters of the city.

However, there was a distinction drawn between the dangerous members of the poorer classes and the working class in general. While sometimes prone to bouts of savage violence, the latter were not seen as brutes. Instead, working men tended to be more described as childish, albeit much more aggressive and destructive than real children. The emphasis on childishness pervaded the paternalistic rhetoric of judges and defence attornies who typically described such men as misguided, but not irrevocably evil. Though they were viewed as incomplete in the moral and intellectual sphere, they were none the less blamed for their inability to come up to the standard of bourgeois masculine adulthood. The sentimental vision of childishness as a state of innocence was rarely mentioned; rather the negative connotations of vicious temper tantrums were invariably stressed.

The discussion of female offenders provoked as much ambivalence as that surrounding male criminals. As has been shown, melodrama was a form which women themselves called

[8] For more on the history of Montmartre through the course of the century as a perceived site of crime and illicit pleasure see Louis Chevalier, *Montmartre: Du plaisir et du crime* (Paris, 1980).

upon to describe the abuse they experienced from men. They used it to carve out a limited arena for womanly agency and violent action which was grudgingly accepted by the masculine world. But melodrama was also deployed in a way which sensationalized masculine violence against women. This is apparent in cases which ranged from the murder of prostitutes through the abuse and mutilation of the refined and well-to-do. Then, a veritable myth of male violence would be forged which cast women as perpetually in need of protection, particularly when female victims were left to die in the streets.[9] The atmosphere of terror created was one which could reinforce the doctrine of separate spheres, suggesting that the domestic realm was the only place where women could be shielded from the violent instincts of perverted male criminals. The discussion of violence against women was thus mystified by the emphasis on isolated masculine brutality since, then as now, the majority of women were beaten and murdered at home rather than on the streets.

My discussion of *criminelles passionnelles* noted that the analysis of female violence was inflected by contemporary attitudes about the 'woman's question'. Women who were seduced, abandoned, and left with child could gain sympathy in many cases because judges, doctors, and jurors adhered to the double standard and openly sympathized with the plight of the otherwise respectable women who had been led astray by duplicitous men. Many upheld rather conservative views on the family and seemed to condone feminine violence in the cause of a more rigid sexual morality, one which made a distinction between worthy and unworthy women.

Still others took a more 'feminist' approach to the issue. For example, the Republican and anti-clerical anthropologist Henri Thulié asserted that it was not surprising that women took to the streets with vitriol and revolver, because no legal redress existed for them.[10] The demands of poorer *criminelles passionnelles* actually echoed the moderate mainstream of French feminism by calling for the recognition of their rights to be honestly married and to have their children legitimized

9 For more on the pervasiveness and strength of this myth see Judith Walkowitz, 'Jack the Ripper and the Myth of Male Violence', *Feminist Studies*, 8 (1982), 542–74.

10 H. Thulié, *La Femme: Essai de sociologie physiologique, ce qu'elle a été, ce qu'elle est, les théories de ce qu'elle doit être* (Paris 1887), 1.

and supported. Similarly, the emphasis on the rights of mothers was in step with the increasingly pro-natalist and maternalist bent of French politics, particularly after 1890. The growing cult of motherhood transcended political (and often sexual) boundaries, stressing the importance of bettering the moral, social, and sometimes economic condition of women because of their position as the caretakers of the race.[11]

But even though the rights of seduced and abandoned women were to some extent acknowledged, the representation of woman's psychological and biological 'nature' was none the less pervaded by an inescapable misogyny. For all that women were dismissed, they were also seen as potentially menacing. Doctors argued that feminine sexual functions made them more likely than even the worst men to commit appalling crimes, especially during menstruation. The doctors were hardly original in regarding menstruation as a stigma, but they were innovative in elaborating a refined scientific representation of female animality.[12]

Despite their alleged scientific disinterestedness, some physicians and criminologists admitted to being disturbed by the claims of feminists. They shared with other male members of their class the usual concerns about the future of the family, and referred frequently to the possibly deleterious consequences of women's emancipation. However, their ambivalence towards feminist efforts may well have been based on more specific preoccupations. When discussing the advent of a small number of women into the professions, for example, the criminologist Lacassagne applauded their success; he then proceeded to argue that they would be incapable of undertaking original research, because they did not possess sufficient memory to rank high on the competitive examinations.[13] Such an argument was more than a petty denial of women's possibilities; it seems, rather, to have been strongly affected

[11] See K. Offen, 'Depopulation, Nationalism and Feminism in Fin de Siècle France', 648–75.

[12] For an example of this kind of writing see S. Icard, *La Femme pendant la période menstruelle: Étude de psychologie morbide et de médecine légale* (Paris, 1890).

[13] A. Lacassagne, pref. to R. de Ryckère, *La Femme en prison et devant la mort: Étude de criminologie* (Lyon, 1898), p. viii.

by a fear of increased competition in the labour market. Middle-class feminist aspirations, often articulated within a liberal, individualist ethos of meritocratic achievement, were well suited for unsettling those men who had gained their own social distinction by similar means.

I have chronicled in this book the intensity of the discourse surrounding crime and madness in the *fin de siècle*, the harsh appraisals of degenerates, the wish to rid society of undesirables, and the very real fear of the perilous consequences of not doing so. Given this orientation, which grew in strength right up to the First World War, it is difficult to understand why the judicial system and penal code was not altered more substantially. As I have suggested earlier, a massive transformation of the legal code seemed less necessary when an effective administrative apparatus existed to remove dangerous individuals from circulation and control them once they left the prison system. Although the period between the First and Second World Wars would prove niggardly in penal innovation, the era after 1945 opened up an enlarged sphere for new kinds of 'medico-administrative' organization.[14] Indeed, it seems fair to suggest that much of the intellectual elaboration of modern penology occurred during the pre-First World War era.

The potential for growth of the administrative sphere was not, however, the only reason why the drive to reform the penal code eventually evaporated. For all that criminologists promoted a social interpretation of crime, they held fast to an important belief in personal freedom which was closely in line with their liberal republicanism. Although well aware of the dangers posed by criminality, it seems clear that many reformers were frightened by the implications of a thoroughgoing strategy of social defence and, despite many protestations to the contrary, were uneasy with the implications of scientific management for individual rights and liberties. Similarly, a kind of equilibrium existed between, on the one hand, the perceived need for vigilance against the possible biological, moral, and political inundation by the lower orders, and, on the other, an equally complacent and pervasive

[14] See G. Wright, *Between the Guillotine and Liberty: Two Centuries of the Crime Problem in France* (New York, 1983), 175–218.

assessment that bourgeois society would probably withstand the onslaught.

Finally, for all that criminologists called for a *criminelle politique* designed to promote social defence, they targeted their campaign against individual law-breakers, rather than against the social setting that their analyses implied were ultimately responsible. Degeneration theory and Pasteurian microbiology, so important to the criminological approach, seemed to indicate a far-reaching environmentalism, but none the less concentrated on individual regression and on the lone microbe as the key agents of contamination. The discipline may be ranked therefore with other late nineteenth-century efforts that cast the politics of moral reform in the language of hygienic improvement. Criminology, like crusades against alcoholism, pornography, prostitution, cohabitation, and even bad housing, combined moral disapproval and doomsday prophecy with a striking unwillingness to enact radical measures that would match the scale of the problem described. In line with the social organicism which pervaded *fin de siècle* social theory, criminologists wanted some social improvement and were willing to revise the extreme aspects of *laissez-faire* capitalism to render bourgeois society more secure. However, although they were ready to rub off the edges of class conflict through piecemeal reform, they drew back from the idea of changing the existing class system and the values which supported it.

SELECT BIBLIOGRAPHY

MANUSCRIPT SOURCES

Private Collection (Nancy): Cited with the permission of Mme Tridon, Nancy: *Les Souvenirs inédits de Henri Étienne Beaunis.*

Archives de la Préfecture de police (Paris): B^{A} press coverage of trial of Gabrielle Bompard and Michel Eyraud, Dec. 1890.

Archives de la Seine (Paris): $D^{3}U^{6}$ 32–62, 1880–97 (Arrêts de non-lieu, cartons); $D^{1}U^{8}$ 1880, 1910 (Registres des jugements); $D^{2}U^{8}$ 90–286 (Cour d'assises, cartons).

MURDER CASES CITED

Source: *Archives de la Seine* (Paris).

1880

Marie Magdeleine B . . . $D^{2}U^{8}$ 92, 23 Mar.
Joseph A . . . $D^{2}U^{8}$ 93, 8 Apr.
Pierre Eugène N . . . $D^{2}U^{8}$ 96, 19 July.
Louis Menesclou $D^{2}U^{8}$ 98, 30 July.

1881

Antoine Mathieu C . . . $D^{2}U^{8}$ 114, 22 Aug.
Henri T . . . $D^{2}U^{8}$ 120, 21 Nov.

1882

Antoine Alexandre S . . . $D^{2}U^{8}$ 129, 25 May.
Agathe G . . . $D^{2}U^{8}$ 130, 28 June.
Pierre L . . . $D^{2}U^{8}$ 133, 19 Oct.
Henri W . . . $D^{2}U^{8}$ 134, 11 Nov.
Eulalie Louise Chevalet J . . . $D^{2}U^{8}$ 134, 14 Nov.
Henri Alexis C . . ., Antoine P . . ., Charles Marie A . . . , Ferdinand Gustave P . . ., Eugène B.-G . . . $D^{2}U^{8}$ 136, 26 Dec.

1883

Edmée-Rose G . . . $D^{2}U^{8}$ 139, 29 Mar.
Henri R . . . $D^{2}U^{8}$ 141. 26 May.
Jacques François P . . . $D^{2}U^{8}$ 146, 27 Aug.
Désirée Zéphirine V . . . $D^{2}U^{8}$ 147, 21 Sept.
Jean Alphonse L . . . $D^{2}U^{8}$ 148, 22 Oct.

Amicie Lépée G . . . D^{2}U^8 149, 12 Nov.

1884

Amélie-Marie-Augustine S . . . D^{2}U^8 151, 25 Jan.
Régis M . . . D^{2}U^8 156, 26 Apr.
Marie-Françoise-Léontine F . . . D^{2}U^8 156, 9 May.
Eugène Jean P . . . D^{2}U^8 159, 13/14 June.
Joseph T . . . D^{2}U^8 159, 26 June.
Hippolyte F . . . D^{2}U^8 164, 4 Sept.
Julien-Vital M . . . D^{2}U^8 164, 25 Sept.
Joseph M . . . D^{2}U^8 168, 6 Dec.

1885

Jeanne Royannez Clovis-Hughes D^{2}U^8 169, 8 Jan.
Félix B . . . D^{2}U^8 170, 24 Jan.
Ernest Adrien R . . . D^{2}U^8 175, 1 Apr.
François-Louis M . . . D^{2}U^8 176, 25 Apr.
Marie C . . . D^{2}U^8 178, 9 June.
Jean V . . . Roch D^{2}U^8 183, 20 Aug.

1886

Alphonse C . . . D^{2}U^8 194, 22 Mar.
Louise C . . . D^{2}U^8 195, 28 Apr.
Joseph Henri Euxode de V . . . D^{2}U^8 197, 28 May.
Charles Auguste G . . . D^{2}U^8 199, 15 July.
Pierre S . . . D^{2}U^8 204, 30 Oct.

1887

Marie Velsch P . . . D^{2}U^8 212, 24 Mar.
Eugénie Pathier B . . . D^{2}U^8 217, 25/26 July.
Ernest D . . . D^{2}U^8 225, 9 Nov.
Pierre-Marie G . . . D^{2}U^8 224, 22 Nov.
Joseph K . . . D^{2}U^8 226, 22 Dec.

1888

François-Hippolyte-Alexandre L . . . D^{2}U^8 232, 28 Mar.
Eugène Louis H . . ., Jean-François B . . ., Pierre Marcel F . . ., Émile Tannequy de W . . ., Jean Louis Marie S . . . D^{2}U^8 234, 25/26 June.
Pauline B . . . D^{2}U^8 241, 12/13 Dec.

1889

Englebert G . . . D^{2}U^8 244, 10 Apr.
Gilbert L . . . D^{2}U^8 251, 5 Sept.
Paul B . . . D^{2}U^8 246, 10 Sept.

1890

Pierre Eugène D . . . D^{2}U^8 254, 5 June.
Lucien Auguste C . . . D^{2}U^8 255, 27 June.

D . . . D^2U^8 255, 5 July.
Louis M . . . D^2U^8 258, 6 Aug.
Claude-Marie F . . . D^2U^8 259, 10 Sept.
Joseph H . . . D^2U^8 259, 18 Sept.
Gabrielle Bompard D^2U^8 263, 20 Dec.
Charles François C . . . D^2U^8 261, 30 Dec.

1891
Victor D . . . and Carmine D . . . D^2U^8 263, 2/3 Jan.
Pierre-Laurent-Auguste G . . . D^2U^8 269, 25 June.
Alfred Émile H . . . D^2U^8 278, 27 Oct.

1892
Blanche Augustine D . . . D^2U^8 283, 23 Mar.
Anastasie Deulot S . . . D^2U^8 286, 10 Aug.

PRIMARY JOURNALS CITED

Annales d'hygiène publique et de médecine légale
Annales médico-psychologiques
Archives d'anthropologie criminelle
Archives générales de la médecine
Bulletin de l'Union internationale de droit pénal
Journal de psychologie
Réforme sociale
Revue des deux mondes
Revue de l'hypnotisme
Revue internationale de l'enseignement
Revue pénitentiaire
Revue philosophique
Revue de psychiatrie, de neurologie et d'hypnologie
Séances et travaux de l'académie des sciences morales et politiques

NEWSPAPERS CITED

L'Est républicain
Le Figaro
Le Gaulois
Gazette des tribunaux
L'Illustration
L'Intransigeant
Le Journal
Le Journal illustré
Le Journal de Rouen

Le Monde illustré
Le Paris illustré
Le Petit Parisien

PRIMARY SOURCES

ALBERT, M., *Les Théâtres des Boulevards, 1789–1848* (Paris, 1902).

ALIOTTA, A., *The Idealistic Reaction against Science*, trans. A. McCaskill (London, 1914).

ANON., *Inauguration des bustes de Baillarger et de Falret à l'Hospice de la Salpêtrière* (Paris, 1894).

—— *Le Palais de Justice: Son monde et ses mœurs*, pref. by Alexandre Dumas *fils* (Paris, 1892).

AUBRY, P., *La Contagion du meurtre: Étude d'anthropologie criminelle* (Paris, 1896).

AVIAT, H., *La Question des établissements spéciaux pour la cure de l'alcoolisme: Maison de convalescence, d'abstinence et de travail* (Arcis-sur-Aube, 1900).

BABINSKI, J., *Œuvre scientifique, recueil des principaux travaux* (Paris, 1934).

BAILLARGER, J., *Recherches sur les maladies mentales* (Paris, 1890).

BALLET, G., *Le Langage intérieur et les diverses formes de l'aphasie* (Paris, 1886).

—— *Psychoses et affections nerveuses* (Paris, 1987).

—— *et al.*, *Traité de pathologie mentale* (Paris, 1903).

—— and A. PROUST, *L'Hygiène neurasthénique* (Paris, 1897), trans. *The Treatment of Neurasthenia* (London, 1897).

BARIOD, J.-A., 'Études critiques sur les monomanies instinctives: Non-existence de cette forme de maladie mentale', DM thesis (Paris, 1852).

BAYLE, A.-L.-J., *Nouvelle doctrine des maladies mentales* (Paris, 1825).

—— *Traité des maladies du cerveau et de ses membranes* (Paris, 1826).

BECCARIA, C., *Traité des délits et des peines*, trans. from the Italian by André Mordlet (Paris, 1766).

BELLANGER, A. R., *Le Magnétisme: Vérités et chimères de cette science occulte; un drame dans le somnambulisme, épisode historique, les tables tournantes, etc.* (Paris, 1852).

BÉRARD DES GLAJEUX, A., *Souvenirs d'un président d'assises*, 2 vols. (Paris, 1893).

BERNARD, C., *L'Introduction à la médecine expérimentale* (Paris, 1865).

BERNHEIM, H., *Hypnotisme, suggestion et psychothérapie* (Paris, 1891).

—— *De la suggestion dans l'état hypnotique et dans l'état de veille* (Paris, 1884).

—— *De la suggestion et ses applications à la thérapeutique*, 2nd edn. (Paris, 1888).

BERTAUT, J., *La Jeune Fille dans la littérature française* (Paris, 1910).

BERTILLON, J., *La Dépopulation de la France, ses conséquences, ses causes, et des mesures à prendre pour La combattre* (Paris, 1910).
BINET, A. and C. FÉRÉ, *Le Magnétisme animal* (Paris, 1887).
BLUM, L. *Du Mariage* (Paris, 1907).
BONJEAN, G., *Enfants révoltés et parents coupables: Études sur la désorganisation de la famille et ses conséquences sociales* (Paris, 1895).
BOURGET, P., *Le Disciple* (Paris, 1889).
BOURNEVILLE, D.-M., *La Possession de Jeanne Fery: Religieuse professee du couvent des sœurs noires de la ville de Mons* (Paris, 1886).
—— *Science et miracle: Louise Lateau ou la stigmatisée belge* (Paris, 1875).
—— and P. REGNARD, *Iconographie photographique de la Salpêtrière*, 3 vols. (Paris, 1876–80).
BRADA (pseudonym), *La Femme et l'alcoolisme* (Paris, 1913).
BREUER, J. and S. FREUD, *Case Studies in Hysteria*, trans. J. Strachey (New York, 1987).
BRIERRE DE BOISMONT, A.-F.-J., *Des hallucinations ou histoire raisonnée des apparitions, des visions, des songes, de l'extase, des rêves, du magnétisme et du somnambulisme* (Paris, 1845).
BROUARDEL, P., *Les Blessures et les accidents du travail* (Paris, 1906).
—— *L'Exercice de la médecine et du charlatanisme* (Paris, 1899).
—— *Les Intoxications* (Paris, 1903).
—— *La Lutte contre la tuberculose* (Paris, 1901).
—— *Le Mariage, nullité, divorce, grossesse, accouchement* (Paris, (1900).
—— *La Mort et la mort subite* (Paris, 1897).
—— *La Pendaison, la strangulation, la suffocation, la submersion* (Paris, 1897).
—— *La Profession médicale au commencement du XXe siècle* (Paris, 1903).
—— *La Responsabilité médicale; secret médical; déclarations de naissance, inhumations; expertises médico-légales* (Paris, 1898).
—— *Le Secret médical* (Paris, 1887).

CAVILHON, E., *Le Fascinateur magnétique* (Paris, 1882).
CAYLA, F., *Le Vin, le buveur de vin et le buveur d'alcool* (Bordeaux, 1901).
CHARCOT, *La Foi qui guérit* (Paris, 1897).
—— *Les Démoniaques dans l'art* (Paris, 1887).
—— *Leçons du mardi à la Salpêtrière Policlinques, 1887–1888, Notes de cours de MM. Blin, Charcot & H. Colin* (Paris, 1888).
—— *Œuvres complètes*, 9 vols. (Paris, 1885–90).
CHAUVEAU, A. and F. HÉLIE, *Théorie du code pénal*, 8 vols. (Paris, 1834–42).
Congrès international d'hygiène publique (Paris, 1889).

Congrès international de l'hypnotisme expérimental et thérapeutique, tenu à Paris du 8 au 12 août 1889 (Lille, 1889).
Congrès internationale de médecine mentale (Paris, 5–10 Aug. 1889).
Congrès international de 1889: Le Magnétisme humain appliqué au soulagement et à la guérison des maladies (Paris, 1890).
Congrès international de neurologie, de psychiatrie, d'électricité médicale et d'hypnologie (Paris, 1898).
Congrès des médecins aliénistes et neurologistes (Nancy, 1896).
CORRE, A., *L'Ethnographie criminelle* (Paris, 1894).
COURTIS, H., *Étude médico-légale des crimes passionnels*, DM thesis (Toulouse, 1910).
CRUPPI, J., *La Cour d'assises* (Paris, 1898).
—— *Napoléon et le jury* (Paris, 1896).
CUCHE, P., *De la possibilité pour l'école classique d'organiser la répression pénale en dehors du libre arbitre* (Grenoble, 1897).
—— *Traité de science et de législation pénitentiaire* (Paris, 1905).

DALLOZ, V. E., *Les Codes annotés, supplément du code pénal, annoté et expliqué d'après la jurisprudence et la doctrine* (Paris, 1889).
DELBŒUF, J., *Magnétiseurs et médecins* (Paris, 1890).
DESMAZE, C., *Histoire de la médecine légale en France* (Paris, 1880).
DONATO, Prof. (pseudonym), *Cours pratique d'hypnotisme et de magnétisme* (Paris, n.d.).
DUPRÉ, E., *L'Œuvre psychiatrique et médico-légale de l'infirmerie spéciale de la préfecture de police (Lasèque, Legrand du Saulle, P. Garnier)* (Paris, 1905).

ESCOUBE, J., *La Jalousie morbide des alcooliques* (Paris, n.d.).
ESMEIN, A., *A History of Continental Criminal Procedure, with Special Reference to France*, trans. Simpson (Boston, 1913).
ESQUIROL, J.-E.-D., *Des établissements des aliénés en France et les moyens d'améliorer le sort de ces infortunés* (Paris, 1819).
—— *Des maladies mentales considérées sous les rapports médical, hygiénique et médico-legal*, 2 vols. (Paris, 1838).

FALRET, J.-P. *père, Des maladies mentales* (Paris, 1864).
FAURE, F., *La Sociologie dans les facultés de droit de France* (Paris, 1893).
FÉRÉ, C., *La Famille névropathique* (Paris, 1884).
—— *L'Instinct sexuel, évolution et dissolution* (Paris, 1899).
FERRI, E., *Socialism and Positive Science: Darwin, Spencer, Marx*, trans. E. C. Harvey (London, 1902).
FODÉRÉ, F., *Les Lois éclairées par les sciences physiques, ou traité de médecine légale et d'hygiène publique*, 3 vols. (Paris, 1799).
—— *Traité de médecine légale et d'hygiène publique, ou de police de santé, adapté aux codes de l'empire français* (Paris, 1813).

FOUILLÉ, A., *La Science sociale contemporaine*, 6th edn. (Paris, 1922).
—— *L'Idée moderne de droit*, 2nd edn. (Paris, 1923).

GARNIER, P., *La Folie à Paris: Étude statistique, clinique et médico-légale* (Paris, 1890).
—— *Les Fétichistes, pervertis, et invertis sexuels, observations médico-légales* (Paris, 1896).
—— *Les Perversions sexuelles obsédantes et impulsives* (Paris, 1900).
GENIL-PERRIN, G., *Histoire des origines et de l'évolution de l'idée de dégénérescence en médecine mentale* (Paris, 1913).
GEORGET, É., *De la folie* (Paris, 1820).
GILLES DE LA TOURETTE, B., *L'Hypnotisme et les états analogues* (Paris 1887).
GLEY, Prof., 'Discours', *Jubilé du Docteur V. Magnan, 15 Mars 1908* (n.p., n.d.).
GRANIER, C., *La Femme criminelle* (Paris, 1906).
GRASSET, J., *L'Idée médicale dans les romans de Paul Bourget* (Montpellier, 1904).
GUILLOT, A., *Le Jury et les mœurs* (*extrait* de la *Gazette des tribunaux*) (Paris, 1885).
—— *Observations pratiques au sujet des enfants traduits en justice* (Paris, 1890).
—— *Les Prisons du Palais de justice (Dépôt de la préfecture: Conciergerie-Sourcière*) (Melun, 1892).
—— *Les Prisons de Paris et les prisonniers* (Paris, 1890).

HAURIOU, M., *Les Facultés de droit et la sociologie* (Paris, 1893).

ICARD, S., *La Femme pendant la période menstruelle: Étude de psychologie morbide et de médecine légale* (Paris, 1890).
IMBERT-GOURBEYRE, A., *La Stigmatisation* (Clermont-Ferrand/Paris, 1894).
—— *Les Stigmatisées* (Paris, 1873).

JOLLY, H., *Le Crime: Étude sociale* (Paris, 1888).
—— *La France criminelle* (Paris, 1889).
JOURDAN, A., *Des rapports entre le droit et l'économie politique ou philosophie comparée du droit et de l'économie politique* (Paris, 1885).

KAHN, A., *Le Théâtre social en France de 1870 à nos jours* (Paris, 1907).

LASÈGUE, C., *L'Exhibitionisme* (Paris, 1877).
—— *Le Vol aux étalages* (Paris, 1880).
LÈBRE, G. (ed.), *Revue des grands procès contemporains* (Paris, 1889).
LEGRAIN, P.-M. *L'Hygiène, et prophylaxie: Dégénérescence sociale et alcoolisme* (Paris, 1895).
LEYMAIRE, L. DE, *Les Avocats d'aujourd'hui* (Paris, 1893).

LIÉBAULT, A., *Du sommeil et des états analogues considérés surtout au point de vue de l'action du moral sur le physique* (Paris, 1866).

LIÉGEOIS, J., *Origines et théories économiques de l'association des travailleurs* (Nancy, 1872).

—— *De la suggestion et du somnambulisme dans leurs rapports avec la jurisprudence* (Paris, 1889).

LOMBROSO, C. and G. FERRERO, *La Femme criminelle et la prostituée*, trans. L. Meille (Paris, 1896).

—— *The Female Offender*, introd. by W. Douglas Morrison (London, 1895).

MACÉ, G., *La Police parisienne, femmes criminelles* (Paris, 1904).

MAGNAN, V., *De l'alcoolisme, des diverses formes du délire alcoolique et de leur traitement* (Paris, 1874).

—— *Des exhibitionnistes . . . travail communiqué du 12 mai 1890* (Paris, 1890).

—— *Leçons cliniques sur la dipsomanie faites à l'asile Sainte-Anne*, ed. M. Brian (Paris, 1884).

—— and P.-M. LEGRAIN, *Les Dégénérés* (État mental et syndromes épisodiques) (Paris, 1895).

MAIRET, A., *Le Régime des aliénés*: Révision de la loi de 1838 (Paris, 1914).

MARCÉ, L. V., *Traité de la folie des femmes enceintes des nouvelles accouchées et des nourrices et considérations médico-légales qui se rattachent à ce sujet* (Paris, 1858).

MARTIN DU GARD, R., *Le Lieutenant-colonel de Maumort*, ed. A. Daspre (Paris, 1983).

MOISON, L., *Le Péril alcoolique* (Paris, 1911).

MOREAU DE TOURS, J.-J., *Du Hachish et de l'aliénation mentale* (Paris, 1845).

MOREL, B.-A., *Considérations sur les causes du goître et du crétinisme épidémiques à Rosières-aux-Salines (Meurthe)* (Nancy, 1851).

—— *Du goître et du crétinisme, étiologie, prophylaxie, traitement, programme médico-administratif* (Paris, 1864).

—— *Traité des dégénérescences physiques, intellectuelles et morales de l'espèce humaine et des causes qui produisent ces variétés maladives* (Paris, 1857).

—— *Traité des maladies mentales* (Paris, 1860).

MORSELLI, E., *Il Magnetismo animale: La Fascinazione e gli ipnotici* (Turin, 1886).

PANCKOUCKE, C.-C.-F. (ed.), *Dictionnaire des sciences médicales* (Paris, 1819).

PARENT (pseudonym), *Le Rôle de la femme dans la lutte contre l'alcoolisme* (Brussels, 1890).

PASCAUD, H., *De l'autorité paternelle sur la personne et sur les biens des enfants légitimes ou naturels* (Paris, 1893).

PINEL, P., *Médecine clinique ou la médecine rendue plus précise et plus exacte par l'application de l'analyse* (Paris, 1802).
—— *Nosographie philosophique ou la méthode de l'analyse appliquée à la Médecine*, 6th edn. (Paris, 1818).
—— *Traité médico-philosophique sur l'aliénation mentale* (Paris, 1801); 2nd edn. (Paris, 1809).
POULOT, D., *Le Sublime* (1870), ed. A. Cottereau (Paris, 1981).
PROAL, L., *Le Crime et le suicide passionnel* (Paris, 1900).

RAUX, E., *Nos jeunes détenus: Essai sur l'enfance coupable* (Paris, 1890).
RÉGNAULT, E., *Du degré de compétence des médecins dans les questions judiciaires relatives aux aliénations mentales et des théories physiologiques sur la monomanie homicide, la liberté morale, etc.* (Paris, 1830).
REINACH, J., *Contre l'alcoolisme* (Paris, 1911).
RIBOT, T., *De l'hérédité* (Paris, 1872).
—— *Les Maladies de la mémoire* (Paris, 1881).
—— *Les Maladies de la personnalité* (Paris, 1885).
—— *Les Maladies de la volonté*, 2nd. edn. (Paris, 1884).
RICHER, P., *Études cliniques sur l'hystéro-epilepsie ou grande hystérie* (Paris, 1881).
RIVAIL, HIPPOLYTE (pseudonym: ALLAN KARDEC), *Livre des esprits, contenant les principes de la doctrine spirite* (Paris, 1857).
ROUXEL, JEAN (pseudonym: AUGUSTE LEROUX), *Rapports de magnétisme et du spiritisme* (Paris, 1892).
RYCKÈRE R., DE, *La Femme en prison et devant la mort: Étude de criminologie* (Lyons, 1898).

SAILLARD, P., *Le Rôle de l'avocat en matiére criminelle* (Paris, 1905).
SALEILLES, R. *Essai d'une théorie générale des obligations d'aprés le projet du code civil allemand* (Paris, 1890).
—— *L'Individualisation de la peine* (Paris, 1898).
—— *Œuvre juridique de Raymond Saleilles*, ed. M. E. Thaller (Paris, 1914).
—— *Quelques mots sur le rôle de la méthode historique dans l'enseignement du droit* (Paris, 1890).
SAULLE, H. L. DU, *La Folie devant les tribunaux* (Paris, 1864).
—— G. BERRYER, G. POUCHET, *et al.*, *Traité de médecine légale, de jurisprudence médicale et de toxicologie* (Paris, 1886).
SÉMÉLAIGNE, R., *Les Grands Aliénistes français*, vol. i (Paris, 1894).
—— *Philippe Pinel et son œuvre au point de vue de la médecine mentale* (Paris, 1888).
—— *La Psychiatrie française*, vol. i (Paris, 1930).
SÉRIEUX, P., *V. Magnan: Sa vie et son œuvre* (Paris, 1921).
SIMON, T., *Un clinicien: Magnan. Un créateur de la psychologie expérimentale* (Paris, 1918).

SOULIÉ, F., *La Closerie des genêts* (Paris, 1846).
SOURY, J., *Le Système nerveux central, structure et fonctions: Histoire critique des théories et des doctrines* (Paris, 1899).

TAINE, H., *L'Intelligence* (Paris, 1870).
TARDE, G., *La Criminalité comparée* (Paris, 1886).
—— *Les Lois d'imitation* (Paris, 1890).
—— *La Philosophie pénale* (Paris, 1890).
THALLER, E.-E. (ed.), *L'Œuvre juridique de Raymond Saleilles* (Paris 1914).
THULIÉ, H., *La Femme: Essai de Sociologie physiologique, ce qu'elle a été, ce qu'elle est, les théories de ce qu'elle doit être* (Paris, 1887).

VÉTAULT, V., *Étude médico-légale sur l'alcoolisme: Des conditions de la responsabilité au point de vue pénal chez les alcoolisés* (Paris, 1887).

ZOLA, E., *La Vérité en marche*, Introd. and annot. by Colette Becker (Paris, 1969).

SECONDARY SOURCES

AKERKNECHT, E., *Medicine at the Paris Hospitals, 1794–1848* (Baltimore, 1967).
ALEXANDER, M., 'The Administration of Madness and Attitudes towards the Insane in Nineteenth-Century Paris', Ph.D. thesis (Johns Hopkins Univ., 1976).
AUNE, B., *Kant's Theory of Morals* (Princeton, 1979).
AUTIN, A., *Le Disciple de Paul Bourget* (Paris, 1930).

BARROWS, S., 'After the Commune, Alcoholism, Temperance and Literature in the Early Third Republic', in J. Merriman (ed.), *Class Experience in Nineteenth-Century Europe* (New York, 1979), 205–18.
—— *Distorting Mirrors: Visions of the Crowd in Late Nineteenth-Century France* (New Haven, 1981).
BARRUCAND, D., *Histoire de l'hypnose en France* (Paris, 1967).
BARTHES, R., *Selected Writings*, ed. S. Sontag (Oxford, 1982).
BARUK, H., *La Psychiatrie française de Pinel à nos jours* (Paris, 1967).
BENDER, D., 'The Development of French Anthropology', *Journal of the History of the Behavioural Sciences* 1 (1965), 139–51.
BERCHERIE, P., *Les Fondements de la clinique: Histoire et structure du savoir psychiatrique* (Paris, 1980).
BERLANSTEIN, L. R., *The Working People of Paris, 1871–1914* (Baltimore, 1984).

BIDELMAN, P. K., *Pariahs Stand Up! The Founding of the Liberal Feminist Movement in France, 1858–1889* (Westport, Conn. and London, 1982).

BING, F., 'La Théorie de la dégénérescence', in J. Postel and C. Quétel (eds.), *Nouvelle histoire de la psychiatrie* (Toulouse, 1983), 351–6.

BISHOP, L., *The Romantic Hero and his Heirs in French Literature* (American University Studies Series) (New York, 1984).

BLANCHE, J., *Pêche aux souvenirs* (Paris, 1949).

BLANCKAERT, C., *Monogénisme et polygénisme en France de Buffon à P. Broca, 1749–1880*, 3 vols., Ph.D. thesis (Univ. of Paris I, 1981).

BLEANDONU, G., and G. GAUFFEY, 'Naissance des asiles d'aliénés (Auxerre-Paris)', *Annales: Économies, sociétés, croyances*, 20 (1975), 93–121.

BOOTH, M. R. *Victorian Spectacular Theatre, 1850–1910* (London, 1981).

BOREL, J., *Du concept de dégénérescence à la notion d'alcoolisme dans la médecine contemporaine: Les Campagnes anti-alcooliques de 1865 à 1965* (Montpellier, 1968).

BORIE, J., *Mythologies de l'hérédité au XIXe siècle* (Paris, 1981).

BORING, E., *A History of Experimental Physiology* (New York, 1950).

BORSA, S. and C. R. MICHEL, *Des hôpitaux au XIXe siècle* (Paris, 1985).

BRODERICK, A. (ed.), *The French Institutionalists, Maurice Hauriou, Georges Renard and Joseph T. Delos*, trans. M. Welling (Cambridge, Mass., 1970).

BROOKS, P., *The Melodramatic Imagination: Balzac, Henry James, Melodrama and the Mode of Excess* (New Haven, 1976).

BUICAN, D., *Histoire de la génétique et de l'évolutionnisme en France* (Paris, 1984).

BYNUM, W. F., 'Alcoholism and Degeneration in Nineteenth-Century European Medicine and Psychiatry', *British Journal of Addiction*, 79 (1984), 59–70.

—— 'Chronic Alcoholism in the First Half of the Nineteenth Century', *Bulletin of the History of Medicine*, 42 (1968), 160–85.

—— R. PORTER and M. SHEPHERD (eds.), *The Anatomy of Madness: Essays in the History of Psychiatry*, 2 vols. (London, 1985; vol. iii forthcoming).

CANGUILHEM, G., *Études d'histoire et de philosophie des sciences*, 5th edn. (Paris, 1983).

—— *Le Normal et le pathologique*, 3rd. edn. (Paris, 1975).

CARTER, A. E., *The Idea of Decadence in French Literature* (Toronto, 1958).

CASTEL, E., *La Gestion des risques: De l'anti-psychiatrie à l'après-psychanalyse* (Paris, 1981).

CASTEL, R., *L'Ordre psychiatrique, l'âge d'or de l'aliénisme* (Paris, 1976).
—— 'Le Traitement morale: thérapeutique mentale et contrôle social au XIXe siècle', *Topique*, 2 (1970), 109–29.
CHAMBERLAIN, J. and S. GILMAN (eds.), *Degeneration: The Dark Side of Progress* (New York, 1985).
CHAMPENOIS-MARMIER, M.-P. and J. SANSOT, *Droit, Folie, Liberté: La Protection de la personne des malades mentaux (Loi du 30 juin 1838)* (Paris, 1983).
CHESNAIS, J.-C., *Histoire de la violence* (Paris, 1981).
CHEVALIER, L., *Laboring Classes and Dangerous Classes in Paris During the First Half of the Nineteenth Century*, trans. Frank Jellinek, (Princeton, 1973).
—— *Montmartre: Du plaisir et du crime* (Paris, 1980).
CLARK, L. L., *Social Darwinism in France* (Birmingham, Ala., 1984).
CLARK, M. J., 'The Data of Alienism: Evolutionary Neurology, Physiological Psychology, and the Reconstruction of British Psychiatric Theory, *c.*1850–1900', D.Phil. thesis (Univ. of Oxford, 1982).
—— ' "A Plastic Power Ministering to Organisation": Interpretations of the Mind-Body Relation in Late Nineteenth-century British Psychiatry', *Psychological Medicine*, 13 (1983), 487–97.
CLARK, T. N., *Gabriel Tarde: On Communications and Social Influence* (Chicago, 1969).
CLARKE, E. and C. D. O'MALLEY, *The Human Brain and Spinal Cord: A Historical Study Illustrated by Writings from Antiquity to the Twentieth Century* (Berkeley, 1968).
COLEMAN, W., *Biology in the Nineteenth Century: Problems of Form, Function and Transformation* (Cambridge, 1985).
—— *Death is a Social Disease: Public Health and Political Economy in Early Industrial France* (Madison, 1982).
CONRY, Y., *L'Introduction du darwinisme en France au XIXe siècle* (Paris, 1974).
CORBIN, A., *Les Filles de noces: Misère sexuelle au dix-neuvième siècle* (Paris, 1978).
—— *Le Miasme et la jonquille: L'Odorat et l'imaginaire social, XVIIIe–XIXe siècle* (Paris, 1982).
—— 'Le Péril vénérien au début du siècle: Prophylaxie sanitaire et prophylaxie morale', *Recherches: L'Haleine des faubourgs*, 29 (1977), 245–83.
CORSI, P., 'Recent Studies on Italian Reaction to Darwin', in D. Kohn (ed.), *The Darwinian Heritage* (Princeton, 1985), 711–29.
—— and J. WEINDLING, 'Darwinism in Germany, France and Italy', in D. Kohn (ed.), *The Darwinian Heritage* (Princeton, 1985), 683–711.

DARNTON, R., *Mesmerism and the End of the Enlightenment in France* (Cambridge, Mass., 1968).
DELAHAYE, M.-C. (ed.), *L'Absinthe: Histoire de la fée verte* (Paris, 1983).
DIDI-HUBERMAN, G., *Invention de l'hystérie: Charcot et l'iconographie photographique de la Salpêtrière* (Paris, 1982).
—— and P. FÉDIDA, (eds.), J.-M. Charcot, *'Les Démoniaques dans l'art', suivi de: 'La Foi qui guérit'* (Paris, 1984).
DIGEON, C., *La Crise allemande de la pensée française* (Paris, 1959).
DIJKSTRA, B., *Idols of Perversity: Fantasies of Feminine Evil in Fin-de-siècle Culture* (New York, 1986).
DOERNER, K., *Madmen and the Bourgeoisie* (Oxford, 1982).
DONOVAN, J. M., 'Justice Unblind: The Juries and the Criminal Classes in France, 1825–1914', *Journal of Social History*, 15 (1981–2), 89–105.
DONZELOT, J., *L'Invention du social: Essai sur le déclin des passions politiques* (Paris, 1984).
—— *The Policing of Families Welfare v. the State*, trans. R. Hurley (London, 1979).
DOUGLAS. M., *Implicit Meanings: Essays in Anthropology* (London, 1975).
—— *Natural Symbols: Explorations in Cosmology* (London, 1970).
—— *Purity and Danger: An Analysis of Concepts of Pollution and Taboo* (London, 1966).
DOWBIGGAN, I., 'Degeneration and Hereditarianism in French Mental Medicine, 1840–90', in W. F. Bynum, R. Porter, and M. Shepherd (eds.), *The Anatomy of Madness*, i. 188–232.
DRESCHER, S., D. SABEAN and A. SHARLIN (eds.), *Political Symbolism in Modern Europe* (New Brunswick, NJ, 1982).
DWELSHAUVERS, G., *La Psychologie française contemporaine* (Paris, 1920).

ELLENBERGER, H. R., *The Discovery of the Unconscious: The History and Evolution of Dynamic Psychiatry* (New York, 1970).
ELWITT, S., 'Social Reform and Social Order in Late-Nineteenth Century France: The *Musée social* and its Friends', *French Historical Studies*, 11 (1980), 431–51.
—— *The Third Republic Defended: Bourgeois Reform in France, 1880–1914* (Baton Rouge, 1986).
EY, H., 'La Discussion de 1855 à la Société Médico-psychologique sur l'hallucination et l'état actuel du problème de l'activité hallucinatoire', *Annales médico-psychologiques*, 15th ser., 1 (1935), 584–613.
FARLEY, J. and G. L. GEISON, 'Science, Politics and Spontaneous Generation in Nineteenth Century France: The Pasteur–Pouchet Debate', *Bulletin for the History of Medicine*, 48 (1974), 161–98.

FEUILLERAT, A., *Paul Bourget: Histoire d'un esprit sous la Troisième République* (Paris, 1937).

FORRESTER, J., 'Contracting the Disease of Love: Authority and Freedom in the Origins of Psychoanalysis', in W. F. Bynum, R. Porter, and M. Shepherd (eds.), *The Anatomy of Madness*, i. 255–70.

FOUCAULT, M., 'About the Concept of the "Dangerous Individual" in Nineteenth-Century Legal Psychiatry', *International Journal of Law and Psychiatry*, 1 (1978), 1–18.

—— *The Birth of the Clinic: An Archeology of Medical Perception*, trans. A. M. Sheridan Smith (New York, 1975).

—— *Discipline and Punish: The Birth of the Prison*, trans. R. Hurley (New York, 1980).

—— (ed.), *Généalogie des équipements de normalisation, les équipements sanitaires* (Paris, 1976).

—— (ed.), *I, Pierre Rivière, Having Slaughtered my Mother, my Sister, and my Brother . . .* (London, 1978).

—— *Power/Knowledge, Selected Interviews and Other Writings, 1972–1977*, ed. C. Gordon (London, 1980).

FOX, R. and G. WEISZ (eds.), *The Organization of Science and Technology in France, 1808–1914* (Cambridge, 1980).

FRIEDLANDER, R., 'B.-A. Morel and the Theory of Degeneration: The Introduction of Anthropology into Psychiatry' Ph.D. thesis, (Univ. of Calif., 1973).

GALLAGHER, C. and T. LACQUER (eds.), *The Making of the Modern Body: Sexuality and Society in the Nineteenth Century* (Berkeley, 1987).

GANNE DE BEAUCOUDRY, E., *La Psychologie et la métaphysique des idées-forces chez Alfred Fouillé* (Paris, 1936).

GARÇON, M., *Histoire de la justice sous la IIIᵉ République*, 3 vols. (Paris, 1957).

—— *La Justice contemporaine, 1870–1932* (Paris, 1933).

GARNER, J. W., 'Criminal Procedure in France', *Yale Law Journal*, 25 (1916), 255–84.

GAUCHET, M. and G. SWAIN, *La Pratique de l'esprit humain: L'Institution asilaire et la révolution démocratique* (Paris, 1980).

GAY, P., *The Bourgeois Experience: Victoria to Freud, Education of the Senses* (New York, 1984).

GEISERT, H., *Le Système criminaliste de Tarde* (Paris, 1935).

GEISON, G. L. (ed.), *Professions and the French State, 1700–1900* (Philadelphia, 1984).

GELFAND, E. D., *Imagination in Confinement: Women's Writing from French Prisons* (Ithaca, 1983).

GLICK, T. F., *The Comparative Reception of Darwinism* (Austin, 1972).

GINSBURG, C., 'Signes, traces, pistes: Racines d'un paradigme de l'indice', *Le Débat*, 6 (Nov. 1980), 3–44.

GOLDSTEIN, J. E., *Console and Classify: The French Psychiatric Profession in the Nineteenth Century* (New York, 1987).

—— 'French Psychiatry in Social and Political Context: The Formation of a New Profession, 1820–1860', Ph.D. thesis (Univ. of Columbia, 1978).

—— 'The Hysteria Diagnosis and the Politics of Anti-Clericalism in Late Nineteenth-Century France', *Journal of Modern History*, 54 (1982), 209–39.

—— ' "Moral Contagion": A Professional Ideology of Medicine and Psychiatry in Eighteenth and Nineteenth Century France', in G. L. Geison (ed.), *Professions and the French State, 1700–1900* (Philadelphia, 1984), 181–222.

GOUBRAN, C., *L'Influence de l'ivresse sur la responsabilité pénale: Étude de la doctrine et de la jurisprudence française* (Paris, 1925).

GOULD, S. J., *The Mismeasure of Man* (New York, 1981).

GRIFFITHS, R., *The Reactionary Revolution: The Catholic Revival in French Literature, 1870–1914* (New York, 1965).

GRMEK, M. D., *Raissonnement expérimental et recherches toxicologiques chez Claude Bernard* (Geneva and Paris, 1972).

GUILLAIS, J., *La Chair de l'autre: Le Crime passionnel au XIXe siècle* (Paris, 1986).

GUILLAUME, P., *Du désespoir au salut: Les Tuberculeux aux 19e et 20e siècles* (Paris, 1986).

GUILLY, P.-J.-L., *Duchenne de Boulogne* (Paris, 1936).

GUNN, J. A., 'Ribot and his Contribution to Psychology', *The Monist*, 34 (1924) 1–14.

HABERMAS, J., *Toward a Rational Society, Student Protest, Science and Politics*, trans. J. J. Shapiro (Boston, 1970).

HAINE, W. S., 'I go to the café to create my relations: Sociability and Strategy in Parisian Working-Class Cafés. 1870–1890', Ph.D. thesis (Univ. of Wisconsin, 1984).

—— 'The Regulation of Taverns, Cabarets and Cafés in France from the Old Regime to 1880', MA thesis (Univ. of Wisconsin, 1980).

HALBECQ, M., *L'État, son autorité, son pouvoir, 1880–1962* (Paris, 1965).

HALÉVY, E., *The Growth of Philosophic Radicalism*, trans. M. Morris (Clifton, NJ, 1972).

HARRINGTON, A., 'Hemisphere Differences and "Duality of Mind" in Nineteenth-Century Medical Science, *c*.1760–1900', D.Phil. thesis (Univ. of Oxford, 1985).

HARRINGTON, A., 'Hysteria, Hypnosis and the Lure of the Invisible: The Rise of Neo-mesmerism in fin-de-siècle medicine', in W. F. Bynum, R. Porter, and M. Shepherd (eds.), *The Anatomy of Madness*, vol. iii (forthcoming).

—— *Medicine, Mind and the Double Brain: A Study in Nineteenth-Century Thought* (Princeton, 1987).

HARRIS, R., 'Murder under Hypnosis in the Case of Gabrielle Bompard: Psychiatry in the Belle Epoque Courtroom', in W. F. Bynum, R. Porter and M. Shepherd (eds.), *The Anatomy of Madness*, ii., 197–241.

HARTMANN, M., *Victorian Murderesses: A True History of Thirteen Respectable French and English Women Accused of Unspeakable Crimes* (New York, 1977).

HAUSE, S. (with A. R. KENNY), *Women's Suffrage and Social Politics in the French Third Republic* (Princeton, 1984).

HAYWARD, J. E. S., 'Educational Pressure Groups and the Indoctrination of the Radical Ideology of Solidarism, 1895–1914', *International Review of Social History*, 8 (1963), 1–17.

—— 'The Official Philosophy of the French Third Republic: Léon Bourgeois and Solidarism', *International Review of Social History*, 6 (1916), 20–32.

—— 'The Social History of an Idea in Nineteenth-Century France', *International Review of Social History*, 4 (1959). 261–84.

HILLMANN, R. G., 'A Scientific Study of Mystery; The role of the Medical and Popular Press in the Nancy-Salpêtrière Controversy on Hypnotism, *Bulletin for the History of Medicine*, 39 (1965), 163–72.

HIRST, P. Q., *Durkheim, Bernard and Epistemology* (London, 1975).

HOLMES. F. L., *Claude Bernard and Animal Chemistry* (Cambridge, Mass, 1974).

HUGHES, H. S., *Consciousness and Society: The Reorientation of European Social Thought, 1890–1930* (London, 1959; 2nd edn., New York, 1977).

IGNATIEFF, M., *A Just Measure of Pain: The Penitentiary in the Industrial Revolution, 1750–1850* (New York, 1978).

IHRIG, G. P., *Heroines in French Drama of the Romantic Period, 1829–1848* (New York, 1950).

IMBERT, J. and G. LEVASBEUR, *Le Pouvoir, les juges et les bourreaux* (Paris, 1972).

ISAMBERT, F. A., *Politique, religion et science de l'homme chez Philippe Buchez, 1796–1865* (Paris, 1967).

ISRAEL, L., *L'Hystérique, le sexe et le médecin*, 5th edn. (Paris, 1983).

JACKSON, J. H., 'Evolution and Dissolution of the Nervous System', *Selected Writings of John Hughlings Jackson*, ii (London, 1932), 76–91.

JACQUEMET, G., 'Médecine et "maladies populaires" dans le Paris de la fin de XIXe siècle', *Recherches: L'Haleine des faubourgs*, 29 (1977), 349–65.

JAMES, A. R. W., 'L'Hallucination simple?' *Revue d'histoire littéraire de la France*, 6 (1986), 1024–37.

JAMES, M., 'Therapeutic Practices of J.-M. Charcot in their Historical and Social Context', (forthcoming Ph.D. thesis, Univ. of Essex).

JANET, P., 'L'Œuvre psychologique de Ribot', *Journal de Psychologie*, 11 (1915), 268–82.

JARDIN, A., *Histoire du libéralisme politique: De la crise de l'absolutisme à la constitution de 1875* (Paris, 1985).

JEFFERSON, A., *Reading Realism in Stendhal* (Cambridge, 1988).

JOHNSON, D., *The Dreyfus Affair* (New York, 1966).

JOHNSTON, W., 'The Origin of the Term "Intellectuals" in French Novels and Essays of the 1890s', *Journal of European Studies*, 4 (1974), 43–56.

JONES, G. S., *Outcast London: A Study in the Relations between Classes in Victorian Society* (Oxford, 1971).

JORDANOVA, L. J., 'Earth Science and Environmental Medicine: The Synthesis of the Late Enlightenment', in L. J. Jordanova and R. Porter (eds.), *Images of the Earth* (Chalfont St Giles, 1979), 119–46.

—— (ed.), *Languages of Nature: Critical Essays on Science and Literature* (London, 1986).

—— 'Policing Public Health in France, 1780–1815', in T. Ogawa (ed.), *Public Health: Proceedings of the Fifth International Symposium on the Comparative History of Medicine, East and West* (Tokyo, 1981), 12–32.

—— 'Romantic Science? Michelet, Morals and Nature', *British Journal for the History of Science*, 13 (1980), 44–50.

—— and R. PORTER (eds.), *Images of the Earth* (Chalfont St Giles, 1979).

KISSEL, P., 'L'École neuro-psychiatrique de Nancy: Le Professeur Bernheim', *Médecine de France*, 68 (1969), 11–13.

KNIEBHLER, Y. and C. FOUQUET, *La Femme et les médecins: Analyse historique* (Paris, 1983).

KOHLER, P. A. and H. F. ZACHER (eds.), *The Evolution of Social Insurance, 1881–1981: Studies of Great Britain, France, Switzerland, Austria and Germany* (London, 1982).

KOHN, D. (ed.), *The Darwinian Heritage* (Princeton, 1985).

KOLAKOWSKI, L., *Positivist Philosophy*, 2nd edn. (Harmondsworth, 1972).

KOPELL, B. S., 'Pierre Janet's Description of Hypnotic Sleep Provoked from a Distance', followed by trans. of 'M. Pierre Janet, Report on Some Phenomena of Somnambulism', in *Journal of the History of the Behavioural Sciences*, 4 (1968), 119–131.

LALOUETTE, J., 'Le Débit de boisson en France, 1871–1919', Ph.D. thesis, 2 vols. (Univ. of Paris I, 1979).

—— 'Le Débit de boisson urbain entre 1880–1914', *Ethnologie française*, 12 (1982), 131–6.

—— 'Le Discours bourgeois sur les débits de boisson aux alentours de 1900', *Recherches: L'Haleine des faubourgs*, 29 (1977), 315–46.

LANDUCCI, G., *Darwinismo a Firenze: Tra Scienze e ideologia, 1860–1900* (Florence, 1977).

LANTERI-LAURA, G., 'La Chronicité dans la psychiatrie française moderne', *Annales: Economies, sociéties, croyances*, 27 (1972), 548–68.

—— *Histoire de la phrénologie* (Paris, 1970).

—— *Lecture des perversions: Histoire de leur appropriation médicale* (Paris, 1980).

LATOUR, B., 'La Théâtre de la preuve', in C. Salomon-Bayet, *Pasteur et la revolution pastorienne* (Paris, 1986), 335–84.

LENOIR, R., 'The Psychology of Ribot and Contemporary Thought', *The Monist*, 30 (1920), 365–94.

LÉONARD, J., 'Comment peut-on être pastorien?', in C. Salomon-Bayet (ed.), *Pasteur et la révolution pastorienne* (Paris, 1986), 143–79.

—— *La Médecine entre les pouvoirs et les savoirs, Histoire intellectuelle et politique de la médecine française au XIXe siècle* (Paris, 1981).

LESCH, J. E., *Science and Medicine in France: The Emergence of Experimental Physiology, 1790–1855* (Cambridge, Mass., 1984).

LESSELIER, C., 'Les Femmes et la prison, 1820–1939', in J. Petit (ed.), *La Prison, la bagne et l'histoire* (Paris, 1984), 115–28.

LEVADE, M., *La Délinquance des jeunes en France, 1825–1968* (Paris, 1972).

LÉVY-BRUHL, L., *History of Modern Philosophy in France*, trans. anon. (Chicago, 1924).

LIOURE, M., *Le Drame de Diderot à Ionesco* (Paris, 1973).

LOGUE, W., *From Philosophy to Sociology: The Evolution of French Liberalism, 1870–1914* (Dekalb, Ill., 1983).

LUKES, S., *Émile Durkheim: His Life and Work: A Historical and Critical Study* (Harmondsworth, 1973).

—— and A. SCULL, *Durkheim and the Law* (Oxford, 1984).

MACCORMACK, G. M. and M. STRATHERN (eds.), *Nature, Culture and Gender* (Cambridge, 1980).

MACINTYRE, A., *After Virtue: A Study in Moral Theory* (London, 1981).
MCLAREN, A., *Sexuality and Social Order: The Debate over the Fertility of Women and Workers in France, 1770–1920* (New York, 1983).
MCMILLAN, J., *Housewife or Harlot: The Place of Women in French Society, 1870–1914* (London, 1981).
MAIRE, C. L., *Les Convulsionnaires de Saint-Médard: Miracles, convulsions et prophéties à Paris au XVIIIe siècle* (Paris, 1985).
MANDELBAUM, M., *History, Man and Reason: A Study in Nineteenth-Century Thought* (Baltimore, 1971).
MANNHEIM, H. (ed.), *Pioneers in Criminology* (London, 1960).
MARRUS, M., 'Social Drinking in the Belle Époque', *Journal of Social History*, 7 (1974), 115–41.
MARTIN, B. F., 'The Courts, The Magistrature, and Promotions in Third Republic France, 1871–1914', *American Historical Review*, 87 (1982), 977–1009.
—— *The Hypocrisy of Justice in the Belle Époque* (Baton Rouge, 1984).
MARTIN, C., *La Dégénérescence dans l'œuvre de B. A. Morel et dans sa postérité*, Ph.D. thesis (L'École pratique des hautes études, 1983–4).
MAYER, J.-M., *Un Prêtre démocrate: L'Abbé Lemire, 1853–1928* (Paris, 1968).
MERRIMAN, J. (ed.), *Class Experience in Nineteenth Century Europe* (New York, 1979).
MEYER, P., *The Child and the State: The Intervention of the State in French Family Life*, trans. J. Ennew and J. Lloyd (Cambridge, 1983).
MICALE, M. S., 'Diagnostic Discriminations: Jean-Martin Charcot and the Nineteenth-Century Idea of Masculine Hysterical Neurosis', Ph.D. thesis (Yale Univ., 1987).
—— 'The Salpêtrière in the Age of Charcot: An Institutional Perspective on Medical History in the Late Nineteenth Century', *Journal of Contemporary History*, 20 (1985), 703–31.
MICHAUD, G., *Message poétique du symbolisme* (Paris, 1947).
MICHAUD, S., 'Science, droit, religion: Trois contes sur les deux natures', *Romantisme*, 13 (1976), 23–40.
MIGNOT, R., 'Magnan et ses études sur l'alcoolisme', *Annales médico-psychologiques*, 15th ser., 1 (1935), 738–47.
MILLER, D., 'From Workers' Diseases to Occupational Diseases: The Impact of Experts' Concepts on Workers' Attitudes', in P. Weindling (ed.), *The Social History of Occupational Health* (London, 1985), 55–78.
MILLER, M. B., *The Bon Marché: Bourgeois Culture and the Department Store, 1869–1920* (London, 1981).
MITCHELL, H., 'Rationality and Control in French Eighteenth-

century Medical Views of the Peasantry', *Comparative Studies in Society and History*, 21 (1979), 82–112.

MONESTIER, A. (ed.), *Le Fait divers* (Musée national des arts et traditions populaires, Paris, 19 Nov. 1982–18 Apr. 1983).

MOORE, J. R., 'Could Darwinism be Introduced in France?' (Essay Review of Yvette Conry, *L'Introduction du darwinisme en France* . . .), in *British Journal for the History of Science*, 10 (1977), 246–51.

MOORE, M. S., *Law and Psychiatry: Rethinking the Relationship* (Cambridge, 1984).

MOREAU, T., *Le Sang de l'histoire: Michelet, l'histoire et l'idée de la Femme au XIXe siècle* (Paris, 1982).

MOREL, P. and C. QUÉTEL, *Les Médecins de la folie* (Paris, 1985).

NYE, R., *Crime, Madness and Politics in Modern France: The Medical Concept of National Decline* (Princeton, 1984).

—— 'Degeneration and the Medical Model of Cultural Crisis in the French Belle Époque', in S. Drescher, D. Sabean, and A. Sharlin (eds.), *Political Symbolism in Modern Europe* (New Brunswick, NJ, 1982), 19–41.

—— 'Heredity or Milieu: The Foundations of Modern European Criminological Theory', *Isis*, 67 (1976), 335–55.

—— 'Heredity, Pathology and Psychoneuroses in Durkheim's Early Work', *Knowledge and Society*, 4 (1982), 103–42.

—— *The Origins of Crowd Psychology: Gustave LeBon and the Crisis of the Mass Democracy in the Third Republic* (London and Beverly Hills, 1975).

O'BRIEN, P., 'The Kleptomania Diagnosis: Bourgeois Women and Theft in late Nineteenth-century France', *Journal of Social History*, 17 (1983), 65–77.

—— *The Promise of Punishment: Prisons in Nineteenth-Century France* (Princeton, 1981).

OFFEN, K., 'Depopulation, Nationalism and Feminism in Fin de Siècle France', *American Historical Review*, 89 (1984), 648–75.

—— ' "First Wave" Feminism in France: New Work and Resources', *Women's Studies International Forum*, 5 (1982), 685–9.

OGAWA, T. (ed.), *Public Health: Proceedings of the Fifth International Symposium on the Comparative History of Medicine, East and West* (Tokyo, 1981).

OLRIK, H., 'Le Sang impur: Notes sur le concept de prostituée-née chez Lombroso', *Romantisme*, 31 (1981), 168–78.

OWEN, A. R. G., *Hysteria, Hypnosis and Healing: The Work of J.-M. Charcot* (London, 1971).

PANCALDI, G., *Darwin in Italia: Impresa Scientifica e Frontiere Culturali* (Bologna, 1983).

PASQUINO, P., 'Criminology: The Birth of a Special *savoir*', *Ideology and Consciousness: Technologies of the Human Sciences*, 7 (Autumn 1980), 17–32.

PASSMORE, J., *A Hundred Years of Philosophy* (New York, 1966).

PAUL, H. W., 'The Debate Over the Bankruptcy of Science in 1895', *French Historical Studies*, 5 (1967–8), 299–327.

PEEL, J. D. Yeadon, *Herbert Spencer: The Evolution of a Sociologist* (New York, 1971).

PERROT, M., 'Dans la France de la Belle Époque, les "apaches", premières bandes des Jeunes', in *Les Marginaux et les exclus dans l'histoire, Cahiers Jussieu*, 5 (Paris, 1979), 387–407.

—— 'Délinquence et système pénitentiaire en France au XIXe siècle', *Annales: Économies, sociétés, croyances*, 30 (1975), 67–91.

—— (ed.), *L'Impossible Prison: Recherches sur le système pénitentiaire au XIXe siècle* (Paris, 1980).

PETIT, J. (ed.), *la Prison, Le bagne et l'histoire* (Paris, 1984).

PICK, D., 'The Conception and Descent of Degeneration, 1848–1914', Ph.D. thesis (Univ. of Cambridge, 1987).

—— 'The Faces of Anarchy: Lombroso and the Politics of Criminal Science in Post-Unification Italy', *History Workshop*, 21 (1986), 60–86.

PICKSTONE, J., 'Bureaucracy, Liberalism and the Body in Post-Revolutionary France: Bichat's Physiology and the Paris School of Medicine, *History of Science*, 19 (1981), 115–42.

PIERROT, J., *The Decadent Imagination, 1880–1900*, trans. D. Coltman (Chicago, 1981).

PITT-RIVERS, J., *The Fate of Shechem or the Politics of Sex: Essays in the Anthropology of the Mediterranean* (Cambridge, 1977).

POOVEY, M. ' "Scenes of an Indelicate Character": The Medical "Treatment" of Victorian Women', *Representations*, 14 (1986), 137–68.

POSTEL, J. and C. QUÉTEL (eds.), *Nouvelle histoire de la psychiatrie* (Toulouse, 1983).

PRAZ, M., *The Romantic Agony*, trans. A. Davidson (London, 1933).

PRESTWICH, P. E., 'French Workers and the Temperance Movement, *International Review of Social History*, 25 (1980), 35–52.

—— 'Temperance in France: The Curious Case of Absinthe', *Historical Reflections/Réflexions Historiques* (1979), 301–19.

QUÉTEL, C., 'L'Asile d'aliénés en 1900', *L'Histoire*, 7 (1978), 25–34.

RABINOVITCH, L., *Les Crimes passionnels* (Paris, 1931).

REARICK, C., *Pleasures of the Belle Époque: Entertainment and Festivity in Turn-of-the-century France* (New Haven, 1985).

REUCHLIN, M., 'The Historical Background for National Trends in Psychology: France', *Journal of the History of the Behavioural Sciences* 1 (1965), 115–23.

RHODES, H. T. F., *Alphonse Bertillon: Father of Scientific Detection* (London, 1956).

ROBERTS, J. S., *Drink, Temperance and the Working-Class in Nineteenth-century Germany* (Boston, 1984).

ROSEN, C., *From Medical Police to Social Medicine: Essays in the History of Health Care* (New York, 1974).

ROSENBERG, C. E., *No Other Gods: On Science and American Social Thought* (Baltimore, 1976).

ROSHSCHUH, K. E. (ed.), *Die Entwicklung der kontinentalen Physiologie im 18. und 19. Jahrhundert mit besonderer Berücksichtigung der Neurophysiologie* (Stuttgart, 1964).

ROSS, E., ' "Fierce Questions and Taunts": Married Life in Working-Class London, 1870–1914', *Feminist Studies*, 8 (1982), 575–602.

SAINT-JOURS, Y., 'France', in P. A. Kohler (ed.), *The Evolution of Social Insurance* (London, 1982), 93–149.

SALOMON-BAYET, C. (ed.), *Pasteur et la révolution pastorienne* (Paris, 1986).

SARBIN, T. R. and J. B. JUHASZ, 'The Historical Background of the Concept of Hallucination', *Journal of the History of the Behavioural Sciences*, 3 (1967), 339–58.

SAVEY-CASARD, P., *La Peine de mort* (Geneva, 1968).

SCHILLER, F., *Paul Broca; Founder of French Anthropology, Explorer of the Brain* (Berkeley, 1979).

SCHILLER, J., *Claude Bernard et les problèmes scientifiques de son temps* (Paris, 1967).

SCHNAPPER, B., 'La Correction paternelle et le mouvement des idées au dix-neuvième siècle, 1789–1935', *Revue historique*, 263 (1980), 319–50.

SCOTT, J. A., *Republican Ideas and the Liberal Tradition in France, 1870–1914* (New York, 1966).

SCULL, A. T., *Museums of Madness: The Social Organization of Insanity in Nineteenth-Century England* (London, 1979).

SEGUIN, J.-P., *Les Canards illustrés du 19ᵉ siècle: Fascination du fait divers* (Musée-galerie de la Séita, Paris, 9 Nov. 1982–30 Jan. 1983).

SÉLIGMAN, E., *La Justice en France pendant la révolution*, 1789–1792 (Paris, 1901) vol. i.

SELIN, T., 'Enrico Ferri', in H. Mannheim (ed.), *Pioneers in Criminology* (London, 1960), 277–300.

SEN, A. and B. WILLIAMS (eds.), *Utilitarianism and Beyond* (Cambridge, 1982).

SHAPIRO, A.-L., *Housing the Poor of Paris, 1850–1902* (Madison, 1985).

SIEGEL, J., *Bohemian Paris: Culture, Politics and Boundaries of Bourgeois Life, 1830–1930* (New York and Harmondsworth, 1986).

SMITH, R., 'The Background of Physiological Psychology in Natural Philosophy', *History of Science*, 11 (1973), 75–123.

—— 'Expertise and Causal Attribution in Deciding between Crime and Mental Disorder', *Social Studies in Science*, 15 (1985), 67–98.

—— *Trial by Medicine: Insanity and Responsibility in Victorian Trials* (Edinburgh, 1981).

SOURNIA, J.-C., *Histoire de l'alcoolisme* (Paris, 1986).

SOWERWINE, C., *Sisters or Citizens? Women and Socialism in France since 1876* (Cambridge, 1982).

SPITZER, A. B., *Old Hatreds and Young Hopes: The French Carbonari against the Bourbon Restoration* (Cambridge, Mass., 1971).

STEBBINS, R. E., 'France', in Thomas F. Glick, *The Comparative Reception of Darwinism* (Austin, 1972), 117–67.

STERNHELL, Z., *La Droite révolutionnaire, 1885–1914: Les Origines françaises du fascisme* (Paris, 1978).

—— *Maurice Barrès et le nationalisme français* (Paris, 1972).

STOCKING, G. W., *Race, Culture and Evolution: Essays in the History of Anthropology* (New York, 1968).

SWAIN, *Le Sujet de la folie: Naissance de la psychiatrie* (Toulouse, 1977).

SWART, K., *The Sense of Decadence in Nineteenth Century France* (The Hague, 1964).

TEMKIN, O., *The Falling Sickness*, 2nd edn. (Baltimore, 1971).

VEITH, I., *Hysteria: The History of a Disease* (Chicago, 1965).

VILLEY, R., *Histoire du secret médical* (Paris, 1986).

VOGT, F. W., 'Progress, Science, History and Evolution in Anthropology', *Journal of the History of the Behavioural Sciences*, 3 (1967), 132–55.

VURPAS, C., 'Les Obsessions, les impulsions et les perversions sexuelles dans l'œuvre de Magnan', *Annales médico-psychologiques*, 15th ser. 1 (1935), 748–59.

WAJEMAN, G., *Le Maître et l'hystérique* (Paris, 1982).

WALKOWITZ, J., 'Jack the Ripper and the Myth of Male Violence', *Feminist Studies*, 8 (1982), 542–74.

WEBER, E., *France: Fin de siècle* (Cambridge, Mass., 1986).

—— *Peasants into Frenchmen: The Modernization of Rural France, 1870–1914* (Stanford, 1976).

WEEKS, J., *Sex, Politics and Society: The Regulations of Sexuality since 1800* (London, 1981).

WEINDLING, P. (ed.), *The Social History of Occupational Health* (London, 1985).

WEINER, D., 'The Apprenticeship of Philippe Pinel', *Clio Medica*, 13 (1978), 125–33.

WEISZ, G., *The Emergence of Modern Universities in France, 1863–1914* (Princeton, 1983).

WILLIAMS, J. P., 'The Making of Victorian Psychical Research: An Intellectual Élite's Approach to the Spiritual World', Ph.D. thesis (Univ. of Cambridge, 1984).

—— 'Psychical Research and Psychiatry in late Victorian Britain: Trance as Ecstasy or Trance as Insanity', in W. F. Bynum, R. Porter, and M. Shepherd (eds.), *The Anatomy of Madness*, i., 233–54.

WILSON, S., *Ideology and Experience: Anti-Semitism in France at the Time of the Dreyfus Affair* (London, 1982).

WOLFGANG, M. E., 'Cesare Lombroso', in H. Mannheim (ed.), *Pioneers in Criminology* (London, 1960), 168–227.

WRIGHT, G., *Between the Guillotine and Liberty: Two Centuries of the Crime Problem in France* (New York, 1983).

WRIGHT, P. and A. TREACHER, *The Problem of Medical Knowledge: Examining the Social Construction of Medicine* (Edinburgh, 1982).

YOUNG, R., *Mind, Brain and Adaptation in the Nineteenth Century* (Oxford, 1970).

ZEHR, H., *Crime and the Development of Modern Society: Patterns of Criminality in Nineteenth Century Germany and France* (London, 1976).

INDEX

All laws are to be found grouped together under the entry for 'laws'